INSIGHT GUIDES

SWITZERLAND

Discovery CHANNEL

APA PUBLICATIONS L

Part of the Langenscheidt Publishing Group

INSIGHT GUIDE
SWITZERLAND

Editorial
Editor
Joanna Potts
Editorial Director
Brian Bell

Distribution

UK & Ireland
GeoCenter International Ltd
Meridian House, Churchill Way West
Basingstoke, Hampshire RG21 6YR
Fax: (44) 1256 817988

United States
Langenscheidt Publishers, Inc.
36–36 33rd Street, 4th Floor
Long Island City, NY 11106
Fax: 1 (718) 784 0640

Australia
Universal Publishers
1 Waterloo Road
Macquarie Park, NSW 2113
Fax: (61) 2 9888 9074

New Zealand
Hema Maps New Zealand Ltd (HNZ)
Unit D, 24 Ra ORA Drive
East Tamaki, Auckland
Fax: (64) 9 273 6479

Worldwide
Apa Publications GmbH & Co.
Verlag KG (Singapore branch)
38 Joo Koon Road, Singapore 628990
Tel: (65) 6865 1600. Fax: (65) 6861 6438

Printing

Insight Print Services (Pte) Ltd
38 Joo Koon Road, Singapore 628990
Tel: (65) 6865 1600. Fax: (65) 6861 6438

©2008 Apa Publications GmbH & Co.
Verlag KG (Singapore branch)
All Rights Reserved

First Edition 1993
Fourth Edition (Updated) 2007
Reprinted 2008

CONTACTING THE EDITORS
We would appreciate it if readers
would alert us to errors or out-
dated information by writing to:
**Insight Guides, P.O. Box 7910,
London SE1 1WE, England.
Fax: (44) 20 7403 0290.
insight@apaguide.co.uk**

NO part of this book may be reproduced,
stored in a retrieval system or transmitted
in any form or means electronic, mechanical, photocopying, recording or otherwise, without prior written permission of
Apa Publications. Brief text quotations
with use of photographs are exempted
for book review purposes only. Information has been obtained from sources
believed to be reliable, but its accuracy
and completeness, and the opinions
based thereon, are not guaranteed.

www.insightguides.com
In North America:
www.insighttravelguides.com

ABOUT THIS BOOK

The first Insight Guide pioneered
the use of creative full-colour photography in travel guides in 1970.
Since then, we have expanded our
range to cater for our readers' need
not only for reliable information about
their chosen destination but also for
a real understanding of the culture
and workings of that destination.
Now, when the internet can supply inexhaustible (but not always reliable)
facts, our books marry text and pictures to provide those much more
elusive qualities: knowledge and dis-
cernment. To achieve this, they rely
heavily on the authority and experience of locally based writers and
photographers.

How to use this book
Insight Guide: Switzerland is structured to convey an understanding of
the country and its culture and
guide readers through its sights and
activities:

◆ The **Features** section, indicated by
a yellow bar at the top of each page,
covers the history and culture of the
country in a series of lively and infor-
mative essays.

◆ The main **Places** section, indicated by a blue bar, is a complete
guide to all the sights and areas
worth visiting. Places of special
interest are coordinated by number
with the maps.

◆ The **Travel Tips** listings section,
with an orange bar, contains comprehensive information on travel,
hotels, restaurants etc.

The contributors
This edition of *Insight Guide: Switzerland* was updated by **David Dalton**,

Map Legend

▬ ▬▪▪	International Boundary
▬ ▬ ▬ ▬	Canton Boundary
⊖	Border Crossing
▪▪▪	National Park/Reserve
✈ ✈	Airport: International/Regional
🚍	Bus Station
❶	Tourist Information
✉	Post Office
† † ⟨⟩	Church/Ruins
†	Monastery
☾	Mosque
✡	Synagogue
▦ ▥	Castle/Ruins
∴	Archaeological Site
∩	Cave
⚊	Statue/Monument
★	Place of Interest

laborator, who travelled the length and breadth of Switzerland to help bring the **Places** section up to date. By his account, he "clung to the edges of waterfalls in the Bernese Oberland, tiptoed around cows in Wengen, walked the streets of Geneva from end to end, rode the most beautiful train rides in the world and burnt the midnight oil in Basel".

There are four picture stories in this edition of the book that offer a close-up view of the famously efficient Swiss railway network and its picture postcard resorts, and some fascinating revelations about its historic buildings and rural traditions: Alpine Railways, written by **Anthony Lambert**; Architecture, by **Vivien Stone**; Country Life, by **Danny Aeberhard**; and Tourism, by **Mike Ivory**.

The **Travel Tips** were updated and extensively enlarged by **David Dalton**, bringing up to date the earlier contributions by **Jael Bertschinger**, a professional harpist from Zürich who plays with the Ensemble Pyramide chamber music group. With her musical background, Bertschinger was able to add details in particular about the wealth of arts and music festivals taking place all over Switzerland throughout the year.

Insight Guide: Switzerland maintains the high standard of photography for which the Insight series is renowned, with many images taken by **Jerry Dennis**, one of Insight's regular photographers and contributors.

This updated edition was proofread by **Sylvia Suddes**, and was indexed by **Elizabeth Cook**.

a Switzerland-based writer and editor, building on the contributions made by the team of writers in previous editions, including **Marianne Flueler-Grauwiler**, **Rowlinson Carter** and **Klaus Speich**.

The **Features** section has previously been expanded to reflect the growing boom in outdoor and special interest holidays, for which Switzerland offers an excellent range of opportunities.

Chapters have been written on the following subjects: The Arts, and Food and Drink, by **Paul Wade**; People, by **Kathy Arnold**; Flora and Fauna, by **Vivien Stone**; Lakes and Mountains, by **Mike Ivory**; and Outdoor Adventure, by Swiss-born **Danny Aeberhard**.

Other contributors include **Paul Karr**, a frequent Insight Guides col-

The main places of interest in the Places section are coordinated by number with a full-colour map (e.g. ❶), and a symbol at the top of every right-hand page tells you where to find the map.

INSIGHT GUIDE
SWITZERLAND

CONTENTS

Maps

Inside front cover:
Western Switzerland
Inside back cover:
Eastern Switzerland

Winter Wonderland
in Wengen

Travel Tips

Places

THE BEST OF SWITZERLAND

*Spectacular scenery, world class resorts, picturesque railways,
historic castles, festivals and museums... Here, at a glance,
are our top recommendations for a visit to Switzerland*

MAJOR HIGHLIGHTS

- **Conquer the Jungfrau** Take the train up to Jungfraujoch, the highest railway station in Europe, and admire the views from near the very peak of this mighty mountain. *See page 133.*
- **Visit Zermatt and see the Matterhorn** Explore this chic mountain resort, from where there are spectacular views of the iconic mountain. *See page 181.*
- **Zürich** Wander through the atmospheric old town, eat in fashionable restaurants and shop till you drop on Bahnhofstrasse. *See pages 233–49.*
- **Explore Bern's old town** The medieval walled area of the federal capital is a warren of historic landmarks and welcoming restaurants, bounded on three sides by the beautiful Aare River. *See page 119.*
- **Take a boat trip on Lake Luzern** Steamers depart regularly during the summer from the quays in front of the train station. *See page 302.*
- **All aboard the Glacier Express** There's barely a dull moment on this wonderful 8-hour journey from St. Moritz to Zermatt. *See pages 138 & 226.*

BEST WINTER SPORTS RESORTS

- **Klosters** Authentic Alpine charm in the Engadine – and a favourite haunt of British Royals. *See page 218.*
- **Gstaad** Film stars, tycoons and sports stars call it home. The skiing isn't bad either. *See page 137.*
- **Zermatt** Skiing and snowboarding for all levels, including off-piste experts, in the shadow of the Matterhorn. *See page 181.*
- **Kandersteg** Small, peaceful resort in the Bernese Oberland better known for cross-country skiing than downhill, although it's got that too. *See page 135.*
- **Wengen** The purist's ski resort, high in the Bernese Oberland, with a vast network of runs for all levels and the bonus of Eiger views. *See page 134.*
- **Saas Fee** Car-free resort in Valais with more than 95 km (60 miles) of runs in winter and a glacier if you fancy some summer skiing. *See page 182.*
- **Verbier** One of the finest interconnecting skiing networks on the planet, with more than 400 km (250 miles) of marked pistes. *See page 176.*

TOP: the Matterhorn. **LEFT:** the astronomical clock and building decoration in old Bern. **BELOW:** high-octane skiing.

BEST WALKING

- **Adelboden** High in the Bernese Oberland this traditional and peaceful Alpine resort has more summer trails than you could walk in a lifetime. *See page 135.*
- **Lake Uri** Walk around the lake's wooden shores and through Inner Switzerland on the 35-km (22-mile) "Swiss Path", which is best tackled over two days. *See pages 103 & 315.*
- **Leukerbad** Mountain trails from this spa town take you across the Bernese Alps between magnificent peaks including Wildstrubel and Balmhorn. *See page 179.*
- **Jura** Up around Laufen the rolling landscape close to the French border offers undemanding walking on some of Switzerland's quietest but most scenic trails. *See pages 103 & 284.*
- **Titlis** A network of cable cars and chairlifts links hundreds of kilometres of trails around Titlis, the tallest peak in Inner Switzerland. *See page 314.*

SPA TOWNS

- **Leukerbad** The premier spa town in Valais, Leukerbad's thermal baths are open year-round (covered and open-air). Bathe in natural 50°C (122°F) waters among snow-covered mountains. *See page 179.*
- **Bad Ragaz** The restored 19th-century baths in this historic spa town in the Rhein Valley offer various bathing experiences, including private thermal baths. *See page 264.*
- **Therme Vals** The remote Hotel Therme in Graubünden has open-air thermal baths, while a wellness centre offers additional spa treatments. Hotel guests can also enjoy night-bathing in the stunningly lit pools. *See page 211.*
- **Scuol** Scuol's mineral water is known locally as the "Champagne of the Alps". Also with a wellness centre and sauna, the highlight of this beautifully located spa in the Engadine are the Roman-Irish thermal baths. *See page 218.*

BEST ADVENTURES

- **Bungee jumping** The most terrifying of Switzerland's jumps is the 220-metre (770-ft) plunge from the Verzasca Dam in Ticino, made famous in the Bond film *Goldeneye*. *See page 105.*
- **Cresta Run** First-timers can book in advance for the thrill of a lifetime in St Moritz. *See pages 102 & 106–7.*
- **Hit the trails** Hike the rugged mountains of the Swiss National Park in Graubünden. *See pages 103 & 220.*
- **Paraglide in Interlaken** You can book a thrilling first-time tandem flight at the local tourist office or even sign up for lessons and go solo. *See page 128.*
- **Mountain climbing** There are a number of centres where you can get training for anything from a short ice climb to a full-scale attempt on the Eiger. *See page 104.*
- **Sledding** There are specially prepared runs throughout the country in winter; in summer there are toboggan runs with metal tracks. One of the best of these is in Kandersteg. *See page 135.*

TOP: take a hike; the legendary Cresta Run.
RIGHT: relaxing at a spa.

BEST EVENTS

- **Fasnacht** Many Swiss cities enjoy this Lenten festival, but Basel's Fasnacht is the biggest and the best. *See page 274.*
- **Locarno Film Festival** Held over 10 days in August, this popular event includes new films shown on a giant screen in the beautiful Piazza Grande. *See page 196.*
- **Zürich Street Parade** Wild but friendly alfresco rave attended by tens of thousands of euro-youths every summer. *See page 241.*

- **Montreux Jazz Festival** Major names from the jazz, blues and pop worlds converge on this lakeside town every July. *See page 168.*
- **Sechseläuten** A bizarre but entertaining pageant in Zürich that sees the medieval guilds on parade with a giant snowman. *See page 242.*
- **Hot Air Ballooning Week** Annual January event that brings visitors to Château d'Oex in the Bernese Oberland for rides and colourful racing events. *See page 137.*
- **Chästeilet** Friendly mountain festival near Lake Thun that has sprung from the old farming tradition of cheese-sharing. *See page 131.*
- **Willisau Festival** This pleasant fortified town holds a major summer music festival that includes everything from rock to rap. *See page 305.*

BEST LITTLE TRAIN JOURNEYS

- **Mount Rigi** Take one of two Alpine railways that run up the "Queen of the Mountains" to the east of Luzern. From the summit you can see the snow-capped giants of the Jungfrau region. *See page 139.*
- **Niesen** A quaint funicular runs to the top of "the Swiss Pyramid", from where the views of the Eiger, Mönch and Jungfrau are simply the best. *See page 127.*
- **Mount Pilatus** The country's steepest rack railway runs from Alpnachstad to the summit of Pilatus. *See page 313.*
- **St Moritz to Zermatt** The Glacier Express covers this route, but so do regular trains, crossing the Bernese Alps and offering terrific vistas at every turn. *See page 138.*
- **Monte San Salvatore and Monte Brè** Both these mountains in Ticino can be scaled by funicular. On a clear day you can see all the way to Milan. *See page 198.*

BEST MUSEUMS

- **Einsteinhaus** It may be small, but don't miss the chance to see the modest apartment in Bern where the genius did some of his greatest work. *See page 121.*
- **Schweizerisches Alpines Museum** In Bern, an absolute must for anyone with an interest in the Alps and the Alpine lifestyle. *See page 122.*
- **Sherlock Holmes Museum** It's only a replica of the great detective's Baker Street lodgings, but for Holmes fans Meiringen is a mandatory pilgrimage. *See page 124.*
- **Schweizerisches Landesmuseum** Visit Zürich's most well-

known museum for a fascinating overview of Swiss history, politics and culture. *See page 235.*
- **Musée du Vieux Genève** The elegant 14th-century Maison Tavel, the oldest remaining domicile in the city, is a museum in itself. *See page 158.*

TOP: Jungfraubahn and the Eiger; altarpiece at the Schweizerisches Landesmuseum. **LEFT:** a Fasnacht drummer.

BEST MARKETS

- **Laufen** Farmers' market with lots of good wine, cheese and sausage every Tuesday and Saturday in the pretty main street. *See page 284.*
- **Bern** Produce from the Oberland as well as stalls selling handicrafts, antiques and delicious organic snacks and lunches. *See page 119.*
- **Lugano** Lakefront market with a distinctly Italian flavour including hundreds of stalls selling everything from pasta and olives to designer jeans and bric-a-brac. *See page 198.*

- **Fribourg** This quaint old town hosts one of the biggest markets in Switzerland every Saturday, with produce from the Fribourg Alpen and lots of ethnic goods such as bags and rugs. *See page 143.*
- **Bulle** The main feature here is an extensive range of Gruyère cheese from local producers. Every Thursday in summer there's cheese tasting and in winter lots of fondue stalls. *See page 145.*

TOP: a colourful stall in Bern. **RIGHT:** Castelgrande. **BELOW:** a budget ride.

BEST CASTLES

- **Château Chillon** Beneath this wonderful lakeside castle lies the dungeon of Francois de Bonivard, the prisoner whose fate inspired Lord Byron to write one of his most famous poems. *See page 168.*
- **Habsburg Castle** A few kilometres southwest of Brugg, this is the obvious place to head for if you're interested in the dynasty of the same name. *See page 306.*
- **Schloss Tarasp** Small but fascinating 11th-century castle in Scuol with a violent history; it was largely controlled by the Austrians until 1803. *See page 218.*
- **Château de Gruyères** For centuries the counts of Gruyères called this redoubtable edifice home. There's a collection of period art and a wonderfully dank dungeon to explore. *See page 144.*
- **Castelgrande** Bellinzona's biggest fortification is in the town centre and has an excellent museum. It can be reached either by a spiral of stairs or in a lift from Piazza del Sole. *See page 193.*

MONEY-SAVING TIPS

Public Transportation Switzerland has a number of different passes offering discounted travel. Most comprehensive is the Swiss Pass: a personal network ticket which enables its bearer unlimited mileage on SBB and many private railways, postbuses and boats (and in 30 cities and towns on buses and trams too). *See page 325.*

Accommodation You can save money by staying in hostels or smaller hotels and inns. You can also stay in private rooms (ask at the tourist office) and even sleep on straw at some farms. *See page 330.*

Meals Eating out can be expensive, but there are plenty of self-service and fast food restaurants in most towns and cities where you can eat for less. A good tip is to go to the cafes at the main railway station, which will usually have reasonably priced food. Department stores such as Migros and Coop also have inexpensive restaurants. *See page 336.*

Admission Fees Many attractions have discounts for under sixteens and children (under 12) are often free. The Swiss Museum Pass enables visitors to have free entry to more than 420 museums throughout Switzerland. The Swiss Pass public transport card also entitles you to free admission at all museums in the Swiss Museum Pass scheme. An International Student Identity Card (ISIC) entitles the holder to all sorts of discounts. *See page 348.*

A MAGNET FOR MYTHS

*A country of cliché-defying contradictions, Switzerland
has long been romanticised and misrepresented*

The popular image of Switzerland is so riddled with myth that books which propose to set the record straight hardly know where to begin. Most famously, it has had to live with the dialogue of Orson Welles in *The Third Man*, which pronounced that the only product of centuries of Swiss civilisation was the cuckoo clock. Studying that civilisation, a Swissophile and academic confessed that he began to question whether Switzerland could – or even should – exist. The home of William Tell has no natural frontiers, no common language, no unifying culture and no dominant religion.

It has been a holiday destination since 1863 when Thomas Cook first organised a package tour from Britain. Byron's *The Prisoner of Chillon* and Conan Doyle's climactic struggle between Sherlock Holmes and Professor Moriarty at the Reichenbach Falls helped romanticise the mountainous country, as did Johanna Spyri with her popular Heidi stories. Visitors have not always been kind, however. Ernest Hemingway found the streets so clean he expressed a desire to foul them.

The picture of bankers and milkmaids, chocolate and watches, ski resorts and yodelling is hard to reconcile even with the origins of Switzerland's name. It was the invention of the Habsburgs, who gave their motley collection of southern neighbours the title of their most pugnacious members, the Schwyz. This played on the German word for "sweat", implying a people not too fussy about hygiene.

The "peace-loving" Swiss were, up to about 150 years ago, almost constantly at war with themselves or others; many of these conflicts were orchestrated by powerful neighbours in order to keep the Swiss state intact and neutral, but domestic squabbles threatening this haven included civil war, peasant uprisings and religious disputes. Somehow, the Swiss always managed to pull themselves back from the brink.

Significant developments taking place in other European countries were often dismissed by the Swiss. In deciding to "opt out" in this way, Switzerland subconsciously set the early parameters for making the country what it is today. Nineteenth-century nationalists advocated language ties as a prime criterion for setting the frontiers of modern Europe. The Swiss ignored this, as they did the idea that centralised government was desirable or that a monarch was necessary. "The Swiss believe," says one of them, "that they are rational and realistic. They are not. They will take pains to define a principle, immediately think of a dozen exceptions to the rule, then say it's better to use common sense. In other words, they believe in the principle of no principles." ❑

PRECEDING PAGES: trekking on the Obergabelhorn; paragliding over the Alps.
LEFT: flying the flag.

AETH . . . . . . PANTONES XIII OHRT der EIDGENOSSSCHAFT 1 ZURICH 2 BERN 3 LUCERN 4 URI 5 SCHWEIZ 6 . . RV
S GALLEN ART . . . N STATT 2 PUNDTEN 3 WALLIS 4 MULHAUSEN 6 BIEL 7 NEUBURG NEUFCHATEL 8 GENET GENEVE 9 BISCHOFF BASEL. T . . . . . .
FREYE AMPTER . . . . IN THAL . . . . . . Abbatcellanis . Toureau. Bremgarten. Lucernensibus Urip. Suitensibus. Solothurno. Thogenbure. Glaronensibus. qu VIII Cantonos Vetcoss . . . . . . part BADEN . . . XII
USCHALENS 4 ORBE 5 GRANSON Crocum. Suitersunt et SubvePrumoruni sunt 6 BELLINZONA 7 RIVIERA 8 VALLEBREGNIA PALENSERTHAL. Sutoruni et Glarunculum GASTER CASTRARH S

NOUVELLE CARTE
DE LA
SUISSE
Divisée en ses
TREIZE CANTONS
SES ALLIEZ ET SES SUJETS
par . . . . Jacob . . . . . .
de Zurich
Docteur en Medecine

A AMSTERDAM
Chez COVENS et CORNELIS MORTIER
Geographes

BOURGOGNE

Lac de Joux

LEMANUS LACUS Lac de GENEVE

SAVOYE

BAILLAGE
DE
GEX

DE... 8 GLARUS 9 BASEL 10 FREIBURG 11 SOLOTHURN 12 SCHAFFHAUSEN 13 APPENZELL. CONFŒDERATI ZUGEWANDTEORRT
Cing. Sax ... Sux, sodes Sapax, Trgmachus, Glanorachus, qui VII Cantone, ucbera, VII alle Obrt vulgo vocantur parent 1 THURGEU infectis in reionrabiles Bevorulibe, Friborgenibu, et Sohoburodibu 2 SARGANS
Sargana, parte cum japanvergi Præfectura Transalpaul 3 LAUIS LUGANO 4 LUGGARUS LOCARNO 5 MENDRIS 6 MEINTHAL Bemenlom et Friborgenum Dominis subiect 1 MURTEN 2 SCHWAERZENBURG
8 Sux jaris sunt 1 RAPERSCHWEIL 2 ENGELBERG 3 GERSAU   AMSTELODAMI Apud IOANNEM COVENS et CORNELIUM MORTIER Geographos

HELVETIÆ ANTIQUÆ
GEOGRAPHICUS INDEX

Decisive Dates

PREHISTORY

c. 10,000 BC: Following the thaw after the great Ice Age, hunter-fisher folk settle in the Mittelland.

c. 400 BC: Rhaetians enter the southeastern parts of the country; Celtic tribes settle in the southwest. By 58 BC Germanic tribes force the powerful Celtic Helvetii tribe to migrate to Gaul.

ROMAN AND HOLY ROMAN EMPIRES

58 BC: Julius Caesar pursues the Helvetii, defeating them at Bibracte in Burgundy.

58 BC – AD 400: The Romans occupy a defensive area along the Rhein and Danube, settling with the Celts in relative harmony.

c. 500: The Alemanni tribes invade from Germany, driving out the Romans, and taking possession of northern Switzerland, while the Burgundians take the south. The Rhaetians hold out in Grisons.

c. 600: Irish monks St Colomba and St Gallus bring Christianity to Switzerland.

614: Founding of the St Gallen monastery, later to become one of Europe's major seats of learning.

771: King Charles, later to become Charlemagne, unites Switzerland as the kingdom of the Franks. The country is divided up into shires, which form the basis of the present canton demarcation.

834: The Treaty of Verdun divides the country up into the old kingdoms of the French Burgundians and the Germanic Alemanni.

1032: The Battle of Morat, in which Conrad II of Germany takes over the Kingdom of Burgundy, incorporating it into the Holy Roman Empire.

RISE OF THE SWISS CONFEDERATION

12th and 13th centuries: Noble dynasties, including the Habsburgs, Savoys and Zahringens, found many of today's main cities, developing power bases and autonomous regional authorities.

1291: Death of Habsburg Emperor Rudolf triggers instability, which leads to the historic Oath at Rutli Meadow, proclaiming the Swiss Confederation. Origins of heroic legend of William Tell.

1315: The Battle of Morgarten: defeat of the Austrian Habsburgs by the Schwyz peasants, leading to the admittance into the Confederation of Luzern in 1332.

1351–53: Zürich, Bern, Glarus and Zug join the Confederation, which now numbers eight cantons.

1386: The Battle of Sempach: the Confederation defeats the Austrians again, killing Duke Leopold III; heroic performance of Arnold Von Winkelried.

1389: Vienna Peace Treaty signed, following another defeat of the Austrians at the 1388 Battle of Nafels, guaranteeing peace for seven years and confirming the legitimacy of the Confederation.

1415: Twenty-year peace treaty signed between Austria and the Confederation.

1476: Bern declares war on Charles the Bold of Burgundy, in the name of the Confederation. Charles's defeat and subsequent death almost leads to civil war, averted by the hermit-saint Niklaus von Flue.

1499: Basel Peace Treaty, incorporating the city into the Confederation and establishing Swiss independence from the empire.

1501–13: Enlargement of the Confederation to 13 cantons, adding Schaffhausen and Appenzell.

1513: The Battle of Novara, in which Hans Waldmann, Burgomaster of Zürich, is executed.

1515: The Battle of Marignano, between Francis I of France and the Confederation. The defeat of Switzerland demotes the country to lowly status in Europe.

THE AGE OF RELIGIOUS CONFLICT

1518: Reformist cleric Ulrich Zwingli gives rousing sermon in Zürich, attacking Catholic conventions.

1524: Zwingli marries a rich widow, scandalising the church for his breach of celibacy.

1524–28: Reformation spreads, splitting the Confederation; Schaffhausen, Bern, Basel, Grisons and St Gallen join the reformists, while Zug, Fribourg and Solothurn remain Catholic.

1529: Zürich declares war on the Forest Cantons, and again in 1531, when Zwingli is killed.

1535: Vaud, incorporating Lake Geneva, is annexed by Bern reformists. John Calvin, French humanist, establishes the Church of Geneva.

1555: Growth of new movement in reaction to the Reformation, further dividing the Confederation and forcing Protestants to seek refuge in Zürich.

1616–48: The Thirty Years War, in which Switzerland remains neutral and retains its sovereignty at the Peace of Westphalia.

THE ENLIGHTENMENT

1712: The Peace of Aargau, which settles equal status of Catholics and Protestants. The Swiss economy flourishes, with countryside remaining pastoral and agricultural and urban centres developing booming industries, particularly watch- and clockmaking.

1755: Voltaire's arrival in Geneva rocks the Calvinist establishment; after several attempts, he establishes a theatre in the city in 1766.

1798: Napoleon's army sacks Bern and conquers Switzerland. The Confederation is remodelled on the new revolutionary French system, and renamed the "Helvetian Republic".

1814: The Congress of Vienna: Switzerland appeals for neutral status, but invades France.

1815: The Treaty of Paris, which grants the Swiss permanent recognition of its neutrality.

1844: Renewed conflict between Catholics and Protestants in Luzern leads to outbreak of civil war.

1848: Federal Constitution introduced, establishing democratic institutions in the cantons and centralising powers in a national government.

1859: New law introduced, imposing further restrictions on Swiss mercenary activity abroad.

1864: Signing of the first Geneva Convention and founding of the Red Cross Organisation.

STILL NEUTRAL THROUGH TWO WORLD WARS

1901: Henri Dunant, founder of the Red Cross Organisation, wins the first ever Nobel Peace Prize.

1914–18: World War I; Swiss again preserve their neutrality. Influx of refugees leads to General Strike suppressed by the army.

1920: First meeting of League of Nations, Geneva.

PRECEDING PAGES: map of the Swiss Confederation when it had 13 members.
LEFT: Lombard cross from the 7th century.
RIGHT: United Nations' Palais des Nations, Geneva.

1939–45: World War II; Switzerland neutral but sets up defence strategy. Swiss contribute generously to post-war economic reparations.

1945: Founding of United Nations, with Geneva as European headquarters.

1955: Opening in Geneva of European Centre of Nuclear Energy (CERN).

1959: Swiss Parliament rejects women's bid for the right to vote and stand for national elections. Both are finally granted in 1971.

1979: The region of Jura is made into a canton.

1980: The Gotthard Tunnel, linking Switzerland to Italy, opens to road traffic.

1997: Swiss banks reveal that about $57 million

exists in dormant accounts, many of which were opened by German Jews before World War II. The Swiss Banking Union publishes a list of names of account holders for the first time, and a compensation fund is set up.

2001: The Swiss vote to stay outside the EU.

2002: The country votes to join the United Nations, and a bilateral agreement is signed with the EU.

2003: The right-wing Swiss People's Party (SVP) becomes the biggest force in parliament after winning almost 28 percent of the vote in general elections.

2005: Referendum vote goes in favour of opening job market to workers from the 10 newest European Union countries. ❑

BEGINNINGS

*The earliest settlers in Switzerland were Celts who built their
wooden homes on stilts by the shores of its now famous lakes*

During the unusually severe winter of 1853 the level of Lake Zürich fell to an unprecedented low level, exposing a swathe of sticky mud around the shoreline. Enterprising residents realised that shoring up the perimeter would provide a windfall of free land, and with that they got busy with spade and shovel.

The eager opportunists of Obermeilen, a village about 39 km (24 miles) from Zürich, found their digging impeded by what appeared to be a forest of wooden props just beneath the surface. Someone had the sense to summon the distinguished Dr Ferdinand Keller from Zürich and he, probably with the ancient Greek historian Herodotus in mind, was able to proclaim the discovery of one of the vital missing links in Switzerland's prehistory. The props, he concluded, were evidence of an ancient Celtic tribe who built their houses on stilts over water.

Cro-Magnon ancestors

Tools found among the props were made of stone and bone rather than metal, indicating a date earlier than the Bronze Age, which is generally put at about 1500 BC onwards. Traces of human presence in Switzerland of course go back much further. A fragment of jaw found in the Jura has been identified as belonging to a woman who lived about 50,000 years ago; a more complete skull from Neuchâtel is that of a young Cro-Magnon adult of about 12,000 BC. Caves which housed prehistoric troglodytes have been found near Geneva, Villeneuve and Thayngen. The significance of the submerged props near Obermeilen was as evidence of people who constructed their homes, and quite elaborate ones at that.

Hundreds of similar aquatic villages, some with as many as 40,000 piles driven into the mud, have subsequently been discovered in lakes, rivers and swamps. The Swiss lake-dwellers, like the troglodytes before them and

the so-called Beaker people of western Europe afterwards, remain shrouded in prehistory. The transition to recorded history begins with Roman literature of the 1st century BC. The lake-dwellers had by then been replaced by other Celts and a branch of the Etruscans, the Rhaeti (Raeti), a people probably Celtic in origin who inhabited

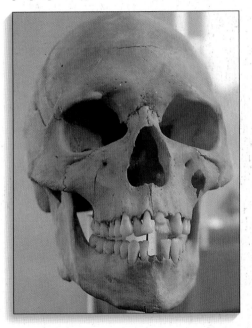

what is now southern and eastern Switzerland and were defeated by the Romans in 16 AD.

The Romans annexed present-day Switzerland to the Roman Empire in 15 BC. Because the Swiss "province" lay between Italy and the Roman defensive lines along the Rhein and the Danube, it was crucial to the security of the Roman world; Romans fortified key mountain passes and applied all their renowned road-building skills to the territory.

Switzerland is much richer in Roman remains than is popularly supposed. Baden, a well-known spa near Zürich, was described by Tacitus as "a place which during long years of peace had grown to be a city, much frequented on account

---

LEFT: the Celt, as romanticised in Swiss painting, an image used on the Swiss 2-franc, 1-franc and 50-rappen coins.
RIGHT: a 12,000-year-old skull from the Jura.

of the attraction of its salubrious waters". The greatest Roman city, though, was Aventicum, the modern Avenches, where a complex of palaces, temples and triumphal arches was enclosed by a wall some 7 km (4 miles) in circumference.

The Alemanni

Roman ruins bear testimony to the empire buckling under the pressure of the Germanic tribes at the turn of the 5th century AD. The Alemanni took possession of northern Switzerland; the Burgundians seized the south. Secure in the mountain fastnesses of Graubünden, the Rhaeti alone escaped almost untouched, whereas what is now

Ticino was driven closer to Italy, sharing that country's fate under the Ostrogoths and Lombards well into the Middle Ages. The foundations were laid for the German-French-Romansch-Italian components of modern Switzerland.

The mutual hostility of the Alemanni and Burgundians was tempered by the common threat of the Franks under Clovis, but to no avail. The Franks were routed in 469 and the Burgundians in 534 at Autun, where the Romans had turned back their Celtic predecessors. The whole of modern Switzerland, Ticino excepted, was again united in subjugation to a single power, its future bound up with the vary-

RESISTING THE ROMANS

The Helvetii were the most powerful of the Celtic tribes and lived between lakes Constance and Geneva, in the Alps and on the Jura. By 58 BC, pressure from German tribes had forced the Helvetii to migrate en masse to Gaul. With their bridges burnt behind them, 368,000 men, women and children assembled in Geneva on 28 March 58 BC for the exodus, only to find their exit across the Rhone barred.

The barrier was Julius Caesar and his army, then embarking on his conquest of Gaul. The emigrants slipped past the Roman cordon but they were pursued and caught at Bibracte, near the modern town of Autun in Burgundy. In his *Commentaries on the Gallic Wars*, Caesar pays tribute

to the fighting spirit of the Helvetii, whose last stand was behind a makeshift barricade of oxcarts. Their resistance held out from 1pm until sunset, but the outcome against the drilled legions was inevitable and they were obliged to return whence they had come, albeit with the promise of Roman protection in future and a large measure of self-government in what became known as Helvetia.

The Etruscan Rhaeti refused to succumb to Rome for another 40 years, and one of the more colourful accounts of their resistance has Rhaeti women, frustrated by their lack of weapons, hurling their suckling children at the conquerors "through sheer exasperation".

ing vicissitudes of the Merovingian, Carolingian and Frankish rulers for centuries to come.

Clovis had sworn that if he defeated the Alemanni he would convert to Christianity, and he was duly baptised on Christmas Day, 496. As the champion of orthodox Christianity, he was as opposed to the heretical Arian Christians as he was to heathens. The Burgundians were numbered among the former, the Alemanni among the latter; so, the history of Switzerland from the Merovingian kings to Charlemagne's coronation as Holy Roman Emperor in 800 was closely allied to the religious upheavals of the age.

LINGUA ROMANA

The legacy of the Romans in Switzerland is apparent in the Romansch language, still spoken in Graubünden, which is a combination of Roman Latin and the Tuscan dialect of the Rhaeti.

Band of Irish monks

The task of reasserting orthodoxy in Switzerland fell, curiously, to a caravan of tattooed, long-haired Irish monks who set out in 610 under the leadership of St Columba, armed with stout sticks and with a spare pair of boots slung round their necks. They followed the course of the Limmat River past Zürich to the lakeside village of Tuggen. "This place pleased them," says a chronicle of 771, "but not the evil ways of the dwellers. Cruelty and mischief ruled in their midst, and they were given over unto heathen superstitions." These included toasting their gods with beer. Gall, Columba's zealous assistant, threw the images of the local gods and the drinking vessels into the lake, whereupon the enraged Alemanni drove them away.

The monks transferred their attention to Pregentia (Bregenz), which they were advised was a hotbed of heathen practices. Gall found this to be true and again destroyed the local icons.

Ordered out of the country for his actions, Columba led his band of monks across the Alps into Italy, but Gall was too unwell to travel and stayed behind in the forest east of Arbon. In 614 he founded the famous monastery which bears his name *(see pages 260–1)*.

Alemannia, which had so doggedly resisted Christianity, became the seat of other great monasteries: Rheinau, founded in 724 by the Visigoth Pirminius, Pfäfers and Einsiedeln. Each of these monasteries established a network of

parish churches which accelerated the complete conversion of Switzerland, effected a revolution in agriculture and cleared huge expanses of forest.

Conflict with the Pope

As the Merovingian kingdom collapsed under the weight of its crimes and incapacity, it split into what were known as Austrasia and Neustria, in effect the same Burgundian-Alemannic dichotomy which existed in microcosm in Switzerland. Eventually the two halves were reunited as the Kingdom of the Franks

under Charles, later Charlemagne, in 771. Crowned Holy Roman Emperor by Pope Hadrian in 800, Charlemagne suddenly found himself almost on a level with the Pope, who, however, exceeded the secular power of kings by virtue of vast papal estates and wealth. The papacy and the imperial throne were then closely matched rivals for the leadership of the Western world.

As long as Charlemagne and Pope Hadrian remained on fairly friendly terms, conflict did not materialise, but the danger signs were evident in Switzerland. Clerical land barons were not inclined to take their orders from the secular counts. They insisted on a legal immunity which made them answerable only to the impe-

LEFT: Caesar's army confront the Helvetii, near Geneva (58 BC).
RIGHT: Clovis I, the first Christian king.

rial crown. An ambiguous chain of command spelt potential trouble.

The threat was realised soon after Charlemagne's death in 814. His heir, Ludwig the Pious, was barely able to contain four rebellious sons, and on his death the empire was carved up among the three survivors: Lothar, Ludwig the German and Charles the Bald. The division, ratified by the Treaty of Verdun in 834, split Switzerland along the old lines. The Teutonic Alemanni joined the other subjects of Ludwig the German, and the Romanised Burgundians those of Lothar.

The Kingdom of Burgundy, of which the Swiss "Kingdom of Transjurane" was but a small portion, eventually succumbed to the sheer incompetence of its successive kings and in 1032 it was swallowed up by Conrad II of Germany after the battle of Morat. Swiss Alemannia fared little better. Two attempts to revive an independent Duchy of Alemannia failed, so that the two principal parts of Switzerland fell under the sway of the German empire. Ticino, in the south, was wrapped up in Italian affairs, while the three so-called Forest Cantons of Switzerland were considered too remote to be of interest.

Family feuds

During the 12th and 13th centuries, most of Switzerland was ruled by the German kings and emperors, but beneath that was a feudal patchwork which produced four great families, each of whom attempted to wrest Switzerland for itself. All failed utterly, although two of them, the Savoys and Habsburgs, ended up elsewhere with a kingdom (Italy) and a dynastic empire (Austria-Hungary) apiece.

The other two families, the Zähringers and the Hohenstaufens, continued the 11th-century struggle between Henry IV – both King of Germany and Holy Roman Emperor – and Pope Gregory VII. When the dust settled the Hohenstaufen family emerged as the shaky holders of the Duchy of Alemannia while the Zähringers had created a power base in the town and estates of Zürich, one which they used as a springboard to become the masters of almost all of modern Switzerland by 1127.

The system of defence with which the Zähringers attempted to consolidate their hold had a profound effect on the future shape of the country. They fortified a number of strategic villages and converted them into cities with chartered privileges. A small settlement on the banks of the Sarine became Fribourg; others grew into Burgdorf, Morat and Thun. The centre of the defensive line between Fribourg and Burgdorf formed a stronghold at Bern.

A further 100 or more fledgling towns were founded in the following century, and it was reckoned that a traveller in the lowlands passed a town gate every 20 km (13 miles) or so. Not all the towns survived, but the successful ones steadily attained a measure of independence which they were ready to defend against any aggressor. As they were seldom strong enough to do so alone, they sought alliances with kindred communities or powerful princes, and

Charlemagne

THE FIRST CHRISTIANS

According to tradition, Christianity first put in an appearance in Roman Helvetia in the person of Mauritius, the commander of a Christian legion posted there from Egypt. He fell victim to a purge of Christians by the Emperor Maximilian and was executed at a place in the present-day Valais, whose name was later changed to St Maurice to honour his martyrdom.

In any case, it seems that Switzerland had a bishop, either Theodor or Theodul, as early as 381. In general, however, this was a false dawn for the new religion and over the course of a couple of centuries the remnants seem to have been infused with a good deal of heresy.

Switzerland began to resemble a scaled-down version of the Greek city-states. The urban population remained relatively modest: by the end of the Middle Ages, Basel had between 9,000 and 12,000 inhabitants; Geneva, Zürich, Bern, Lausanne and Fribourg had about 5,000 each.

Holy deadlock

Berchtold V's death in 1218 without an heir unleashed a violent struggle for possession of his estates between two formidable rivals, Thomas of Savoy and Count Rudolf of Habs-

INTELLECTUAL FOUNTAIN

Flattered by Charlemagne's many visits to the city, Zürich still refers to the Holy Roman Emperor as the "fountain of its intellectual life".

which way to turn during the deadlock over the succession to the Kingdom of Germany and the Holy Roman Empire. The powerful church estates, recognising no temporal authority within the country, were torn between loyalty to the semi-divine imperial crown and their duty to the papacy.

Thrust to greatness

Pope Gregory's ultimatum to the German princes was that if they could not agree among themselves on a new emperor he would impose one. Their response was to submit the name of

burg. In a decisive battle at Chillon, on the shore of Lake Geneva, Thomas defeated Rudolf's forces, but he did not have long to relish his victory. He died a few months later (in 1268) on his way home from a trip to Italy. His achievements were squandered by the gross incompetence of his brother, Philip.

The future of Switzerland hung in the balance and the territory might easily have disintegrated. Added to all the independently minded new towns were scores of princelings not knowing

a supposed nonentity whom they could keep under their thumb. The nominee was Count Rudolf of Habsburg, then 55 years of age. He could number among his accomplishments "great slaughter" of forces loyal to troublesome bishops, a stirring battle (at Zürich's behest) against the unsavoury Count of Regensburg, and the capture of a few castles. In the Terrible Times, however, that made him a rather ordinary German princeling and not necessarily imperial material.

Newly crowned nevertheless, Rudolf set about laying the foundations of the great Habsburg dynasty. His aims in Switzerland were first to cut Philip of Savoy down to size

LEFT: Charlemagne, the Holy Roman Emperor.
ABOVE: fortified cave dwellings in St Gallen canton, dating from the 12th–13th century.

and then to acquire as much land as he could, especially from the abbeys.

The abbots of St Gallen were forced to cede land and farms; the monastery of Murbach, then in financial difficulties, was made to surrender Luzern. Any estate whose ownership was in doubt went straight into the Habsburg bag. Rudolf's gobbling up of Switzerland is considered to be the catalyst of Swiss political history. All that had gone before served merely as a prologue to the Swiss Confederation.

> ### TELL – THE TRUTH
>
> The authenticity of William Tell's heroics has long been disputed, even by Voltaire, who observed that "this whole business about the apple is highly suspect."

Rebellion of the forest cantons

The setting for these contentious events is the three so-called forest cantons – Unterwalden, Schwyz and Uri – on Lake Luzern, north of the Alps. What distinguished the Alemanni inhabitants of this region from the rest of the nation was that in their remote station they had escaped rigorous feudalism. Since time immemorial the valleys of Uri and Schwyz had enjoyed virtual self-government under popular assemblies – *Markgenossenschaft* – which ran contrary to the structured tiers of feudalism.

Subsequent events in Uri are rather confusing and as such are typical of the general mêlée surrounding the birth of the Swiss Confederation.

While the nuns of the Abbey of Our Lady in Zürich collected the tax revenue, political overlordship was given first to the Zähringers and then, when that family petered out, to the Habsburgs when they acquired the governorship of Zürichgau, an extensive district which included all three forest cantons.

The fact that most of the population were free peasants, and thus had the right to bear arms and to serve abroad, gave them delusions of grandeur and importance. They believed they were free of all feudal obligations except to the emperor himself. The coronation of Rudolf as emperor brought matters to a head: the emperor whom they were prepared to love and the titular overlord whom they instinctively hated were at a stroke one and the same person. Which would it be: love or hate?

The traditional version of events provides one answer. It says that Rudolf could have been loved if he had been willing to adjudicate personally over the theft of goats and other items of parochial business, but as emperor he was far too busy. He appointed agents to deal with such things, and they were not good enough for the proud free peasants. The conventional view is that the agents were "covetous and cruel tyrants who taxed, fined, imprisoned, and reviled the unfortunate inhabitants".

The tyranny of Rudolf's agents, most notably Landenberg and Gessler, of William Tell fame, drove the forest canton people to unite in rebellion, asserting their allegiance in the historic pact of 1291 *(see page 29)*. The resultant birth of Swiss liberty was not a spontaneous explosion against Habsburg tyranny, however, but a refinement of earlier alliances among communities who probably derived the idea of such leagues from Italy. In fact, some say, there was no Habsburg tyranny.

Nevertheless, the inhabitants of the forest cantons would have had enough to alarm them in the remorseless expansion of the Habsburg estates which created a de-facto cordon around them. The Swiss whom William Tell symbolised were undoubtedly exceptionally sensitive to the threat of outside interference. ❑

LEFT: a medieval Swiss knight in battle – an activity which accounted for much of the Middle Ages.

William Tell

The origins of Switzerland's most famous folk hero are rooted in the country's early history, when Emperor Rudolf held sway over his subjects, through the tyrannical activities of tax-collecting bailiffs. One of the most unpopular of Rudolf's men was Herman Gessler, who was based in the canton of Uri. The haughty and spiteful Gessler placed his hat on a pole in the town marketplace of Altdorf, and gave orders that all passing should show due reverence to it.

A local countryman named William Tell blatantly ignored the hat and was arrested. The biting sarcasm in the exchange between a furious Gessler and the unrepentant Tell gets lost in translation, but the well-known outcome was Tell being ordered to shoot an apple off his son's head. The arrow was right on target, but that led to questions about a second arrow in Tell's quiver. "Had I injured my child," Tell told Gessler, "this second shaft should not have missed thy heart." Right, said the governor, lock him up!

Tell was taken in chains to Gessler's dungeon in Axenstein, which meant crossing the lake by boat. When a violent storm threatened to engulf the boat, the oarsmen, who were unfamiliar with these waters, untied Tell and told him to steer them to safety. On reaching the shore he was able to jump out and push the boat adrift with his captors, including Gessler, still in it. Gessler and crew managed to save themselves, but by then Tell had vanished. He had not gone far, however. Tell knew the route Gessler would take back to his castle, and he was lying in ambush at a suitable spot near Kussnacht when the governor appeared. The arrow held in reserve now found its mark through Gessler's heart. "This is Tell's shaft," Gessler gasped with his dying breath.

The basic story and various embellishments, culminating in the dissidents in the meadow at Rütli taking their cue from Tell and launching a full-scale rebellion, paint a picture of freedom-loving Alpine republicans who were willing to submit themselves to a decent German king like Frederick II but were more than capable of delivering a devastating riposte to tyrants like the ghastly Habsburgs.

"All this seems to have been invented," observed the sceptical Swiss historian François Guilliman in a private letter in 1607, "to nourish hatred against Austria."

Ironically, Guilliman was one of those responsible for nurturing the figure of William Tell, but the story owes its universal currency to a play by Schiller in 1804 and Rossini's well-known opera, which was first performed in 1829. Schiller, a German, never set foot in Switzerland and his knowledge of Swiss history was largely gleaned from Johannes von Müller's *History of Switzerland*, which appeared during the French Revolution. The William Tell story, which von Müller believed totally, was offered as Switzerland's contribution to the rampant spirit of Liberty, Equality and Fraternity.

"The first to challenge the fact that there ever was a man named William Tell, or a bailiff named Gessler," says the waspish historian Christopher Herold, "was saved from national disgrace and possible lynching only by the fact that his books were so dull and unreadable that few people were aware of their existence."

Von Müller's research was taken up by other historians, however, and was boosted by the discovery of the original document of the Pact of 1291, detailed in the next chapter. It transpired that very similar legends (the archer, the object on his son's head, the second arrow held in reserve) crop up in mythology over northern and central Europe and even in Asia Minor. ❑

RIGHT: man or myth, William Tell remains Switzerland's most enduring national hero.

SWISS CONFEDERATION

An independent Switzerland emerged at the end of the Middle Ages, during which it established its prowess at cunning and ruthless warfare

The three forest cantons signed their "Perpetual League" pact on 1 August 1291, barely two weeks after Rudolf's death. "The people of the valley of Uri," it proclaimed in Latin, "the democracy of the valley of Schwyz, and the community of the mountaineers of the Lower Valley, seeing the malice of the age... have promised in good faith to assist each other with aid, with every counsel and every favour, with person and goods, within the valleys and without, with might and main, against one and all, who may inflict upon any one of them any violence, molestation or injury, or may plot any evil against their persons or goods…"

The declaration laid down the basis of a legal code with the proviso that "we will accept or receive no judge in the aforesaid valleys, who shall have obtained his office for any price, or for money in any way whatever, or one who shall not be a native or a resident with us."

Rudolf died bitterly disappointed that he had not been able to secure the non-hereditary succession to the imperial throne for his son Albrecht, and the family reverted to being mere dukes when the crown went instead to Adolf of Nassau. The loss of imperial status made the Habsburgs a less imposing force in the eyes of the Swiss Confederation, which almost immediately entered into an alliance with Zürich and an anti-Habsburg coalition which sprang up in eastern Switzerland.

Zürich attacked Winterthur, a Habsburg town, in 1292, but was severely defeated. The Habsburg Duke Albrecht retaliated by besieging Zürich and eventually regaining the crown for the Habsburgs. Albrecht was subsequently assassinated in an ambush, however, and on his death the German crown slipped away from the family again, this time to Count Henry of Luxembourg.

LEFT: the historic oath at Rütli (1291), as perceived at the time of the French Revolution.
RIGHT: the Swiss "family tree" of confederate cantons up to 1815.

Night of violence

The violence was not one-sided. In 1314 a band of Schwyz men attacked the Habsburgs' abbey at Einsiedeln and made off with the monks as prisoners, even taking the monastery's cattle. The following year, in 1315, the infuriated Habsburgs resumed hostilities.

Duke Leopold assembled at Zug an army which included contingents from Luzern, Winterthur and, remarkably, Zürich. On reaching the hamlet of Haselmatt, near Aegeri, his ill-prepared force began the steep ascent of Morgarten.

Above a particularly tricky part of the ascent the defenders were waiting for them. Weighed down by heavy armour, the Austrians and their Swiss allies barely had time to look up when an avalanche of rocks and tree trunks descended on them from the Figlerfluh, a spur on the ridge of Morgarten. The Confederates rushed into the confusion brandishing their fearsome halberds (long spears with an axe blade on one side and a pick on the other). The

Austrians could retreat only by the way they had come. The retreat turned into flight, the flight into slaughter; many who escaped as far as a lake were drowned by the weight of their armour.

Peasants triumph

The Battle of Morgarten, a victory celebrated in Switzerland to this day, was possibly the first triumph in medieval Europe of peasants on foot over mounted knights. "When the fight was over," the chronicle records, "the men of Schwyz

ALBRECHT'S MEMORIAL

The monastery of Königsfelden, near Baden, was built in 1308 by Elisabeth, the widow of King Albrecht, on the spot where her husband was slain in ambush by a gang of Swiss nobles.

pulled off the weapons of the killed and drowned, robbed them also of their other possessions, and enriched themselves with arms and money." The occasion was commemorated by the construction of a chapel to St Jacob, but perhaps the best epitaph is a quotation attributed to the Austrian duke's fool before the action: "You have taken counsel how best to get into the country, but have given no explanation of how you are going to get out again."

The surprise victory over the Austrians boosted the forest cantons' prestige among their peers and more regions were drawn into the Confederation. In 1332 Luzern was the first town to join up, followed by Zürich (1351),

Glarus and Zug (1352), and Bern (1353), making a total of eight members. After Bern, however, the rural cantons were wary of the balance tilting towards the cities, and no more cities were admitted until 1481. Zürich seceded from the Confederation but rejoined when not even the military assistance of Charles VII of France could stave off defeat.

A similar league was formed in Rhaetia, where the city of Chur joined surrounding villages and valleys in the "League of the House of God". The spread of such leagues was propelled by the bankruptcy of the smaller feudal lords in an economic climate devastated by the Black Death, bad harvests and starvation. Forced to pawn their feudal rights, they saw them being snapped up by prosperous cities. Bern bought the Hasli Valley from the impoverished lords of Weissenburg and with it the feudal rights over its inhabitants. Ironically, the new "lords" in such circumstances were in no hurry to extend to their acquired subjects the freedom which they valued so highly for themselves.

The Vienna Peace Treaty

Successive Habsburg dukes never gave up the idea of reclaiming the Swiss lands lost to the Confederation and for a while succeeded in regaining Zug. Zürich was the main target, however, and it was only saved in 1351 by the intervention of the forest cantons. In time, the Swiss took the offensive. Luzern launched attacks on surrounding Austrian strongholds, Zug on the castle of St Andreas near Cham, Zürich on Rapperswil, and Schwyz on Einsiedeln. In June 1386, Duke Leopold III, nephew of the loser at Morgarten, proposed to deal with the Swiss once and for all, at the Battle of Sempach (*see box, right*).

In 1389, after another Austrian defeat, this time at Näfels, a seven-year peace treaty was signed at Vienna which gave the Confederation undisputed possession of conquered lands, which is not to say that the Habsburgs did not attempt to seduce Zürich back into the fold by various diplomatic subterfuges. A 20-year

LEFT: Burgundian troops, Switzerland's opponents.
RIGHT: Arnold von Winkelried's heroic death in the Battle of Sempach (1386).

peace treaty signed in 1415 was an altogether more reliable indication of Austria's willingness to accept what had happened. Although the Confederation was still technically within the German Empire, the bond was growing meaningless. Germans began to refer to the inhabitants of the confederate states collectively as Die Schweiz, after Schwyz, the state which to them seemed most representative of their increasingly distant neighbours.

In spite of apparent progress towards a constitution, the Confederation still fell some way short of a comprehensive government. It was a union of the loosest kind, in which the members were neither fully equal nor all bound to one another. Zürich kept a rather frigid distance from Luzern, for example, and Luzern from Glarus. The charters of each of the various states were very different. The rural cantons tended to be quite genuinely democratic, with magistrates appointed by popular assemblies, while in the cities the supreme power was lodged with the magistrate, who dispensed liberality downwards more or less as he pleased.

Nevertheless, during the 15th century Switzerland began to assume the proportions of a major European power. Its military prowess had already been amply demonstrated, and now the

ARNOLD VON WINKELRIED

The victory of the Confederates at the 1386 **Battle of Sempach** was due at least partly to the bravery of one Arnold von Winkelried, a national hero with similar hazy historical origins to those of William Tell.

The Austrians took to the field in full armour; the Swiss infantry faced them in a wedge-shaped formation. Unusually, the Austrian knights dismounted and advanced on the wedge with their halberds levelled. The tactics worked as, even with halberds 2.5 metres (8 ft) long, the Swiss could not get close enough to strike.

The Swiss were dropping like flies and defeat seemed certain when things took a miraculous turn. "A good and pious man," says the chronicler, "stepped forward from the Swiss ranks". The Swiss are reluctant to believe that it was anyone other than Arnold von Winkelried. "I will cut a road for you; take care of my wife and children!" he cried.

The enterprising von Winkelried spread his arms wide and threw himself forward, forcing a number of levelled lances to the ground. His comrades charged over his fallen body and through the gap to engage the enemy at close quarters, the style of fighting at which they excelled.

Duke Leopold himself was killed but when his body was laid out, the Swiss having won a resounding victory, it was noticed that mysteriously his head bore no visible wounds.

economic foundations also looked solid. After the pan-European depression of the 14th century, the Confederation grew rich on cloth, wool and linen or, in the case of Zürich, silk. The attraction of money, as opposed to the barter goods which had generally been the currency previously, took precedence over political power.

This development was not quite as high-minded as it may appear, however, because much of the capital which created the new wealth was plainly and simply war booty, the fruits of victory over the richest ruler in Europe, Charles the Bold of Burgundy.

THE COVENANT OF SEMPACH

The Covenant of Sempach, drawn up after the battle in 1386, has been described as "the first attempt, made by any people, to restrain somewhat the fury of war, to regulate military disciples and leadership by intelligent, humane law." Five centuries before the Geneva Convention, it provided for the humane treatment of the wounded and included such clauses as: "Women should not be attacked unless they warned the enemy by an outcry or fought themselves, in which case they could be punished as they deserved."

The enlightened covenant also reflected the growing identity of the "Schweiz" as a separate nation.

The Burgundian war

The Swiss were so confident of their military superiority that they looked on foreign wars as unremarkable business opportunities. They did not realise that in this instance they were being manipulated by the notoriously wily Louis of France. The war was undertaken, says one historian, "at the instigation of France, for the interest of France, and in the pay of France".

Hostilities commenced in 1476, with Bern declaring war on Charles the Bold in the name of the Confederation. While Charles was away in Germany, Bernese troops invaded Burgundy and took Héricourt. On his return, Charles marched on Bern by way of Lake Neuchâtel, pausing to take the town of Grandson and either hanging or drowning 412 prisoners.

The first engagement proper at Neuchâtel took place on 2 March 1476 when, after an initial skirmish, the Burgundians were surprised by a sudden Swiss offensive. Their retreat was so hasty and disorderly that the booty left behind was unbelievable. Among 420 pieces of artillery and a huge quantity of general stores, there were also diamonds and a golden casket containing holy relics including nothing less than pieces of the true cross and the crown of thorns. It was said that the booty included enough silk to enable the Confederate peasants to scorn clothing made from anything less for years. In contrast, the loss of life was minor.

Charles returned within a few weeks with a force of 25,000 men and laid siege to Morat, pounding the city with artillery fire which tore down part of the town wall and destroyed houses. Knowing that Bern would be next if Morat fell, the Confederate forces marched to the city with a force as large as the Burgundian besiegers, who included a number of English archers. The result was one-sided: between 8,000 and 10,000 of Charles's men were killed, against a few hundred Swiss losses.

Two days after the battle, a decisive victory for Charles's opponent, the Duke of Lorraine, a body was recovered from a frozen lake. It had been half-eaten by wolves but the exceptionally long fingernails – an affectation of Charles the Bold – left little doubt as to its identity.

Dividing the booty

The spoils of the Burgundian war were colossal but their division, as far as the rural cantons were concerned, was so loaded in favour of the cities that the question of admitting yet more cities to the Confederation, in this instance Fribourg and Solothurn, brought the country to the brink of civil war.

Providentially, however, peace was maintained by the future saint, Niklaus von Flue. He worked out a compromise which admitted the towns to the Confederation in return for abandoning their other alliances. He proposed a new covenant, the *Stanser-verkommnis* (Agreement of Stans), which would in future regulate the

GORY GRANDSON

"It is a horrible, fearful sight, that of so many dangling corpses," reported the Duke of Milan's ambassador with the Burgundian forces at Grandson, taken by Charles the Bold in 1476.

ranean. Now, the Low Countries were able to reassert their own identities, and what had so recently been Louis XI's relatively insignificant kingdom assumed the dominant role in what became modern France. The role of the Swiss in bringing about Charles's demise was not as significant as his own bad judgement, but Swiss soldiers won great admiration and were perceived throughout Europe as the most useful to have on one's side.

Charles the Bold's terminal difficulties began

division of spoils. Niklaus's canonisation followed some five centuries later.

Mary and Maximilian

The death of Charles the Bold and the disintegration of the Duchy of Burgundy in the 15th century was as momentous and unexpected as the collapse of the Soviet Union would be in the 20th. The duchy was in reality an empire which included the Netherlands and Belgium and went all the way south to the Mediter-

LEFT: Charles the Bold (1433–77).
ABOVE: *Death and the Mercenary*, from the *Danse Macabre*, by Niklaus Manuel (*c.* 1484–1530).

with a hitch in the proposed marriage between his daughter Mary and Maximilian, son of the Habsburg Emperor Frederick.

The marriage eventually took place and rescued Habsburg finances in what was undoubtedly their darkest hour. The Swiss soldier who had to a large extent paved Maximilian's way to a handsome inheritance was, with perfect impartiality, reaching for Maximilian's throat.

Maximilian's mistake was to offer the Swiss the hand of friendship. He suggested they forget about their Confederation and join instead the Swabian Bund, a new league headed by himself. War was soon raging along the whole line of the Rhein, from Basel to the borders of

Vorarlberg and Graubünden, at the very idea. The so-called Swabian War lasted six months and was punctuated by the acts of valour now expected of Swiss troops.

Severing German links

The peace treaty signed at Basel on 22 September 1499 secured the liberation of Rhaetia from the German Empire, incorporating it into the Swiss Confederation, and effectively reducing the links between the Confederation and the empire to a mere formality. This

step was tantamount to acknowledging its independence. Formal independence, however, was not declared until the Peace of Westphalia, 150 years later.

The Confederation's burgeoning prestige attracted applications for membership from Basel and Schaffhausen in 1501. When Appenzell joined the Confederation in 1513 the number of members stood at 13, and there it remained for the following three centuries.

The activities of Swiss mercenaries from the 15th to 19th centuries really belong to the history of other nations' problems rather than Switzerland's, but in the interest of symmetry it may be worth noting that having helped France

and the Habsburgs in their difficulties with Burgundy, and having then turned on the Habsburgs, the Swiss again demonstrated perfect impartiality by taking up cudgels against France.

Italian alliance

The Swiss actually began on France's side, the occasion being the invasion of Italy in 1494. The switch in their loyalties was the work of Matthäus Schiner, a man who began life as a street urchin but went on to become a cardinal and a confidant of Pope Julius II. The Pope was of course alarmed by French ambitions in Italy. Schiner suggested to him that the Swiss might be open to an offer of money, indulgences and other incentives. They were: a five-year alliance between the Papal See and Switzerland was duly signed. The Swiss drove their recent allies out of Lombardy and reinstated the Sforzas in Milan, which became a Swiss protectorate. The French bounced back but the issue was settled, so it seemed, at the Battle of Novara, which decided the matter in 1513.

The rural cantons were uncomfortably aware that the balance of power previously shared with the cities was slipping away. Zürich, Bern and Luzern could between them field twice as many men as all the other cantons put together. Zürich, in particular, was behaving like a sovereign state under its "ambitious and readily bribed" burgomaster, Hans Waldmann, "whose manifest opulence gave the lie to his affectation of republican simplicity".

Of humble origins himself and "Squire of Dubelstein" only by a fortuitous marriage, Waldmann personified the contempt of the urban nouveaux riches for the agrarian peasants by ordering them to put down all their large dogs because they were spoiling the hunting.

Torture and execution

Five hundred peasants of Knonau marched on Zürich in protest and, taking Waldmann prisoner, gave him a taste of the rack in the Wellenberg state prison. Waldmann had spent some time in Wellenberg for youthful excesses, and there were not a few jilted mistresses who probably wished he had never been let out, but on this occasion the rack failed to extract a confession which would have invoked the death penalty. Undeterred, the city council voted to let him die anyway. Thousands turned out to watch him being led to the block in a meadow outside the city walls. He is said to have looked back at the city longingly before lowering his head. "May God protect thee, my beloved Zürich, and keep thee from all evil," were his parting words. His death was followed by rioting and many more executions as the plutocrats tightened their grip on the city to the exclusion of the country districts. After centuries of debate Zürich finally elected a monument to Waldmann in 1937.

While enterprising merchants could amass fortunes in the towns, the economy as far as rural people were concerned was still all about mercenary soldiering. Unfortunately for them, warfare was becoming too expensive for prospective employers. Developments like artillery, now essential, put the cost of even small wars beyond the means of minor, bad-tempered princes, traditionally the most regular source of employment. Moreover, the Germans had woken up to what they were missing and their mercenaries were competing for what business there was.

The Battle of Marignano

Novara had been a great triumph for Swiss arms, but, when Francis I acceded to the French throne soon afterwards and immediately marched on Italy to restore French honour, three cantons – Bern, Fribourg and Solothurn – refused to fight. Cardinal Schiner, his sacred mission yielding to the profane, took command of the depleted Swiss forces. The two armies met on the road to Marignano on 13 September 1515. Battle raged inconclusively until midnight, was broken off, and resumed at dawn. In the afternoon, the French destroyed the dykes holding back the Lambro, and the plain on which the majority of the Swiss troops stood was suddenly flooded. The orderly retreat from this impossible predicament so impressed Francis that he ordered his men not to pursue.

There was also some solace in the "Eternal Peace" concluded with France afterwards. The Swiss possession of Ticino was acknowledged,

although the future "Italian" canton was not granted that status until 1805.

The trauma of defeat weighed heavily on the Swiss. They tried immediately to raise another army, but the response was lukewarm. That afternoon on the road to Marignano saw France and Switzerland change places on the ladder of European power. A loose Confederation without a strong central authority was suddenly and dramatically exposed as an inadequate anachronism. Switzerland was reduced at a stroke from a great power to a small neutral state, and it was in no condition to face the schismatic wrench of the Reformation. ❏

LEFT: Matthaus Schiner (*c.* 1465–1522), bishop, cardinal and politician.
RIGHT: the Battle of Marignano (1515), a crushing defeat for the Swiss.

SOLDIERS FOR HIRE

Historian J. Christopher Herold aptly summed up the Swiss skill at balancing war and peace: "Beginning in the Middle Ages, [the Swiss] sold military service to foreign powers in the form of mercenaries. In order to exercise their military profession undisturbed and to enjoy its fruits in peace, they soon adopted a policy of neutrality – that is, the territory of Switzerland became neutral, while its citizens took part, on an impartial basis, in every European war for several centuries. The Swiss, who now consider themselves the first free and peaceful nation of the Continent, gave their name to an occupation usually involving both servitude and belligerency."

THE REFORMATION

Switzerland stood at the heart of Europe's religious upheaval, its cities erupting in flames as redoubtable reform leaders challenged the authorities

The impact of the Reformation was doubly hard on Switzerland because, while Martin Luther in Germany concentrated on theology and was content to leave politics to the princes, Ulrich Zwingli drew no such distinction between religion and politics. He wanted a total overhaul of Swiss society, top to bottom.

Zwingli rouses the masses

Born in Wildhaus in 1484, Zwingli was educated in Basel and Bern with a view to entering the church. He was a gifted student and entered into serious correspondence with scholars like Erasmus in Holland.

Never a natural bookworm, however, Zwingli went campaigning in Italy, although he became increasingly sceptical about the Swiss mercenary tradition and expressed his objections so forcefully that a public uproar made it prudent to retreat for two years to the abbey at Einsiedeln. The abuses within so appalled him that he re-directed his critical energies, and this brought him to the attention of the Zürich council, which had decided that the city's reputation for wickedness required a vigorous remedy.

Zwingli's first sermon as the newly appointed "plebanus" was a rousing address which had people talking about "a new Moses who had arisen to save his people from spiritual bondage". The scholar Platter, sitting in the congregation, "felt himself lifted off the ground by his hair". Unlike Luther, Zwingli did not challenge papal authority over the sale of indulgences and the like. He was at first more inclined to outline a new state modelled on the Greek ideal, but he came round to the view that in order to build a new society it was necessary first to destroy the old. His targets were the mass and the worship of images.

The forest cantons rebel

In 1524 Zwingli showed what he thought of clerical celibacy by marrying a rich widow, and in the same year he was supported by the government in ordering the removal of all pictures and images from churches. By cutting ties with the diocese of Constance, Zwingli created in Zürich what was virtually its own state religion. The reforms were adopted readily in the northern and eastern cantons, but the forest cantons were steadfastly conservative and Roman Catholic. The Reformation was to them a product of the cities and for that reason alone suspicious if not downright evil. The forest cantons issued a warrant for Zwingli's arrest in case he entered their territory.

The Swiss factions looked beyond their borders for support, the Reformers to Germany and the Catholics to Austria. The split deepened and in 1529 Zürich declared war on the forest cantons. The confrontation of the two armies at Kappel was cooled at the last moment by diplomacy. Zwingli was disgusted by this pact and predicted that the Catholics would one day hold sway and then there would be no mercy.

In a way, Zwingli was right, because when the armies squared up again in the same place two years later the forest cantons had four times as many men as the Zürich force. On this occasion battle was not averted, and Zwingli was killed, along with many of his relatives and most of the Zürich city council. His body was quartered, burnt and "scattered to the wind". Leadership of the Zürich movement passed to his son-in-law Heinrich Bullinger, who found it expedient to concentrate on ecclesiastical matters and leave politics alone.

DECADENT GENEVA

The 16th-century Genevese were the most decadent citizens of Switzerland. Their moral plateau was a city statute that levied a modest charge on men who kept more than one mistress at a time.

Calvin's cause

In one sense, John Calvin, the second giant of the Swiss Reformation, picked up where Zwingli left off, but Zwingli's work was mainly about Zürich and the conversion of German-speaking Switzerland while Calvin's was about Geneva and French-speaking Switzerland. Calvin and Geneva were improbable bedfellows. He was born in Picardy, northern France, in 1509, "a northern Frenchman of superior intelligence and learning, but of a gloomy, austere disposition." The Genevese were the least austere people in Switzerland. They were gamblers and wine-lovers, and kept a red-light district busy.

After the collapse of the Roman Empire, the city was passed around various masters, but at an early date it became an episcopal see, the bishops reaching some kind of accommodation with the House of Savoy which controlled the territory all about. In 1421, however, Duke Amadeus VIII of Savoy usurped the see and it was entrusted to a motley collection of Savoyard hangers-on and royal offspring.

Geneva hot-bloods

Rebellion against the Savoyards produced the three musketeers of Geneva's history: Bezanson Hugues, Philibert Berthelier and François Bonivard, the last immortalised – with poetic licence – in Byron's romantic poem, *The Prisoner of Chillon*. They were a slightly anarchistic band of hot-bloods known as the "Children of Geneva". The first was decapitated by the bishops in 1519, the second fled, and Bonivard, about whose life Byron actually knew very little, was imprisoned in Chillon.

LEFT: Ulrich Zwingli (1484–1531), pioneering humanist reformer, based in Zürich.
RIGHT: John Calvin, his successor in Geneva.

Wishing to rid themselves of the autocratic Savoyards, the Genevese turned to the Swiss Confederation, then at the pinnacle of its military prestige, and to Bern in particular. Bern was by then under Zwingli's influence and the price of its support was that the Genevese had to reform. Guillaume Farel, a fanatical preacher from Neuchâtel, was chosen as the man for the job.

Farel's arrival in 1532, two years after Bonivard had been locked up for the second time, precipitated a storm, the city

I. CALVIN

dividing into supporters of the Confederation, known as the Eydguenots, and those who realised they preferred Savoy, the so-called Mamelukes. Egged on by Farel, the former invaded the cathedral in 1535, ripped apart everything except its walls, and led their dogs and mules inside the hallowed walls to add the proverbial insult to injury. Defrocked priests trampled on their robes while the beleaguered Catholics could only pray for a miracle.

It was Geneva's misfortune at the height of this religious tension suddenly to become the coveted target of three avaricious neighbours: Francis I, the victor at Marignano, the Emperor Charles V and Geneva's supposed ally, Bern itself. Bern got there first with a force of 6,000 men but fear of French intervention inhibited them and saved the city from annexation. The Bernese forces captured the castle of Chillon, however, and freed Bonivard.

Bonivard discovered that Geneva had changed in his enforced absence. His abbey had been seized and secularised, and the whole city looked gloomy. The difference was John Calvin, whom the fiery Farel had taken on to help him clean things up. For the moment, Calvin's proposed remedy was altogether too rigorous for the Genevese and in 1538 both he and Farel were banished. Farel returned to

Neuchâtel and stayed there for the rest of his life, but within three years violent infighting on the Geneva council and the renewed threat of a Bernese occupation led to an invitation to Calvin to return.

Calvin's moral crusade

Accepting Geneva's offer – on his own terms – Calvin now set about his mission with a vengeance. The Genevese were less aware of the intricacies of his doctrine of pre-destination than of the impact of the Consistory, his tribunal of 12 civic worthies who passed judgement on all spiritual and moral matters, public and private. They had the power to enter houses on suspicion of depravity, and laid down the law on the clothes, including the colour, and on what and how much people ate. Drunkenness, blasphemy and agnosticism were put into the same criminal category as murder.

In 1556 John Knox, the Scottish Calvinist, visited Geneva and described it as "the maist perfyt schoole of Chryst that ever was in the erth since the dayis of the Apostillis." By then, most of Calvin's opponents had bolted from the city, but his writings, which could be construed as a charter for capitalism in that they sanctioned the charging of interest on loans, went down well in Scotland and New England. No fewer than 24 printing presses ran day and night churning out his works in a number of languages. More than 2,000 of his sermons and 4,721 letters survive. "His religious enthusiasm was able to triumph over bodily ailments" says one of the more sympathetic biographers.

Last lecture

Calvin died in 1564, his parting words being a stern lecture to those who came to pay their respects. The institutions he left behind in Geneva were soon severely tested by the gentler form of persuasion employed by St Francis of Sales, the champion of the Counter Reformation. By eliminating the more scandalous abuses of the Catholic Church, he managed to win back the entire countryside south of Lake Geneva. The city itself remained loyal to Calvinism and it was at the risk of his life that St Francis, while officially the Bishop of Geneva, paid one or two clandestine visits.

The Genevese took – and take – considerable pride in the way they saw off a perfidious attack on their religion in 1602 by Charles Emmanuel I of Savoy, who was re-living the old Savoyard dream of making Geneva his own. The Savoyards crept up on the city on the night of 11 December and several were halfway up the walls when the alarm was given. Citizens in nightshirts rushed out and the invaders were beaten off at the cost of several lives. To guard against any repetition, Geneva signed a treaty with Henry IV of France, but the treaty did not come cheap. The city had to surrender to him its main agricultural hinterland, the Pays de

PUBLIC BURNING

The Spanish scholar Servetus unwisely passed through Calvin's Geneva on his way to Italy. He was not only a Unitarian but unsound on infant baptism. Servetus was publicly burnt to death.

Europe to shreds. The Swiss cantons were neutral, but atavistic instincts were aroused by war swirling around them and the Swiss population was divided, rooting for one side or the other.

Huguenot wealth

Geneva had difficulty feeding itself with the loss of the Pays de Gex to Henry IV of France, but the French Huguenots provided the solution. They were artisans, watchmakers and jewellers, merchants and, above all, financiers. In little more than a

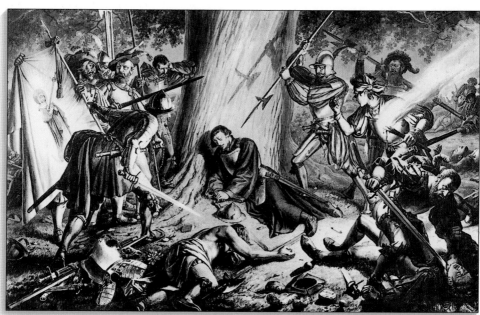

Gex, and it was hard to imagine how Geneva would be able to feed itself.

Continual conflict

Unpleasant as the Reformation and Counter Reformation had been in Switzerland, the discomfort paled in comparison with the Thirty Years' War, which began at the start of the 17th century as a war about Bohemia and religion, developed into a trial of strength between France and the Habsburgs, and tore central

LEFT: Calvin *(right)* and Farel *(left)* in Geneva, which was rocked by their zealous reform uprisings.
ABOVE: the death of Zwingli in the Battle of Kappel.

century, Geneva became one of the wealthiest cities in Europe. On the political front, the Peace of Westphalia, which concluded the Thirty Years' War, ratified Swiss independence. The Swiss states were no longer, even in the loose sense which had long been the case, part of the German Empire.

The Swiss, quiet and prosperous while the rest of Europe was at war, used the Peace of Westphalia as a cue to fight among themselves and let the economic advances slip away. It was almost as if the Confederation needed an external threat to remain in one piece. Without it, the states went off on their own. Neuchâtel and St Gallen were paragons of unbending

Voltaire's theatre

Geneva was roused from its Calvinistic state of self-denial when Voltaire arrived in the city in 1755 and introduced its citizens to the theatre, with all its perceived vices. The French author spent most of the last 20 years of his life in Switzerland, although he returned to Paris just before he died in 1778.

Voltaire's writing to date would not have been at all to the taste of the previously libertine but now thoroughly chastened burghers. He found his métier in writing a wicked satire on the pompous

Duke d'Orléans which earned him a six-month banishment from Paris. He continued to comment on the unfortunate duke's character and was therefore brought back to be thrown into the Bastille. A spell in England opened his eyes to the intellectual traditional of Isaac Newton, John Locke and other empiricist philosophers of the 18th century.

By now, Voltaire was producing an impressive flow of literature, and on returning to France showed a hitherto unsuspected talent for making money, buying shares in the government lottery and selling corn to the army.

Voltaire's romantic attachments kept pace with his rising fame and fortune and earned him the patronage of Madame de Pompadour. Nevertheless,

he carried on pricking personalities, including the Prussian Frederick the Great, for whom he happened to be working at the time, living in one of Frederick's palaces and drawing a pension of 20,000 francs. When Voltaire then showed up in Geneva, an unlikely place for someone with his kind of background, it was a matter of waiting to see what he would get up to next in spite of his protestations about being on the brink of death and wishing only to lead a quiet life.

In the event, Voltaire bought an estate, Les Délices, on the outskirts of Geneva, pottered about his garden, and was charming to everyone he met in Genevese society. He invited a select gathering to meet his house guest Lekain, the greatest French actor of the day. Lekain, Voltaire and his niece, Mme Denis, gave a reading from one of his works, *Zaire*. "Never saw I so many tears shed," Voltaire wrote later, "never were the Calvinists so tender..." His mind was made up – Geneva must have a theatre.

At his announcement of this, Geneva caught its breath. The Consistory fulfilled expectations with such an explosion of moral outrage that even Voltaire, to whom controversy was meat and drink, thought it prudent to decamp to Lausanne until things cooled down.

Outraging Rousseau

Voltaire returned quietly the following year but soon revived the issue by writing in the *Encyclopaedia* that Geneva needed a theatre that would "unite the wisdom of Sparta with the polish of Athens". This apparently inoffensive claim nevertheless raised the hackles of the other great man of contemporary Switzerland, and former friend, Jean-Jacques Rousseau, who fumed that while he had nothing against theatre, per se, it would corrupt the innocent Genevese, leading them to the road to levity, ruin and perdition.

Undaunted, Voltaire opened his theatre at Les Délices; the city closed it down. He tried again at several other locations, always with the same result. Geneva at last got a purpose-built wooden theatre in 1766 and the Puritans promptly put a torch to it. Voltaire swore that Rousseau was responsible. The flames attracted a crowd of citizens armed with buckets, but on realising that it was the theatre they are reputed to have emptied the buckets with a cry of "Let those who wanted a theatre put it out!" The ironic outcome to this feud is that when Rousseau died he was buried in the Pantheon in Paris – alongside Voltaire. ❑

LEFT: Voltaire, *bête noire* of the Calvinists.

absolutism; Bern, Fribourg, Solothurn and Luzern aped the oligarchies based on birth and inheritance. Only the forest cantons were even remotely democratic. Society split along class lines too: a minor peasant protest against new taxation struck such a popular chord that a proletarian uprising exploded over much of central Switzerland.

The peasants themselves were "hards" pitted against "softs", the former chopping off the beards, ears or both of those who were thought not to be pulling their weight. The poorly equipped peasants were no match for their common enemy, however, and both their principal

Catholics wished to carry the cross upright in a procession through the streets. The Second Villmergen War, which again saw St Gallen in the thick of the action, was over who should provide the labour for the construction of a new road. The Pope was drawn into the dispute and it was only settled after a bloody victory by the combined Zürich and Bern armies.

The manipulative hand of Louis XIV of France was behind much of the religious ill-feeling of the 17th century. To begin with, he needed Swiss mercenaries – between 6,000 and 16,000 a year – for his wars and was prepared to offer commercial privileges in return.

leaders, Christian Schibi and Nicholas Leuenberger, were captured, tortured and executed.

Second wave

The religious wars were fought all over again on slight pretexts. The First Villmergen War (1656) was sparked by the imperiously Catholic Schwyz sending three of the handful of Protestants living in the canton to be dealt with by the Inquisition in Milan, and eventually had Bern and Zürich at war with all five Catholic states. War threatened in St Gallen in 1697 because

ABOVE: John Calvin (1509–64) delivers his parting lecture on his death bed, zealous to the very end.

Switzerland ended up, though, as a dependency of the French Crown in all but name, and things might not have stopped there had France not been kept in rein by Britain and the Netherlands. Swiss envoys were treated to lavish entertainment at the French court and it was said that they were beguiled into playing the king's poodles. When Louis XIV remarked that all the money he had paid for Swiss troops would have paved the road from Paris to Basel with gold pieces, the Swiss replied – in one celebrated exception to their sycophancy: "You forget Sir, that with the Swiss blood spilt in the French service you might fill a canal from Basel to Paris."

In the 17th and 18th centuries the leading cities of the Confederation took on different characters. Zürich was the seat of liberal and intellectual progress, Bern of politics and finance, and Geneva of science. Zürich, like all fully fledged members of the Confederation, had its subject lands, and the liberal tendencies stopped there to be replaced by the sort of patriarchal governor much admired by Goethe. Landolt von Greifensee, a case in point, "hated enlightened peasants and modern revolutionary ideas". He advocated compulsory church attendance and believed that flogging was an effective means of discipline.

> ### THE SOCIAL CONTRACT
>
> "Man is born free; and everywhere he is in chains" – the resounding opening to Rousseau's Social Contract.

citizens led by a certain Henzi presented a petition asking for some of these regulations to be relaxed. Henzi paid for the presumption with his life.

Geneva, which we have previously seen under the heel of Calvin's Consistory, was rocked to its foundations in 1755 by the arrival of Voltaire. He was there, he said blandly, to see out his twilight years (he was then 61), but those who assumed this meant a mellow, uncontroversial retirement were in for a rude awakening (see box, page 40).

French elite

Bern was resolutely French in language and manners. Its constitution was elitist, with all power vested in 360 families. The middle class had no political rights but were given the run of trade, education and religion. The lower class, which included foreigners, were not permitted to own houses or have their children baptised in the city. They were not allowed to enter the market before 11am, by which time their betters (or their betters' servants) were supposed to have done their shopping. In 1744 a group of

Revolutionary shock

As France had long been Switzerland's most powerful ally, the Revolution sent shockwaves through the Confederation. It was opposed, naturally enough, by those with a vested interest in the divinely appointed social and political order: the cantonal governments, the privileged urban classes, the church and, of course, the French aristocratic refugees, most of whom congregated in Solothurn, Fribourg and Neuchâtel. It was supported by the subject territories, the French-speaking parts and by Swiss émigrés in Paris. The opponents could have found an ally in imperial Austria, but there was always the fear of Austrian territorial ambition in Switzerland. France, whatever its government, was seen as the best available guarantee against Austrian aggrandisement. All in all, it suited Switzerland to be neutral.

Franco-Swiss relations, on tenterhooks because of the Revolution, were tested to the limit on 10 August 1792 when the Paris mob stormed the Palace of the Tuileries, where the job of protecting the French royals was in the hands of the Swiss Guard. It seems that once his personal safety had been secured, Louis XIV ordered a ceasefire, whereupon the mob turned on the guard and massacred nearly 800 of them. Ten days after the incident, the French Assembly dismissed the Swiss mercenaries serving elsewhere and sent them all home without pay. Many of them, particularly the officers, promptly switched sides, fighting for the anti-revolutionary coalition under Austrian command and British pay.

The Swiss revolutionaries in Paris shook off the general Swiss outrage at the massacre of the Guard to press for the French "liberation" of Switzerland. The French Government was cautious. Almost the whole of Europe had imposed a blockade on France, and only the Swiss frontier was open to admit a long list of materials provided by indiscriminating suppliers in Austria, Italy and Hungary.

In 1798 French attitudes hardened under the growing influence of Napoleon Bonaparte. A pretext was found to occupy the southern shore of Lake Geneva, the first such foreign invasion in the Confederation's history. Laharpe, who had long borne a grudge against Bern, reminded Napoleon that the city possessed a treasure trove of gold. Bern was the military mainstay of the Confederation but, abandoned by the other members and paralysed by internal dissent, it could not withstand a French assault.

The sack of Bern

On 5 March the French Army entered the city and went to work. The contents of the treasury were carted off in 11 wagons together with the city's three mascots, bears named Erlach, Steiger and Weiss.

LEFT: *The Elephant Carousel* by Antoine Caron: the elephant represents Geneva, its "Turk" passengers are Protestant infidels, and both are under attack from Catholic forces.

RIGHT: Jean-Jacques Rousseau.

The 10 city cantons acquiesced in the Helvetic Republic proclaimed by France, but the three forest cantons were defiant. They would be "burnt beneath their blazing roofs", they said, "rather than submit to the dictates of the foreigner". They were hopelessly outnumbered, however, and after the fall of Glarus and Schwyz the resistance focused on the town of Stans, in Nidwalden.

The French commander called 9 September 1798 the hottest day of his life: "Like furies, the black legion of the French galley-slaves slew and raged the district through." The defiance ended in smoke and blood that night. ❑

TRADITIONAL COUNTRY LIFE

Life continues in much the same way as it always has in the rural communities of the Alps, with their distinctive music, crafts and style of dress

One of the most remarkable features of Switzerland is the coexistence of two contrasting economies: the dynamic, ultramodern one of industry and business and the rural, farming economy that is, at least in mountain areas, highly traditional. Upland farming is still conducted on a small family scale, and high government subsidies have helped to stem the ongoing generational drift away from the land. Consequently, Switzerland has been less affected by the pervading western European phenomenon whereby rural communities rapidly transmute into commuter villages, and the Swiss in general take tremendous pride in their traditional countryside heritage that embodies much more than the caricature of bearded, yodelling, alphorn-playing, flag-tossing farmers in traditional dress that you'll find in touristy folklore shows.

THE SOUND OF MUSIC

Yodelling, with its ululating high falsetto and low chest notes, was developed from the calls of Swiss herdsmen and, like the national instrument, the melancholy alphorn, was used as a way of communicating across mountain valleys.

The alphorn, made of a hollowed pine trunk up to 4 metres (13 ft) in length, was first described in 1555 and originated in the traditional rural village of Appenzell and the Bernese Oberland. By the early 19th century, the alphorn had come perilously close to disappearing from use but, from the 1820s, a cultural revival rescued it from this ignominious fate.

Apparently, herdsmen used to play it to soothe the cows while they were being milked.

▷ **ACROSS THE ALPS**
Cows graze in pasture near the Paso del Lucomagno (Lukmanier Pass), which, with the St Gotthard, is one of the most important north–south routes across the Alps.

△ **ALPINE WELCOME**
A man in Col du Pillon, from where visitors can take local transport to the glacier at Les Diablerets, a small village in the Alps Vaudoises.

◁ **BASKET CASE**
Country life can be hard and involve back-breaking work. This basket, pictured in Val Bregaglia, was made to carry fodder.

▷ **A COUNTRY SEAT**
Early Swiss design is on display in museums across the country, and through them the culture is preserved. This chair and footstool in a rural kitchen are characteristic.

THE ART OF WOODCARVING

Around Lake Brienz is a community of craftsmen who use local wood such as linden to create works of art – from music boxes and trinkets to sculptures. Even the architecture and the buildings with heavy, ornate wooden balconies reveal the craftsmanship which has made the town of Brienz the unofficial woodcarving centre of Switzerland.

Woodworkers have passed on ancient skills from generation to generation creating the ornamental objects and practical items which are sold in the region's studios and craft shops. Traditional skills are preserved at the Kantonale Schnitzerschule Brienz (Woodcarving School and Museum; open daily 8–11.30am and 2–5pm during term time; tel: 033-952 17 51). Opposite is a violin-making school, which runs courses throughout the year, and nearby is the Jobin Living Museum, which claims to have the largest collection of antique carvings and wooden Swiss music boxes.

◁ **SOMETHING CHEESY**
Traditional cheesemaking survives in Château d'Oex. In Swiss valleys and mountains old-time methods are used to process fresh milk.

▽ **RURAL COMFORT**
A charming and typical Appenzell country bedroom, reconstructed in the Open-air Museum at Ballenberg, near Brienz in the Bernese Oberland.

△ **SWISS WOODCRAFT**
Nothing compares to the elaborate carving and designs that can be seen in Brienz, Switzerland's woodcarving centre.

▷ **TRADITIONAL DRESS**
There is an astonishing variety of traditional regional dress: some 400 different types have been recorded. Right is one from Emmental.

THE MAKING OF MODERN SWITZERLAND

The country preserved its neutrality through two world wars, and ended up
even richer and more stable than before

The Helvetic Republic was formed physically and politically to suit the purposes of France. Bits of the south were chopped off and given to French-controlled Italy, Neuchâtel was completely cut off and Mulhausen

was attached to France. The remainder was divided into 23 cantons under a rigidly centralised executive directory, as in France. The constitution duplicated the individual liberties introduced by the Revolution but these were less appreciated than the loss of local autonomy was mourned. The ultimate humiliation was the choice between signing a perpetual military alliance with France (effectively ending Swiss neutrality) and outright annexation.

The constitution was made unworkable by constant squabbling among the Swiss and six changes to it between 1798 and 1803 made no difference. By 1803 Napoleon had had enough: they could have their quasi-sovereign cantons,

their neutrality and even their judicial torture. The perpetual alliance was reduced to 50 years, and Napoleon reserved the right to recruit 16,000 men in Switzerland. Under his Act of Mediation Napoleon took the title Mediator of the Swiss Confederation and for a while the country was able to dress the wounds.

The road to neutrality

The Congress of Vienna, convened to unstitch the Napoleonic Empire after its collapse in 1814, saw the Swiss patricians lobbying furiously to regain their former rights, and it was only through much banging of Swiss heads that the Big Four – Austria, England, Russia and Prussia – got them to agree to a loose federation. The cantons, now numbering 23, would be almost autonomous with just a few federal functions exercised by rota among Bern, Zürich and Luzern. These deliberations were dramatically interrupted, however, by news of Napoleon's escape from Elba. Switzerland, whose neutrality was on the table awaiting ratification, was coerced into declaring war on France, the argument being that neutrality would be worthless if Napoleon were able to re-establish himself.

The Swiss Army invaded France on 3 July 1815, halted on the 22nd, and simply went home. With Napoleon finally disposed of, the Treaty of Paris recognised the perpetual neutrality of Switzerland on 20 November 1815.

Switzerland's borders were established by the treaty as they are today. The Confederation lost Mulhouse but regained an enlarged Geneva, the Valais and Neuchâtel. The former territory of Basel was shared with Bern.

While the international status and map of Switzerland were now secure, the domestic scene during the next 15 years of "Restoration" was chaotic. Cantons insisted on coining their own currency and customs barriers between them were so cumbersome that international traders used other routes.

In 1830, inspired by the example of the Revolution in France, "Restoration" was transformed into "Regeneration", a curious misnomer unless it is understood to mean the regeneration of forces capable of turning confusion into utter chaos. Disgruntled peasants in the various cantons pursued their respective dreams which, apart from a general desire to cut the aristocracy down to size, reflected the spectrum of differences. The reactionary old order fought back with the kind of mindless logic which saw the French-speaking aristocrats in Fribourg demanding German as the official language because German it had been until 1798.

The Federal Diet was impotent, so much so that in 1832 seven cantons, including Luzern and Zürich, formed a federation of sorts within the federation, and other groupings followed suit. These groupings then re-arrranged themselves so that the Confederation was effectively two bitterly antagonistic camps: "an ominous state of affairs, calculated to make every patriot tremble for the result…"

As tension mounted between opposing religious factions, the canton of Aargau "set the whole country ablaze" by abolishing all monasteries and nunneries, thereby antagonising the Pope and the Emperor of Austria whose ancestors had founded Muri, one of the monasteries in question. The compromise was to save the nunneries but to get rid of the monasteries.

Council of War

In 1844, Luzern, one of the Catholic cantons, decided that its religious interests would best be served by handing over its education to the Jesuits. Extremist Protestants launched guerrilla raids on the city, in one of which 100 paramilitary volunteers were killed and 1,900 captured. The seven predominantly Catholic cantons linked up as the *Sonderbund*, declared an Act of Succession and appointed a Council of War. Prince Metternich, the Austrian Chancellor who had been one of the architects of the "new" Switzerland at the Congress of Vienna, watched these developments aghast. "Switzer-

---

LEFT: detail from *The Famous of the Nation*, a painting of 1829.
RIGHT: cover of the Confederate Agreement of 1815.

> ### ANTI-JESUIT FERVOUR
>
> On the eve of the civil war, the editor of the *Basler Zeitung*, Jacob Burckhardt, raged that "Jesuits are a curse on all those lands and persons who fall into their hands".

land," he wrote, "presents the most perfect image of a state in the process of social disintegration… Switzerland stands alone today in Europe as a republic and serves troublemakers of every sort as a free haven. Instead of improving its situation by appropriate means, the Confederation staggers from evils into upheavals and represents for itself and for its neighbours an inexhaustible spring of unrest and disturbance."

The civil war pitted the 415,000 inhabitants of the seven *Sonderbund* cantons against nearly

2 million of the "federal" cantons. The Sonderbund, moreover, was difficult to defend. The forest cantons held a strong central position, but Fribourg was completely isolated and Valais was connected to the others only by high Alpine passes. Understandably, the federal forces picked off Fribourg first and then closed in on Luzern from all sides. The city surrendered without a fight, and the others soon followed. The campaign was over within 20 days at the cost of 78 dead and 260 wounded.

The victors were lenient, the principal victims being the Jesuits, who were expelled. A new constitution was put to the vote, and although seven cantons opposed it they agreed to go along with the majority. The Federal Constitution of 1848 put foreign affairs and other institutions like the post office and customs under central control, restricted mercenary activities abroad and ensured that for the first time all cantons had democratic institutions. The Swiss had a plausible national government at last and were in a position to catch up with the rest of Europe.

In the years that followed, Zürich played a prominent role in federal affairs, and under the dynamic leadership of its liberal mayor, Jonas

Furrer, enjoyed an unprecedented period of cosmopolitan cultural renaissance.

Neuchâtel crisis

Revitalised by their growing democracy, the Swiss felt cocky enough to contemplate going to war with Prussia over the curious business of Neuchâtel, the first crisis of foreign policy the young state had to face. Neuchâtel had been something of an oddity since 1707 when, in order to spurn the advances of Louis XIV of France it had put itself under the ducal sway of Frederick II of Prussia. It remained a Prussian possession even after admission as a canton in 1814; it was thus a monarchical enclave within

a republican confederation. These royalists refused to join the federal forces against the *Sonderbund* in 1847 and were overthrown by republican sympathisers.

Two-day coup

The following year, however, the Great Powers reinstated the Prussian king as "Prince of Neuchâtel". The Swiss would have none of it and went on recognising the republican usurpers. On 2 September Count Frédéric Pourtalès usurped the usurpers in a royalist coup and Neuchâtel was Prussian again – but only for two days. A hundred or so royalists were taken prisoner in the counter coup, but Frederick William IV of Prussia mobilised, and the Swiss responded by raising a force of 30,000.

Napoleon III, who did not wish to see the Prussian Army rolling up on his southeastern flank, offered to mediate, and Britain's Lord Palmerston reminded Frederick William of the guarantees of Swiss neutrality.

The agreement reached was that Switzerland would release the royalist prisoners, who would then return to Prussia, Neuchâtel would be given full cantonal rights within the Swiss Confederation, and Frederick William would give up his sovereign rights for all time although he could, if he liked, go on calling himself Prince of Neuchâtel. It was the last of the old struggles between Swiss and foreign authorities.

Mercenaries and refugees

The twin problems caused by Swiss mercenaries abroad and political refugees remained unsolved. The 1848 Federal Constitution had forbidden any more military capitulations (ie, contracts to supply mercenaries) but it did not abolish those already in existence, two of which were with King Bomba of Naples and the Pope. These meant that, whether they liked it or not, Swiss troops were mixed up in the wars of the Italian Risorgimento, a situation which continued in defiance of the issuing of a new federal law in 1859 which tightened the ban on mercenary service.

In the same year a papal Swiss regiment was accused of atrocities after capturing Perugia; another unit was badly beaten the following year at Castelfidardo by an Italian army marching to join Garibaldi. About 4,000 Swiss

---

A CAUTION FOR KINGS

When royalists were imprisoned following the Neuchâtel coup, Frederick Willliam IV of Prussia called it a "slap in the face for all the monarchs of Europe".

"volunteers" fought in the American Civil War, mostly for the South, and 7,000 were killed fighting for France in World War I. Volunteering – even for the French Foreign Legion – was banned in 1927, the only exception being the Vatican Guard, founded in 1505 by Pope Julius II, whose contracts stipulate no combat duties.

The political convulsions of the mid-19th century created a flood of fugitives who chose to interpret Switzerland's internationally guaranteed neutrality as a safe haven for them. The country showed both profit and loss on its popular reputation as an asylum.

Napoleon defused the danger by leaving Swiss territory and moving to London.

Louise-Philippe's actions reflected the not uncommon attitude that the price of Swiss neutrality was *not* harbouring fugitives. The Swiss of course did not agree and, at least to begin with, the majority of the population welcomed the refugees as martyrs, trying to find them work. The welcome cooled when the volume swelled to thousands and, unable to find work, they became public nuisances. The refugee question became a grave embarrassment to Switzerland, and its shadow today is the feeling, perhaps, that the vaunted secrecy of the

Swiss Napoleon

Louis-Philippe, the future "citizen-king" of the French, spent some years in Graubünden as a mathematics teacher, but on assuming the throne he objected violently when Louis Napoleon, who later succeeded him as Napoleon III, claimed asylum in Switzerland. Napoleon was in fact a naturalised Swiss and had become a captain in the Swiss Army. When the Diet refused to expel him, Louis-Philippe sent an army of 25,000 men to fetch him.

LEFT: French troops near Hüningen (c. 1798).
ABOVE: planting the "Tree of Liberty" on Münsterplatz, in Basel.

country's banking system may shield rather too many unworthy causes.

In spite of difficulties with Neuchâtel, mercenaries and refugees, federal Swiss enjoyed internal peace, economic prosperity and even respectability in foreign relations.

War again

As long as the European balance of power remained stable, the independence and neutrality of Switzerland were safe. When the balance was upset, cracks showed in the fabric. The 1870 Franco-Prussian War was a particular case in point because of the country's racial and religious composition. The political minority

The Red Cross

International Geneva, familiar as the backdrop to so many peace conferences and summit meetings, is practically a state within a city. It is the address for scores of international organisations and even has its own postmark for their outgoing mail. It is no coincidence that the famous Red Cross which has fluttered above ambulances in countless wars is actually the Swiss flag with its colours reversed, nor that the Red Cross headquarters should be in Geneva. The two are closely linked, but the origin of that association

is a largely forgotten story worth recounting.

Henri Dunant, the founder of the Red Cross (pictured above), was born in Geneva in 1828 and made his fortune in Algeria as a grain speculator. He returned to Geneva to try to raise more capital but, faced with bureaucratic obstacles, decided to go to the top, to Napoleon III personally.

Dunant's efforts to secure an audience with Napoleon set something of a benchmark in sycophancy. He wrote a book, which proved beyond a doubt that Napoleon was, among other things, heir to the Emperor Augustus, a fact only vaguely implicit in the title. It was The Empire of Charlemagne Reestablished or The Holy Roman Empire Reconstituted by His Majesty the Emperor Napoleon III, by J.

Henri Dunant, director and president of the Financial and Industrial Society of Mons-Djemila (Algeria), member of the Asiatic Society of Paris, of the Oriental Society of France, of the Geographic Societies of Paris and Geneva, of the Historical Society of Algiers, etc. Dunant had one copy printed, and then had to deliver it.

He tracked down Napoleon in Italy on the eve of the Battle of Solferino (1859). Understandably, the emperor had other things on his mind and, in the morning, so did Dunant. He found himself in the middle of one of the bloodiest battles in history – 33,000 casualties on the first day alone. Dunant threw himself into washing wounds and generally helping as casualties poured in at the rate of 55 a minute. After two days and nights without sleep, the man was a legend. It was almost irrelevant that Napoleon glanced at the book and said that for political reasons he could not accept it.

Dunant returned to Geneva and wrote a moving account of the horrors he had seen. A Souvenir of Solferino was a powerful plea for the creation of a neutral organisation which would care for the casualties of war. M Gustave Moynier, president of the Society for Public Usefulness of Geneva, read it and thought the idea good. Dunant toured Europe drumming up support; the result was the signing of the first Geneva Convention in 1864.

Three years after the foundation of the Red Cross, however, Dunant left Geneva, bankrupt. Wandering penniless, he thought of other ambitious schemes, such as putting the Levant under Napoleon's protection and creating a Jewish state in Palestine. These came to nothing and pursuit by his creditors meant he could not stay in one place for long.

In 1887 Dunant returned to a semi-incognito existence in Switzerland, living like a hermit in the village of Heiden in Appenzell. A journalist discovered the fate of the founder of the Red Cross, and his scoop was quickly followed up by other newspapers. In 1901 the white-bearded hermit of Heiden jointly won the first Nobel Peace Prize – seized on by his creditors as an opportunity to renew their claims. Embarrassed by the financial failure of one of its own, Geneva questioned his claim to have founded the Red Cross.

Dunant had the last word. When he died in 1910, he left the Nobel Prize money he had saved to charitable institutions in Norway and Switzerland. His remaining creditors got nothing. ❏

LEFT: Henri Dunant, founder of the Red Cross.

of Catholic Conservatives and the linguistic minority of the Radical-Democratic French cantons were united by the dread of Protestant Germanisation, as exemplified by the growth of Prussia. The threat existed in the possible Germanisation of the federal government, so logically they dug in their heels in favour of cantonal autonomy. The division between Centralists and Federalists was therefore a racial and cultural one, championed respectively by the Vaudois Louis Ruchonnet and the Federal Councillor

of voters back from Europe and all the way from America. The result was a draw but, under the majority system, the Conservatives gained two-thirds of the seats.

The Radicals took the law into their own hands, seizing public buildings, imprisoning the municipal council and declaring a provisional government. The arrival of two battalions of federal troops and a promise of proportional representation calmed things down. In 1892, the Radicals were returned to power.

NOTABLE VISITORS

Instead of persecuted Protestants, 19th-century refugees in Switzerland included leading political figures such as Mazzini and Lenin, and, later, Mussolini.

Emil Welti, the latter campaigning on the slogan "One law, one army."

The obvious outsider in the fundamental Swiss split was Italian-speaking Ticino, where Conservatives and Radicals were practically of equal strength. Complaints of dishonest electoral practices led to demonstrations, riots and bloodshed, and for a while civil war within the canton looked likely. Elections in 1889 to test some democratic innovations brought Ticinese living abroad streaming home to vote. The parties even chartered ships to bring hundreds

ABOVE: exchange of fire during the civil war between Basel District and Basel Town (1831).

EARLY TOURISM

Following two visits to the Alps by Queen Victoria, Switzerland suddenly became the fashionable holiday destination for the European middle classes.

According to one contemporary report, however, visitors got a far more mixed reception than is the norm today: "For three months the only vegetables that we had were potatoes. In fact a person coming here for health gains greatly as regards climate, but loses greatly for want of good food and ordinary home comforts."

Anticipating the boom in winter sports nevertheless, the first form of entertainment was joy-riding downhill on *Schlitten*, or toboggans, borrowed from villagers.

The new economy

A neutral Switzerland provided one carefree flank for all its neighbours; the critical question was whether Switzerland had the will and the power to prevent its neutrality from being invaded by someone else. It was probably as much as Switzerland could do in this respect to announce large increases in the mobility and striking force of its army and, all the while, lend its neutral territory profitably as the seat for international organisations.

STRATEGIC PAWN

Switzerland's size meant that it would only ever be a pawn in Europe's power game, but the opening of the Gotthard Tunnel in 1882 made it a key player, with the best route from north to south.

ever, exposed the Swiss farmer to competition from as far afield as Russia. Swiss production costs and prices were too high compared to foreign cereals which, thanks to better transport, could now be imported with ease.

Swiss farmers turned to other things, and the cereal mountain shrank. By the end of the 19th century, the country was producing only what was needed to cover domestic consumption for six months.

Swiss farmers realised that they had turned

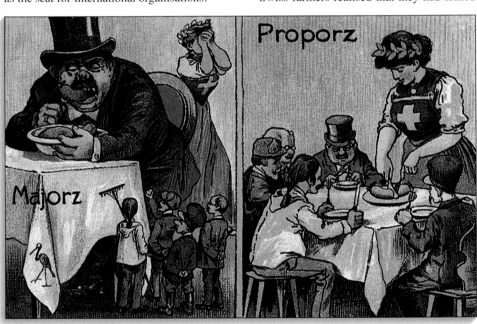

The new tunnels, roads and railways were bad news for farmers, or so it seemed. The military efficacy of embryonic Switzerland depended to a very large extent on a pastoral economy, that is to say non-labour-intensive stock-raising. Over the course of centuries, the forest cantons were joined and progressively dominated by others whose land was more conducive to mixed farming. Agriculture evolved so that by the middle of the 19th century the main activity overall was cereal production.

In the circumstances, cereal production increased so that the country generally had enough grain to cover domestic consumption for 300 days. Modern means of transport, how-

full circle. Conditions were still excellent for stock-raising and dairy farming, so they once again invested their energies in these. Some things had changed. The demand from abroad was no longer for horse meat but for beef.

Cheese sold so well that it eventually accounted for more than a third of agriculture exports. The dairy industry also produced two novelties which have since become synonymous with Switzerland – chocolate and condensed milk.

Swiss watches

The watch- and clockmaking industry was forced (especially after World War I) to adopt factory methods for export sales. The industry as a whole went for volume, rising to control nearly 90 percent of total world production. By the 1970s it had slipped to about 40 percent and was still falling as the Swiss franc gained against the currencies in the watch industry's main export markets. A falling dollar meant that competitive American watches were cheaper, and of course the entry of the super-efficient Japanese manufacturers re-wrote the rules from top to bottom.

Looming world war

In time, political conversation in Switzerland, as in the rest of Europe, hinged on the domino effect that began with the Habsburg Archduke Ferdinand's assassination in Sarajevo and resulted in World War I.

French-speaking Switzerland, as before, was suspicious of Germany, exceptionally so after its invasion of Belgium, and of the German outlook which had been gaining ground within the country. More than 220,000 "pure" Germans were living in Switzerland, half of them in Basel and Zürich alone. French-speaking Switzerland's sympathies were entirely with France and Britain. The Italian-speaking Ticinese were for Italy. For their part, German-speaking Swiss felt a kinship with Germany and admired its rise in technology, industry and commerce. Many deplored the invasion of Belgium but they still believed in Germany.

"On general cultural grounds as well as political I believe that a German victory is desirable," wrote Karl Scheurer, head of the Military Department of Bern canton in August 1914. A month later, the German minister in Bern reported to his superiors: "From the very first day since the outbreak of war Switzerland has discreetly placed at our disposal her entire secret military intelligence service…"

The arrest and trial of two of Commander-in-Chief General Wille's staff officers for passing secrets to the Germans and Austrians led to calls for his resignation, which did nothing for the morale of an army on uneventful, boring frontier duties. A few bombs were dropped but there were no serious breaches of neutrality. The real war, for Switzerland, was economic.

LEFT: satirical cartoon representing the late 19th-century campaign for proportional representation.
RIGHT: a poster supporting women's cantonal voting rights in Zürich.

Depleted agriculture was insufficient to feed the people and there was always the danger of being cut off not only from imported food supplies but also from the raw materials which kept industry running. An agreement with the central powers in 1915 provided for the import of German and Austrian goods but the Allies were not so cooperative. The United States guaranteed the supply of bread.

Some Swiss were ruined by the war; others did well. In the absence of foreign competition, it was like old times for farmers. The worst economic pressures fell on the working class. The bitterness of the workers was exacerbated by

Aktionskomitee für das Frauenstimmrecht im Kanton Zürich

the large number of foreigners who flooded in during the war – profiteers, deserters, conscientious objectors, and even more Russian revolutionaries like Lenin, Trotsky, Zinoviev, Axelrod and Martov. Their presence alone made Switzerland look like the revolutionary capital of the world, and Swiss socialists were impressionable. The idea of a general strike took shape.

The Federal Council moved quickly to stifle the strike. The army was sent into Zürich to prevent the Social Democrats from holding a demonstration to celebrate the anniversary of the Russian Revolution and the entire Soviet legation in Bern was frog-marched to the frontier. The strike was only partially effective, and the Social Democrats succumbed to a federal order to call it off. Some of the strike leaders went to prison for short spells, but many of their demands, such as that for a 48-hour week, were quickly met.

World War II

With the prospect of a second war ever more likely, Switzerland took precautions against being caught out as before by filling its granaries. Neutrality in the event of hostilities was taken for granted, but sight of an official German training manual gave a shock: its maps put Switzerland firmly within the boundaries of the Third Reich. The German Swiss were no less alarmed than the rest and it made them realise that, after all, they were rather different from real Germans, certainly from the Fascists. When war broke out, Switzerland's Commander-in-Chief was again elected, and the choice fell on the French-Swiss Henri Guisan of Vaud, a significant change from the previous German bias among the military. Mobilisation led to the call-up of 400,000 men, later increased to 850,000 with the inclusion of auxiliary services and the home guard, out of a total population of only 4 million. In the early stages of the war, Swiss troops took up their usual positions along the borders, but with the

THE LEAGUE OF NATIONS

Switzerland was enthusiastic about the proposed League of Nations after World War I, and, although it took no significant part in its creation, Geneva was selected as the seat of the League. Nevertheless, there was doubt whether Switzerland's neutrality would allow it to join; in 1920 the Declaration of London allowed Switzerland in "by reason of an ancient tradition". The Confederation would not be called on to take part in military operations, but it would be bound to observe economic sanctions as imposed by the League. When the chance to join was put to the Swiss electorate, the population voted in favour of joining, by 414,830 votes to 322,937.

fall of France, which left the country completely surrounded by the Axis, Guisan adopted a strategy that an enemy would be allowed to roll across the frontiers, where defence was difficult, in order to be met where conditions better suited the Swiss, in and along the Alps.

There is no doubt that the German High Command had plans for a Swiss invasion. They even had a codename, *Tannenbaum* (Fir Tree). Why they were not carried out remains a puzzle. One theory is that Hitler thought that the number of troops required could not be justified by what Switzerland represented in the way of raw materials. Moreover, he needed and already had the use of the Gotthard Tunnel to get coal to his Italian allies. The Swiss, he knew, had mined the tunnel and would blow it up at the first sign of an invasion, a potential loss which would make the invasion counterproductive. Hitler had a ready-made excuse to invade if he needed one: his troops had uncovered in French headquarters at La Charité-sur-Loire the terms of a secret agreement on the exchange of information between Swiss and French intelligence, an ironic postscript to World War I. In any case, after the Allied landings in North Africa and France, Hitler had other things on his mind.

Post-war help

When peace was concluded, Switzerland devoted a generous proportion of its intact economy to post-war reconstruction. The full implications of Fascism in Germany and Italy ran deep. The various Swiss contingents seemed to decide that they were not bad bedfellows after all.

However, the unified spirit of the wartime years was quickly upset by the effects of the Cold War. From 1948, the Communist Party had a strong influence, and tensions between Communists and opposing factions caused a deep rupture in Swiss society. Nevertheless, the economy purred from one boom to the next, propelled by huge reserves of capital and relatively cheap foreign labour. The question of giving the vote to women, a proposal discarded in 1959, but finally accepted in 1971, suggested the Swiss were not merely quaint but antediluvian. Conservatives and the lower-middle classes broke a taboo by asking aloud whether the country really wanted so many foreign workers. Students no longer blindly upheld the hallowed Swiss virtues, suggesting, for example, that they did without national service.

Even questions about the canton system, which most people assumed had been settled in 1848, arose in connection with the proposal to detach the Jura from Bern canton and make it a canton in its own right. To make matters worse, it emerged that Bern interests opposed to the change had bought votes to prevent it from taking place.

> **WOMEN'S VOTES**
>
> The right of Swiss women to vote and stand for federal elections only came in 1971, and women's right to vote in Appenzell-Rhoden cantonal elections was only passed in April 1991.

In 1997, the Swiss banking industry was found to have about $57 million in dormant accounts, many opened by German Jews before World War II, of which $8.6 million was in accounts under Swiss names. The Nazi Gold Scandal, as it became known, had a deep impact on the collective psyche but no tangible effect.

The Swiss, with their comfortable lifestyles, have traditionally regarded themselves as being immune from the rest of the world, and the average citizen is not interested in big changes

that might disturb the peaceful equilibrium of life. However, in a landmark referendum in 2002, the country voted by a small margin to join the United Nations, thus overturning the result of a similar referendum held in 1986.

Gradually, Switzerland is increasing its political integration with the rest of Europe. Despite voting against joining the European Union in 2001, a bilateral agreement, which makes it easier for EU nationals to live in Switzerland, came into force in 2002. In 2005 a referendum went in favour of opening the job market to workers from the 10 newest EU countries. However, in 2006 voters backed plans to make Switzerland's asylum laws among the toughest in the West. ❏

LEFT: farming women making hay.
RIGHT: General Henri Guisan, French-Swiss Commander-in-Chief during World War II.

THE SWISS

Renowned for being efficient, thrifty and staid, the diverse people of this wealthy nation also display some uncredited and unexpected characteristics

Although Switzerland is now one of the world's richest nations, for most of its history this tiny, landlocked country was one of the poorest. With no natural resources, its young men went abroad to earn a living, often serving as mercenaries. At home, the philosophy of "waste not, want not" became part of the national character.

Careful with money, tidy-minded and environmentally conscious, the Swiss have a highly developed attention to detail. No wonder they are good at running banks, hotels and railways, as well as making watches and executing complex engineering projects.

Curse of the stereotype

The Swiss still suffer from the international perception that they are either faceless bankers in grey business suits or bearded farmers, wearing quaint leather shorts. While examples of these stereotypes do exist, the reality is that the population is surprisingly varied. Just think of the innumerable dialects.

Not that the Swiss themselves are free of the curse of stereotyping. Despite its long record of external neutrality, Switzerland suffers considerable inner tension. As relatively recently as 1847 there was a minor civil war, and internal disputes are common. Although women were given the vote only in 1971, its 7 million inhabitants have a degree of independence unknown elsewhere in the world.

Not only does each canton have its own tax-raising powers, it also has its own schools, police and courts. Beneath that level are 3,000 communities, each of which has the power to decide everything from utilities to public holidays and road maintenance.

Major decisions are decided by referenda. All this results in considerable, though understated, pride about where you come from. Locals are

---

PRECEDING PAGES: a hiker takes a well-earned rest; the new year procession at Urnäsch, Appenzell.
LEFT: bathing in Ticino's Val Verzasca.
RIGHT: delivering the daily bread.

rarely complimentary about the folks who live over the hill, or, more often, mountain.

Each region loves to mock its neighbours. Characterised as slow and dull, the Bernese bear the brunt of the equivalent of Irish or Polish jokes. Tending to follow the dictum "if it ain't broke, don't fix it", they rarely vote for new

ideas, except for stronger environmental controls. These conservative folk are divided from their Francophone neighbours to the west by the River Sarine, and an imaginary line called the *Röstigraben*, the Rösti ditch. This witty label conjured up by the Swiss press is a reminder that *Rösti*, the crispy potato cake, is a Swiss-German delicacy. The Swiss-French population talk about the Bernese region east of the river as Outre-Sarine, as if it were overseas, or even outer space.

The citizens of Zürich consider their eastern neighbours in Appenzell as the most workaholic, obstinate and even the most backward of all the Swiss. The German speakers, proud of their work ethic, tend to scorn the French speakers in the west, labelling them as lazy. As recently as 1978, the French speakers in Bern Canton broke away to form the new canton of Jura.

The rest of Switzerland regards the Italian-speaking community in Ticino with suspicion because the Ticinese look as if they enjoy life too much. As for the folk in the Valais, they are regarded merely as "strange": most speak French, and the rest speak a German dialect that is incomprehensible to outsiders. There are even mixed emotions about the Romansch-speaking inhabitants of Graubünden, who wear traditional dress daily, and with admirable pride.

their glasses to one another with great ceremony before drinking. They also fly national and cantonal flags as often as possible.

There have been considerable social changes during the past decade, however. The gap between forward-thinking city dwellers and the rural traditionalists has widened. This is especially true when it comes to the question of the European Union. The idea of entry has been regularly blocked by the conservative country vote. In the national referendum of 2001, the Swiss voted to stay outside the EU – 22 out of the 26 cantons (including some French-speaking ones) voted no. In 2002, however, bilateral

Zürich, with its city slickers, reckons it is far superior to Bern, even if Bern is the nation's capital. As for Basel and Geneva, Zurchers and Berners see them as borderline cases, barely in Switzerland at all.

Swiss roles

There are, however, national characteristics that override regional differences. The thriftiest nation on earth, the Swiss abhor the idea of buying on credit, preferring to save up conscientiously for major purchases. At the same time, wealth is never, ever discussed, let alone flaunted. In general, the Swiss are polite, always shaking hands whenever they meet and bid farewell. They raise

agreements between Switzerland and the EU came into force – the result of the first pro-European vote in recent Swiss history.

Despite the rift between old and new, the Swiss retain a passion for their roots. On Christmas Eve, they flock back to their native villages, ready to meet and greet childhood friends, to sing carols and to celebrate. At the same time, there is also a noticeable brain drain, mainly to North America, as highly qualified young Swiss move to jobs with better prospects.

There are also more and more outside influences. With as many as 20 percent of the population foreign-born, Arabic speakers now outnumber Romansch-speakers.

Technical skills

Another essential facet of the Swiss character is ingenuity. Over the centuries, innovation has helped to overcome the lack of natural resources. Back in 1513, Urs Graf developed etching, the art of making prints from an etched metal plate. In the 18th and 19th centuries, skilled watchmakers in the Jura made names like Rolex, Ebel and Rado world-famous. The world's first electric oven was switched on at the Hotel Bernina, St Moritz in 1889.

UNFAIR APPRAISAL

F. Scott Fitzgerald maintained that Switzerland was a place where few things begin but many things end. However, the psychiatrist Karl Jung and the painter Paul Klee are among Switzerland's influential innovators.

practical, the recessions of the 1980s and 1990s revived the spirit of enterprise, proving that the words Swiss and stuffiness did not belong in the same sentence. Think of the Swatch watch, the Smart car, and even the *trotinette*, the trendy micro-scooter that crowds sidewalks across the world.

This is also a sports-loving nation, where men and women excel internationally at snow and ice sports, such as skiing, tobogganing, bobsleighing and curling. Thanks to the inspi-

Switzerland has long been at the leading edge of technology. In 1981, at IBM's Zürich laboratory, Gerd Binning and Heinrich Rohrer won the Nobel Prize for their work on the scanning tunnelling microscope. Through work at CERN (the European Centre for Nuclear Research), a particle physics research facility near Geneva, quarks are part of everyday life. CERN was also where, in 1990, the Internet was born, when physicist Tim Berners-Lee created the first browser-editor.

Although most inventions have been strictly

ration and invention of British holidaymakers over a century ago, the Swiss took up downhill skiing and have never looked back. The first world Alpine championships were staged at Mürren in 1931. The mountainous terrain is also ideal for producing champions in air sports such as hang-gliding, while on flatter land Swiss equestrian competitors have an excellent record at international level in showjumping, dressage and carriage driving. World-class rowers and sailors thrive on the numerous lakes, as evidenced by the Swiss Alinghi team winning the 2003 America's Cup.

Many claim that competitive rifle shooting was born in Switzerland. Certainly, records show that

LEFT: woman from Val Bregaglia, Graubunden *(far left)* and station platform guard from Zürich.
ABOVE: domestic life in Meiringen, Bernese Oberland.

the Luzern Shooting Guild, founded in 1446, was the world's first shooting club, and the tradition continues. A newer sport, tennis, is experiencing a boom among the young, thanks to the success of Martina Hingis and Roger Federer, who became the world number one in 2004.

Although brochures used to advertise traditional sports, such as *Schwingen* (wrestling), Switzerland is trying to update its image. Today, for every photo of a monastery or mountain, you will find a picture of youngsters enjoying "extreme sports": bungee jumping, snowboarding, ice climbing or sky surfing. The scarier it is the better. Landlocked Switzerland even

boasts a surf team on the international circuit.

Switzerland's combination of neutrality and tolerance has attracted a curious collection of celebrities over the centuries. Many have been French or German, exiles with easy access to their homelands, such as John Calvin (1509–64). The French Protestant reformer moved to Basel, then Geneva, where he put into practice his theories that the church should control the state. He ruled Geneva like a dictator for 20 years.

In the 20th century, the famous residents ranged from political radicals to reactionaries. Lenin, the archetypal communist (1870–1924), left Russia to live in Zürich in 1914, where he wrote *Imperialism, the Highest State of Capitalism* (1917). Italian Fascist leader Benito Mussolini (1883–1945) fled to Switzerland as a young man in 1902, where he began preaching revolution. He was thrown out for causing unrest. Among many exiled rulers have been the Shah of Iran, Mohammed Reza Pahlavi (1918–1980), and dictators such as Sese Seko Mobutu, president of Zaire (1930–1997).

Then there was Einstein. Long before he became famous, German physicist Albert Einstein (1879–1955) took Swiss nationality in 1901 when he went to work in the Patent Office in Bern. Four years later, he published four highly advanced papers, one of which dealt with the theory of relativity.

Haven of the well-heeled

Nowadays, Switzerland is seen as a hideaway for the fabulously rich. Untrammelled by paparazzi and sensational newspapers, residents range from Greek shipping billionaires to wealthy playboys.

Some made their own fortunes, such as Ingvar Kamprad, founder of the Swedish firm of IKEA; others inherited their millions, such as France's Léonard Lauder, of the Estée Lauder cosmetic empire. In 1952, comedian Charlie Chaplin (1889–1977) escaped the McCarthy political witch-hunts in the USA to settle in Corsier, near Vevey, and started a trend among the entertainment industry. As well as film stars such as Audrey Hepburn, Switzerland has been home to writer and wit Noel Coward, rock star Phil Collins and actor and writer Peter Ustinov.

Famous alumnae of the posh finishing schools included the late Diana, Princess of Wales, a former pupil at Rougemont. ❑

SWISS TAX APPEAL

When Johnny Halliday, France's "Elvis", arrived by helicopter in the ritzy ski resort of Gstaad in 2006, Gstaad residents shrugged. Halliday had just become another in the long line of celebrities who have homes in the town, among them Elizabeth Taylor, Sean Connery, Elle Macpherson and Mohamed al-Fayed. Switzerland has become a fiscal paradise for the rich because of a friendly tax environment that in Halliday's case saw a generous reduction in his liabilities from the best part of $3 million a year in France to $105,000 in Switzerland. Small wonder Halliday chose Gstaad as the location to build a modest $3-million timber chalet.

LEFT: showing support for the Swiss football team.

Language

Surely the Swiss are polyglots who switch between flawless German, French and Italian and usually throw in serviceable English as well? No, not quite. The Swiss-German majority, for a start, read and write a language they do not usually speak (German), and speak one which is neither official nor national (Swiss-German Schwyzerdütsch) and is incomprehensible across the border in Germany. Secondly, official French as disgorged in writing by bureaucrats makes purists cringe, while the vernacular French is not at all bad, although each area has its own idiosyncracies. Italian Swiss can speak standard Italian, the third official language, but generally use dialects which would draw blank stares in Italy.

Romansch, national but not official, sounds something like a mixture of Italian and Schwyzerdütsch but is Latin and Etruscan. Romansch is a legacy of the Rhaeti, who resisted the Romans, and of the Romans themselves. It is used by only 50,000 Swiss in Graubünden and splits into five different dialects in the following areas: Upper Engadine, Lower Engadine, Vorderrheintal, Rheintal and the region of Oberhalbstein. Romansch was declared a national language in 1938 to thwart Mussolini, who argued that Romansch was Italian and Graubünden suitable for annexation.

Government documents are in the three official languages, while officials are addressed in the "national" language of the region. That is the theory; the practice is more complicated. The best way to make any sense of it is to follow the chronology.

German arrived in Switzerland with the Alemanni, who expelled the Romans, and Schwyzerdütsch is collectively three bands of the Alemannic dialect known as "Low", "High" and "Highest" Alemannic. The grammar is very different from standard German, a relatively recent convention created by Luther's translation of the Bible.

The Swiss read their newspapers and official documents in standard German, but they speak one form or another of Alemannic. Highest Alemannic is, appropriately, the dialect of the people of the very high Alps, and while they can understand the lower forms of Schwyzerdütsch those lower down cannot always understand them. Unlike accents in England, the varieties say nothing about class but they

reveal where someone comes from and therefore their character. Thus a person is presumed to be aggressive if audibly from Zürich, witty if from Basel, and so on. The educated classes can speak and read standard German but are not inclined to do so. Radio and television use both German and Schwyzerdütsch. Swiss writers by their own admission generally come across as stilted when they write in German.

The history of French in Switzerland is a little less complex. In about AD 500, Helvetic territory split between the Alemanni and the Burgundians, who were also Germanic but gradually adopted the Romance language, which became French. In so

doing they earned the derision of those who remained loyal to Alemannic. As for Romansch, that was "Kauderwelsch" or, roughly, gibberish.

Those of Burgundian stock held their ground and today about one-fifth of the Swiss population speak French, concentrated in six cantons: Geneva, Waadt, Jura, Neuchâtel, and large parts of Fribourg and Valais. The Swiss-French feel very much part of the cultural world of France. The one common point that never fails to make French blood in Paris or Geneva boil is what the Swiss-Germans do to their language.

Italian is the common language in Ticino and in parts of Graubünden. Local Italian dialects amount to private languages, so someone from northern Ticino would be baffled by what is said in the south. ❑

RIGHT: in Geneva, dogs speak French: "I don't foul the pavements".

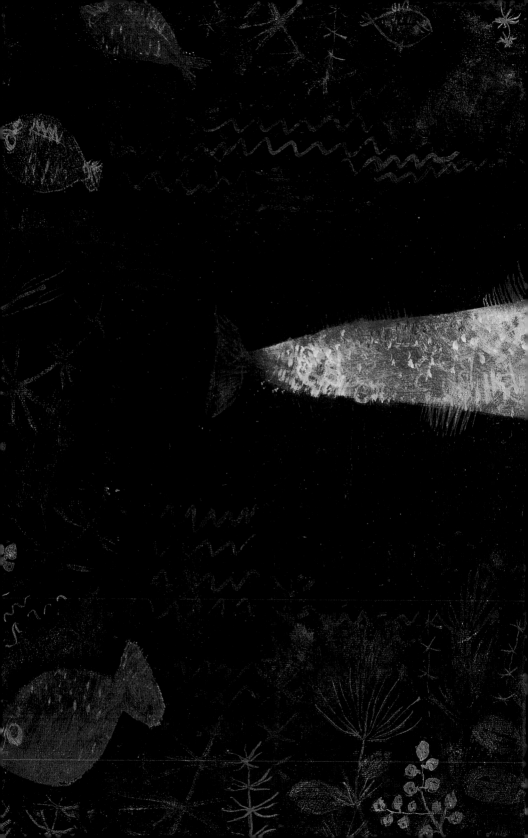

THE ARTS

*For a supposedly conservative nation, Switzerland has produced some
highly innovative artists and art forms during the past 100 years*

To get a sense of how seriously the Swiss take their culture, just take a look at their money. Every banknote features a personality from the arts: architect Le Corbusier on the 10 SFr note, composer Arthur Honegger on the 20 SFr note, painter Sophie Taeuber-Arp on the 50 SFr note, writer and poet Charles Ferdi-

on bottles and shouting poems through hats, they were witnessing the birth of a new art movement: Dadaism. One of the artists behind the chaos was Jean Arp (1887–1966), born in France but resident in Switzerland from about 1909, when he also met Paul Klee. One of the giants of the 20th century, Bern's Paul Klee (1879–1940)

nand Ramuz on the 200 SFr note and, finally, the art and culture historian Jacob Burckhardt on the 100 SFr note. The 20th century saw a blossoming of the arts in Switzerland, with museums and galleries opening in small towns as well as cities. A wide variety of concerts are well attended throughout the year, with summer festivals popular with visitors and locals alike.

Painting

This seemingly conservative nation inspired groundbreaking art forms in the 20th century. Imagine the astonishment of an audience at an arts club called the Cabaret Voltaire in Zürich, on 8 February 1916. Confronted by artists banging

is the most recognisable Swiss painter. Despite his association with movements like the Bauhaus designers, he retained an individuality, using strong colour to convey his personal fantasies.

The self-taught Symbolist Ferdinand Hodler (1853–1918) left striking canvases of Swiss landscapes, many of which are on display at the major museums in Bern and Zürich.

Sculpture

Some of the 20th century's greatest sculptors were Swiss. The most innovative was Alberto Giacometti (1901–1966), the son of Impressionist painter Giovanni. Able to draw and paint fluently as a child, he was 14 when he first sculpted his brother, Diego. Creating the first of his spindly figures in 1935, he worked on them with a passion for the rest of his life.

Few sculptors intrigue the general public as much as Jean Tinguely (1925–1991) from Fribourg. He invented mechanical sculptures, including some that even painted pictures. In 1959, his *"metamatic-automobile-odorante-et-sonore"* created 40,000 abstract paintings while it was exhibited at the first Paris Biennial. Although his sculptures look eccentric, they carry an artistic message: "The machine allows me, above anything, to reach poetry," he said, and "The only stable thing is movement." Other prominent Swiss sculptors include Robert Müller (1920–) and Max Bill (1908–94). Müller works with black-painted sheet metal, as well as chunks of scrap metal, all highly polished and finished to eliminate the "junk" look. Bill's all-round talent included architecture, painting, writing and graphic design. Inspired by mathematics, his sculptures were often based on a helix or a spiral. Continuing Switzerland's innovative sculpting is Pipilotti Rist (1962–), whose installations, video and computer works are displayed worldwide.

> **CORBUSIER'S LEGACIES**
>
> The creations of leading 20th-century architect Le Corbusier can be seen all around the world: from Chandigarh in the Punjab and the Museum of Modern Art in Tokyo to Rio de Janeiro in Brazil.

Architecture

Perhaps the most influential architect of the 20th century was Swiss: Le Corbusier (1887–1965). A modest painter (under his real name, Charles-Edouard Jeanneret), he was heavily influenced by the Cubists. For him, simplification of design was a priority. Today's buildings still rely on his five-point guidelines for construction, ranging from the free-standing pillar to the roof garden. For him, a house was "a machine for living", and you can still see the villas that he designed in his home town of La Chaux-de-Fonds. Le Corbusier was multi-talented: his 1929 Barcelona chair is a design classic, displayed in museums.

Other influential Swiss architects include Ticino's Mario Botta (1943–), who designed the SFMOMA gallery in San Francisco, and Jacques Herzog and Pierre de Meuron, who – at the turn

of the new millennium – won international acclaim for their conversion of a former power station into the Tate Modern gallery in London. At home, they are best known for their signal box outside Basel railway station, and their green doctor's surgery, now a tourist attraction in Basel.

Galleries

Every major city has an impressive *Kunsthaus* (art gallery): Zürich, Geneva, Luzern, Lausanne and Bern, where a Klee museum and arts centre, the Zen-

trum Paul Klee, was opened in 2005. Always check to see what is on at the Migros Museum in Zürich, where special exhibitions often juxtapose young Swiss talent with works by well-known artists. In Basel, there are two unmissable sites. One is in Solitude Park: the Mario Botta-designed Jean Tinguely museum, dedicated to his ingenious kinetic sculptures. The other is nearby, at Riehen, in a striking building designed by Renzo Piano. This houses the outstanding private collection of art dealer Ernst Beyeler, whose artist friends included Pablo Picasso.

In addition to these major galleries, Switzerland has some unexpected gems. Since 1978, the Fondation Pierre Gianadda, set among vineyards

---

PRECEDING PAGES: *The Golden Fish* by Paul Klee (1925).

LEFT: *Café*, by Sophie Taueber Arp, wife of French-born Dadaist Jean Arp (1928).

RIGHT: *Liebespaar*, by Herman Scherer (1924).

in Martigny, has staged crowd-pulling exhibitions of works by Gauguin, Modigliani and Matisse. The permanent collection includes Picasso, Toulouse-Lautrec and Cézanne, as well as outdoor sculptures by Arp, Brancusi, Rodin and Moore. These are regularly complemented by concerts featuring major international stars, such as Cecilia Bartoli and Itzhak Perlman. St Gallen has its traditional Kunstmuseum and the Museum im Lagerhaus, dedicated to modern art. However, the main talking point here is the Hauser und Wirt exhibition space (a sibling of the Zürich Hauser und Wirt gallery). Find it next to the railway station, in what was the turning shed for engines.

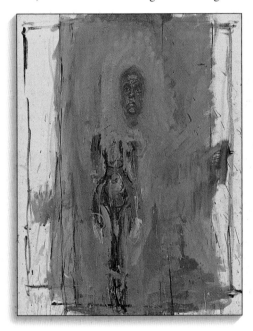

Music, ballet and film

Love of music starts at grass-roots level in Switzerland. Every village has a *Musikverein*, a music club, often with a *Hudigääggeler*, a combo of double bass, clarinet and the ubiquitous accordion. Traditional instruments still played include the *Hackbrett*, a stringed instrument, laid flat and played with wooden spoons. The haunting echoes of the alphorn, the long, long horn, still fill the valleys on 1 August, the Swiss national day. Yodelling, the vocal way to send messages from one isolated community to another, is now used for entertainment.

Close to Germany, France and Italy, Switzerland has long been a retreat for world-famous musicians. In 1848, Richard Wagner (1813–83) fled Germany after the May Uprising. He settled in Zürich, where he worked on his towering opera, *Der Ring des Nibelungen*. Some 60 years later, Russian composer Igor Stravinsky (1882–1971) wrote *The Rite of Spring* (1913) at Clarens, near Montreux. Although he was a member of a French group of composers nicknamed *Les Six*, Arthur Honegger (1892–1955) is Switzerland's most famous musical son. He wrote for chamber orchestra and piano, for ballet and symphony orchestras. His *Symphony No. 4* was dedicated to Basel, while his 1923 tone poem, *Pacific 231*, is all about a railway engine.

Other noteworthy composers include Frank Martin (1890–1974) and Othmar Schöck (1866–1957). Thanks to contemporary composers, such as the oboeist and conductor Heinz Holliger (1939–), modern music has a high profile in Zürich and Bern. Under the baton of Ernest Ansermet (1883–1969), Geneva's Orchestre de la Suisse Romande built an international reputation, since matched by the Basel Sinfonietta, the Festival Strings Luzern and the Züricher Kammerorchester. Over in Basel, innovative artistic director Heinz Spoerli's ballet company is highly rated, even though there are no Swiss dancers in the company; while TECS (Tanz Ensemble Cathy Sharp) is run by US choreographer Cathy Sharp. Lausanne is home to French-born choreographer Maurice Béjart, and his inspired ballet company.

Many Swiss are avid jazz fans. In Montreux, the summer Jazz Festival attracts over 170,000 fans to listen to the world's leading musicians at the Miles Davis Hall and the Stravinski Auditorium, while the Festival-Off features free concerts in the surrounding communities. In Verbier, the classical-music festival is held in a giant tent, with spectacular views of the surrounding mountains, while Luzern's *Musikfestwochen* (Music Festival Weeks) are staged in the striking new lakeside concert hall. Nyon's Paléo summer festival is more youth-oriented. Recent concerts have featured Goldfrapp and The Who, while each August, Locarno's international film festival is rated among the top half-dozen in the world.

The Swiss also have an affinity with country music, with festivals held during summer. The biggest, Country Night In Gstaad, has drawn some major names since it was first held in 1989, including Emmylou Harris, Travis Tritt and Dwight Yaokam.

Literature

Two of the 20th century's leading German language writers were Swiss. One was dramatist Friedrich Dürrenmatt (1921–90). His plays, such as *The Visit*, performed both on Broadway and in London, and *The Physicists*, a surreal look at scientists, demonstrate his excellent plots and sense of theatre, as well as his acute perception of moral dilemmas and black humour. Max Frisch (1911–91) typified the extraordinary, all-round talent of so many

ARTISTS' HAVEN

Switzerland has long been a popular home for musicians, artists and writers. When English poet Lord Byron left Britain for good in 1816, he lived in Geneva with fellow poet Shelley.

Geneva attracted writers and philosophers, such as Voltaire and Madame de Stael.

German-speaking authors who lived and worked in Switzerland included the Austrian poet Rainer Maria Rilke (1875–1926) and German Nobel Prize author Thomas Mann (1875–1955). In *The Magic Mountain* (1924), Mann used a Swiss sanatorium to represent a microcosm of European society. Another German novelist, Herman Hesse (1877–1962) moved to Ticino in 1911, where he wrote *Steppenwolf* (1927).

Swiss artists. In his time both a philosopher and a journalist, Frisch designed and built his first house in 1943, the year his first novel was published. No wonder Edna O'Brien called him "a European brain that is as witty as it is adult." His play, *The Fire Raisers*, is regarded as a key text in the Theatre of the Absurd.

Until the 19th century, Switzerland inspired foreign writers rather than home-grown talent. Geneva was a hugely influential city in the early 18th century. The birthplace of the philosopher and writer Jean-Jacques Rousseau (1712–78),

LEFT: *Femme et tête*, by Alberto Giacometti (1965).
ABOVE: *Sudliche küste abends*, by Paul Klee (1925).

Other foreign novelists included Ireland's James Joyce (1882–1941), who spent five years in Zürich, where he wrote *A Portrait of the Artist as a Young Man* (1916). Other residents included prolific Belgian novelist Georges Simenon (1903–89), creator of Maigret, the detective, and Graham Greene (1904–91). In *The Third Man*, the film of Greene's novel, Harry Lime comments that "In Switzerland they had brotherly love, 500 years of democracy and peace, and what did they produce…? The cuckoo clock." Added to the script by Orson Welles, those lines epitomise the cynicism of Harry Lime; but Welles was wrong about the cuckoo clock. It was invented in Germany. ❏

FROM ROMAN RUINS TO GLASS TOWERS

Although famous for its natural architecture, Switzerland's towns and cities contain an array of fascinating buildings dating back to Roman times

Gothic architecture is symbolised by Europe's magnificent cathedrals. Switzerland has wonderful examples in Lausanne and Bern. More art than architecture, Lausanne's stained-glass rose window and the magnificent gilded triptych in Chur cathedral represent the heights of perfection reached by Gothic style. The cool, classical lines of Renaissance style can be seen in some of the mansions of the wealthy and in a few churches, for example San Lorenzo in Lugano. There are also beautiful baroque buildings; most notable are the cathedral and abbey at St Gallen dating from the 18th century. The abbey library, with its fabulous wooden inlaid floor, is a masterpiece of rococo style. Neoclassical styles and industrial architecture represent the preoccupations of the 19th century. In the 20th century Switzerland embraced the key architectural styles fashionable in the rest of Europe, from the *belle-époque* hotels of Montreux to Modernist buildings such as Le Corbusier's La Clarté glass and steel apartment block in Geneva. Postmodernism also has Swiss exponents including Bernhard Tschumi.

FROM ANTIQUITY

Avenches and Martigny contain fine Roman amphitheatres, and another has been discovered at Nyon. Romanesque style can be seen in Zürich's Grossmünster *(right)* and the cathedral in Chur. Although much altered in later centuries, the St Gallen Portal of Basel's sandstone cathedral is a fine example of late-Romanesque style and decoration.

△ **ROMANSCH HERITAGE**
A traditional facade in Guarda, Lower Engadine. The cream stuccoed buildings are adorned with Romansch (the local language) script and ornate designs.

◁ **ROMANESQUE STYLE**
The twin towers of the Romanesque Grossmünster in Zürich dominate the city skyscape. They were rebuilt in the original and Gothic style after a fire in 1763.

▷ **VILLAGE CHARM**
A pretty flower-filled wooden balcony in Langwies, north of Arosa, is a typical sight in hillside resort towns and villages.

MODERNIST MEDLEY

Swiss architects have made the most of the 20th-century development of reinforced concrete. Some of the country's most ingenious architecture has been employed in the building of impressive bridges and tunnels in the Alps. The opening of the world's longest road tunnel, the Gotthard, in 1980, was an engineering achievement which architects Rino Tami and Christian Menn designed to work well with the natural landscape. Known as the "father of Swiss architecture", Karl Moser designed numerous buildings, including St Antonius Kirche in Basel (1931) which imaginatively used the then new medium of concrete. Le Corbusier's last building (1967), the predominantly glass Maison de l'Homme, is in Zürich. Architect Mario Botta designed the Banca Gottardo (*above*), and the Tinguely Museum in Basel in 1996, capitalising on its riverside setting.

◁ **THE LAST JUDGEMENT**
The Münster in Bern is a treasure chest of religious art including the *Last Judgement*, a stunning stained-glass window in the Matter Chapel.

▷ **ROMAN INFLUENCE**
A mosaic detail displayed in the Roman Museum at Avenches, in western Switzerland, where valuable ruins and artefacts have been unearthed by archaeologists.

◁ **A BAROQUE BEAUTY**
The abbey at Disentis is a fine example of baroque design. The white exterior contrasts with the impressive gilt and stuccoed interior.

▷ **LOFTY TOWER**
Arresting architecture at La Chaux-de-Fonds, birthplace of the architect Le Corbusier and of quality timepieces.

FOOD AND WINE

*There is a lot more to Swiss cuisine than chocolate, fondue
and* rösti, *but they make a fine introduction to further delights*

When it comes to food, Switzerland has specialities that are known worldwide. What could be more indulgent than a bar of Swiss chocolate? What could be more sensible than a bowl of muesli for breakfast? What could be more sociable than sharing a fondue? Yet these mouthfuls are only a taste of the culinary story. This tiny nation crams in a host of local and regional dishes, often based on French, German and Italian traditions. However, in the Switzerland of today, you will also find modern, light and creative dishes, as well as the usual array of restaurants from around the world.

The Swiss love good, healthy food. Cookery lessons, for both boys and girls, are on the curriculum of many primary and secondary schools. In markets, the fresh fruit and vegetables delight the eye and many of these locally grown staples are organically produced. Common to all regions is careful preparation, with an emphasis on bold, unfussy flavours. Dishes still tend to complement the seasons, with portions appropriate to the weather. In winter, high in the mountains, they are hearty; in summer, down by the lakes, they are lighter. They are always satisfying, however; seldom has anyone stood up from a Swiss meal still feeling hungry.

Famous chefs

Switzerland has produced hundreds of talented chefs. Some are, or have been, international stars: Freddie Girardet in Crissier (Vaud), Roland Jöhri at Jöhri's Talvo on the outskirts of St Moritz, or Roland Pierroz at the Hotel Rosalp in Verbier.

Many Swiss chefs have made their reputations abroad. Anton Mosimann, proud holder of a royal warrant, has lived and worked in London for over 30 years. One of the first media stars of the kitchen, he takes pride in his former students, many of whom are now well-

PRECEDING PAGES: a well-to-do family at table (1643).
LEFT: a platter of Swiss meats and cheese.
RIGHT: fresh chanterelles at the market.

known chefs too. Yet, the dishes that make him homesick are simple Swiss classics: simply prepared lake fish such as perch, meaty sausages cooked on an outdoor grill and crispy *rösti*. First and foremost is bread, fresh from a wood-fired oven, with an aroma to tempt even the most jaded taste buds.

Daily bread

Bread is on the table at every meal in Switzerland. Although each bakery sells a wide range of breads, many were once regional or festive specialities. In the western French-speaking cantons, for example, bread tends to be white and crusty, often inscribed with a motif: diamonds in Geneva, a bishop's crosier in the Jura. Walnuts are incorporated into the dense, rye-based Valais loaves, and rye is also the main ingredient in the hearty Graubünden bread. For the country-style *Burebrot* (farmer's bread), white, rye and wholewheat flours are mixed together. Breads once eaten only on high days and holy days are now bought for Sunday brunch or a party: *Züpfe*, yeasty plaited loaves, or *taillaule*, a brioche-like bread from Neuchâtel. Popular all over Switzerland is the Ticino-style *torta di pane*, an exotic bread pudding, made with stale bread, raisins and brandy.

Filling favourites

Some of Switzerland's best-known dishes, however, are among the simplest. Popular with hikers is the cheesy *Älplermakkaronen*. This belly-bursting version of macaroni cheese, with chunks of bacon and lots of cream, is often

> ### WILD MUSHROOMS
>
> Thousands of Swiss regularly comb the forests for a multicoloured array of fungi (Ilze, ceps or funghi), which are eaten fresh, or preserved and pickled for the months ahead.

served in a wooden bowl at mountain huts during the summer. If there is one national dish, it has to be *Zürigschnätzlets*. Originally from Zürich, this dish of diced veal gently cooked with cream and mushrooms is now found on menus across the country, often accompanied by potatoes or by the pasta-like *Spätzli* (which means "little sparrows").

Charcuterie is another forte. Like so many dishes, these home-made sausages and dried meats reflect the harder times of old, when mountain communities relied on well-stocked larders to survive the winter. Nowadays, wind-dried beef is a delicacy, served in paper-thin slices. Best-known is the tender and flavour-

some *Bündnerfleisch* (from Graubünden), but the herb-flavoured *Walliserfleisch* (from the Valais) and *Mostbröckli* (cured beef) are equally popular in the eastern cantons. Every butcher takes pride in his own secret recipes for sausages. With onions and a beer, nothing slides down more easily than the hotdog-like *Kalbsbratwurst* (veal sausage) – unless it is a *Bratwurst* (pork sausage) or a spicier *Bauernbratwurst* (farmer's sausage). Only very hungry skiers and hikers, however, can do justice to the Bernese challenge of a *Berner Platte*, a casserole of sauerkraut and beans, garnished with meats such as *Zungenwurst* (tongue sausage), *Rippli* (smoked ribs) and *Siedfleisch* (boiled beef).

Potatoes and fish

Having long been a staple food, potatoes are transformed into a variety of dishes. Among the tastiest is *rösti*, a flat, round and crusty potato cake. Much crisper than hash browns, the potatoes are boiled, grated and then fried.

Freshwater fish is also highly prized. As well as trout, lakeside restaurants serve delicate, salmon-like *Felchen*, and *Egli* or *perchette* (perch), all in a variety of creative dishes.

Muesli

One dish ensures that Swiss food has a healthy image. Around the world, muesli has become a fashionable modern breakfast dish. As ever, the packet version bears little resemblance to the original. Invented in 1897 by dietary expert Dr Bircher-Benner in Zürich, muesli is often eaten in Switzerland as a light snack, rather than a breakfast dish. The Swiss call it *Birchermuesli*, in honour of its inventor, and today's muesli can be quite a creamy concoction.

The ingredients of oat flakes, nuts and grated apple with a splash of water and lemon juice are often enriched with dried fruits and soaked overnight in creamy milk. Next day, it is served with a blob of yoghurt.

Seasonal specialities

Some dishes are prepared only for special festivals or religious celebrations. In early December, entire households bake huge batches of *Weihnachtsguetzli*, Christmas cookies, which are presented to all visitors. At New

Year, families in Basel give *Läckerli* (spiced honey biscuits) to their friends. Zürich has its own version, called *Züri-leckerli* and *tirggeli*.

As elsewhere in the world, the start of Lent is a time of indulgence before fasting. In Basel, look for *Zibelewaie*, a type of creamy onion quiche. Calorie-laden treats include the *Fasnachtskiechli*, or *merveilles*, sugary fritters, and *Zigerchugeli* and *Zigerchröpfli*. These deep-fried turnovers, stuffed with cinnamon and hazelnut-flavoured soft cheese, are delicious

has festivals, often marking the end of the harvest. The five-centuries-old Basel Autumn Fair is an excuse to eat *Lebkuchen* (gingerbread), *Magenbrot* (chocolate loaf) and *Rosenkiechli* (waffles).

As Christmas approaches, you can nibble on *Lebkuchen*, *Änisbrötli* (aniseed-flavoured cookies) or *Mailänderli* (shortbread). Look for regional specialities, such as *Zimmetstern* (cinnamon stars) from Chur, almondy *Biberli* from Appenzell and *Brunsli* (chocolate "brownies") from Basel.

ROYAL BUNS

On 6 January, a family treat is the *gateau des rois*, or *Dreikönigskuchen*, a crown of sticky buns with a hidden prize. If you find the small plastic king in your bun, you will be crowned king for the day.

eaten fresh from the baker. In Ticino, local variations include *ravioli di carnavale*, pastries stuffed with prune purée. The Ticinese also have a communal feast, featuring *luganiga* (Lugano sausage), served with enormous vats of saffron-yellow risotto.

On Easter Sunday, goat and lamb are the traditional main course in many parts of the country. In the German-speaking areas, *Osterfladen* is a must for dessert. With dried fruits, eggs and almonds, this is a pie or a rice tart, with a melt-in-the-mouth crust. In the autumn, every region

CHOCOLATE

When it comes to fine chocolate, the Swiss and the Belgians vie for top honours. Many of the world-famous brand names were innovators, dreaming up delights that we now take for granted: Charles-Amadée Kohler (hazelnut chocolate), Tobler (Toblerone bar), Daniel Peter (milk chocolate), Lindt (chocolat fondant). Chocaholics may flock to Zürich to indulge themselves at nirvana-like stores such as Sprüngli on Paradeplatz, or Teuscher on Storchengasse, but all small towns have specialist *chocolatiers* who often invent their own signature goodies. The best chocolate shops often have a café, where rich pastries and coffee tempt you to stay.

LEFT: a mouth-watering array of chocolate.
RIGHT: bringing the milk to the dairy.

Swiss wines

The reputation of Swiss wines has been steadily improving in recent years with many growers deciding to concentrate on grape varieties such as Petite Arvine, Cornalin and Fendent, which are hard to grow elsewhere. Despite this, Swiss wine is still relatively unknown in the rest of the world. Vintners say the problem with the Swiss wine industry is a lack of investment brought about by liberalisation, which means that the Swiss drink most of the annual output themselves: only 1 percent of the production leaves the country. Yet, the 15,000 hectares (37,000 acres) under vines is 50 percent greater than the better-known wine producing nation of New Zealand. Fortunately for visitors, you are never far from a vineyard, whose best wines are always featured proudly in local restaurants.

Popular Swiss wines include Fendant, an easy-drinking, fresh white wine, made from the Chasselas grape, and Johannisberg, made from the Sylvaner grape, which the locals call Rhin. The dominant red wine is Dôle, a traditional blend of Pinot Noir and Gamay. Vintners have their own recipes, based on the balance between the varieties. Goron, a lighter, fruitier version of Dôle, is often on wine lists in *Stuebli* (pubs).

The greatest wine production is in the upper Rhône valley of the Valais, particularly between Visp and Martigny. Although the climatic conditions are ideal, the steep, dry hillsides demand intense manual labour for both irrigation and maintenance. Most characteristic of the area are the local whites, made from Petite Arvine and Heida, while Humagne Rouge and Cornalin provide the most interesting reds. There is also some Syrah, the classic French Côte du Rhône grape, grown here near the headwaters of the same river. In 2000, one of the international gold-medal winners was a Cayas Syrah du Valais from the vineyards of the ambitious Germanier family, near Sion.

The vertiginous vineyards of the Vaud are all planted with Chasselas grapes, producing flinty, often heady white wines. Most come from the picturesque regions of La Côte, Lavaux and Chablais, where the vines look south over Lake Geneva. Circling the lakes in western Switzerland are patches of vines, producing light white wines that make for convivial evenings.

Bordering on Italy with its viticultural traditions is Ticino, where the best of the rich, dark Merlots rarely leave the region. Mature Merlots from the Mendrisiotto are powerful, yet smooth, full-bodied reds. Hoarded in the deep cellars of restaurants great and small, they are a revelation to most visitors. Everyday wines, however, also provide drinking pleasure. Take a seat in a small grotto (Ticino pub) and order a carafe of red, produced from the host's own plot, and a plate of his salamis: gustatory memories are made of this.

Vineyards are expanding everywhere. A new generation of winemakers using modern techniques are making award-winning wines in tiny enclaves. In villages like Malans, in the Bündner Herrschaft, for example, the Pinot Noirs are noteworthy. The best-kept secret of all is the sweet Swiss wines, which are a perfect foil for foie gras or dessert. Gemma, for example, made in Salgesch, Valais, is matured in barrels from October to June high in a cave in the Rhône glacier. With its high acidity, this is the sort of wine where you really want a second glass. ❑

VALAIS GIRLS

In the Valais, everyone seems to have a private wine plot. The vast areas under vines are split among 22,000 owners. As locals quip, "It's impossible to marry a girl who has no vineyard."

LEFT: chardonnay from the leading Swiss vineyard region of Valais.

Cheese

Swiss cheese with holes – as featured in countless *Tom and Jerry* cartoons – is Emmentaler, and just one of hundreds of different varieties. The holes are bubbles made by carbonic acid during the fermentation process. The more symmetrical the holes, the more expert the fermentation.

The Swiss were making cheese before their recorded history began, and, as Roman records indicate that the cheese they imported over the Alpine passes had holes in it, it was almost certainly a kind of Emmentaler.

In any case, Emmentaler is now produced all over the world: the appearance is similar, but even identical processing cannot achieve the flavour imparted by the Alpine herbs which the cows eat on the high pastures during the summer months.

With the end of the Pax Romana, the Swiss must have used goat's milk for their cheese because only goats would have survived all year round at the kind of altitude to which herdsmen were restricted by hostilities below. It was only the security brought about by the military victories at Morgarten and Sempach in the 14th century that created safe grazing for cattle in the forest cantons, Entlebuch, the Oberemmental, the Bernese Oberland and the Gruyère region, the heart of the future dairy industry. At a later stage in their history, the herdsmen had to decide between growing cereals for their own consumption or devoting the acreage to grazing. The cows won.

"The products that can be obtained from milk and from cattle are the precious and divine materials of our mountains and bring gold, silver, and much wealth into our country," wrote a 17th-century chronicler of Luzern.

After Emmentaler and Gruyère, the best-known cheese is Sbrinz, a hard variety which becomes easily digestible after being left to ripen for about three years. On a smaller scale, Schabziger from Glarus, Vacherin Fribourgeois, Tomme Vaudoise, Tête de Moine, Appenzell Rässe and Ticino Formaggini are notable delicacies.

Two of the most popular Swiss dishes are based on cheese. A genuine fondue is made of three melted cheeses (Emmentaler, Gruyère and Vacherin), plus a glass of Kirsch (cherry eau-de-vie). This communal dish is shared among friends, who use chunks of bread to scoop up the hot, creamy liquid. Another cheese-based dish is *raclette*. The traditional preparation starts with a wheel of cheese from the Valais, set before a fire. As the cheese melts, it is scraped straight onto boiled potatoes, and eaten with gherkins and pickled onions. Both *raclette* and fondue are more than a meal, they are rituals, enjoyed not just by locals but also by visitors, particularly on skiing holidays.

The popularity of cheese fondues in general and *raclettes* of Valaisan cheese in particular has spread well beyond Switzerland in recent years. Some of the contraptions now used to melt the

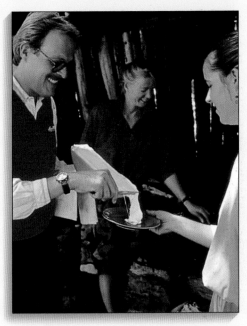

cheese are designed along the lines of an electric chair, but in fact both fondue and *raclette* are ancient dishes. Dairymen stuck in the Alps used to melt their cheese and mix it with milk; it was the Valaisans who first introduced the refinement of pouring it over potatoes.

Purists insist that the *raclette* should use halves of Goms cheese only, which are scraped after being melted by an open fire or a large charcoal oven. Potatoes (often in their jackets), pickled onions and gherkins are among the approved accompaniments. Fancy equipment erected on individual tables, exotic sauces and so on are frowned upon and polite visitors are likely to find that they are left with no choice in this respect. ❑

RIGHT: serving *raclette* – melted Swiss cheese dish, in Saas Fee, Valais.

FLORA AND FAUNA

From the emblematic edelweiss to soaring eagles, the Swiss landscape
has an unexpectedly wide range of wildlife

Switzerland's varied landscape creates ideal conditions for a diverse collection of plants and animals, much of which can be seen against spectacular forest backdrops or mountain vistas. From the snow-tipped Alpine peaks of western Switzerland to the warm lake shores of Ticino, few European countries can boast such a range of vegetation and natural life. While many of the most spectacular species are shy, live predominately in woodlands or are nocturnal, in a short period of time visitors can still see a host of wildlife, from palm trees and other tropical plants in the east to edelweiss, gentians and abundant wild orchids and other delicate flowers in the Alpine pastures. Bearded vultures now again grace the skies over the Alps, while in western Switzerland re-introduced species such as the lynx and ibex are making a strong comeback.

Changing face of wildlife

A combination of forces has resulted in some major changes to the flora and fauna of Switzerland and neighbouring Alpine countries. Glaciation and changing climate patterns wiped out the last of the dinosaurs many millions of years ago. Traces of this remarkable era can still be found in rock outcrops in the central Valais. Less accessible are a collection of 200 footprints thought to have been made by prosauropods and theropods in the Swiss National Park in the canton of Graubünden. Skeletons of giant lions, panthers and bears have been recovered from many parts of the country – witness to a rich former fauna.

These species died out largely from natural causes, but human interference has more recently caused the demise of many other wildlife species, among them the wolf, brown bear, lynx and ibex, largely as a result of over-hunting. Through careful conservation and

management programmes many of these species have now begun to appear again – although some of the re-introductions have been, and continue to be, quite controversial. Nevertheless, it is hoped that the return of these native species will eventually restore some of the country's former natural diversity.

Into the woods

Switzerland's forests are a haven for much of the country's most spectacular wildlife. Although highly managed for commercial purposes – as well as serving as important barriers to avalanches – forests cover some 30 percent of the country. While the last vestiges of its old-growth forests have all but disappeared, much of the forest and woodland one sees today, while managed, is composed of an interesting mixture of species which is far more beneficial to wildlife than pure stands of monoculture.

Among the many species to be seen is the remarkable capercaillie, the largest bird you are likely to spot in Switzerland's forests. Most

PRECEDING PAGES: a group of ibex, rarely seen residents of the higher Alpine slopes.
LEFT: a chamois goat and its offspring.
RIGHT: the edelweiss – an unmistakable Swiss flower.

people's first encounter with this species is through its raucous cry, which starts with a resonant rattle and ends with a noise that resembles a cork being pulled and liquid poured from a long-necked bottle, followed by a crashing sound made by the bird scraping its wing feathers along the ground.

If you want to trace the source of this startling performance – the purpose of which is to alert other capercaillies to its presence – you should look for a blackish-grey, turkey-sized bird with a distinctive green throat, chestnut and white patches on the side and wings, and a large, black tail.

Wildcats

Another woodland dweller along the Jura of western Switzerland that makes a rare appearance is the wildcat. Substantially larger and far more aggressive than the average domestic cat, these superb hunters are mainly nocturnal and feed primarily on small rodents and ground-nesting birds.

Slightly larger than the wildcat, but equally secretive, is the European lynx, which is again making a comeback to Switzerland following a re-introduction programme in 1970. With an increasing population, sightings are becoming more frequent along the Jura, in central

LAST OF THE BIG CARNIVORES

The years 1871 and 1904 marked the end of an era for Switzerland's wolf and brown bear populations. Up until this time, they roamed the countryside. In this traditionally pastoral country, however, domesticated species were the priority, and hunters gradually wiped out the wild predators.

Ironically, the Val Mingèr, where the last bear was shot, is now part of the exemplary Swiss National Park in eastern Switzerland. Sightings of wolves are reported occasionally and a debate is under way concerning the possible re-introduction of brown bears and wolves. A single brown bear appeared in the Müstair Valley in southeast Switzerland in 2005, but it was believed to have crossed over from Italy.

Switzerland and the Valais, in the southwest, although you should take care not to approach if you are lucky enough to spot one of these animals, especially in spring and early summer when female lynx might be guarding cubs.

At higher altitudes, in pine forests, look out for the nutcracker. The presence of this characteristic brown and white spotted bird is often betrayed by heaps of broken pine cones on the ground. One of this bird's most curious acts is its food-hoarding behaviour. Each autumn, nutcrackers pluck mature cones from the pine trees and extract the nutritious seeds at the base of the soft outer scales. With up to 90 seeds in its gullet, the bird then flies to another part of its territory, where it proceeds to bury the seeds by digging small holes in the forest floor and embankments. What is remarkable is that around 85 percent of these stored seeds are recovered: nutcrackers depend on this food source from October to June, when snow covers the soil and when no other foods are available. At any one time an individual nutcracker may have up to 100,000 pine seeds hidden within its territory. Those they fail to recover often germinate, and grow into new trees.

BIRDWATCHING SITES

Top places for birdwatching include: Verbois (Geneva), Lac de Pérolles (Fribourg), Grangettes (Vaud), Erlimoos (Bern), Barrage de Klingmann (Aargau) and Bolle di Magadino (Ticino).

by sightings of the European beaver – or at least their homes. Large mounds of logs and branches are hauled into place and built into an almost impregnable dam by hard work and abundant applications of mud. While beavers actually do live in chambers beneath these "huts", as the entrance is underwater your best hope of a sighting is when they are swimming to and from the hut, or when grooming or undertaking the regular maintenance to the outside of the mound.

Strange encounters may arise with two intro-

Life in rivers and lakes

River banks and lake shores make great birdwatching sites: considerable numbers of resident and migratory species, including black and white storks, red- and black-throated divers, kingfishers, ring ouzels, dippers, little bitterns, little and great-crested grebes, together with many wildfowl species, are all commonly seen.

Strolls along some of the quieter backwaters of rivers in western Switzerland, as well as the lower reaches of the Rhône, might be rewarded

LEFT: the European lynx, whose numbers in Switzerland are on the increase.
ABOVE: courtship display of the great-crested grebe.

duced species, the coypu, a native of South America, and the muskrat, from North America. These species are found in northwestern Switzerland and along the River Aare, respectively.

Although otters are occasionally spotted in streams in western and northwestern Switzerland, sadly, this animal, which was once abundant in Switzerland, can no longer be considered a resident, following severe persecution in the first half of the 20th century.

Keep an eye out also for some of Switzerland's smaller aquatic fauna such as the water shrew, a small insect-eating mammal which is characterised by its pointed snout, long tail and striking colour contrast of black fur on its back and a white underside. Water shrews are widespread throughout the country – except at high altitudes – and are most often seen scurrying along river banks or eating or grooming on exposed rocks midstream.

Alpine pastures

Between the mountains and the valleys, the Alpine pastures lying at 800 to 3,000 metres (2,600 to 9,800 ft) are havens for wild plants. As the spring snows melt away, carpets of low ground plants such as wild crocuses and gentians poke through the still boggy soil,

> ### LOOK – BUT DON'T PICK
>
> Many of the species of Alpine wild flowers are protected by law, so the policy of "leave only footprints and take only memories and photographs" should apply here.

Switzerland's other native reptiles, such as grass snakes, smooth snakes and adders.

Up to the tree line

Most often heard before they are seen, the shrill, high-pitched whistles of marmots in the Alps serve as warning calls of danger – usually from eagles or foxes, but also the occasional walker that ventures too close to their colonies. Hibernating in underground burrows and chambers for the winter months, marmots give birth during the spring, but the

waiting to erupt in a profusion of colour that transforms pastures almost overnight. Species to look out for are blue and yellow gentians, lilies, Alpine snowbells, Alpine columbine, Alpine asters, cyclamens and the edelweiss.

A rare inhabitant of Alpine meadows, woodlands, rubble slopes and quarries of northern Switzerland is the Alpine salamander. After over-wintering below ground for 7–8 months, the totally black salamander generally emerges in May and disappears again in October. Early morning, especially during moist, cool conditions, is the best time to look for this rare species. On exposed rocky, scree slopes you might have chance encounters with some of

young only emerge around June–July, when their playful antics are a joy to watch.

Usually found in groups of anything from 5 to 50, Alpine ibex, easily recognised by their large, ridged, backward-curving horns, are found as high as 4,000 metres (13,000 ft), preferring cliffs and sheer rock areas above the tree line. In summer, ibex graze on the rich high-Alpine flora, descending in winter and spring to lower, south-facing cliffs. At the onset of the rutting season, solitary males are often seen duelling – rising up on their hind legs and

LEFT: Alpine asters, with Mt Blanc in the background.
RIGHT: a soaring golden eagle.

crashing down against each other with resounding cracks of their horns – for the right to breed with females. Exterminated in Switzerland in the 19th century, the ibex has made a spectacular comeback thanks to careful management. The largest groupings of ibex – which in total number more than 16,000 today – are found on Mont Pleureur and Aletsch (Valais), Graue Hörner (St Gallen) and Albris (Graubünden).

Other, even more abundant, ungulates to watch for are chamois, characterised by their short pointed horns and nimble footwork as they perform what often seem impossible movements along sheer mountainsides. Two small groups of mouflon – another type of mountain goat, originally from Corsica and Sardinia – occur in Morgins and around Champéry.

The high fliers

Lofty peaks are also the empires of many species of raptors, among the most spectacular being golden eagles and bearded vultures. Feeding on anything from small mice and marmots to birds such as grouse, ptarmigan and partridge, golden eagles may also prey on sick, weak animals such as roe deer and chamois fawns – a service which contributes to the maintenance of healthy populations of wildlife.

Bearded vultures (or *Lämmergeier*) perform an equally important clean-up service. This vulture is an extreme food specialist, feeding mainly on bones from animal carcasses – unusual for such a large bird: their wingspan can reach almost 3 metres (10 ft). Few other carrion-feeders bother with what might appear to be an unappetising meal, but by breaking open the bones – which they do by dropping

them onto scree slopes from great heights – they can reach the soft inner marrow. Driven out of the Alps by 1913, the re-introduction programme under way to bring this majestic species back to its former haunts is proving that such initiatives can be possible. Some 70 birds have been released at various sites in the Alps over the past few years: the reward for decades of hard work came in spring 1997 when a young bearded vulture hatched in the French Alps. In Switzerland, releases have been taking place in the Swiss National Park since 1991. For best viewing opportunities, contact the park's information centre. ❑

THE SWISS NATIONAL PARK

One of the last unspoilt areas of Europe, the Swiss National Park is described as a "sanctuary where nature is protected from all human interference and where the entire flora and fauna are left to their natural development".

Stemming from a desire to establish a wilderness area in eastern Switzerland in 1907, a commission was established by the Swiss Society of Naturalists to pursue this vision. Starting with a lease on 21 sq. km (8 sq. miles) of land in 1909, the park has grown over the years to its current 172 sq. km (66 sq. miles). Rigorously preserving its original declaration, the park provides a safe home to many species of flora and fauna, including some that are either endangered or extinct elsewhere in the country, as well as some recently re-introduced species.

It is now clear, however, that this area is too small to allow adequate conservation of such a wide range of species: further expansion is being seriously considered. Visitors to the park are required to remain on the more than 80 km (50 miles) of well-defined paths throughout, but there is a range of interesting walks to follow which permits ample opportunity to enjoy a varied landscape and learn more about the natural systems of this enchanting region.

● *For practical details about visiting the Swiss National Park, see the Southeast chapter, page 220.*

LAKES AND MOUNTAINS

Switzerland's steep valleys and soaring peaks were formed by powerful
geological upheavals and the erosive effects of the great Ice Ages

Famous for its superb mountain backdrop, no less than 60 percent of Swiss territory forms part of the Alps, the great rocky barrier dividing northern Europe from the Mediterranean world and extending in a 1,200-km (750-mile) long arc from the French Riviera to the gates of Vienna. Another, lesser range of mountains, the Jura, defines the country's northwestern frontier with France, while between the Alps and the Jura extend the varied landscapes of the Plateau or Mittelland. In this latter, relatively low-lying area the majority of the country's population live and work, many of them clustered around the glorious lakes which make up for the country's lack of a sea coast.

The shaping of the mountains

Infinitely complex in detail, with every valley and every peak quite distinct from every other, the geology of the Alps is relatively simple, though the extensive timescale involved and the tectonic forces exerted are almost beyond human comprehension.

The country's first foundation consisted of an enormously thick layer of crystalline rock. Around 300 million years ago, this bedrock was subjected to great pressure and folded into what are sometimes referred to as the "first Alps". These predecessors of today's mountains eventually sank beneath the surface of an ocean, which gradually filled up with sediments, many of them rich in fossils. This process extended over tens of millions of years, until it was interrupted by the northward drift of the ancient continent of Africa.

Beginning roughly 100 million years ago, rock material which had once extended over a distance of about 500 km (300 miles) from north to south was compressed into an area no more than 200 km (120 miles) across. The more or less orderly layering of rocks in chronological sequence was disturbed almost beyond recog-

nition, as the remorseless pressure folded one layer over another, forming a wave-like surface. In places, the Earth's crust fractured, and magma from the interior spewed from volcanoes. About 3 million years ago, a final thrust heaved the rocks skyward to form a high mountain range, the basis of today's Alps.

The action of the ice

The present outline of the mountains is mainly the result of successive Ice Ages, the last only ending some 10,000 years ago. At one point, virtually the whole of Switzerland lay buried beneath a vast sheet of ice, from which only the occasional peak protruded. This was the era of the glaciers, the slow but relentless movement of which sculpted much of the landscape into its present form. The characteristic U-shape of many an Alpine valley is a sure sign of its former occupation by a glacier, while many of the country's lakes fill basins originally scooped out by ice, then dammed by material deposited when a glacier had come to a

LEFT: glorious Alpine valley in the Appenzell canton.
RIGHT: as global temperatures rise, the glaciers retreat. Summer 2003 was Switzerland's warmest on record.

temporary halt. Mighty ancestors of today's Rhein, Rhône and lesser rivers flowed out from the glaciers, sweeping rocky debris with them which, when dropped, gave the lowlands their present shape. As the ice sheets underwent their final (to date!) retreat, the climate improved, and the land they had bared was colonised again by plants and animals, first by a tundra-like vegetation of mosses, lichens, dwarf shrubs and trees, then by the conifers (pines, firs, spruces) which rise to today's tree line, then by the deciduous trees (alder, willow, oak, beech, ash and sycamore) which form the woodlands of the plateau and the alpine valleys.

exposure to the sun, or the presence of a great body of water helping to maintain more stable conditions; thus the steep north shore of Lake Geneva is one great vineyard, while the highest vines in Europe are to be found in the canton of Valais above the valley of the Rhône, where fine wines are made from grapes harvested at an altitude of 1,100 metres (3,600 ft). Together with the other southern cantons of Ticino and Graubünden, the Valais is known in German as the "Sonnenland", where the bare rock and contorted arolla pines of the heights contrast with a luxuriant Mediterranean vegetation of figs and chestnut trees on the lower slopes and in the valleys. Sur-

Swiss climates

Switzerland is affected by Atlantic, continental and Mediterranean weather systems, while the intricate combinations of altitude, slope and exposure to the sun mean that many parts of the country have a whole range of local climates within a very limited area. This is very obvious in many an east-west Alpine valley, where the shaded, north-facing (ie, southern) slopes of the valley will be clad in dense coniferous forest, while the sunny, south-facing (ie, northern) side of the valley is a cheerful patchwork of villages, farm buildings, fields and meadows. The severity of the climate increases rapidly with height, but this can be offset by a southerly location,

WINDS OF CHANGE

Landlocked Switzerland is subject to seasonal winds that blow through its valleys from the farthest corners of the continental landmass.

One such wind is the cold, dry **Bise**, which sweeps in across the Vaud and Neuchâtel plateau from eastern Europe. The northern side of the Alps is much affected by another wind: the **Föhn**. Blowing from the south, the warm Föhn unloads its moisture as it rises, crosses the ridge line and, warm and dry, sweeps down the northern valleys, melting snow, scorching plants and giving people headaches, or even depression. When villages were built of wood, devastating Föhn fires were common.

prisingly warm conditions prevail too in the low-lying parts of the cantons of Vaud and Neuchâtel, protected from Atlantic winds and rain by the great wall of the Jura Mountains.

Environmental threats

Nowadays, the Föhn (see box, left) is of less concern than global warming, acid rain and pollution generally. The country's 1,828 glaciers are good indicators of climatic change, and most have been retreating for some time. They lost 18 percent of their surface between 1985 and 2000 and the consequences are dramatic. The tongue of the Rhône glacier once reached the valley floor at Gletsch, but visitors wanting to admire this mighty natural phenomenon at close quarters now have to make their way much further up the valley. The sudden melting is also creating instability in mountainous regions; for example, massive rockfalls from the Eiger in 2006 were blamed on a retreating glacier that was no longer supporting some areas of the mountain.

Environmental pollution has been an issue for some time in this small, landlocked country. Chemical spills in the Rhein have made the headlines, as has the sudden mass death of fish in the country's lakes, but the most taxing environmental problem has been the erosion of Alpine forests, aggravated by atmospheric pollution from motor vehicles, in particular from the thousands of trucks driving daily through the Alps.

In Switzerland, mountain forests are not simply admired for their beauty, they frequently have a vital function as avalanche inhibitors and soil stabilisers. The death of trees, particularly conifers, because of acid rain, is not therefore simply an aesthetic issue, but one of the survival of Alpine communities and the safeguarding of communication routes.

The Jura

Rising to a high point of 1,723 metres (5,650 ft), the 200-km (120-mile) long Jura range consists of a regular succession of rounded ridges and trough-like valleys running southwest/northeast and looking from above very much like "a sea which has been petrified in a storm" (Emil Egli, Swiss author). The mountains are made of lime-

MELTING ICE

In the course of the 20th century, more than a quarter of the area of Switzerland's permanent ice, covering about 100 sq. km (38 sq. miles), disappeared, as a result of climatic change and pollution.

stone, formed in the Jurassic era, which bears their name, and squeezed into these shapes by the same forces which shaped the Alps. On the French side of the border they descend in a series of stepped plateaux, while on the Swiss side they form a formidable cliff up to 1,000 metres (3,000 ft) high.

Cattle graze on the upland pastures and most slopes carry forests of beech or spruce, while most human activity is concentrated in the parallel valleys where roads and railways run. Communication between the valleys

is via cluses, transversal ravines cut perhaps by the rivers. As so often in Switzerland, lakes form a transition between mountains and lowland regions; the Jura dips its toe into two beautiful bodies of water, the Bieler See and the Lac de Neuchâtel. From the crest of the range, there is a magnificent prospect of the Savoy Alps on the French shore of Lake Geneva, Europe's largest Alpine lake, 310 metres (1,000 ft) deep and covering an area of 580 sq. km (220 sq. miles).

The Mittelland

Plateau it may be, but the Swiss Mittelland is far from flat; lying at a height of 350–1,200 metres (1,100–3,600 ft), most of it consists of

LEFT: the ice-worn rock of the San Bernardino Pass.
RIGHT: the Gletscherschlucht, near Grindelwald.

undulating hillsides interspersed with level areas along the bigger rivers or on dried-out lake beds. Farmland alternates with woodland, villages with towns and larger cities, all linked by a dense network of roads and railways.

Though the plateau only occupies 30 percent of the area of Switzerland, it is the home of two-thirds of the country's inhabitants. At its junction with the mountains, lakes have formed, providing favourable sites for great cities like Geneva, Zürich and Luzern. In the western part of the

> **MIGHTY ICE CUBE**
>
> High in the Bernese Oberland is the greatest expanse of ice in central Europe, the Aletsch Glacier, covering nearly 169 sq. km (65 sq. miles).

plateau, from the rim of Lake Geneva northeastwards towards Zürich, the favourable climate and the fertility of the soil encourage arable farming, even the cultivation of crops such as tobacco.

Further east, beyond Zürich, in the cantons of Thurgau, St Gallen and and Appenzell, rainfall is heavier and grazing is dominant, with rich grasslands enhanced by the presence of fruit trees and orchards whose blossom makes a splendid spectacle in springtime.

The southern edge of the plateau is overlooked at a number of points by great ramparts of rock seeming to guard the approach to the Alps. Lake Luzern is dominated by Rigi, Bürgenstock and Pilatus, the Appenzell country by the Säntis.

The famous peaks

The Alpine heartlands are further south, reaching their greatest elevation in the Valais Alps, which extend eastward from the massif of Mont Blanc. Here stands the awesome pyramid of the Matterhorn (4,477 metres/ 14,700 ft), close to the country's highest peak, the Dufourspitze (4,634 metres/ 15,200 ft). To the north, beyond the valley of the Rhône, are the summits of the Bernese Oberland, culminating in the Finsteraarhorn (4,274 metres/ 14,000 ft) and the far more famous Jungfrau (4,158 metres/13,600 ft) – accessible even to daytrippers by cog railway.

For all their grandeur of bare rock, snow and ice, few parts of the Alps are nowadays really remote. The mountain valleys have long been areas of human settlement as well as important corridors of communication. The Oberland and the Valais Alps are separated by the deep cleft occupied by the Rhône, prolonged eastwards by the valley of the Vorderrhein. This is one of the most prominent features in any map of Switzerland, an east-west trench running from Martigny in the Valais right across the southern part of the country to Chur in the canton of Graubünden. At Andermatt, this valley meets the ancient trade route coming up the valley of the Reuss towards the Gotthard Pass and the cities of northern Italy, thereby forming one of the great crossroads of Europe.

The traffic-filled roads and busy rail networks of these major corridors contrast with lesser valleys, where a traditional way of life has only recently begun to be transformed. Hanging high above the Rhône is the valley of the little River Lonza, the Lötschental, its string of villages still made up of severe, dark timber houses. Until the beginning of the 20th century, when a rail tunnel was bored beneath the Lötschberg and a station was built at the bottom of the valley, the only connection with the outside world was on foot over the high Lötschenpass, or by steep mule track to the valley of the Rhône. A road only climbed up to the Lötschental to end its isolation in the 1970s. ❑

LEFT: weathered limestone outcrop in the Schynige Platte, near Interlaken.
RIGHT: the glacial waters of the River Gander, in the Gastern Valley, near Kandersteg.

OUTDOOR ADVENTURE

Whether you are after white-knuckle thrills or a gentle, pastoral meander,

Switzerland is one of the great outdoor playgrounds

Unless you happen to be addicted to surf, there is no better destination in Europe for sporting pursuits than Switzerland, which is, in many ways, the original outdoor destination, certainly as far as winter sports and mountaineering are concerned. Whether your interest lies in gentle walking or diving head-long into heart-pumping adventure sports, you will not be short of choice, and with such a remarkable array of beautiful natural settings, a healthy climate and world-class facilities it is small wonder that huge numbers of Swiss are active outdoor sports people.

Before plunging into the Swiss sporting experience, be sure that your insurance covers you fully, particularly for sports like mountaineering and skiing, where your policy should cover helicopter rescues. In addition, always try to minimise your environmental impact, and remember that mountain ecosystems are especially fragile: if hiking or mountain biking, please stay on the paths and do not pick Alpine flowers; skiers should stick to the pistes or designated off-piste areas.

Skiing

Switzerland cannot claim to be the birthplace of skiing – the Scandinavians had been using skis for cross-country transport for thousands of years before skis first came here in the late 1850s – but it was here, from the 1880s, where skiing grew up to be a glamour child, developing into a downhill sport. As with so many of the winter sports, the pioneers were British (either holidaymakers or recovering convalescents), whose activities were viewed at the time as rather eccentric. Nevertheless, the fledgling sport soon spread in popularity, numbering the likes of Arthur Conan Doyle among its aficionados. During those early years, practitioners would labour up the slopes on foot, but the

situation improved once funicular railways started operating winter services, and then with inventions like the T-bar drag lift in the 1930s, the chairlift and, by the 1960s, the cable car. The first downhill race was staged in 1911 in Montana in the Valais, and, in 1921, the Briton Arnold Lunn invented the slalom in the small

mountain village of Mürren in the Bernese Oberland, arranging the first race the year after.

Lunn also organised what some see as the true ancestor of all ski races, the mad Inferno, first held here in 1928, covering almost 15 km (9 miles; not all of it downhill) from the summit of the Schilthorn to the village of Lauterbrunnen. It is still an annual event, open to all comers, and is held in mid-January. Even more challenging, and better known, is the annual Lauberhorn race at Wengen *(see box on following page)*.

Nowadays, more than 2 million people ski the Swiss Alps annually. There are hundreds of places you could visit, ranging from small

---

PRECEDING PAGES: the Cabane des Vignettes, Val d'Hérens, in Valais canton.
LEFT: cross-country skiing on the Pigne d'Arolla.
RIGHT: snowboarding, hands-free thrills.

villages offering nothing more than a couple of beginners' drag lifts over local cow pastures to world-famous resorts in Graubünden, and the higher ones of the Valais and the Bernese Oberland.

Swiss resorts are typically scenic, village-based places, with more traditional chalet-style hotels than the type of purpose-built high-rise resorts to be found in France – and though the sport is not cheap by the time you have hired equipment (about 50 SFr a day) and bought yourself a lift pass (roughly the same price), you will get some of the best skiing in the world for your money.

The top ski resorts

In eastern Switzerland you will find perhaps the most famous resort of all: **St Moritz**, the patriarch of winter sports ever since the first party of British tourists overwintered here for free on the invitation of a local hotelier, Johannes Badrutt, in 1864. Famous for its sunny climate and chic designer boutiques, it also has some great skiing as well as a host of other winter sports. **Davos** and the more sedate **Klosters** are two similarly well-heeled resorts, the latter being favoured by the British royal family. Both of these resorts use the large Parsenn skiing area around the Weissfluh, and they are famous for

THE LAUBERHORN RACE

The most famous high-speed ski race in Switzerland today is the blue-riband Lauberhorn race held in the Bernese Oberland resort of Wengen, in early January. In the World Cup competitive downhill calendar, only Kitzbühel's Hahnenkamm in Austria can rival this terrifying descent in terms of both prestige and fear, and the cacophony of cowbells and hollering that psyches up local Swiss competitors as they career down the course lends atmospheric charge to the thrilling spectacle.

To win, racers attempt to complete the 4.2-km (2.6-mile) course – the longest on the international circuit – in under two-and-a-half thigh-burning minutes. Except for

the period just before the race, you can, if you are a confident skier, try out the course for yourself.

For the Swiss, no sporting champions are held in such high acclaim as native-born heroes of the slopes and, in the wake of a recent run of relatively barren years, they are fervently hoping for a new Pirmin Zurbriggen or Vreni Schneider (stars in the 1980s and 1990s in the men's and women's championships respectively) to wrest dominance from their arch rivals, the Austrians.

Finding accommodation in Wengen during the Lauberhorn race can be very difficult; contact the tourist office (www.wengen.com) for details of hotel vacancies.

long, cruisy pistes, up to 12 km (7½ miles) long. **Arosa** is popular as an attractive family resort with plenty of intermediate runs, and up-and-coming **Flims-Laax-Falera** is carving out a reputation for some first-rate snowboarding, good-value accommodation and a relaxed atmosphere.

Verbier, to the east of Martigny in the Valais, has one of the finest interconnecting networks in the country, the Four Valleys, with over 400 km (250 miles) of marked pistes. Its lifts run right up to Mont-Fort (3,329

SNOWBOARD CONTEST

Every March, Verbier is home to the international O'Neill Xtreme Snowboard Contest, one of the world's most prestigious events for this activity, held on the mountainside of Bec de Rosses.

ing World Championships: though a famous name, it is not the most attractive of resort developments. You will get some fine panoramic views when skiing, and there is good boarding, but it offers less challenging pistes than either Verbier or the Valais' third major skiing destination, **Zermatt**. This charming, car-free resort village has unbeatable views of the Matterhorn and neighbouring Alpine giants. Other bonuses about Zermatt are that there is some great eating in the piste-side

metres/10,920 ft), with its sensational views of most of the grandest peaks in the Alps, including Mont Blanc, the Weisshorn and the Matterhorn (here called by its French name, Cervin).

Verbier, whose accommodation is based more around self-catering chalets than hotels, is also one of the best bets for fine late-season skiing, plus world-class off-piste and snowboarding options.

Northeast of Verbier, near the town of Sierre, is **Crans-Montana**, which hosted the 1992 ski-

restaurants, and a healthy (or unhealthy) dose of nightlife in the village. Just to the east of Zermatt is the resort of **Saas Fee**, with plenty of glaciers nearby that make it an ideal destination for summer skiing. Summer glacier skiing is likewise available in Zermatt, Verbier and other high-level resorts.

Bernese Oberland resorts

Skiing in the Bernese Oberland centres on the majestic Jungfrau region, with connecting resorts such as the car-less village of Mürren, set high up on a plateau above the Lauterbrunnen Valley, and whose skiing commands wonderful views of the Eiger, Mönch and Jungfrau; busier

LEFT: snowboarding in the Davos/Klosters region, which offers 320 km/200 miles of downhill runs.
ABOVE: paraskiing over Zermatt, Valais canton.

Grindelwald, surrounded by savage mountain peaks; and Wengen. Trains from the last two will sweep you up to Kleine Scheidegg, where you can find dramatic skiing at the foot of the Eiger's north face. Another famous Bernese ski centre is the chic little village of Gstaad, renowned less for its skiing (which is scenic but comparatively tame), than for being a playground for Europe's rich aristocracy, who take up residence for the season in its opulent hotels.

Ski schools

All Swiss mountain resorts have ski schools, staffed by extremely professional instructors, many of whom are multilingual. If you want to escape the pistes and have both the money to seek out high-altitude virgin powder and the skill to ski it, you can arrange heli-skiing at any of the major resorts. You will be whisked up as high as 4,000 metres (13,000 ft) and dropped off to ski with your guide – mandatory on all such trips to ensure that you do not get caught out by the very real danger of avalanches.

For those who would prefer to appreciate the mountain scenery at a more sedate pace, Switzerland has wonderful options for cross-country ski-

ing (called *Langlauf* in German; *ski de fond* or *ski nordique* in French). Graubünden is a popular destination, but there is a huge network of trails: some of these are free, but for the majority, you will need to purchase a reasonably priced pass from the local ski centre.

Other winter sports

In addition to ice-skating, the frozen waters of St Moritz's local lake plays host to skijoring, a risky sport whose competitors get dragged on skis by a galloping horse: experienced skiers only might like to give it a try. St Moritz's most famous site is the Cresta Run *(see page 106)*, the world-famous toboggan track, founded in 1884, and where the fastest daredevils have touched speeds of 150 km (90 miles) an hour. Once the last big race of the season is over in mid-February, the run is opened up to guests of members of this British-run club, who pay a sizeable whack for the privilege of making five runs. Non-members can book online as a beginner (www.cresta-run.com). It is most definitely not for the faint-hearted, and, in a touch of old-boy chauvinism, women are not allowed.

Do not confuse the toboggan (also called "skeleton") with the luge (which is similar, but riders travel feet-first) or the bobsleigh, also invented in St Moritz. Both are practised at the resort's famous 1,600-metre (5,250-ft) Olympic bob track. For a thrill, you can hail the four-man "bob taxi", for one 130 km (80 mile) per hour run. It books up fast and they start taking reservations in July (tel: 081 830 02 00).

Cycling

The idea of making Europe's most mountainous country a destination for a cycling holiday might, at first, seem ludicrous. However, travelling Switzerland by bike is one of the most rewarding ways of exploring the country, and, if you are concerned that your fitness is not up to the mountains, stick to the lowlands and valleys, or jump on a train with your bike for a difficult stretch. Swiss roads are fantastic, its drivers are generally very respectful of cyclists, and the country's acute environmental awareness is characterised by encouraging the activity at all turns. Cities such as Zug and Zürich, for example, have free bike-loan schemes: all you need is your passport and a small deposit.

WEATHER WARNINGS

For daily, up-to-date reports on the weather, snow conditions and avalanche alerts, check the Swiss Tourism website at www.myswitzerland.com

There are nine national cycling routes, which form part of an interlinking, 3,300-km (2,050-mile) network of regular road routes and mountain-bike trails, all of which are marked on maps called *Velokarten* (available in bookshops; 1:100,000 scale). Make use, too, of the wonderful national scheme whereby you can rent well-maintained bikes from most train stations. Choose between a touring bike or a slightly more expensive 21-speed mountain bike, and for a small charge (family rates also available), you can return your bike to any other recognised station, which allows you tremendous flexibility in planning a route.

areas near Locarno, for example, like **Maggia**, **Verzasca** or **Centovalli** – with their tiny stone-built villages and thick forests.

You can walk around the steep, wooded shores of **Lake Uri** (Urnersee), the nation's historical core, on the highly recommended 35-km (22-mile) "Swiss Trail", developed to celebrate the 700th anniversary of the birth of the Swiss Federation in 1291, and best done as a two-day walk. Alternatively, check out the dramatic **Churfirsten**, a sheer-sided limestone range that rises in jagged peaks from rolling hills near Appenzell's Walenstadt, in the northeast of the country. Switzerland's network of hiking trails,

Hitting the trails

Switzerland is the kind of country that makes the feet of even confirmed couch potatoes begin to itch. You might like to hike the rugged mountain scenery of the Swiss National Park in Graubünden, looking out for ibex, or trek around the high peaks of the Valais and Bernese Oberland. There is a trail that crosses the entire range of low, forested Jura Mountains; or you can explore the exquisite valleys of Ticino –

LEFT: glacier walking demands proper equipment, not to mention preparation for the unexpected.
ABOVE: Swiss Alpine valleys are well served with hiking trails, aided by signposts and mountain huts.

CROSS-COUNTRY SLEDGING

If you fancy a gentler ride than St Moritz's bob sleigh or toboggan circuits, there is a delightful alternative, to the northeast of the town. This is the classic 5-km (3-mile) sledging route through the spectacular Albula (or Alora) Valley from Preda to Bergün.

Rent a sled in Preda and set off without fear: the road is closed to cars and its specially banked corners prevent mishaps. At the other end, buy a day pass for the Rhätische Bahn train and jump aboard to be ferried back up to the start. The route is floodlit, so you can carry on well into the night, staving off the cold with a hot chocolate or *Glühwein* while you wait for the train.

marked with a clear and reliable system of sign-posting, is second to none. Yellow signs designate normal hiking trails *(Wanderweg, chemin de randonnée* or *sentiero)*, for which you do not need anything better than decent walking shoes. Yellow signs tipped by a white-red-white direction pointer designate higher mountain trails *(Bergweg, chemin de montagne)*, and though trails are well-marked you will need at least hiking boots with decent ankle support for these. Check the weather with the local tourist office before setting out, and when up in the mountains never underestimate the need for proper outdoor clothing, sun protection and water: day-hikers tend to be caught out more often by dehydration, exposure or hypothermia than more serious mountaineers.

Mountain climbing schools

If you are keen to stretch your limits or learn techniques to progress beyond the normal hiking trails, head to one of the 27 mountain climbing centres across Switzerland. The Swiss Association of Mountain Climbing Schools (Verband Bergsportschulen Schweiz, tel: 027 948 13 45, fax: 027 948 00 35; www.bergsportschulen.ch) has a list of these and registered private guides. Centres offer guided hikes in their locality as

MOUNTAIN REFUGES

Mountaineers, climbers and experienced trekkers who want to make longer hikes in higher Alpine terrain can use the fantastic network of reasonably priced mountain refuges *(Berghütten, cabanes de montagne)*, found at altitudes usually well over 2,000 metres (6,560 ft). The huts have communal bunk beds with plenty of blankets (but no sheets), and basic meals are usually available. The Swiss Alpine Club at Monbijoustrasse 61, 3000 Bern (tel: 031 370 18 18; email: info@sac-cas.ch) publishes a book listing all the huts and their telephone numbers. During the busy summer season, book your sleeping berth at least a month in advance.

well as short courses for those interested in rock- and ice-climbing. The service between centres does vary, so if you are planning your holiday around such a trip make arrangements well in advance. Always ensure you get a full list of the equipment and clothing you will need for your proposed activity and where you can rent this: ice axes, crampons, harnesses and helmets are often rented by the respective mountain centre, but you may find it easier to bring items like karabiners, rucksacks, gaiters, boots and clothing with you. In addition, follow the centre up to ensure that they have indeed contracted the services of a guide for your dates, as demand often outstrips supply at peak times of year. Even the best-laid plans, however, can be thwarted by poor weather in the mountains.

From the Bergsteigerzentrum in Grindelwald, you can arrange challenging treks in the region of the **Eiger**, **Mönch** and **Jungfrau** massif. The Eiger's brooding North Wall (2,000 metres/6,600 ft) remains one of the world's classic technical rock-climbing challenges, despite having been first successfully negotiated as far back as 1938. Tragically, ice- and rock-falls down its face claim several climbers' lives every year. Hikers who merely want a look at this rock face from close up can hop on the train to Alpiglen and take the trail that leads to its foot; while those who would prefer to climb the North Wall from the comfort of their own living room can buy a video detailing the ascent in Grindelwald's or Wengen's shops.

Other famous Swiss destinations for mountaineers and climbers are Pontresina near St Moritz and, naturally, Zermatt with its Matterhorn *(see page 180)*.

Sailing and watersports

The lakes of Switzerland provide marvellous venues for a whole host of watersports, ranging from diving and waterskiing to windsurfing and sailing, whereas several rivers are being touted for their whitewater rafting and canoeing potential. Some of the best sailing lakes are **Lake Thun** in the centre of the country, and lakes **Silser** and **Silvaplaner** in the east, between St Moritz and Maloja. Beautiful lakes like Lake Luzern and Lake Lugano are better suited to motorboats than to sailing, as conditions are less regularly windy. In midsummer, even some high Alpine lakes reach swimmable temperatures, but you will need a wetsuit if you are going to be staying in for long.

High-adrenaline adventure sports

If all else fails to satisfy your craving for an adrenaline buzz, do not lose hope. Track down the 45-metre (150-ft) canyon jump at the spectacular Gletscherschlucht ravine in Grindelwald, or you can plunge 120 metres (395 ft) on

---

THE HIKING SEASON

The Alps' main hiking season lasts from May to mid-October, and late May and early June are generally excellent times for enjoying the glorious Alpine meadow flowers that appear after the spring thaw.

---

a bungee cord from the Stockhorn cable car, also in the Bernese Oberland, near Thun.

Other cable-car jumps exist across Switzerland, but the most hair-raising bungee jump of all – and, at 220 metres (720 ft), reputedly the world's highest, is just to the northeast of Locarno, made famous by the death-defying opening scene of the James Bond film, *Goldeneye*. Here is the spectacular **Verzasca Dam**, where you can take a bungee jump down its sheer concrete face, between the months of

April and October, either during the day or by full moon (contact Trekking Team, tel: 091 780 78 00, fax: 091 780 78 01, www.trekking.ch). In addition, you will find a host of places across the country advertising hot-air ballooning, tandem skydiving, hang-gliding, paragliding and parascending.

One final word: normally a country synonymous with safety, Switzerland had a big wake-up call in 1999, when 21 young people were drowned in the Interlaken area while on a canyoning trip (a different activity from canyon jumping) after warnings of possible flash floods went unheeded. The company involved has since been closed down. ❑

LEFT: the reward of spectacular views, at the summit of the Breithorn (4,165 metres/13,665 ft), near Zermatt.
RIGHT: waterskiing on Lake Geneva/Lac Léman.

The Cresta Run

Before the motorcar and aeroplane, the fastest men on earth were an amiable group of eccentrics including the author and literary critic John Addington Symonds who, strictly speaking, should have been tucked up in bed in the Swiss hospital in which he was staying.

Instead, Symonds and company, some of whom were also in Switzerland on doctors' orders, begged and borrowed *Schlitten* which the Swiss used as their ordinary means of winter transport and, hurling themselves down a hill near the Belvedere

Hotel in Davos and down the Clavadel Road leading to Klosters, invented the sport of tobogganing and hence its offspring, bobsleighing.

By 1903, the year in which the Wright brothers nursed *Kitty Hawk* into the air, they were attaining speeds of some 130 km (80 miles) an hour. This was at a time when motorcars were still being preceded by pedestrians waving red flags.

An entry in Symonds's diary is one of the earliest references to how the sport started. After a dinner which lasted until two in the morning, complete with a zither and guitar player, he and two friends "descended on one toboggan in a dense snow-storm. It was quite dark and drifty beyond description." They got down all right, the diary notes,

but not so "Miss I" who was on another toboggan. She completely lost control, flew over a photographer's hut and landed "on the back of her head on the frozen post-road. I fully expected to find her dead. She was only stunned, however."

The original *Schlitten* was simply a pair of flat iron runners screwed to a wooden frame on which riders sat upright. Canadian settlers discovered that the Indians used something similar, and in 1870 they were tearing down Mt Royal in Montreal.

The English invalids founded the Davos Tobogganing Club in 1883 and in that year issued a challenge to all other nationalities to a race down the twisting road from Davos to Klosters. Two Australians, one Canadian, two Germans, one Dutchman and 12 Swiss accepted. The race was a dead heat between the Australian, one George Robertson, and a Swiss bus conductor, Peter Minsch.

In the meantime, the St Moritz invalids had also made a rough-and-ready run alongside the Kulm Hotel. The general standard of behaviour among these invalids was very open to reproach: "A good deal of gambling and drinking took place at times and flirtation led to many scandals, all of which used to stop when the spring came and the invalids scattered with the melting of the snow."

Realising the commercial potential of the new craze, the owner of the Kulm Hotel contributed towards the cost of building a better run to woo custom away from Davos. The result was the most famous toboggan run of all, the Cresta, and competitions between the two fledgling resorts were soon being organised on a regular basis.

The 1886 competition provided a sensation. Up until that year riders had invariably sat upright on the toboggan but, as the local *Alpine Post* newspaper dramatically reported: "Mr Cornish… lay his body on the toboggan, grasping its sides well to the front, his legs alternating between a flourish in mid air and an occasional contact with mother earth… To see him coming head first down the leap is what the Scotch call uncanny… Unfortunately, however, he came to grief more than once during the race, though the extraordinary quickness of his recovery astonished the onlookers."

The following year provided an even greater thrill. A New Yorker, a Mr L.P. Child, "who had considerable experience of tobogganing in the United States", asked a local carpenter to run up a toboggan to his own specifications. He named it *America*. It was long, low, built of solid wood and had spring steel runners attached fore and aft.

Mr Childs thrashed the opposition down the

Clavadel road. The shocked regulars wanted the device banned, but others could see the writing on the wall and rushed off to see their carpenters. The genesis of the bobsleigh was produced by a blacksmith on behalf of a Mr Wilson Smith.

Tobogganers seemed routinely to die, but it was from tuberculosis or whatever complaint had brought them to Switzerland, rather than the sport, in the first instance. The first death to occur on the run was that of a 27-year-old British Army captain, Henry Pennell, who had ironically won the Victoria Cross on the Indian North West Frontier. The second death followed less than a month later and involved another heroic character, Count Jules de Bylandt, a

event. The British regarded the Cresta as their pet invention and entered two lords, Brabazon and Northesk, but the former was eliminated by a crash at Shuttlecock during practice which left him with broken ribs and a badly bruised face. In the end the event was won by two American brothers, Jennison and Jack Heaton.

Over the years since the 1928 Olympics, the Cresta Run has been tackled by any number of celebrities, some of them lulled into trying by an oleaginous veteran who would sidle up to visitors to St Moritz and say: "Let me introduce you to a sport that requires no work at all. All you have to do is lie on a toboggan…"

Dutch big-game hunter. De Bylandt crashed into the level crossing which controlled traffic where, before a tunnel was built, the run crossed a road.

The scene of Captain Pennell's accident was a particular curve, known as Shuttlecock, which caused so many horrific tumbles that in 1934 a club was formed, and an annual dinner given, by those who survived. As is the custom of such clubs in other spheres, members instituted their own peculiar rites, and wore elbow pads over their dinner jackets.

The 1928 Winter Olympic Games were held in St Moritz and six nations took part in the toboggan

There is a story that Errol Flynn stopped at Shuttlecock, knocked back a glass of champagne proffered by an astonishingly beautiful blonde, and continued to a chauffeur-driven Rolls-Royce at the bottom. Brigitte Bardot used to be a familiar sight at the Cresta while she was married to Gunther Sachs, the industrialist and pillar of the club in more recent years.

The Cresta is not all about fabulous wealth and glamour, however. The most successful rider of the run's history, and therefore by definition the most absurd, was Nino Bibbia, who hailed from St Moritz and was a greengrocer. It's possible for absolute beginners to ride the Cresta, but you need to book well in advance (www.cresta-run.com).   ❏

LEFT: poised for adventure.
ABOVE: boys with toys at the end-of-season line-up.

PLACES

*A detailed guide to the entire country, with principal sites
clearly cross-referenced by number to the maps*

Switzerland is an attractive destination at any time of year, and its dramatic divisions of landscape and major differences in elevation mean different regions can be rewarding in different ways, depending on the season. Eastern Switzerland and the low-lands, with their blossoming orchards and forested hills, are at their best in spring, while in summer visitors tend to gravitate towards the banks of the country's numerous Alpine lakes, or to the walking trails of the Alps. Windsurfers and yachtsmen are fond of western Switzerland, the ice-cold yet always breezy Alpine lakes of inner Switzerland, and the Grisons.

Autumn, with the promise of crisp, misty mornings and clear after-noon skies, can be enjoyed in many ways: in the vineyards of the Valais or the Vaud, in the bright-yellow larch forests of the Engadine or the southern valleys of the Grisons. In Ticino, autumn can be sig-nificantly warmer than in the rest of Swizerland and this, combined with the absence of summer crowds, makes it the perfect time to visit. Finally, winter provides innumerable possibilities throughout the Alpine region for winter sports or trekking through the snow. It is also an excellent time to discover the atmospheric wintry delights of cities such as Zürich, Bern and Lausanne.

Switzerland may be small, but many visitors make the mistake of sticking to the through-routes and of zipping around the country with-out actually having got to know anywhere in depth. That is why this Insight Guide has been organised in such a way that the most widely dif-fering areas are covered from a large city or a regional centre via com-fortable day trips in all directions.

In contrast to tourists of the past, who were compelled to explore the still undiscovered Alpine country of Switzerland on foot, on the backs of mules, or in buses with little if any suspension, today's trav-ellers have an astonishingly thorough and comprehensive traffic sys-tem at their disposal. Thanks to the many and varied means of travel available – whether rail, bus, cable railway or boat – it is very tempt-ing to leave the car at home, and to get to know really large areas of the country in a relatively short time. Every railway station in Switzerland can provide detailed information about these types of roundtrip, and combination tickets for different modes of transport are available everywhere. ❑

PRECEDING PAGES: the majestic Matterhorn; Château Aigle in the Valais canton; Foroglio in the Val Bavona.
LEFT: looking down the Lauterbrunnen Valley in the Bernese Oberland.

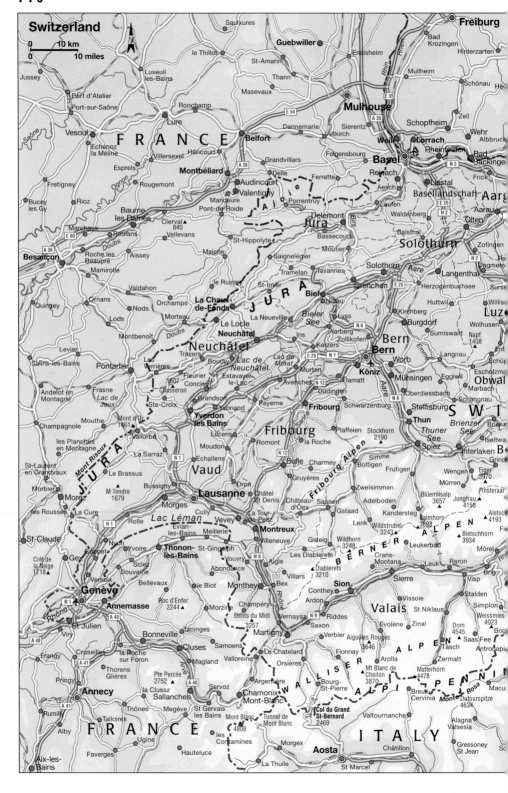

THE BERNESE OBERLAND

With its massive peaks, typified by the craggy Eiger, its immaculate villages and its indefatigable mountain rail network, this central region is Switzerland's prime holiday heartland

Maps:
City 120
Area 122

The region to the southeast of Switzerland's capital of Bern, extending up to the Bernese Oberland – also known as the Bernese Alps – and its famous Alpine peaks, is characterised not just by great mountains, but by all three types of Swiss topography: the lowlands, the Alpine foothills and the Alpine massif. The Oberland, in swift succession, also reflects the economic strengths of each of these regions. As you travel southwards from Bern, industry becomes less important, and agriculture and tourism more so. Further east, cattled meadows dominate; animal husbandry and Alpine dairy farming are still big business in the Oberland. Not far to the south of Bern rises the great wall of the Alps themselves, dominated by the three famous peaks of the Mönch, the Eiger and the Jungfrau.

The federal capital

The charming city of **Bern ❶**, in contrast to most other European capitals, is not obviously international in any way. The complexities of Swiss history have not left the country with any one centre where the nation's greats forged their and their country's destiny. There was never a unifying, inspiring personality around whom the upper echelons of society would gather, as there was, say, in the case of Europe's monarchies. Rather, Bern is the result of the hegemony of a few patrician families who managed to retain their claim to a leading role for centuries.

LEFT: a bear on a fountain at Zahringen, Bern.
BELOW: view over Bern.

The old town can be visited no matter what the weather: even in torrential rain, you will not get too wet because the old streets are lined with covered arcades, 6 km (3½ miles) in length. The main streets run roughly parallel with the end of the rocky outcrop skirted by the **Aare River**. Outside these rows of buildings in the city centre, the land falls off steeply on three sides down to the Aare. This area beneath the town forms the "lower town" where the level of life was once lower socially as well as topographically. The view from the **Münster-Plattform** illustrates the point perfectly: deep below, at the foot of a mighty retaining wall, lies the area known as the **Matte**. Once a workers' and artisans' quarter, it is now particularly favoured by the arty set.

Bern was founded in 1191 by Duke Berchtold V of Zähringen. When the Zähringen dynasty died out the town became free. Bern's compact structure is an accurate reflection of its single-minded spirit. Its victory over Burgundy and the ensuing policy of expansion transformed Bern into the largest city-state north of the Alps. Even internal unrest could not bring the absolutist rule of the patricians to an end. It was only in 1798 when the French Army marched in that the old Bernese power structure finally collapsed. This political consistency has left its mark on the enclosed, unified-looking streets of the old town. Medieval and baroque facades blend

Bearing up nicely –
one of the residents
of the Bärengraben.

harmoniously. Today, the arcades are given over to rows of shops and, even if you are not keen on shopping, you may still appreciate the architectural details of the arcades, both by day and also when illuminated at night.

The city contains numerous restaurants; note, though, that their doors are quite often disguised as cellar entrances, with steep flights of steps leading down from the street.

You do not need to visit museums or art galleries to enjoy Bern. The streets themselves hold plenty to interest visitors, including 11 historical fountains from the mid-16th century, from which figures such as *Justitia* (Justice) and the dreaded *Kindlifresser* (child-devourer) peer down on the bustling streets below. Bern's most recent, and controversial, fountain (1983) was the creation of a famous artist, Meret Oppenheim.

Bears everywhere

There is much to see in Bern, including plenty of bears, the city's and the canton's emblem. From the railway station it is a nearly straight walk or tram ride of a bit less than 2 km (1¼ miles) to the **Bärengraben** Ⓐ (Bear Pits), just across the river (open daily 9am–5.30pm summer, 9am–4pm winter; entrance fee); bears, small and large, can be seen rolling about, and concern about their continued health and happiness helps to ensure that they have as much care as possible (or at least as much as is feasible for a wild animal kept in a pit in the middle of a city). Bears have lived in these pits since the 16th century and the bear emblem crops up all over town in many different guises, including a local teddy-bear-shaped biscuit. Bern has two tourist offices – one at the main railway station and one at the Bear Pits. The office at the Bear Pits also has the Bern

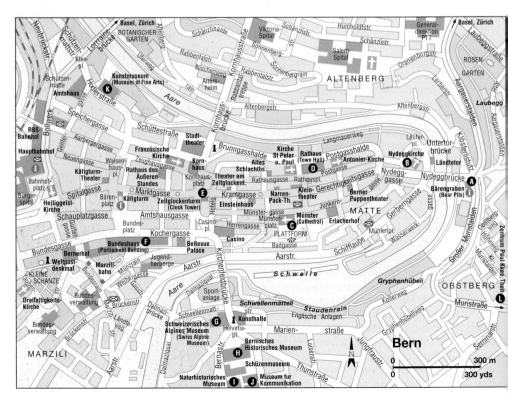

Show, a delightful overview of the city's history presented in a small theatre using impressive models and special effects. It lasts about 20 minutes and is a fun way to get acquainted with Bern (open daily 9am–5pm, shows every 30 minutes in English, French and German; free).

The bear emblem commemorates the founding of Bern by Duke Berchtold. Horace Walpole, English man of letters, explained the significance of the bear in a letter to a fellow countryman, George Montagu, in 1766: "The most faire City Bern hath the name of Beares in the Dutch tongue, because Berchtold Duke of Zeringen, being to build the Citie, and going forth to hunt, thought good to give it the name of the first beast he should meete and kill."

On the way back to town, you cross the old **Nydeggbrücke** bridge and the **Nydeggkirche** ⓑ, a 14th-century structure built over the ruins of the original city fortifications (open daily 10am–noon and 2pm–5.30pm, closed Sunday mornings; free).

The old city centre

A few blocks west and south of the bridge brings you to the city's spiritual centre: the **Münster** ⓒ (open Easter–Oct Tues–Sat 10am–noon and 2–4pm, Sun 11.30am–5pm, rest of the year Tues–Fri 10am–noon and 2–4pm, Sat until 5pm, Sun 11.30am–2pm; free; tel: 031 312 04 62). This is the most important late-Gothic cathedral in Switzerland; the three-aisled pillared basilica, begun in 1421, was designed by Matthäus Ensinger of Ulm. The tower, however, was not completed until 1893. Inside, its most notable features include finely carved choir stalls (1523), and a Gothic font. Over the main portal is a wonderfully intricate sculpture of the Last Judgement. From here, detour due north via the lanes, almost to the river, to see the early-15th-century **Rathaus** ⓓ (Town Hall), which unfortunately is not open to the public. Its fine facade is worth a closer look, however, with columns decorated with figures such as St George, dating from 1406. Much was reconstructed after World War II.

Back on the main street (**Kramgasse**), walk west past the **Einsteinhaus** (open Tues–Sat 10am–4pm; entrance fee; tel 031 312 00 91), where the great scientist lived for a time as he worked out the Theory of Relativity. From here it's a short walk uphill to the **Zeitglockenturm** ⓔ (Clock Tower), another important symbol of the city. Its clock, on the east side, was made in 1530 and is also an astronomical clock. If you can, try to be there four minutes before the clock strikes the hour when its mechanical figures are set in motion – the whimsical procession has to be seen to be believed. Just a block north is the city **Kornhaus** (Granary), now an intriguing exhibition centre with art galleries and a restaurant.

The final stop in Bern's old city centre is the **Bundeshaus** ⓕ (Parliament Building; open Mon–Fri 9am–4pm, Sun 9am–3pm, depending on Parliament business; free; tel: 031 322 97 11), which overlooks the River Aare; to reach it from the clock tower, walk two blocks south and turn west for two more. Meetings of the national parliament take place here. Tours are given daily on the hour except at noon and 1pm.

Map on page 120

TIP

If you are in central Bern on the fourth Monday in November, the **Zibelemärit** (onion market) is well worth a visit, with impressive stalls draped with plaited strings of onions.

BELOW: the Zeitglockenturm is at the end of Kramgasse.

The Kindlifresser-brunnen.

Museums galore

Being the national capital, Bern has plenty of museums. Most are concentrated in a complex south of Kramgasse across another bridge. Walking south across the **Kirchenfeldbrücke** (bridge), you first come to **Helvetiaplatz**, home of the predictable but still eye-opening **Schweizerisches Alpines Museum**  (open Mon 2–5pm, rest of the week 10am–5pm, sometimes closed during lunch in winter; entrance fee; tel: 031 351 04 40), with some detailed maps and models of the Alps, histories of mountain rescues, displays of famous summit ascents and mapmaking in the region. Just through the square you will then find, in succession, the excellent **Bernisches Historisches Museum** (open Tues–Sun 10am–5pm, Wed until 8pm; entrance fee; tel: 031 350 77 11), with Niklaus Manuel's famous *Danse Macabre* panels *(picture on page 33)*, other works of art and local historical items; the **Naturhistorisches Museum** (open Mon 2–5pm, Tues–Sun 9am–5pm, Sat and Sun 10am–5pm; entrance fee; tel: 031 350 71 11), among whose collection of rocks, minerals and wildlife diorama is the stuffed

Bernese Oberland

body of a St Bernard dog that made more than 40 mountain rescues; and the **Museum für Kommunikation** (open Tues–Sun 10am–5pm; entrance fee; tel: 031 357 55 55), which shows the development of the Swiss postal service, integrating even the country's remote and inaccessible corners.

North of the city centre and river, return to the railway station and go downhill, away from the other museums, to the **Kunstmuseum** (open Tues 10am–9pm, Wed–Sun 10am–5pm; entrance fee; tel: 031 328 09 44), on Hodlerstrasse 8–12, which includes an important collection of Swiss art, Italian works from the 14th–16th century, and a large collection of works by French artists of the 19th century. Its Paul Klee collection is the largest in the world.

Finally, to the east of Bern, a short trip from the railway station on the No. 10 bus, is the new **Zentrum Paul Klee** (open Tues–Sun 10am–5pm, Thur 10am–9pm; entrance fee; tel: 031 359 01 01), much of which is given over to the work of the great Swiss artist. Of the 10,000 or so works that make up Klee's oeuvre, about 40 percent – 4,000 paintings, watercolours and drawings as well as archives and biographical material – can be seen here.

Bernese castles

The whole Bernese-controlled region is full of castles that the gracious lords of Bern either had built or restored as country seats. Many are still in private hands, sometimes those of the original patrician families. Hieronymus von Erlach commissioned the baroque **Erlacherhof** (begun in 1746), a horseshoe-shaped palace in the French style in Bern's **Junkerngasse**. He also owned a country seat in **Hindelbank**, 12 km (8 miles) northeast of Bern. Hindelbank has been a women's prison since 1896, although the original construction remains largely intact.

Approximately 10 km (6 miles) to the north of Hindelbank, near **Utzenstorf**, lies **Schloss Landshut** ❷, the only moated castle in the canton of Bern. It houses the **Swiss Museum for Hunting and Protection of Wildlife**. Another interesting trip is into the **Seeland** – known as the canton's "vegetable garden" – northwest of Bern near Lake Biel and the Murtensee.

The Emmental region

Turning eastward and going via Burgdorf, we reach the **Emmental**. Emmentaler – the ultimate traditional Swiss cheese – is sold all over the world. Everywhere one looks in the hilly landscape here, streams have cut their way into the sediment left by the glaciers, making it impractical for large areas of land to be cultivated from one centre alone. These small farmsteads and their family cheese producers are, sadly, finding it hard going competing against the bigger firms, and many have closed down. Just to the east of Langnau in **Barau**, you will find one that has not: Bārau-Chäfti (tel: 034 402 16 34, fax: 034 402 80 51). Their shop sells wonderful, fully matured 2½-year-old Emmentaler cheese, which tastes quite unlike the young product marketed worldwide *(see also Cheese, page 81)*.

Emmental's sedate regional capital, 20 km (12 miles) to the south, is **Langnau** ❸, with one of the most beautiful village squares you will find anywhere in Switzerland. Langnau is a decent enough old town, if a bit

Maps:
City 120
Area 122

TIP

If you are in the Emmental region and want a good, strong cheese, ask for one that is "Reif, Gelagert und Gepflegt".

BELOW:
Schloss Landshut.

Sherlock Holmes: the final drama

The Reichenbach Falls, near Meiringen, were described by Sir Arthur Conan Doyle in *The Final Problem* as "a fearful place. The torrent, swollen by the melting snow, plunges into a tremendous abyss, from which the spray rolls up like the smoke from a burning house. The shaft into which the river hurls itself is an immense chasm, lined by glistening coal-black rock, and narrowing into a creaming, boiling pit of incalculable depth, which brims over and shoots the stream onward over its jagged lip. The long sweep of green water roaring forever down, and the thick flickering curtain of spray hissing forever upward, turn a man giddy with their constant whirr and clamour..."

Thus was recorded the scene of one of the most dramatic moments in Victorian English literature. Here, at the Reichenbach Falls *(see page 130)*, Sherlock Holmes apparent-

ly met his end in a fatal fight with Professor James Moriarty, "The Napoleon of Crime".

The Final Problem, the story which should have been the last word on the world's greatest detective, appeared in *The Strand* magazine in 1893 and it was based on a trip Conan Doyle had just made to the falls. In the story, Dr Watson was not present, but had been sent away on a ruse to treat a consumptive woman in Davos.

In real life Conan Doyle's wife, Louise, had been diagnosed as consumptive, and the author, who was also a doctor, blamed himself for not spotting her condition before they had embarked on what had been a gruelling journey. According to Conan Doyle's biographer, Charles Higham, the consumptive Louise brought about the death of Holmes, simply because she required Conan Doyle's attention, and the scene of his "death" was deliberate, as the visit to the falls had aggravated her illness and he had soon afterwards taken her to Davos.

Although Conan Doyle confessed he had had an "overdose" of his hero, as in the best soaps the hero was brought back to life by popular demand. Yet the site of the fight is still remembered by hundreds who make a pilgrimage to it every year. A rack railway goes by the falls and a bronze plaque at the bottom of the chasm commemorates the desperate struggle.

In nearby Meiringen, meanwhile, a complete replica *(pictured left)* of the fictitious 221B Baker Street, London, lodgings of Sherlock Holmes forms a museum to the illustrious detective (open May–Sept daily 1.30–6pm, Oct–Apr Wed–Sun 3pm–6pm, entrance fee; tel: 033 971 42 21). The **Sherlock Holmes Museum**, in the basement of the former English Church, was inaugurated in 1991 on the centenary of Holmes's "death" and the square outside has been named Conan Doyle Place.

In the town, there is also a statue of Sherlock Holmes, by John Doubleday, which contains clues to each of the 60 Holmes stories, and gives visitors and members of the worldwide Sherlock Holmes Society, of whom there are more than 1,000, an opportunity to use their sleuthing skills. ❑

LEFT: a statue of the great man himself, at the Meiringen Sherlock Holmes Museum.

pedestrian, but its real value lies in the fact that several good hikes up mountains with better views begin close by. Also nearby is **Affoltern**, with its Emmental show dairy (*schaukaeserei*; open daily 8.30am–6.30pm; free; tel: 034 435 16 11).

Map on page 122

The Napf region

Thrusting its way between Bern and Luzern far into the lowlands is the Napf region, a small-scale farming area riven by deep valleys radiating from Napf Peak (1,411 metres/4,630 ft). The slopes of the Napf provide popular walking and hiking trails, accessible by road from the pretty village of **Trubschachen** to the south.

To the west of the Napf region, on Bernese soil, lies **Burgdorf** ❹, a flourishing industrial town built on a hill above the Emme River. The oldest parts of its mighty castle go back to the 12th century. Today the castle houses a museum of local history, the **Schlossmuseum** (open April–Oct Mon–Sat 2–5pm, Sun 11am–5pm; entrance fee; tel: 034 423 02 14) and the first Gold Museum in Switzerland (same opening times as above; tel: 034 422 86 86): an estimated 34 kg (75 lb) of gold ore was extracted from the Emme region between 1523 and 1800. Also well worth a visit is the **Swiss Folklore Museum** (open Apr–Oct Mon–Sat 2–5pm, Sun 11am–5pm; entrance fee; tel: 034 423 02 14) in the Kornhaus at the foot of the hill by the town centre ring road, which has an impressive collection of musical instruments and occasionally holds yodelling concerts.

River landscape

To the southeast of the Napf region, the Kleine Emme River flows in the direction of the Reuss, and eventually joins it below Luzern. The people here, like those from the nearby Emmental, were accurately portrayed by the novelist

BELOW: a traditional horse and cart in the Emmental.

Jeremias Gotthelf (1797–1854), who was pastor at Lützelflüh. Even today they are well known for their unmistakably independent streak.

It is via the valley of the Aare that the **Bernese Oberland** proper is finally entered. The course of the Aare River between Bern and Thun, with its meadows, forests, reed grasses, sedge and backwaters, is one of Switzerland's most precious river landscapes. Much of it is a nature reserve.

The course of the Aare and its tributaries determined the regional layout of the Bernese Oberland. It can be broadly defined by the east-west course of the Aare with its two basins, **Lake Brienz** and **Lake Thun**. South of this line, the lateral valleys run almost parallel to each other, from north to south: the **Simmental**, **Frutigtal**, **Engstligental**, **Kandertal**, **Lauterbrunnental** and **Haslital** – far over to the east – where the Aare has its source.

To the west of the Aare, and separated by a small range of hills, lies the **Gürbetal**. The gateway to this side valley is formed by **Kehrsatz**, 5 km (3 miles) south of Bern. The neoclassical **Lohn Country House**, now owned by the Confederation, is situated here. It is often used for official receptions, and for accommodating guests of the Swiss Government. Another 15 km (9 miles) south along the valley, we reach **Rümligen 5**. This little village prides itself on having had a real Bernese patrician among its denizens; Elisabeth de Meuron (1882–1980), a famous Bern eccentric, inhabited Rümligen Castle. She once locked up a suspected thief in a tower, claiming ancient legal rights to do so.

The real gateway to the Oberland is the town of **Thun 6**. Situated 25 km (15 miles) south of Bern at the point where the Aare flows out of Lake Thun, it is dominated by its **castle** (now a history museum; open mid-May–mid-Oct Mon 2–5pm, Tues–Sun 11am–5pm; entrance fee; tel: 033 223 20 01), perched up on

BELOW:
Schloss Oberhofen
by Lake Thun.

a steep hill above the roofs of the town. The castle's charming interior has a neoGothic dining room, and the gardens are splendid. The 12th-century keep, with its four corner towers, is reminiscent of a Norman castle. There are quite a number of castles in the area, and the Lake Thun tourism office here provides a handy brochure describing them all.

Map on page 122

Alongside the attractive old town are military barracks and the **Wocher-Panorama**. This circular picture, painted between 1808 and 1814 by Marquard Wocher, is a lifelike representation of Thun in the Biedermeier period, and is situated in a round building in the park of **Schloss Schadau**.

The landscape of the southern side of Lake Thun is dominated by the 2,360-metre (7,700-ft) high **Niesen**. The Niesen separates the entry to the Simmental from that to the Kandertal Valley. It can thus be circumnavigated on three sides. There is a good view of the entire Lake Thun region from the top. At the foot of the mountain, right next to the lake, is **Spiez ❼**, with its harbourside castle (now a museum; open mid-Apr–mid-Oct daily 10am–5pm, except Mon open only pm; entrance fee; tel: 033 654 15 06) and, adjacent, its Church of St Columba (open daily dawn to dusk; free). Both buildings are more than 1,000 years old, and still retain many of their Romanesque features.

Shutters and a coat of arms on Schloss Oberhofen.

On the opposite side of the lake, the **Beatushöhlen** (caverns) are hidden beneath the sunny slopes of the **Beatenberg**. Visitors are allowed to venture at least 1,000 metres (3,300 ft) inside. About 8 km (5 miles) of caves have been explored so far, but this represents only a small fraction of the whole system. The mountain itself is named after St Beatus who, legend has it, once drove a dragon out of its cave here. The saint probably belonged to a group of Irish monks who came and settled in Switzerland in the 6th century.

BELOW: heading up the hill to Thun castle.

NAPF VALLEY FARMING

Like most places in Switzerland, the mountainous landscape of the Napf region has forced the residents to adapt to survive. The valleys radiate out in a star pattern from the region's main peak, the Napf. Their waters collect in a valley that forms an almost perfect circle. The road as well as the railway makes use of this ring valley, but this region is not crossed by any major traffic routes.

Because of the high rainfall the Napf is suited to pastoral farming and some crop-raising. The very deep valleys make it impossible for just a few centrally situated villages to look after the fields, instead of which the farmsteads are situated right in the middle of the land they have to till, and many of them are completely surrounded by forest.

These farmsteads comprise a whole series of different buildings and, from afar, they can often look like small hamlets. Each farm has a farmhouse, barn and a somewhat smaller, richly decorated wooden building, the storehouse, in which food supplies and valuable objects used to be kept. Keeping the buildings apart minimised the danger of spreading fire. Nowadays, the storehouse has lost its former significance, and quite often the farmers have built an additional small house some distance away, as a retirement home for their elderly parents.

TIP

Performances of
Schiller's *William Tell*
are held in the open
air in Rugen Forest, on
the outskirts of
Interlaken, from mid-
June to early
September. Tickets
are available from
Tellspielburo
(tel: 033 822 37 22,
www. tellspiele.ch).

BELOW:
the Giessbach
Falls Grand Hotel
near Brienz.

A region rich in tradition

From Spiez, the River Aare continues eastwards, connecting Lake Thun with Lake Brienz. In between these two great lakes sits the aptly named town of **Interlaken** ❽. This popular resort town is noticeably full of splendid hotel buildings. They serve as a reminder of the health-spa-oriented, cosmopolitan lifestyle of the upper classes in both Europe and the rest of the world in the second half of the 19th century.

That is not surprising once you learn that this may be the place where modern-style tourism all started. Lord Byron and Felix Mendelssohn Bartholdy both stayed here as guests, and the cultural tradition has continued; today the town is famous for its William Tell outdoor theatre, its classical music festival, a casino, and droves of young backpackers who bunk down here before setting off into the overhanging mountains.

What would Byron think of all this? Local adventure companies specialise in packages of "extreme" adventure sports such as bungee jumping into gorges, paragliding off cliffs, and a bizarre sport known as "canyoning" – whereby the participants raft swiftly down the rushing chute of a canyon river. It is so dangerous that 21 tourists (mostly Australians) were killed in a horrific 1999 accident when a storm caused a flash flood, drowning them. The Swiss and Australian governments put pressure on outfitters to halt canyoning expeditions, and since then safety measures have been tightened. Other nail-biting excursions continue as normal, however.

For those who are not up to such white-knuckle extremes, quite a few of the *fin-de-siècle* hotels are now used as retirement homes or congress centres. There is also quite an active nightlife in the town centre; several good museums,

Map
on page
122

plenty of Internet-access points for the home-weary and some splendid ivy-covered holiday cottages tucked away from the tourist excess.

The small town of **Brienz** ❾ at the eastern end of Lake Brienz is famous for its woodcarvings, which can be bought in every souvenir shop in the Oberland. There is a glut of souvenir shops selling carvings, which are mostly of people and animals, but you can also see the artisans in action, which does at least prove that they are not mass-produced in Taiwan. Brienz can be approached by bicycle, boat, train, car or even on foot, but tourists traditionally take the boat. A trip around this mountain lake, which is 14 km (9 miles) long, takes some 2 ½ hours. The best means of transport to choose for this is the *Lötschberg*, a paddle steamer every bit as good as its Mississippi counterparts, and the pride of the Brienz fleet.

Tourism in the old days

Elisabeth Grossmann, the "boatwoman of Lake Brienz", was depicted in countless paintings. More than 150 years ago, she wept bitter tears over her unrequited love for a young professor. The grieving woman was immortalised by the painter Johann Emanuel Locher (1769–1820). His picture of *La Belle Batelière* was one of the bestselling colour etchings of its time.

She was one of the local girls who used to row the tourists to **Giessbach**, and who were always mentioned in any accounts of journeys. The German physicist and astronomer Johann Friedrich Benzenberg, who visited Giessbach in 1810, had this to say: "The maidens who acted as our guides were also skilled in the art of song, and did not take much prompting. The maidens here have the reputation of being the best singers of all the farm-girls in the Haslital."

BELOW: view over Lake Brienz.

Rural arts and crafts, such as wood-carving, are preserved at Freilichtmuseum Ballenberg.

BELOW: Giessbach's famous falls.

The real promoter of Haslital Valley turned out to be Hans Kehrli, a teacher from Brienz, at the beginning of the 19th century. In 1818 he built a footpath to waterfalls above the lake's southern shore, the **Giessbachfälle ⑩**, and erected a simple mountain hut there. On pleasant days the whole family would take up position and sing songs for the visitors, with father Kehrli himself playing along on an alphorn. The family became so famous that one of the many landscape painters of that time captured them in a picture entitled *The Giessbach and the Singing Family on its Alp*. In those days, landscape painting was a thriving industry, and there were studios in which employees would copy masterpieces or colour etchings, and these were the forerunners of today's picture postcards.

Giessbach's falls became one of the major attractions for 19th-century visitors to Switzerland and gradually Giessbach began to be developed to accommodate tourists more comfortably. In 1840 a guesthouse appeared; 1872 saw the opening of the first hotel, which was replaced by a larger, more lavishly furnished building after a fire in 1883. Franz Weber, the environmentalist, managed to save it from destruction in 1983 and had it restored to its former glory. It prospers under the motto "Giessbach belongs to the Swiss". Today, people cross the lake in a steamer and the funicular, commissioned in 1879, still provides tourists with a comfortable ride from the docking area to their hotel.

The 2,350-metre (7,700-ft) **Brienzer Rothorn** towers above the town of Brienz. The Brienz-Rothorn-Bahn, the only steam-operated rack railway in Switzerland, travels up to an altitude of 2,240 metres (7,300 ft) in one hour. The line was built at the end of the 19th century and copes with an average gradient of 22.5 percent. The railway operates only in the summer, but anyone who wants to enjoy the view from the Rothorn in winter can get there by cable car from the town of **Sörenberg** in the canton of Luzern to the north.

Following the course of the Aare

Before reaching the area where the Aare has its source, pay a visit to the **Freilichtmuseum Ballenberg** (Swiss Open-air Museum; open mid-Apr–Oct daily 10am–5pm; entrance fee; tel: 033 952 10 30; www.ballenberg.ch) at **Ballenberg ⑪**, 5 km (3 miles) east of Brienz, just past Hofstetten. Some 100 original buildings have been brought to this 270-hectare (660-acre) site from all over Switzerland. They are dismantled, transported piecemeal and rebuilt, section by section, here. Many buildings hundreds of years old have thus been saved from demolition. The museum provides a picture of rural life throughout Switzerland – complete with 250 native farmyard animals – and also features demonstrations of rural crafts; afterwards, you might like to sample some hearty typical Swiss fare in one of the three inns on the premises.

Haslital Valley, on the eastern edge of the Bernese Alps, is where the Aare has its source, and it ends at the catchment basin formed by the **Grimsel Pass**, the only adequately surfaced road between the Upper Valais and northern Switzerland. The higher one goes in the valley the rougher the landscape becomes, and it leads into the largest continuous glacier region of the Alps, covering a surface area of 300 sq. km (190

Map on page 122

sq. miles); among the many glaciers here are the **Aare**, **Rhône** and **Aletsch**. They are all conservation areas. Their water not only supplies the surrounding region but also flows into the Mediterranean via the Rhône and into the North Sea, too, via the Aare, in combination with the Rhein from the nearby Graubünden Alps.

Like everywhere else in the Swiss Alpine region, the plentiful water supply is put to good use. Reservoirs and pressure pipes collect huge masses of seething mountain water with which to drive mighty turbines and generators, providing Switzerland with much of its hydroelectric power. The power stations themselves are situated inside the mountains and are an important source of employment in the mountain areas where they help to stem the emigration of the local population.

Holiday destinations

One of the best-known holiday areas in the Haslital is the region around **Meiringen** ⑫ and **Hasliberg**. High up here on the Hasliberg, on the **Mägisalp** and in the **Justistal Valley** above Lake Thun, a special festival has developed: the Chästeilet (cheese-sharing). The cheese produced on an Alp has to be divided up among the various farmers in relation to the "milk-efficiency" of the cows that grazed on the Alp. In the old days this took place without any great ceremony, but the farmers of today have turned the whole thing into a small folk festival. Sales booths are set up on the Alp and tourists and locals alike have the opportunity to buy the cheese directly. The food, drink and music add an extra dimension to the view of the mountain peaks around the Alp.

"The Giessbach falls like heaps of snow or like laces of shining rice. The smaller falls in it shew gaily sprigged, fretted and curled edges dancing down like the crispest endive."

— GERARD
MANLEY HOPKINS

BELOW: lake on the Grimsel Pass.

TIP

Meiringen is a starting point for a road tour by postbus, known as the Three Alpine Pass Tour, a circular day trip crossing the Susten, Furka and Grimsel passes. You can use a Swiss Pass towards the cost of the bus ticket. The tour runs on Tuesdays from July to September.

BELOW: the classic trio: Eiger, Mönch and Jungfrau.

If you are in Meiringen, it is worth making a trip to the 200-metre (650-ft) deep Aareschlucht or **Aare Gorge** (open Apr–Oct; entrance fee; tel: 033 971 40 48). Between **Innertkirchen** and Meiringen the river has to cut its way through a rocky ridge 1,600 metres (5,200 ft) in length. The footpath through the high and narrow rocky walls runs partly via suspended walkways and partly via galleries hewn out of the rock. If you take the path through the gorge in only one direction you can be taken back to the carpark by bus.

If you follow the **Lütschine River** upstream (that is south) from Interlaken you will find that the valley divides after only 10 km (6 miles) or so, leading eastwards to Grindelwald and southwards to the **Lauterbrunnental**. The whole valley is separated from the Haslital by rocky massifs, some as high as 4,000 metres (13,000 ft) above sea level, and they all form part of the glacier conservation area. The **Finsteraarhorn** (4,274 metres/14,000 ft), situated at the centre of this glacier region, is the highest point in the Bernese Alps.

Here we leave the valley of the White Lütschine River and arrive at Grindelwald, in the valley of the Black Lütschine River. (The "Black" river is so called because its water is the colour of slate from the Black Mountain.) It is possible to get to **Grindelwald** ⑬ by public transport; better yet, however, you can make a rigorous but grand full-day hike over the Grosse Scheidegg from Meiringen. It is a walk for the physically fit, but transportation – via the occasionally passing, bright yellow postbus – can help out along the way if you find the thin air daunting; these are the only motorised vehicles allowed to use the road across the pass. Views of the surrounding glaciers are splendid.

The town of Grindelwald has sold its soul to tourism, no doubt about it. This has been true for quite some time: after the village burned down in 1892 – the

wooden houses provided the flames with more than enough fuel – the new buildings were adapted to suit economic factors, which had changed since the original settlement was built. As was the case in most of the mountain regions, the first tourists had been the English, who paid their first winter visits here in 1860. In 1891 an Englishman amazed the people of Grindelwald by bringing a pair of skis along with him. The area would never quite be the same.

Still, it is exceptionally well located. A day visiting the ice grottoes or glacial gorges, and the spectacular sight (when the clouds of mist part, that is) of the three peaks towering high above, is almost enough to make you forget the sprawl of chalets, bars and souvenir shops spilling along the main street.

The Alpine region

A whole series of mighty mountain peaks lies directly on the border separating the cantons of Bern and the Valais. Foremost among them are the **Eiger**, **Mönch** and **Jungfrau**; these are perhaps the most famous and are almost always thought of as a trio. Since 1912 there has been a railway line leading up to the **Jungfraujoch**. Information is provided in several languages during the journey and the train covers most of the distance inside the mountain itself, although intermediate stations with panoramic windows provide views of the mighty scene. A modern restaurant at the end of the line, 3,454 metres (11,333 ft) above sea level, provides food and drink.

The summit of the Jungfrau is 4,158 metres (13,500 ft) above sea level, and averages temperatures below zero even at the height of summer. The weather station up on the Jungfrau collects important data for meteorologists.

The cable-car ride up past **Gimmelwald** to the **Schilthorn** begins near the high resort village of **Mürren** ⓴ (closed to cars), below the Jungfrau group and at the upper end of the Lauterbrunnental. To get to Mürren from Grindelwald by rail you have to return down the line towards Interlaken and change trains at Zweilutschinen, where the Lutschine Valley divides. Traditionally uniformed and bewhiskered station guards are on hand to direct lost passengers to the correct platform. From the top of the Schilthorn there is a magnificent all-round view of the entire Alpine region. This panorama can also be enjoyed during a meal. The revolving restaurant at the top takes an hour to do one complete revolution. The cable-car scenes and ski-chase sequences from the James Bond film *On Her Majesty's Secret Service* were shot on the Schilthorn, and brochures still refer to it as "Piz Gloria" – its name in the film.

One very unusual attraction in Mürren is the **Sport und Ballon Museum** (open all year daily 4–6pm, Thur to 8pm; free; tel: 033 856 86 86) of the International Spelterini Society. The name refers to the first crossing of the Alps by gas balloon, undertaken by Spelterini (a native of Mürren) in 1910. The **International Alpine Balloon Festival** is held every summer in the Lauterbrunnental in memory of this pioneering achievement.

Heading back up the Lütschine Valley towards Interlaken, another spectacle are the astounding **Staubbach Falls**, outside the picturesque village of

Map on page 122

Souvenir cowbells to remind you of their unmistakable echo around the Alps.

BELOW:
the Chästeilet in the Justistal.

Goethe was inspired by the Staubbach Falls to write his poem "Song of the Spirits over the Water."

Lauterbrunnen ⓯. So impossibly tall that they appear to be a trick of the eye until you get closer, the water crashes over a wall of rock 280 metres (900 ft) high, dissolving almost entirely into fine spray as it does so. When there is a lot of water, in the summer, this spray hangs suspended in the air and can often be felt as far away as the village itself.

Wengen and the Schynige Platte

Wengen ⓰, another village without cars, lies just to the north of Lauterbrunnen up a branch cog railway line. Wengen's main claim to the tourist market is in the winter when it hosts the annual international skiing contest on the **Lauberhorn**. This popular event attracts the crowds, who pay to watch the race and for the practice sessions. Being car-free, Wengen is an especially quiet place for the rest of the year but for the pleasing racket of cowbells and the frequent clanking and braking of the cog railway grinding its way up and down the steep gradient to the valley. For a small town, it is well supplied with amenities, including a cinema, tennis courts and a pool hall. After dark, Wengen's nightlife gets going – more so in the winter, when the glitterati show up for the ski event. It is possible to follow marked trails just uphill from the little station for a bit of pleasant walking through pastures and past rustic, log-heated homes, or you can walk back downhill to Lauterbrunnen in about one hour. Get a good trail map if you will be going further into the backcountry.

Returning to Interlaken, a cog railway line leads up to the **Schynige Platte** ⓱, a rock shelf situated at the entrance to the Lütschinen Valley. The Alpine Botanical Gardens, containing more than 500 species of plants native to the Swiss Alps, have been planted in over 8 hectares (20 acres) of lush meadows. If you do not want to read all the information provided, you can simply admire the visual beauty of these plants. Beware of picking any of these wild flowers, however, as they are protected by law (garden open June–mid-Sept 9am–6pm; entrance fee; tel: 033 822 28 35).

The way to the Valais

Another key traffic junction in the Alps, in addition to the St Gotthard, is the **Lötschberg Tunnel**. It provides a connection with the Valais that is passable even in winter and saves having to go the long way round the Alps via the Lower Valais. The chance to load their cars onto a train also provides motorists with a well-earned break on their journey towards the south. This stretch of railway opened in 1913.

The route to the Lötschberg leads south from **Spiez** and through the **Kandertal**, the third of the four huge valleys of the Bernese Oberland. (The others are the **Frutigtal**, **Kiental** and **Engstligental**.)

The valleys are flanked to the west by the Niesen range. **Reichenbach** is a rather inconspicuous little village on the lower reaches of the **River Kander**, in the Frutigtal. Most of its houses were built in the 18th century, and are examples of the fine carpentry that has been a feature of the Bernese Oberland for centuries. The village's main street is lined with solid-looking wooden houses, each decorated with richly carved and painted facades.

BELOW: the imposing Eiger north wall dwarfs passing trains.

Rivers and waterfalls

Frutigen, the main town in the Engstligental area, stands at the junction of the Kander and the Engstligenbach rivers. The strong erosion of the currents has given the valley its "V"-shape, as powerful torrents of water have cut deeply into the soft rock layers of the Niesen range. Despite these obstacles, the industrious Swiss have built bridges and flights of steps right next to the rivers, some of which provide spectacular views of the frothing action. The numerous local waterfalls and dramatically eroded rocks form a superb natural spectacle.

Adelboden ⑱, a resort occupying a sunny position at the head of the Engstligental, some 15 km (9 miles) from Frutigen, is an exceptionally popular holiday resort and offers a broad range of winter and summer activities including over 300 km (180 miles) of walking trails. Buildings such as the church, constructed in 1433, are consequently often disregarded, but are worth a look. Its exterior wall has a late-Gothic painting of the Last Judgement dating from 1471, and inside there is modern stained glass by Alberto Giacometti *(see The Arts, page 68)*.

Kandersteg ⑲, a beautifully situated resort and mountaineering centre of long standing, lies at the entrance to the Lötschberg Tunnel about 12 km (8 miles) south of Frutigen. In the 18th century considerable trading took place here, with the north exchanging cattle for spices from the south. The porters involved in this trading gradually adapted to the increasing needs of tourism, and whole dynasties of mountain guides arose. The **Blümlisalp Massif** is an ideal destination for mountaineers. Water sports are also possible: the **Öschinensee**, which lies 1,578 metres (5,000 ft) above sea level, is just the place for an Alpine swim. This lake was produced by a landslide in the latter part of the Ice Age. The water flows out from the lake underground, and is used to produce electricity.

Map on page 122

Kandersteg has plenty of seasonal activities on offer, including 750 metres (2,500 ft) of summer toboggan run.

BELOW: on the Schilthorn, also referred to as the "Piz Gloria".

An accordion player entertains in Château d'Oex.

BELOW: the Simmentaler cow is part of the Swiss Alpine landscape.

The Simmental

The last of the large valley communities in the Bernese Oberland, the **Simmental** has belonged to Bern since 1386. At the end of the 14th century, the city-state of Bern took over political control of the region from the monastery at Interlaken. The inhabitants of the valley were, however, far from convinced by the Reformation in the 16th century and most of them remained loyal to their Catholic faith. Despite this, the Simmental did not become alienated from Bern. One conspicuous illustration of this is the Bern coat-of-arms that can be seen at **Schloss Wimmis**, marking the entrance to the Simmental.

The **Lower Simmental River** winds its way westwards through the mountain ranges and then describes a large bend before heading off southwards again as the **Upper Simmental**. The observant traveller – shortly after having entered the **Diemtigtal Valley** (noted for its *Papierschnitzerie* – richly decorated paper cutouts depicting scenes of forests and animals) – will have already noticed the typical Simmental houses in **Erlenbach** as well as in **Därstetten**. The **Knuttihaus**, built in 1756, is considered one of the finest farmhouses in Europe. With its whitened cellar and first storey and loft above it, it is the archetypal Simmental house.

The village of **Bad Weissenburg**, beyond Därstetten, flourished thanks to a mineral spa. It was here, shortly before the outbreak of World War II, that Juliana, later to become Queen of the Netherlands, became engaged to Prince Bernhard. The water is still bottled and sold today, but the spa itself stopped operating long ago. Further up the valley, the road forks off, at **Boltigen** (itself 35 km/22 miles southwest of Thun), west into the **Jaun Pass**. This leads off into the French-speaking region of Gruyère. Further along the Simme, the valley changes from the Lower into the Upper Simmental.

SIMMENTALER COWS

Herds of placidly ruminating, golden-honey-coloured cows are as much a part of the Swiss Alpine landscape as are kangaroos in the Australian outback.

Among all the different varieties found in Switzerland, the undisputed crème de la crème are the beautiful Simmentaler cows from the villages in the Lower Simmental Valley, which runs from east to west at the foot of the Fribourg Alps, to the west of Spiez.

Until a short time ago, the Simmentaler cow was the Swiss cow *par excellence*, and is still one of the most widespread breeds of cattle in the world. These large, sturdy animals ideally weigh around 600 kg (1,300 lb) and are exploited not only for their milk and beef but even as a means of farm traction in areas where mechanised transport is not possible. The breed is generally dappled reddish-beige and white, and horned. The cows are extremely attractive, docile creatures and quite friendly (even the oxen of the Simmental region are said to radiate friendliness).

Unfortunately, this reliable breed is disappearing in favour of the high-milk-yield cows. It has recently been cross-bred with the Red Holsteiner, which has altered its appearance somewhat but not diminished its good looks.

Zweisimmen ⑳ is, from the point of view of transport at least, the most important town in the Upper Simmental – it is right on the main lines stretching to Spiez, Interlaken and even Geneva via the attractive Golden Pass line, which runs through these hills several times a day (though only once nonstop). From here one can either follow the Simme further up to the spa town of Lenk, or go off westwards into the Saanetal, the easternmost projection of the canton of Vaud. The **church** in Zweisimmen is all that remains of the old village, for the town was destroyed by fire in 1862, just as Grindelwald would be 30 years later. The 15th-century church, consecrated to the Virgin Mary, is decorated both inside and out with late-Gothic frescoes which survived the conflagration. The small **Heimathuus** (Obersimmental Local Museum) can introduce you to more history and folklore if you have the time – and happen to be here during one of the three days each week when it is open (mid-May–mid-Oct, Wed, Sat and Sun only, 10am–noon and 2–4.30pm; entrance fee; tel: 033 722 02 01). The museum is housed in a typical Swiss 18th-century building, and contains period furniture, household items, farm implements and local crafts (such as *Papierschnitzerie* – the region's intricate scissor-work).

On the 12-km (8-mile) drive south to **Lenk**, note the preponderance of finely crafted, painted and decorated wooden homes; this is known as the Simmental House Trail, and makes for a pleasing diversion along the road. Lenk, like Zweisimmen, lives mainly from tourism, but it also has a sulphur spring that has been in commercial use since the 17th century.

Gstaad

The **Saanetal**, just west, has the town of **Gstaad** ㉑, also on the Golden Pass route, to thank for its fame. High society from all over the world meets up in the winter months. Gstaad, as well as nearby **Gsteig** 10 km (6 mile) south, is also a summer resort and, despite its snooty image, is as keen on receiving year-round visitors as any other town. The local Gstaad Alpine Centre carries a staff of guides who lead rafting expeditions on the Saane River, maintain a tricky ropes course and run a programme of other pulse-pounding adventures in the surrounding mountains and rivers.

From **Saanen** – more of a country town and without much of the overbearing wealth of its showier neighbour Gstaad – the **River Saane** continues west as the Sarine (its French name) into the Pays d'Enhaut in the Vaud, later to flow into the Swiss-French lowlands and eventually into the Aare. However, if, south of Château d'Oex, you cross one of two passes – the **Col des Mosses**, or the **Col du Pillon** – from Gsteig, you find yourself in the Rhône basin heading for the Mediterranean. If you leave the Pays d'Enhaut in a northerly direction and go up the Sarine you reach the canton of Fribourg.

Château d'Oex ㉒ does make a fine last stop in the area. Not technically part of the Oberland, it is nonetheless a breath of fresh air – literally – with the popular annual International Hot-air Ballooning Week that brings in the visitors every January, offering rides and some spectacular race events. ❏

Map on page 122

*Cyril Connolly noted the potential of **Gstaad** as early as 1946: "Gstaad is an up-and-coming Kitzbuhel, not too high, not too enclosed…the whole ambience has that exquisite stimulation of a mountain resort assured of a future."*

BELOW: hot-air balloon racing in Château d'Oex.

SWITZERLAND'S ALPINE RAILWAYS

Trains snake their way through picturesque valleys and up steep mountains offering views of lush green hillsides and snowcapped peaks

No other country in the world is so dependent on its mountain railways as Switzerland, whether it be to take milk down from the Alpine pastures or to ferry skiers to the pistes. To help trains climb steep gradients on conventional railways, a "rack" between the rails allows the pinions of a cog on the train to engage the rack and claw its way up the slope – or brake its descent. Although the rack system was pioneered in the United States, it was Swiss engineers who developed it and exported equipment all over the world, from Sumatra to North Wales. Another means of mountain climbing was the funicular, using a cable to balance ascending and descending cars.

SPECTACULAR ALPINE VIEWS

To travel on the extensive mountain rail network is one of the greatest pleasures Switzerland has to offer. Most famous of all journeys is the Glacier Express, which conveys passengers in generously glazed, air-conditioned splendour between St Moritz and Zermatt. Though an 8-hour journey, there is barely a dull minute, and the lunch served in the restaurant car is astonishingly good for food on the move. Wine is served in glasses with angled stems to compensate for the steep slopes.

For the photographer and those who relish bracing Alpine air, some trains on the spectacular Bernina line between St Moritz and Tirano in Italy have open carriages from which to enjoy the glacial blue-green of Lago Bianco and the mountains surrounding the highest rail crossing of the Alps.

△ **WORKING RAILWAYS**
Alpine railways are vital to the rural economy; milk from a nearby farming district is loaded at Col-de-Bretaye which lies above the resort of Villars in the canton of Vaud.

◁ **VALLEY CROSSING**
A train crosses a viaduct on the international Centovalli line, which runs between Locarno and Domodossola. It is one of the lesser-known great railway journeys.

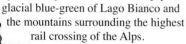

◁ **AN OPEN-TOP RIDE**
The open cab of a steam locomotive on the railway line which travels up Mount Rigi, a viewpoint favoured by Queen Victoria.

◁ **TO THE PLATEAU**
One of the most popular mountain railways in the Bernese Oberland climbs through the valley, up to Schynige Platte at 1,987 metres (6,519 ft).

△ **THE GLACIER EXPRESS**
All aboard the Glacier Express, which runs from St Moritz to Zermatt. Passengers in the panoramic cars can enjoy splendid views of Swiss mountains and valleys.

UP MOUNT RIGI ON THE RACK RAILWAY

Long before the opening of Europe's first Alpine railway up Mount Rigi in 1871, the peak, known as "the Queen of Mountains", was one of *the* Swiss summits to climb. Hikers enjoyed watching the sun set and rise over the magnificent panorama of peaks 805 km (500 miles) in circumference.

To cater for these visitors, the first hotel close to the summit opened in 1816. It was progressively enlarged, resulting in the Hotel Schreiber, which opened in 1875 with accommodation for 300 guests. Both César Ritz and Auguste Escoffier worked at the Schreiber as head waiter and chef respectively before becoming famous.

The idea for the first rack railway in Europe was apparently suggested by the Swiss Consul-General in Washington, John Hitz, during a visit to the works of Niklaus Riggenbach in Olten, a small engineering town in the Jura. Using a rack system he had patented in Paris, Riggenbach began building work in September 1869, and after delays in the delivery of rails and passenger vehicles caused by the Franco-Prussian War, it opened in 1871 with Riggen-bach at the controls of the first train.

▷ **VITAL RAIL LINK**
A train rattles out of the rail tunnel underneath the St Gotthard Pass, *circa* 1882. The tunnel provides a vital link between north and south.

▽ **SKI WAGONS**
Special wagons for skis are attached to some winter trains (such as the one pictured below at Col-de-Bretaye), which are often the only way to reach the pistes.

▽ **THROUGH THE VALAIS**
The emblem of the Martigny–Châtelard line, a rail link between the Valais in Switzerland and France which is well known for its spectacular views over the broad valley and the Rhône.

20

Pierre Joseph
Dumas, Maître Charpentier.
Sous le N° 49

THE WEST

Map on page 144

*This region, comprising two cantons tucked around
Lac de Neuchâtel, is characterised by small-scale dairy villages
and, of course, Gruyère cheese*

The cantons of **Vaud** and **Fribourg** between them form the lowlands and the Alpine foothills of French-speaking western Switzerland, with the valleys of the rivers Thielle, Broye and Sarine running almost parallel to one another. The strangely contorted borders in the **Broye Valley** and their many enclaves of Catholics are a reminder of the time when the city-republics of Bern and Fribourg captured the former Savoy Vaud (which extended from Bieler See to Lac Léman/Lake Geneva) in 1536.

At the time of the revolution, the areas captured by Fribourg – which had remained Catholic – did not want to be connected with the Protestant canton of Vaud for confessional reasons. This region, with its gentle hills and low mountains, its fields of waving corn, its green meadows and its spick-and-span towns has – if one discounts **Morat** (Murten in German) and **Gruyères** (Greyerz) – been spared may of the worst aspects of mass tourism.

Despite industrialisation, Fribourg remains the most markedly rural of Switzerland's cantons: one in six employed people works in agriculture (the figure was as high as 39 percent in 1950), more than three times the number in Switzerland as a whole. The canton has its own breed of cattle, patriotically sporting the black-and-white colours of the canton, and two types of cheese: Gruyère and Vacherin, a fondue cheese. The language border is also a "cheese border": the French-Swiss part of Fribourg produces Gruyère, the Swiss-German part produces the large-holed Emmentaler.

Fribourg, the bridge town

Within a loop described by the River Sarine lies the cantonal capital, **Fribourg** ❶. The fine townscape is dominated by the tower of the Cathedrale St Nicholas (St Nicholas' Cathedral), which has the Last Judgement depicted on its western portal. The Sarine marks the linguistic border. Fribourg is – both literally and metaphorically – a bridge town; for nearly a millennium it has formed a bridge between German- and French-speaking Switzerland. Its setting is spectacular. At the end of the 18th century, the English historian William Coxe was so impressed by its aspect that he was driven to one of his not infrequent flights of fancy: "Many [of the buildings] overhang the edge of a precipice in such a manner that, on looking down, a weak head would be apt to turn giddy…."

Fribourg, founded as a *Freie Burg* in 1157 by Berchtold IV of Zähringen, on a peninsula in the River Sarine, was bigger than both Bern and Zürich when it entered the Confederation, and in terms of prosperity it was easily on a par with Basel and Geneva. Trade and business flourished; the woollen cloth and leather the town produced were sought-after commodities.

PRECEDING PAGES: inside the Gruyère Museum in Bulle. **LEFT:** Fribourg: the old town and the cathedral. **BELOW:** quiet main street in Gruyères.

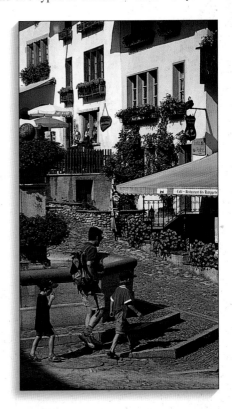

A cheesemaker from Moléson, near Gruyères. The Moléson Cheese Factory, dating from 1686, is open to visitors May–Oct daily 9.30am–7pm; entrance fee; (tel: 026 921 10 44; www.moleson.ch).

After the Reformation – Fribourg stayed with the "old faith" – its economic power declined, even though the town managed to extend its dependencies, and it wasn't until the second half of the 20th century that Fribourg emerged from its somnolence and rapidly industrialised.

As an island of Catholicism in a Protestant land, the town went through a period of decline. The country was preparing to supply mercenaries to foreign princes (particularly to Their Most Christian Majesties of France), and the patrician upper classes became fossilised in class prejudice.

The Gruyère region

To the south of Fribourg is the Valley of Gruyère, through which the River Sarine flows. The valley is a microcosm of Switzerland: a plateau surrounded by mountain peaks, and right in the middle, in a commanding position, a small town with a château, whose lords have ruled the region for centuries. The whole Gruyère region is steeped in history.

Every year over a million people visit the small town of **Gruyères** ❷ and its château, some 30 km (19 miles) from Fribourg. Just outside the town is the **Fromagerie** (Cheese Dairy), so clean that it looks more like a laboratory than the popular image of a rural dairy. The town has only one street, so can be walked through quickly. The **château**, no longer in private hands, has been turned into a major tourist attraction complete with restaurants and souvenir shops. The corridors once walked by counts and their ladies are now packed with tourists from as far away as San Francisco and Tokyo.

As in German-speaking Switzerland, a rich cow-herding culture has developed in the Alpine foothills. Folk artists immortalised the *Poya* – the ceremonial

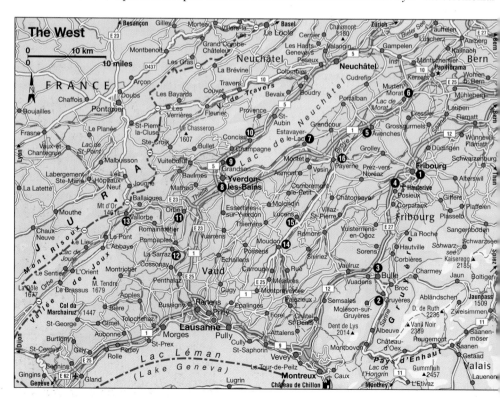

Map on page 144

driving of livestock to the summer pastures – in colourful paintings (especially from the 18th century onwards), which decorated crossbeams and barn doors. Many depict the cows, along with a horse piled high with luggage, a pig and several goats, zigzagging their way up the mountainside, accompanied by herdsmen with rucksacks and walking-sticks on their way to the alpine hut. A fascinating collection of this farm art, so typical of the Gruyère region, can be found in the **Musée Gruérien** (open Tues–Sat 10am–noon and 2–5pm; entrance fee; tel: 026 912 72 60), in **Bulle** ❸, a rewarding place to visit a few kilometres to the north of Gruyères on the road to Fribourg; the museum's exhibition of costumes and farm tools is also worth a look.

Alongside the River Sarine just to the south of Fribourg is the Cistercian **Abbaye de Hauterive** ❹ near **Posieux**. The 12th-century monastery is Switzerland's only remaining abbey belonging to Cistercian monks. Also unique is the 13th-century **Monastère de La Valsainte** near **Charmey**, to the east of Bulle, the only Carthusian monastery in Switzerland, inhabited today by members of this austere order who live as semi-recluses in rows of individual cells, each with its own garden.

Roman amphitheatre at Avenches.

A landscape steeped in history

Most Swiss lakes were formed during the Ice Age; as it ended the glaciers gradually melted and their basins filled with water. After the Rhône glacier had receded, an area of water 100 km (60 miles) in length, covering the base of the Jura all the way to Solothurn, formed northeast of the continental divide of La Sarraz. This "Lake Solothurn" finally split up into three distinct parts: Lac de Morat, Biel and the lakes of Neuchâtel. After the lake had receded, the Orbe plateau developed, and today this Plateau provides fertile agricultural land.

In **Avenches** ❺, to the northwest of Fribourg, are the extensive and well-preserved **Roman ruins** of the Helvetian capital of *Aventicum*. They contain an amphitheatre, temple, baths, theatre and museum, making for a very pleasant short walk from the town (open daily; free entry to ruins). While here, you might wish to visit the adjacent **Musée Romain d'Avenches** (open daily except Mon 10am–noon and 1–5pm, Oct–Mar 2–5pm; entrance fee; tel: 026 675 17 27).

To the north of Avenches, on the shore of the Lac de Morat, is the town of **Murten** ❻. This exceptionally well-preserved town has walls topped with towers, a castle, 15th-century churches and a good little historic museum in what was once a windmill, with interesting prehistoric artefacts found in the lake (open May–Oct Tues–Sun 11am–5pm, Nov–Apr 2–5pm; entrance fee; tel: 026 670 31 00).

East of Murten, near Kerzers, the tropical gardens at **Papiliorama** (open daily 9am–5pm, summer until 6pm; entrance fee; tel: 031 756 04 61; www.papiliorama.ch) feature a heated dome housing tropical butterflies, birds and fish, and another for nocturnal creatures.

Lake Neuchâtel

West of Morat, lying in the shadow of the rugged Jura range, is the large Lac de Neuchâtel, around the shores of which you can visit an eclectic range of historic sites, including more Roman settlements. In **Estavayer-le-**

BELOW: Corpus Christi procession in Romont.

TIP

On 1 October, Murten holds a road race to Fribourg, in memory of an army messenger who collapsed and died in Fribourg after relaying the news of the German victory at Murten in 1032.

Lac ❼, halfway down the lake's eastern side, is the **Château de Chenaux**, founded in the 13th century (not open to the public). The town's local history museum contains, among other things, a collection of frogs preserved in glass jars (open Mar–Oct Tues–Sun 10am–noon and 2–5pm, Nov–Feb Sat and Sun 2–5pm; entrance fee). At the lake's southern tip lies **Yverdon-les-Bains ❽**, a small industrial town with its own thermal baths (sulphur springs). Between 1805 and 1823, the famous teacher Heinrich Pestalozzi ran his world-renowned education institute from the **château** here. Today it houses an **Ethnological Collection** (open Tues–Sun, June–Sept 10am–noon and 2–5pm, Oct–May 2–5pm; entrance fee; tel: 024 425 93 10), which includes prehistoric items recovered from Lac de Neuchâtel.

Just to the north of Yverdon is the historic town of **Grandson ❾**, where the Confederate army defeated Charles the Bold of Burgundy in 1476. Grandson is famous for its mighty **castle** (open Apr–Oct daily 9am–6pm, Nov–Mar Mon–Sat 9–11.30am and 3–5pm, Sun 9am–5pm; entrance fee; tel: 024 445 29 26), which is today the repository for a collection of old cars, motorcycles and bicycles. No less fascinating a building is the Romanesque church of **St John the Baptist**.

Further up the west bank of Lac de Neuchâtel, beyond **Concise ❿** (2.5 km/1½ miles on foot from the railway station, and also accessible by car from the main road), lies the Roman quarry of **La Lance**. Wooden stakes were hammered into the unworked limestone and soaked with water until they cracked the rock: traces of this technique can be clearly seen in the stone today. Ships would then transport the stone across the lake to **Yverdon** (*Eburodunum*) or via the Broye over to the Helvetic capital of *Aventicum*, today's Avenches.

Near the little town of **Orbe ⓫**, 9 km (6 miles) or so south of Yverdon, at **La Boscéaz**, there are some splendid mosaics to be seen, which once decorated

BELOW: monk at work in the Valsainte Monastery.

the floors of a grand Roman villa (open Apr–Oct Mon–Fri 9am–noon and 1.30–5pm, Sat and Sun 1.30–5.30pm; entrance fee).

Map on page 144

The continental divide

The centre of the world for the ancient Greeks was Delphi; for the people of western Switzerland, it is close to the small town of **La Sarraz** ⑫, strategically located midway between lakes Léman/Geneva and Neuchâtel. If the streams leading from the nearby millpond were not barred off, the trout inside could choose which way they wanted to go: to the North Sea via the Rhine or to the Mediterranean via the Rhône. Local people have named the pond Le Milieu du Monde – the centre of the world. People here have dreamt for centuries of a trans-Helvetian and trans-European waterway. As we shall see, to an extent that dream was realised.

This continental divide between the Mediterranean and the North Sea is comparable to the St Gotthard Pass. The railway here, however, has no northern and southern slopes to climb and has few bends (it only twice enters a tunnel). **Eclépens**, on the La Sarraz watershed and 455 metres (1,500 ft) above sea level, is only 18 metres (60 ft) higher than the station in Biel. At the foot of the Jura, the train from German-speaking Switzerland, after passing Yverdon and the Orbe Plateau, crosses the foothills of the Jura known as the **Mormont**, which forms a kind of barrier between the Rhine and Rhône river regions.

It is thought that the name of **La Sarraz** is based on the Latin *serrata* (saw-shaped): the road here squeezes its way between the Jura and the Mormont. On a rocky hill, nearly 1,000 years ago, the lords of Grandson built a **castle**, from which they could supervise this access route. A descendant of the lords turned the castle into a museum in 1911. On his death, his widow made it a

BELOW: chewing the cud in a summer pasture near Charmey.

The gory tomb of Franz of La Sarraz.

centre where people working in the arts could meet and find inspiration: she invited the Russian film director Sergei Eisenstein, the German painter Max Ernst and the Swiss-French architect Le Corbusier to the castle, organised an architects' conference and, in 1929, hosted the first congress of independent film makers. The castle stables house an interesting Horse Museum (both castle and museum are open June–Aug daily except Mon 10am–5pm, Apr–May and Sept–Oct weekends only 1–5pm; entrance fee; tel: 021 866 64 23).

Near the castle there is a Gothic **chapel**, containing the tomb of Franz of La Sarraz, on which his decaying corpse has been rendered in stone. It is a very graphic depiction of the transition from this world to the next: worms are crawling through the body and the face and the genitals are hidden by toads.

The canal of La Sarraz

In the 17th century, La Sarraz Pass was chosen to become a major European traffic route, to be part of a canal linking the North Sea and the Mediterranean. The idea behind the scheme was to provide The Netherlands with an easy route to India, avoiding not only the Straits of Gibraltar but also their Spanish enemies and the Moorish pirates who plagued the North African coast. Canals already led through Belgium and the County of Burgundy, both under Spanish control. The Netherlands thus planned a trans-European connection through Switzerland.

BELOW: making Gruyère cheese in a Fribourg dairy.

Elie Gouret, a British Huguenot in the service of the Dutch, handed the council in Bern a memorandum with the plans of the ship canal and most of the capital he needed. He also brought with him technicians and carpenters to build the sluices and boats. The plan was to connect Yverdon, on Lac de Neuchâtel, with Lac Léman/Lake Geneva. After two years' labour, construction workers reached **Entreroches** on the Mormont. There, they built a harbour and a harbourmaster's house which can still be seen today. Eight years later, they had got as far as **Cossonay**.

It was at this point that they ran out of money, and the dream of a trans-European canal was shelved. Yet the canal – or at least stretches of it – was used right up to the 19th century. Ships with wine, salt and grain (the Vaud trinity) travelled via the Canal d'Entreroches into Lac de Neuchâtel, and then via the Zihl and the Aare up to Solothurn. Even today, it is easy to make out sections of the old canal. From the station at Eclépens a signpost points the way to the **Canal d'Entreroches**. In a beech and oak forest lies a ravine between some limestone rocks. The deep trench between Cyclopean walls is the ship canal.

The Vaud Jura

Vallorbe ⓭, a strategic border town located 21 km (13 miles) west of La Sarraz on Autoroute No. 9, is the gateway to Vaud's section of the vast Jura Mountains *(see The Jura, pages 281–295)*. One of the town's top attractions is its **Railway Museum** (Musée du Chemin de Fer; Apr–Oct Tues–Sun 9.30am–noon and 1.30–6pm, Mon 1.30–6pm; Nov–Mar open on request; entrance fee; tel: 021 843 25 83), housed in the riverside **Grandes-Forges** building. International TGV rail traffic speeds through here from Paris via Lausanne to the south of France or Italy via the Simplon Pass. The

River Orbe, which once provided power for mills, has its source at the top of La Dôle, the second-highest mountain in the Jura.

The **Dôle** (1,677 metres/5,502 ft) is one of the cornerstone peaks of the Jura, where there is a weather station which serves all of western Switzerland. Tourists, however, tend to prefer the **Col du Marchairuz** (1,447 metres/4,747 ft), just south of Le Brassus, which has Nordic skiing runs. A pass road leads over the Marchairuz from Lac Léman/Lake Geneva into the Jura. Here, at the end of a long and tiring hike, you can relax in a natural paradise, the huge (40 sq. km/15 sq. miles) and many-faceted **Parc Jurassien Vaudois** (Vaud-Jura Park), which stretches south as far as the Col de la Givrine.

To the north, the River Orbe forms the **Lac de Joux**; from there the water flows underground, not re-appearing until it emerges here as the **Source de l'Orbe** in a magnificent cavern. Nearby is another cavern which is particularly famous for its stalactites: the **Grotte de l'Orbe**. The highest mountain in the whole range, **Mont Tendre** (1,679 metres/5,508 ft) sloping up from the Lac de Joux, provides an impressive panoramic view, including the forested **Mont Risoux** to the west.

Map on page 144

Vacherin Mont d'Or, one of Switzerland's most popular cheeses, available only in the winter months, takes its name from the Mont d'Or, overlooking Vallorbe.

Medieval Broye

Finally, returning north again to the Broye Valley (the main route from Lausanne to Bern) there are a clutch of picturesque medieval towns: **Moudon** ⓮ has a delightful old quarter; **Lucens** ⓯, with its château and its Sherlock Holmes Museum *(see page 124)*; and **Payerne** ⓰, which has a Romanesque **abbey** and a parish church with the tomb of the legendary Burgundian queen, Bertha. On a hill east of Lucens, lies **Romont**, whose château contains a museum of stained glass. ❑

BELOW: the town of Murten, seen from Lac de Morat.

THE SONG OF SWITZERLAND

As in German-speaking Switzerland, a rich cowherding culture has developed in the western Alpine foothills, producing a long-standing tradition of folk music. The cowherd's melody became known as the Song of the Swiss and became famous around the world. The song with the dialect refrain "Lioba, lioba, por ario" recalls the *Poya*, driving the cattle up to the Alpine pastures.

It is supposed to be so evocative of life on the Alps that in former days it provoked an uncontrollable feeling of homesickness in Swiss mercenaries. So strong was their nostalgia on hearing the song that they would burst into tears. In 1621, a minister of the King of France is said to have banned Swiss mercenaries serving in France from singing the cowherd's melody. But the melody proved so popular that it found its way into operas and operettas, which were performed across Europe and the United States throughout the 19th and 20th centuries.

Today, there are innumerable arrangements and piano renditions, libretti and arias containing the cowherd's melody. They all sing the praises of the rural Switzerland which the homesick mercenaries longed for, a way of life that in today's Switzerland is best summed up by picturesque Swiss dairy towns such as Gruyères.

LAKE GENEVA

Map on page 160

Known to the French as Lac Léman, this is one of the most famous lakes in the world, instantly recognisable for the soaring Jet d'Eau fountain on its banks and, of course, its lakeshore mansions

The train journey from Zürich and Bern in the direction of Lausanne and Geneva rewards travellers – as they emerge from a tunnel just before Lausanne – with a stunning view of the vast, light-blue expanse of **Lake Geneva**, and of the mountains surrounding it. The sloping vineyard next to the railway line here is jokingly referred to as the "Clos des Billets": Swiss Germans, overcome by the beauty of the landscape, are reputed to fling their return tickets (*billets*) out of the train windows. That is probably a bit of an exaggeration. Still, ever since the days when the poet Byron sang the praises of the region guests have been arriving en masse.

The French name for Lake Geneva – Lac Léman – refers to the legendary Lemanus who is supposed to have given the lake its name of Lacus Lemanus. He was a son of the Trojan prince Paris, who started the Trojan War by abducting the beautiful Helen. The first record of the name Geneva was in the 1st-century BC *Commentaries* of Julius Caesar. The Romans introduced vines to the area, and later on Christian monks cultivated the slopes by the lake.

The perfect spot for vines, Geneva is the third largest wine-growing canton in Switzerland after the Valais and Vaud. It is said that the steep vineyards of Lavaux on Lake Geneva, between Lausanne and Montreux, benefit from the sun's rays three times: when it shines from the sky, when it reflects off the lake, and finally at night-time when its warmth, absorbed during the day, radiates from the vineyard walls. Along the Côte (north shore) between Lausanne and Geneva the vineyards form a rather more gentle slope.

PRECEDING PAGES: Château de Chillon. **LEFT:** Jet d'Eau. **BELOW:** Geneva Cathedral.

Western Europe's largest lake

The largest of the Swiss lakes, Lake Geneva is shaped like a sickle, and is 72 km (45 miles) long, up to 13 km (8 miles) wide near the middle, and 310 metres (1,000 ft) deep. Like the sea, it is subject to tides, though they make only 5 mm or so of difference. Some 348 sq. km (134 sq. miles) of its total surface area of 582 sq. km (225 sq. miles) belong to Switzerland, the rest, on the southern shore, belongs to France.

Such statistics apparently failed to impress the clergy in earlier days, as the following anecdote about Bernard, Abbot of Clairvaux in the 12th century, told by James Cotter Morrison in his book about the abbot, makes clear: "'Do not the mountains drop sweetness? The hills run with honey, and the valleys stand thick with corn?' wrote St Bernard of Clairvaux, but when travelling by the lake of Geneva, after having passed a whole day riding along its shore, in the evening, when his companions were speaking about 'the Lake', he enquired, 'what lake?'"

Lake Geneva, which contains 89 billion cubic

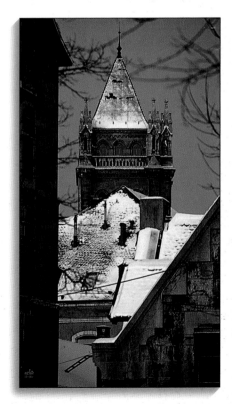

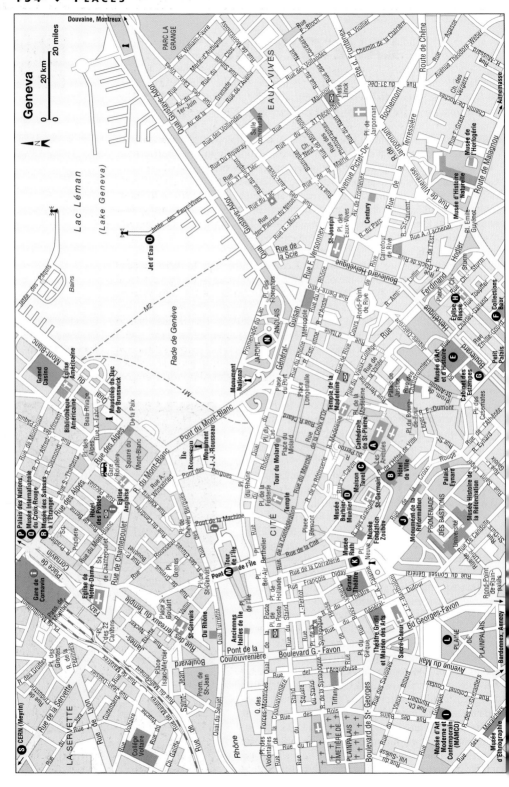

Geneva

metres (3,143 billion cubic feet) of water, is the largest freshwater reservoir in Europe. It contains twice as much water as Lake Constance, six times as much as Lake Neuchâtel and 22 times as much as Lake Zürich. Mathematicians have even made the morbid conclusion that it contains enough water to drown all of humanity: the water level would rise by only 50 cm (20 inches) or so. They have also made it clear that the River Rhône would have to milk the Valais glaciers for 17 years before it could fill an empty lake basin of this size.

Maps:
City 154
Area 160

In spite of all this, Lake Geneva still may not be big enough, however, to absorb progress and population growth. Two centuries ago, water specialists were already predicting that the lake would be destroyed by pollution. Now, as a result mainly of pressure from conservationists, it is slowly making a recovery. On 1 July 1986 Switzerland banned the use of phosphates in washing powders: within only a short time the rarer species of fish, many of which were near extinction in the lake, started to thrive again. The number of waterfowl has also risen substantially since a prolific species of mussel known as *Dreissena polymorpha* began to enrich the range of food available.

There is still some concern about the amount of nitrates in the fertiliser used by farmers in the region but, according to the Lake Geneva Water Protection Commission, "over-fertilisation" with phosphates has been substantially reduced in recent years – the level having been cut by 50 percent since 1986.

It was in 1823 that the steamer *William Tell* belonging to an American named Church first crossed the lake (initially horrifying many of the locals, who thought it was an invention of the devil). Traditionally, freighters with lateen sails were used to bring construction material for the two towns across the lake from Meillerie (Savoy). Unfortunately, there are only two remaining examples of such vessels, the *Vaudoise* in Lausanne and the *Neptune* in Geneva, but it is still possible to experience something of the flavour of lake travel in the early days: paddle steamers take passengers over to the French side of the lake, to Evian-les-Bains (with its casino, Olympic-size swimming pool and a mineral-water source) and Thonon-les-Bains. There are also regular sailings to the flower-bedecked French village of Yvoire and the Château (Castle) of Chillon, on the Swiss side, as well as a selection of half- or full-day roundtrips.

BELOW: Geneva's suburbs seen from afar.

Geneva ❶ (Genève/Genf; city pop. 180,000; canton pop. 410,000) has an international airport, from which it takes only 6 minutes to reach the centre of the city. Yet the city really needs to be approached from the lake (ideally on an old-fashioned steamer) to realise how magnificently situated it is: it nestles among hills and gardens, surrounded by mountain ranges and cradling its broad harbour, "La Rade".

The superb fountain spouting heavenwards at the mouth of the harbour, the Jet d'Eau, can be regarded as symbolic as well as decorative: in its proud history this city-republic has not laid claim to any other regions, and has always maintained an interest in the things of the spirit.

That is not to say that gains of a different kind are not considered desirable. Money has enormous importance in the city. The British actor Robert

A stone memorial at Grand Rue 40, the birthplace of the writer-philosopher Jean-Jacques Rousseau (1712–78).

BELOW:
the entrance to Geneva's Hôtel de Ville.

Morley described Geneva as "this city of wealth by stealth" and there is no doubt about the pioneering role Geneva has played in the creation of the capitalist credit system. The Vaud writer C.F. Ramuz concluded: "Geneva based itself on abstract thinking quite early on; and trading and banking really are abstractions if one compares them to the concrete activity of farming." Nowhere else in Switzerland are arguments indulged in so eagerly, and words bandied about so assiduously as here in Geneva; nowhere else is there so much political discussion.

The fifth continent

Geneva is a city of great influence and famous personalities. In the 16th century the reformer Calvin turned Geneva into a "Protestant Rome", the effects of which were felt worldwide; in the 18th century, the city's "Golden Age", Jean-Jacques Rousseau paved the way for human rights and the French Revolution; engineer Henri Dufour, head of the army in the country's last civil war, became a confederate peacemaker, and the philanthropic businessman Henri Dunant turned his home city into the headquarters of his Red Cross organisation and elevated the Swiss flag – which has the colours reversed – into the international symbol of humanity.

For centuries, the tiny city-state was surrounded by regions controlled by enemy princes – Savoy and France – and completely cut off from the lands in the Confederation. The most important transport connection was across the lake. It was only at the Congress of Vienna of 1814–15 that the border came down and Geneva was finally provided with land access to Switzerland. The umbilical cord is slender: the canton's border with France is 102 km (63 miles) long, while the boundary with the rest of Switzerland measures just 4 km (2 miles).

The German magazine *Stern* once came to the conclusion that Geneva contained "more millionaires than unemployed people". Even Voltaire, who lived in Geneva and nearby Ferney (where his house is now a museum), remarked derisively that the city had "very little else to do but earn money". It is said that the older inhabitants of Geneva grew rich by saving their money. Geneva also has its poor, the victims of prosperity, but they do not make the headlines of the international press. Neither are they that visible, at least not in the places frequented by visitors.

American links

Since the Reformation the coat-of-arms has borne the inscription *Post tenebras lux* (light after darkness). The same words appeared on the title pages of the English Bibles printed in Geneva that the pilgrims took on the *Mayflower* (1620) to America. Calvin's teachings had a worldwide effect: American president Woodrow Wilson, a Calvinist, suggested Geneva as the seat of the League of Nations after World War I.

Geneva makes a great show of championing freedom. In December every year the city celebrates the "Escalade", commemorating the Duke of Savoy's vain attempt to capture the city in 1602. His troops used ladders to climb the city walls but were repelled by the population. In the 19th century, Geneva bankers financed the Greeks' struggle for freedom.

Parks and museums

There are magnificent parks along the edge of the lake. The centre of the old town is on a small rise on the left bank of the Rhône, with the cathedral, the Town Hall, shopping streets and excellent museums. International Geneva is on the right-hand bank, with the Palais des Nations, the International Labour Organisation, the International Committee of the Red Cross and other organisations.

A good place to begin a walking tour of the city centre is at the Place de la Taconnerie. Its centrepiece, the **Cathédrale de Saint-Pierre A** (open June–Sept Mon–Sat 9.30am–6.30pm, Sun noon–6.30pm; Oct–May Mon–Fri 10am–noon and 2–5pm, Sat 10am–5.30pm, Sun noon–5.30pm; free, but there is a fee to climb the tower; tel: 022 310 29 29), has been Protestant since 1536, but dates from the 12th and 13th centuries. The 18th-century west facade is neoclassical. Describing the cathedral, a famous preacher, Pastor Henry Babel, said: "I have never entered the Cathedral St Pierre without the feeling that I was stepping into another world. The reverberating silence of its mighty walls, the shadow of its vaults and the brightness of its stained-glass windows have revealed to me that true greatness derives from a harmony in simplicity. The pillars support the vault towering above them, I told myself, just as science has to support belief."

Just off the cathedral square, you can not miss the large and architecturally interesting **Hôtel de Ville B** (City Hall; free entry) – rightly famous as the place where the Red Cross and the Geneva Conventions were formalised in 1864. Back then this was the place to hammer out international decisions (the

Maps:
City 154
Area 160

Cathédrale de Saint-Pierre sits above an important archaeological site which is open to the public (closed Mon). Here are the remains of church buildings built on the same site dating from the 4th century.

BELOW: Palais des Nations, the headquarters of the United Nations.

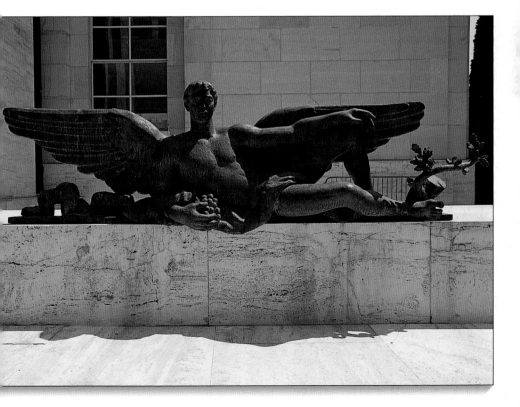

BELOW:
the historic Place
du Bourg-de-Four.
RIGHT: inside
Maison Tavel.

Palais des Nations headquarters building, was not finished until the 1930s).

Just northwest of the cathedral, at Rue du Puits-Saint-Pierre 6, is the **Maison Tavel ⊙**, known for its elegant architecture. The 14th-century house is the oldest remaining domain in the city; it was originally built in the 13th century, but was destroyed by fire and rebuilt in 1334. Inside is the **Musée du Vieux Genève** (open Tues–Sun 10am–5pm; free entry, except during exhibitions; tel: 022 418 37 00); visitors can learn about the fascinating history of Geneva. The museum contains a variety of artefacts from 19th-century Geneva.

A few steps further north of Maison Tavel, up Rue Calvin, bring you to the gorgeous **Musée Barbier-Mueller ⊙** (open daily 11am–5pm; entrance fee; tel: 022 312 02 70), which has collections of fine art from outside Europe.

Back in the cathedral square, head southeast and you will pass through the fountained **Place du Bourg-de-Four**, the city's oldest, and one of its most popular, shopping districts. The Palais de Justice, which has been home to the law courts since 1860, stands in the square.

The **Musée d'Art et d'Histoire ⊜** is at Rue Charles-Galland 2 (open Tues–Sun 10am–5pm; free; tel: 022 418 26 00). Inside the museum the famous altar painting *La Pêche Miraculese* by Konrad Witz (1444) reminds the visitor of Geneva's patron saint, St Peter: it shows Christ walking on the water with the waterfront at Geneva in the background. As well as important collections of fine art, the museum has an interesting Egyptology section.

East of the Musée d'Art et d'Histoire, beyond the confines of the old town, is the well laid-out **Musée d'Histoire Naturelle** (open Tues–Sun 9.30am–5pm; free; tel: 022 418 63 00) on Route de Malagnou. This museum has dinosaur exhibits, dioramas and a useful archive. A little further to the southeast, beyond Place Émile-

Map on page 154

Guyénot, is the **Musée de l'Horlogerie et de l'Emaillerie** (open daily, except Tues, 10am–5pm; free; tel: 022 418 64 70). Also on Route de Malagnou, this museum is worth a visit for its display of Swiss enamel watches and clocks.

Working your way west back toward the heart of the old town, drop by the **Collections Baur ⑥** (open Tues–Sun 2–6pm; entrance fee; tel: 022 346 17 29), at Rue Munier-Romilly 8, to view a private collection of Japanese and Chinese art. Close to the Musée d'Art et d'Histoire, at Promenade du Pin 5, is the museum's collection of prints – **Cabinet des Estampes ⑦** – with 300,000 exhibits spanning 500 years of history (open Tues–Sun 10am–5pm; free; tel: 022 418 27 70). Also nearby is the domed **Église Russe ⑧**, at the end of rues Lefort and François d'Ivernois, more interesting from outside than inside because of its nine gilded domes.

If you still have an appetite for modern art, take a No. 1 bus west past the Plaine de Plainpalais to the **MAMCO ⑨** (Musée d'Art Moderne et Contemporain; open Wed–Sun noon–6pm, until 9pm on Tues; entrance fee; tel: 022 320 61 22), at Rue des Vieux-Grenadiers 10. The museum has many fine examples of late 20th-century art. A couple of blocks south of MAMCO, at Boulevard Carl-Vogt 65–67, is the **Musée d'Éthnographie**, with a large collection of artefacts from around the world (open Tues–Sun 10am–5pm; entrance fee; tel: 022 418 45 50).

Old town to the lake

Proceeding east towards the old town, you come to the **Auditoire de Calvin** which stands between the **Musée Historique de la Réformation** and the **university**. The influential French theologian John Calvin (1509–64) preached his historic Protestant reforms from this auditorium. Closer to the old quarter is

The university in Geneva developed out of an academy set up by John Calvin. It contains the Musée Jean-Jacques Rousseau (open Mon–Fri 9am–noon, 2–5pm, Sat 9am–noon) dedicated to the writer-philosopher.

BELOW: an exhibit at the Museum of the Swiss Abroad: French infantry (Swiss mercenaries are in red).

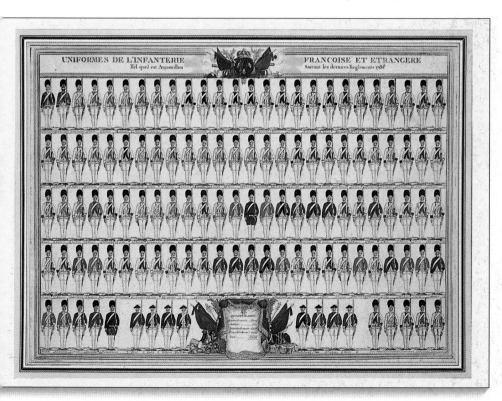

the **Promenade des Bastions** park and its **Monument de la Réformation** ❶, a tall and long stone wall erected in 1917 and incised with the images of the leading members of the Reformation: Farel, Calvin, de Bèze and Knox; it stretches nearly 100 metres (330 ft) and commemorates the key historic events of the Reformation.

Just to the north, on Place Neuve, you come to the **Musée Rath** ❷ (open Thur–Tues 10am–5pm, Wed noon–9pm, closed Mon; entrance fee; tel: 022 418 33 40), a quirky museum, and the first in the city, that hosts visiting exhibitions. Nearby is the base of the city fortifications. To the south, the large **Plaine de Plainpalais** ❸ plaza is the site of outdoor flea markets on Wednesday and Saturday mornings.

Continuing from the museum up Rue de la Corraterie is the river and its **Pont de l'Île** ❹. The **Tour de l'Île** (tower) here is little more than a ruin surviving from a former castle built on the island. Visitors crossing here to the right (north) bank will discover a small fruit and vegetable market and some good restaurants.

Stay on the left (south) bank of the river instead, and it is less than 1 km (½ mile) to the lakeside **Jardin Anglais** ❺, Geneva's largest park and the unofficial gathering place for everyone from disaffected youth to the well-to-do on lunch breaks. This is also the spot to catch the CGN steamer for scenic rides around the lake and even to France. From the park, you get an especially close view of the gushing **Jet d'Eau** ❻. The original fountain was designed in 1886 as a safety feature to reduce pressure on the city's water system. Its touristic potential was subsequently seized upon and today it jets up to 140 metres (460 ft) high, at a force of around 200 kph (120 mph).

You can cross over the water to the north side (right bank) of the city at two

"Pas d'argent, pas de Suisses" (no money, no Swiss) was a popular saying in the days when Swiss soldiers fought around Europe as mercenaries.

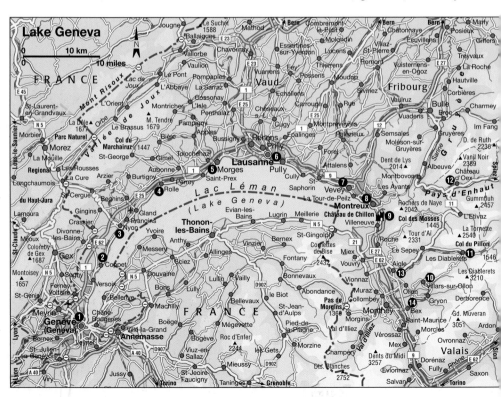

points – the busy **Pont du Mont-Blanc** or the more delightful little **Pont des Bergues**, which falls onto Île Rousseau (with its statue of the philosopher) along the way. Circle the harbour to come to the centre of Cité International, Geneva's international community. The highlight of this is the **Palais des Nations ⓟ** (open weekdays for tours only, July–Aug 9am–5pm, rest of the year 10am–noon and 2–4pm; entrance fee; tel: 022 917 48 96; passport required for tour) at Avenue de la Paix 14. Built between 1929 and 1936 as the headquarters of the League of Nations it is now the European headquarters of the United Nations.

Maps:
City 154
Area 160

Practically steps away, at Avenue de la Paix 17, the **Musée Internationale du Croix-Rouge et du Croissant-Rouge ⓠ** (International Red Cross and Red Crescent Museum; open Wed–Mon 10am–5pm; entrance fee; tel: 022 748 95 25) houses some of the city's most moving displays. The museum is dedicated to human compassion and suffering, highlighting some of history's greatest tragedies – and heroes – through the use of photographs, video footage, a reconstructed cell used to hold prisoners of war, and other exhibits.

The handsome **Penthes Château**, in a magnificent park nearby at Chemin de l'Impératrice 18, houses the **Musée des Suisses dans le Monde ⓡ** (Museum of the Swiss Abroad; open Tues–Sun 10am–noon and 2–6pm; entrance fee; tel: 022 734 90 21), with military memorabilia and cultural artefacts that recall the history of the Swiss who left the country to find their fortune and sometimes their death too: "Pas d'argent, pas de Suisses" (no money, no Swiss), was a popular saying during the days when the Swiss fought in foreign wars as mercenaries.

Ruins from the Roman amphitheatre in Nyon.

Finally, for something different catch a No. 15 bus west from the central Gare de Cornavin train station to **CERN ⓢ** (the European Laboratory for Particle Physics; open Mon–Sat, 9am–5.30pm, closed Mon morning; free; call ahead for tour; tel: 022 767 84 84), located just ouside Meyrin. It has the world's largest ring tunnel (Large Electron Positron Storage Ring; 27 km/17 miles long), used to explore matter. Using this in 1996, scientists at CERN made history as the first people to create antimatter.

BELOW: the International Red Cross Museum.

The villages on Lake Geneva

Leaving Geneva city now, the countryside around its northern lakeshore, **La Côte**, is dotted with pretty, historic villages. Vineyards dominate this area, producing the popular wines of the Vaud.

One of the highlights of La Côte is **Coppet ❷**, about 14 km (8 miles) north of Geneva. Its 18th-century **château**, which is open to visitors (open daily Apr–Oct 2–6pm; July and Aug 10am–noon and 2–6pm; entrance fee; guided tours every 35 minutes; tel: 022 776 10 28), was originally owned by Jacques Necker, a Geneva banker. His daughter Germaine de Staël (1766–1817) was one of the most important figures in European intellectual life. Necker, the Baron of Coppet, was Louis XVI's Minister of Finance. He married off his daughter to Sweden's ambassador in Paris, the Baron of Staël-Holstein. First an admirer, then later a critic, of Napoleon, she was exiled to Switzerland. The leading minds of the age used to meet in the Château de Coppet. Madame de Staël's autobiographical novels are as striking today as they were then in their advocacy of women's

Home of the UN

International Geneva is a city or a state all to itself. The Palais des Nations (guided tours daily) has its own postal service as well as its own stamps – just like Monaco, Liechtenstein or the Vatican. It is larger than the Palais de Versailles, and is the daily place of work for 3,500 international civil servants; it is the most important congress centre in the world, with more than 5,000 meetings every year making it the heart of the economic and sociopolitical UN capital of Geneva.

The international organisations provide 21,000 jobs; the diplomats and civil servants (numbering over 30,000 including their families) live tax-free, admittedly, but they also spend over 1.2 billion Swiss francs a year in Geneva, thus providing a catalyst for the city's prosperity. More than 100 countries, including Switzerland itself, have diplomatic missions in Geneva); the Swiss Embassy in Geneva represents the country in the various international organisations.

Geneva's rise as a famous conference centre began in 1871: a court of arbitration was held in the Town Hall during the row about the sinking of the battle cruiser *Alabama* in the American Civil War. On the first centenary of American independence in 1876, in memory of the arbitration award, US officers handed in their swords, the metal of which was recast into the form of a ploughshare; it can be seen in the "Salle Alabama" in the Town Hall. Geneva's international mission, however, dates back to Calvin and his "Protestant Rome".

Geneva's big moment came in 1919, when it was chosen as the seat of the League of Nations. With the advent of World War II the International Labour Organisation moved to Montreal and New York was chosen as the seat of the United Nations, and it was only thanks to the efforts made by several diplomats that Geneva became the European seat of the UN. Then a whole series of organisations started moving to Geneva: the UN possesses several special institutions, including 14 intergovernmental and 108 non-governmental organisations, and it is now considered the done thing for organisations' headquarters to be based in Geneva. Cardiologists, university chancellors, the World Council of Churches, the Women's League for Peace and Freedom, the World Wildlife Fund, the YMCA and the Boy Scouts all have a base here.

Scarcely any other city in the world receives so many visits from foreign heads of state. Geneva has been the scene of many historically important conferences:

1954: The Indo-China conference ended France's intervention and decided, fatefully, on the division of Vietnam.
1955: The Big Four summit: Eisenhower (USA), Bulganin (USSR), Eden (Britain) and Faure (France). The first meeting of The Conference for the Peaceful Use of Atomic Energy.
1983: Conference on Palestine.
1985: Summit meeting between Ronald Reagan (USA) and Mikhail Gorbachev (USSR) paved the way for the arms reduction agreements and the end of the Cold War.
2003: Unofficial peace proposal, the Geneva Accord, launched in an attempt to resolve the Israeli-Palestinian conflict. ❑

LEFT: the European seat of the United Nations has made Geneva a centre for peace talks.

emancipation, and her political tracts such as *De l'Allemagne* are pleas for European reconciliation.

Further along the shore 9 km (6 miles) north of Coppet is another delightful little town, **Nyon** ❸, originally a Helvetian settlement named Noviodunum, then a Roman fortified town founded by Julius Caesar (Colonia Iulia Equestris). On Rue Maupertuis is the **Musée Romain** (open Apr–Oct Tues–Sat 10am–noon and 2–5pm, Sun 10am–5pm; rest of the year closed mornings Tues–Sat; entrance fee; tel: 022 361 75 91). Housed in the ruins of an ancient basilica the museum documents life in the town during Roman times.

Visitors can buy one ticket which allows entry to both the Roman museum and the **Musée du Léman** (Lake Geneva Museum, Quai Louis-Bonnard; open Apr–Oct Tues–Sat 10am–noon and 2–5pm, Sun 10am–5pm; Nov–Mar Tues–Sat 2–5pm, Sun 10am–5pm; entrance fee; tel: 022 361 09 49), which has paintings, a display of steamships and other lake history. Nyon's fine **château**, housing the Musée Historique and a collection of Nyon porcelain (open Apr–Oct Tues–Sun 10am–5pm, Nov–Mar Tues–Sun 2–5pm; entrance fee; tel: 022 363 8351). The grand **Château de Prangins**, just to the west of Nyon, is a branch of the National Museum of Switzerland and concentrates on the country's 18th- and 19th-century history (open Tues–Sun 10am–5pm; entrance fee; tel: 022 994 88 90).

The attractive little town of **Rolle** ❹, situated on the lakeside about 11 km (7 miles) beyond Nyon, developed around the 13th-century château (closed to the public) built by Savoy Count Amadeus V. The small offshore island called **Île de la Harpe** was created in 1835 from surplus earth during the construction of the harbour. On the island is an obelisk, a monument to Vaud freedom-fighter Frédéric César de la Harpe, who was also a tutor at the court of the Tsar.

Île de la Harpe, which belongs to the town of Rolle, has a yachting community and is also the venue for races.

BELOW: Château Vufflens, a private castle in the Morges countryside.

The headquarters of the International Olympic Committee in Lausanne.

Another 14 km (9 miles) along the lakeshore road, the town of **Morges ⑤** also has a Savoyard château, a huge building which houses the **Musée Militaire Vaudois** (Military Museum; open Sept–June Tues–Fri 10am–noon, 1.30–5pm, Sat & Sun 1.30–5pm; Jul–Aug Tues–Sun 10am–5pm; entrance fee; tel: 021 316 09 90), the old arsenal, a collection of 10,000 lead soldiers and other remnants of war. The **Musée Alexis Forel** (open Mar 15th–Nov 30th Tues–Sun 2–6pm; entrance fee; tel: 021 801 26 47) in Blanchenay was once the home of Alexis Forel, an engraver. Today it contains collections of furniture, dolls and tapestries.

Just on the edge of Morges is one last surprise: the hamlet of **Tolochenaz** is famous in these parts because it was the former home of actress Audrey Hepburn, who lived here from 1963 until her death in 1993.

A little further around the lake, just 3 km (2 miles) before Lausanne, **St Sulpice** has a lakeside Romanesque church originally constructed in the 11th century and rebuilt a century later; it is now the site of summertime concerts.

Cosmopolitan and rural mix

First-time visitors to **Lausanne ⑥**, the capital of Vaud canton, would do best to start a tour by the harbour, at Château Vidy, the seat of the International Olympic Committee. Why not tour the ruins of the Roman harbour city of *Lousanna*, and then proceed to the medieval part of town? Here, a bishop of the Helvetians established a settlement on the hills above Lake Geneva when he was forced to give up his residence in Aventicum. The bishop built a château at the northern end of the old town, which still serves as a seat of government to this day. The city's medieval cathedral, consecrated in 1275 in the presence of both the emperor and the Pope, is considered one of the most beautiful early-Gothic buildings anywhere in Switzerland.

BELOW: the main portal of Lausanne Cathedral.

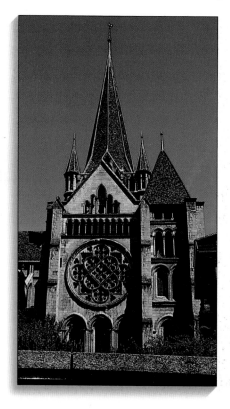

Inland from the harbour on Quai d'Ouchy in the Parc Olympique, the **Musée Olympique** (open Tues–Sun 9am–6pm, Thurs until 8pm; entrance fee; tel: 021 621 65 11) highlights the history of the Games and notable achievements of some of its participants through archive material and multimedia displays. It is an impressive place, and the grand views and good food make it a rewarding lunchtime stop of a few hours.

Also in the parkland, near the waterfront is the **Musée de l'Elysée** (open Tues–Sun 10am–6pm, Thurs until 9pm; entrance fee; tel: 021 316 99 11), which is actually just outside the official borders of Lausanne in the resort of Ouchy. Dedicated to photography, this museum is definitely worth a visit because of its often stunning visiting exhibitions.

Back at the lake, in the harbour is the former fishing village of **Ouchy**, a separate municipality, and now an area that bustles with boating, windsurfing, bathing and other sports during the daytime, then pulses at night with revellers in a string of bars and dance clubs just off the water. Sunset is wonderful here, as is the view of the distant twinkling lights of the towns across the lake. Here, too, lies the brigantine *La Vaudoise*, a reminder of the time when hundreds of freighters with crossed lateen sails ferried rock from Meillerie on the opposite, Savoyard bank of the lake to use in the construction of Geneva and Lausanne.

At the *embarcadère* (quayside), where steamers have been mooring since 1823, a fountain decorated with stone asses' heads bears a mysterious inscription: *En souvenir de l'Académie d'Ouchy*. Did this fishing village have its own academy? The answer is no: the "Académie d'Ouchy" was the name given to the columns of donkeys and pack mules that used to carry the construction material from the freighters up to Lausanne. As the caravan of animals made its way through the vineyards, students and townspeople, in a mocking reference to the professors who went in procession through Lausanne, would jeer: *"Voilà l'Académie d'Ouchy!"*

The rack railway is somewhat ambitiously referred to as the Métro (the former funicular is still popularly referred to as *la ficelle*, the string), but another way up to the **Cathédrale Notre-Dame** (open daily Apr–Oct 7am–7pm, from 8am weekends, rest of the year Mon–Fri 7am–5.30pm, weekends 8am–5.30pm; free; tel: 021 316 71 61) in the old town is on foot. It is not for the faint-hearted and the people of Lausanne are kept fit by all the stair-climbing up the Escaliers du Marché required to reach the cathedral. Climb higher still, up the southwest tower, for a breathtaking view of the city.

From 10 in the evening till two in the morning, just after the cathedral bell rings the hour, a rough male voice resounds through the vicinity: it is the watchman in the tower calling out the time, and calling for order. "Il a sonné douze" (it has struck 12) he shouts down from the tower; the long, drawn-out sound of each vowel echoes through the narrow streets.

Inside the cathedral, visitors can admire the stained glass of the **rose window**, which was built around 1240, the choir ambulatory, and the elegant pillars. The last king of Burgundy, Rudolf III, was crowned here. A sarcophagus contains the mortal remains of Jean Abraham Davel, who tried to start a religious uprising

Map on page 160

TIP

Don't plan a visit to the Cathédrale Notre-Dame on a Sunday morning, unless you wish to attend the service.

BELOW: the wine village of Féchy overlooking Lake Geneva.

against Bern in 1723 and was later executed.

North of the cathedral and the old town is a park, Bois de Sauvabelin, and more good views over hilly Lausanne can be had from Signal de Sauvabelin, a restaurant above the town. Nearby, on Route du Signal, is the **Fondation de l'Hermitage** (open Tues–Sun 10am–6pm, Thurs until 9pm; entrance fee), an art gallery which has a fine permanent collection and a varied schedule of temporary exhibitions.

Head west to Avenue des Bergières and the **Collection de l'Art Brut** (open Tues–Sun 11am–1pm and 2–6pm; entrance fee; tel: 021 647 54 35), well worth a visit for its fascinating collection of works by fringe artists.

If you visit Lausanne in the autumn, watch out for the arrival of the national agricultural fair known as Le Comptoir Suisse (ask at the tourist office for details). Visitors come to this exhibition, held every September at the Palais de Beaulieu, from all over the world, elevating the occasion far above a purely commercial level. Bulls and cows are paraded in front of members of the government and other politicians, while visitors eagerly snap photos.

The Lavaux

Continuing east around Lake Geneva beyond Lausanne, the steeply pitched wine region of **Lavaux** comes into view. The picturesque villages and small towns of the region nestle among vineyards on the terraced slopes or down by the lake itself. In fact, to get to Vevey, there is a choice of two routes: either along the lake, or further up, along the side of the valley. In the two large wine-growing regions of La Côte and Lavaux, carefully plotted vineyard routes and hiking trails lead to winegrowers' cellars *(caveaux)* and village inns *(pintes)*. In the *caveaux*, whether in Mont-sur-Rolle, Aubonne or elsewhere, winegrowers will offer wine

TIP

Vevey's world-renowned wine festival, the **Fête des Vignerons**, is held only four or five times each century (roughly once every 25 years). The last wine festival was in 1999.

BELOW:
La Tour-de-Peilz,
a country château.

LA FÊTE DES VIGNERONS

Annual grape-harvest festivals take place in Lutry, Morges and Russin (Geneva) but Vevey's *Fête des Vignerons* leaves the rest standing. This unique wine festival was celebrated in 1905, 1927, 1955, 1977 and 1999; the date of the next has yet to be fixed.

The roots of the festival go back to the Middle Ages. The local winemakers' guild supervised wine production and awarded prizes to the best workers in the vineyards. Prizewinning vintners were then led in a parade – known as *pourminade* (promenade) – through the town, annually first of all, and then at longer intervals.

In 1730 the event celebrated Bacchus, the Roman god of wine, portrayed in the parade by a boy on a barrel, followed by fauns and bacchants, then by Ceres the Earth Mother; next came Noah and lastly the shepherd goddess Pales. Since 1905 the guard of honour has been led by musicians from Basel and herdsmen from Gruyère.

At the last festival in 1999 the wine guild's banner was carried down to the lake; halberd and pike bearers marched in; and then came the banners of the cantons, at which point the vintners were awarded their prizes.

Finally, the Festival King, a figure resplendent in gold, signalled the beginning of the merry-making.

accompanied by *saucisson* (sausage) with pickled onions and cheese. In the village inns one can find delicious ham, sausage with cabbage *(saucisses aux choux)* and fresh trout from the lake, or – in Vinzel – *Malakoffs*, a kind of cheese doughnut made to a recipe said to have been brought back by veterans from the Crimean War.

Map on page 160

Vevey

Lying some 20 km (12 miles) around the lakeshore from Lausanne, the town of **Vevey ❼**, founded in the Middle Ages, is the base for wine-seeking trips and headquarters of the giant food corporation, Nestlé, west of the centre. On the waterfront is the **Nestlé Alimentarium** (open Tues–Sun 10am–6pm; entrance fee; tel: 21 924 41 11) on Rue du Léman, an attractively laid-out museum on the theme of food and nutrition, which helps their image and publicity. A visit to the **Musée Historique de Vevey** (open Mar–Oct Tues–Sat 10.30am–noon, 2–5.30pm, Sun 11am–5pm, Nov–Feb Tues–Sun 2–5.30pm; entrance fee; tel: 021 921 07 22) on Rue d'Italie, a charming town museum, is also highly recommended. The neighbouring town of Corsier contains the grave of Charlie Chaplin who lived here for 25 years until his death in 1977.

From Vevey, a short "wine train" ride takes you to the Chemin des Vignes, an inland trail looping above the lake concocted by local winegrowers during the mid-1990s to boost tourism; at first the route closely follows the so-called corniche road and its swooping views. Towns along the way include Chexbres (the beginning point), Epesses, Cully, cute St Saphorin – perhaps the most atmospheric of them all – Chardonne and Rivaz, the endpoint for a return to Vevey. Each has local vintners on hand to explain their craft and sell their wares in pleasantly rural surroundings.

A statue of Charlie Chaplin (1889–1977) overlooks the quay at Vevey; he lived in Corsier nearby.

BELOW: a wine festival in Vevey.

The medieval Château de Chillon. Guided tours are available.

Montreux and the Château de Chillon

Back on the lakeshore, the journey continues to **Montreux ❽**, the world-famous spa. The climate here is exceptionally mild, as the palm trees and camellias lining the lake's promenade testify. The town draws people from all over the world. The busiest time to be here is during the annual jazz festival in July. Mountain cable railways lead to Caux, and to the Rochers de Naye, where one can get a magnificent panoramic view of the whole of Lake Geneva.

The big attraction for most visitors, though, is probably the **Château de Chillon ❾** (open daily Apr–Sept 9am–6pm, Mar–Oct 9.30am–5pm; Nov–Feb 10am–4pm; entrance fee; tel: 021 966 89 10), fortified by the counts of Savoy, and captured by Bern in 1536; beneath the château lies the underground dungeon of François de Bonivard, a lay prior from Geneva who was set free when the Bernese arrived. The event inspired Lord Byron to write *The Prisoner of Chillon*, his romantic poem about de Bonivard, in Lausanne, in 1816. This has made the château one of Switzerland's most popular tourist stops. The château overlooks the water and is actually in Veytaux, 3 km (2 miles) from Montreux. Visitors can approach on foot by coastal trail from town, or by boat in the summer.

From Montreux, one splendid day-trip option is to take any of a number of narrow-gauge railway lines up the sharply ascending mountains overhanging the lake. Rail enthusiasts prefer the weekend steam train up to **Blonay**, while sightseers tend to go for the MOB (Montreux-Oberland-Bernois) railway (some trains have panoramic coaches) which climbs to the Les Avants ski area and offers excellent views back down over the lake. Really, any one of the lines brings you to superb meadow walking and inns serving hearty, rustic fare.

BELOW:
Hotel Eden au Lac.

THE PRISONER OF CHILLON

The plight of François de Bonivard, who was imprisoned by the Duke of Savoy for several years in the 16th century, moved Lord Byron (1788–1824) to immortalise him in his poem *The Prisoner of Chillon* in 1816.

From 1530 Bonivard, who came from Saint Victor's priory in Geneva, was held in the dungeon of Château de Chillon and chained to a pillar for preaching about the Reformation, against the explicit wishes of the duke. He was freed after the arrival of the occupying forces of the Bernese in 1536; they remained in Vaud until it became independent in 1798.

Several other writers from the 19th-century Romantic era, such as Jean-Jacques Rousseau, Victor Hugo and Alexandre Dumas, wrote about the château. It is a spectacular structure built on a small islet close to the eastern shore of Lake Geneva, with lofty towers, courtyards, a striking chapel, many rooms full of beautiful furniture, and frescoes on the walls and also on the ceiling of the Great Hall.

Take a walk around the château independently, or join a guided tour available in eight different languages. Visitors should allow at least a couple of hours to explore, and can even visit the dungeon where Bonivard was held.

Skiing and salt mines

The Vaud Alps contain a number of winter health spas, most notably **Villars-sur-Ollon ⑩** (an excellent hiking area in the summer) and **Les Diablerets ⑪**, a trés-chic resort area with a cable car leading up to the **Diablerets Glacier**, 2,940 metres (9,600 ft) above sea level. There is also the **Château d'Oex ⑫**, a mountain cheese-dairy town. Less health-conscious visitors may prefer the winemaking centres along the Rhône Valley, such as **Aigle ⑬** (a château with its own winemaking museum) and **Yvorne**. Most of the region – the town and dominions of Aigle (or Älen in German) – was captured by the city-republic of Bern in 1475 during the Burgundian wars and was the first French-speaking part of Switzerland.

Such towns became particularly valuable when salt was discovered in the region in the 16th century. The saltworks of **Bex ⑭** (pronounced "bay") and Aigle are still in use today, contributing to the town's wealth. They provide the salt for the canton of Vaud and the chemical industry in Monthey, in the Valais.

Today the Bex Saltworks is a tourist attraction: visitors travel on a narrow-gauge railway through the tunnels, halls and corridors through which the brine (rock salt solution) is pumped out of the mountain. The salt deposits are estimated to amount to 10 million tonnes.

In the Middle Ages, salt was as important a natural resource as oil is today. An imperial decree bestowed on princes the right to manufacture salt (the so-called *Salzregal*), and Switzerland's cantons have had a virtual monopoly on the salt trade to this day. Before the salt deposits in Bex were discovered, the republic of Bern used to import its salt from Venice and from saltworks in the Franche Comté region of western France. ❑

Map on page 160

BELOW: hot-air ballooning near Château d'Oex.

THE VALAIS

This large, predominantly French-speaking canton in southwestern Switzerland has some of the country's best ski resorts, and is crowned by the mighty Matterhorn

Map on page 174

T he name of this, the most mountainous region of Switzerland, comes nevertheless from the Latin word for valley – and it really is one big valley, roughly 130 km (80 miles) long, nestling in the chain formed by the Valaisan and Bernese Alps, with their total of 51 mountains over 4,000 metres (13,000 ft) high. The particular attraction of this landscape lies in the stark contrasts on offer within a very confined area; the backdrop formed by the Alps is already immense, even claustrophobic. Nevertheless, the land up at the top of the Goms Valley seems to have an awe-inspiring breadth to it. Here, one of the lowest alpine valleys – its lowest point is just 500 metres (1,600 ft) above sea level – is surrounded by the very highest peaks in all the Alps.

The Valais lies on the Simplon rail line (Paris-Milan) and is connected to the north via the Lötschbergbahn (Bern-Brig). Narrow-gauge railways lead from Brig to St Moritz and to Zermatt (the trip on the "Glacier Express" between Zermatt and St Moritz is one of the most impressive stretches of railway in all the Alps), from Sierre to Montana and from Martigny across to Chamonix in France. The N9 motorway takes you almost to Sierre; the cantonal roads in the main valley as well as those leading off into the side valleys are also in very good condition and make it easy to get around.

PRECEDING PAGES: the Château de Tourbillon, at Sion. **LEFT:** the world-famous profile of the Matterhorn. **BELOW:** woman from Evolène in the Val d'Hérens.

A short history

"Individualists" is the word usually used by the Swiss to describe the people of the Valais, the area lying between the Rhône Glacier and Lake Geneva/Lac Léman. The French-speaking part cannot be treated as a subdivision of western Switzerland, and the German-speaking people of the Upper Valais – who form one-quarter of the canton's population – are very different from German-speaking Swiss in general. The centuries-long dominion of the Upper Valais over the lower part of the canton ended when Napoleon's troops marched in at the close of the 18th century; then, in 1810, the Corsican conqueror annexed the land on the Rhône and gave it the status of "Département du Simplon". The region, impoverished, plundered and burned, could take only one course of action: joining the Swiss Confederation in 1815.

Travellers arriving from the direction of Lake Geneva/Lac Léman make their first acquaintance with the Valais in **St-Maurice** ❶, 30 km (20 miles) south of Montreux on the N9 toll motorway. As well as visiting the 3rd-century Abbaye de St-Maurice, with its church treasures, it is worth spending some time in the centre of the town. There is a military museum (closed Mon), and just outside is the Grotte-aux-fées, (a cave lined with stalactites), whose restaurant offers good views over the town rooftops.

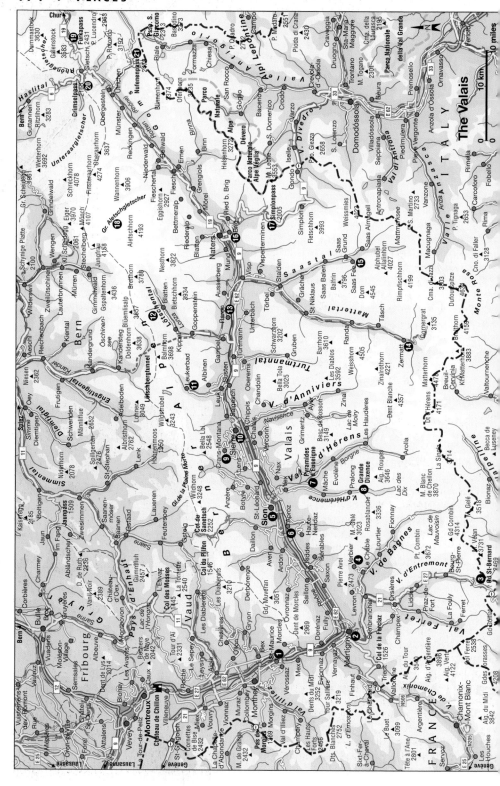

The real cultural and historical centre of the Lower Valais lies 10 km (6 miles) further south, however, up the valley in **Martigny ❷**, where the narrow hollow formed by the lowest part of the Rhône Valley suddenly opens out. This ancient town has developed into an internationally celebrated cultural centre in recent years – in addition to its roles as an industrial centre and an important site of archaeological finds from Roman times.

The town has attracted travellers for centuries. Close to the Town Hall on Place Central is the former inn La Grande Maison, once the town's leading hotel, where both Goethe and Alexandre Dumas stayed during their travels.

The real hub of cultural activity, however, is the **Fondation Pierre Gianadda**, at Rue du Forum 59. This foundation was started by a member of the Gianadda family in memory of a brother who died in an accident. A modern **Cultural Centre** has been built here (open daily June–Nov 9am–7pm, Nov–May 10am–6pm; entrance fee; tel: 027 722 39 78); it incorporates the ruins of a Roman amphitheatre – which has made a name for itself beyond Switzerland's borders. It has hosted exhibitions of works by such great artists as Rodin, Toulouse-Lautrec, Picasso and Giacometti, and the garden contains numerous sculptures.

The building also houses the **Gallo-Roman Museum**, containing finds from excavations at Martigny and bronze statues from Octodurus (discovered in 1883), as well as an **Automobile Museum**. The latter contains a display of some 50 vintage cars dating from 1897 to 1939 – most of them still roadworthy – including the first-generation vehicles of such prestigious names as Rolls-Royce, Mercedes-Benz and Bugatti.

Closely linked to the fate of Martigny is the **Col du Grand St-Bernard ❸**, some 45 km (25 miles) south of Martigny on the E27. Since the road tunnel was

As Switzerland's largest company, Nestlé makes its presence felt all round the country.

BELOW: a real St Bernard, no mere shaggy dog story.

THE GREAT ST BERNARDS

The St Bernard dog – a close relative of the Pyrenean mountain dog – used to save pilgrims and travellers who had lost their way from dying of exposure and exhaustion after sudden storms, and is today saving the Great St Bernard Pass itself from lapsing into obscurity.

The world-famous St Bernards, some 15 or 20 of them altogether, are housed in the **Hospice Museum** (open June to Sept daily 9am–6pm; entrance fee; tel: 027 787 12 36). Unconcerned by the stream of visitors who come to pay tribute to them, the dogs doze all day long and it is only when feeding time comes around after their short morning walk that their 80–100 kg (175–220 lb) frames show any further signs of movement.

This indulgent lifestyle is a far cry from earlier days, when for 200 years, from the end of the 16th century until 1897, some 2,000 travellers were rescued by the brave dogs. Their sturdy bodies and broad chests helped them to force a path through the snow, while their reliable sense of direction enabled them to find their way home even in the midst of the heaviest storms. The barrel of brandy that the dogs are shown wearing around their necks is, however, a fallacy, probably invented by a certain Alpinist named Meissner in 1816.

opened, this route across the Alps, which was also used by Napoleon as a gate of entry into Italy for the decisive battle against Austria at Marengo, might have been all but forgotten – but, ironically, its decline has saved the pass.

A quick trip to **Aosta**, Italy, and a visit to the **Val de Bagnes**, the **Val d'Entremont** and the **Val Ferret** makes a delightful detour at this juncture – but the route leads away from Martigny in an easterly direction. It is best not to use the four-lane autobahn here, but rather take the small side-road which leads past the medieval castle-town of **Saillon**, the setting for many tales and legends.

Heading for the slopes

Accessible via a short branch rail line from Martigny and then a cable-car ride, **Verbier** ❹ is a popular and fashionable Alpine resort. Events like the Xtreme Freeride competition bring an excited crowd here to gawk as young snowboarders shoot down the nearly 45-degree pitch of **Mont Fort's** 3,330-metre (10,920-ft) high walls – and sometimes make spectacular falls. The resort has also published a comprehensive study of skiing and snowboarding injuries on its own slopes – a brave step, given the ski taboo against talking about disaster, and one it hopes will provide some clue about how to make slopes safer while remaining challenging.

Skiing is spectacular here, and the place is not nearly as congested as many similar Swiss resorts (thanks to the services of one of Europe's largest lift systems, and to its remote position). What is interesting about this ski area, too, is that you can lose yourself in the backcountry for a few hours or even days at a time; there are many kilometres of trails of all different sorts, and local outfitters will guide you, provide maps and equipment, and even lift you in a heli-

Octodorus was the Roman name for Martigny, which in the 1st century BC was developed into a fortified outpost by General Servius Galba under Julius Caesar's orders.

BELOW: a snowboarder competes at Verbier.

copter to a remote location (for a hefty price) if you are so inclined. Several schools have also recently opened in and around the town to promote summer adventure sports, such as rugged hikes and daring hang-glides. Don't forget the classical music and poetry festivals in summer, either.

Map on page 174

Sion's surprising culture

Sion ❺, the canton's capital 30 km (20 miles) northeast of Martigny on the No. 9 autobahn, has a reputation among Valaisans for being a boring town full of civil servants. In fact, the Planta Square area where the government building is situated and the old part of the town reveal an astounding cultural and historical heritage. A visit to the **Cathedral of Notre-Dame-du-Glarier** (open daily 9am–4pm; free), the last medieval episcopal church in Switzerland and one of the most impressive religious edifices in the Valais, is highly recommended. Its carved 17th-century choir-stalls, magnificent St Barbara altar and 15th-century bishops' tombs are its most notable treasures. At the foot of the two hills of **Valeria** and **Tourbillon** lie the **Hotel de Ville**, the **Maison Supersaxo** and the cantonal museums which frequently hold interesting exhibitions of local history. The trip up the Valeria on foot, which takes a quarter of an hour, is worth doing if only to take a look at the world's oldest functioning organ in the church on top – though this is a claim that some experts vehemently dispute. A few ruins consisting of hewn grey stone are all that remain of the Tourbillon fortress, erected in the Middle Ages by the once-mighty prince-bishops of the Valais.

What may possibly be a unique Swiss custom, cow-fighting, takes place every spring and autumn all over the canton. Around mid-May, in **Aproz ❻**, just southwest of Sion, the great cantonal championship cow-fight is held. It is

The clock tower of Sion's Hotel de Ville.

BELOW: the Château de Valère, Sion.

a popular spectacle in which the most belligerent representatives of the Eringer breed – not large, but they can be suitably aggressive – are brought face to face. The fights developed from the natural sparring by which hierarchies were established within cow herds in the Alps, and the cows fight only when they feel like it, regally avoid chasing their rivals after they have beaten them, and scarcely ever injure one another.

Further south of Sion, a little way down the **Val d'Hérens** (which eventually leads to the quiet ranges and towns that mark the Italian border), is a striking range of jagged peaks, known as the **Pyramides d'Euseigne ❼**, which have been carved by millennia of wind, water and ice into a kind of Alpine badland. Formed during the last Ice Age, which eroded the surrounding rockscape, these dramatic fangs remained, thanks to their crowns of hard rock. The pyramids make a scenic view from the road, or a walk if you are staying in the area.

Grande Dixence dam

Continuing south from Sion down the **Val d'Hérémence**, you come to another monument – but this time a more recent one: the concrete dam of **Grande Dixence ❽**. Even now, 40 years after its construction – which took from 1951 to 1965 to complete – at 285 metres (935 ft) tall it is still the highest dam in Europe. A statistic-lover's paradise: there are 400 million cubic metres (14 billion cubic ft) of water lurking behind this 700-metre (2,200-ft) long concrete construction. It is 200 metres (650 ft) wide at the bottom and only 15 metres (50 ft) wide at the top, and weighs 15 million tonnes. Construction of this dam – unlike the Mattmark Dam in the Saas Valley where 88 people died in a glacier accident in 1965 – was largely disaster-free.

BELOW: "Les Violettes", skiing region near Crans-Montana.

Wine and spa water

Golf and skiing are the main attractions for the fashionable visitors to **Crans-Montana** ❾, a fancy resort where almost everything comes at a price. This is not the place to find Alpine quiet – you will be amazed by the sprawl, traffic and nightlife in such a tiny valley – but the glacier skiing here is terrific, if not terrifically challenging: the local glacier is nearly level, and it is normal to traverse it on cross-country skis. In late summer, the annual Swiss Open event at the resort's course brings Europe's finest golfers to town.

The **Val d'Anniviers**, 15 km (9 miles) west near Sierre, is one of the valleys of the Central Valais in which nomadic mountain people were still moving between the valley floor and the Alps with the seasons as recently as the mid-20th century. The Austrian poet Rainer Maria Rilke called **Sierre** ❿ a mixture of Provence and Spain – heady praise indeed.

The flat, rocky and chalky vineyards just east of Sierre, and above **Salgesch** and **Varen** on the French to German linguistic border reputedly produce the best red wine in Switzerland. The small vintners in Salgesch and Varen have readily adapted to tourists, and lay on wine-tastings. The **Musée Valaisan de la Vigne et du Vin** (open Apr–Nov Tues–Fri 2–5pm; entrance fee; tel: 027 456 45 25), located in the château at Sierre, offers an in-depth look at the wines of the Valais; a pleasant 4 km (2½ mile) vineyard walk leads to Salgesch and another part of the museum, this time concentrating on the agricultural side of wine production.

On the small, narrow road that leads from Salgesch 15 km (9 miles) north in the direction of Leukerbad, the impressive-looking **Pfynwald** comes into view; it is the largest continuous forest of Arolla pine in central Europe, and much of it is now protected. There is a warm microclimate here, with a rich abundance of flora and fauna.

In the Leukerbad Valley basin, surrounded by the rocky walls of the **Gemmi** (these impressed Goethe even more than the fleas in his tent), are the hot, healing springs of Leukerbad. As its name suggests, the town of **Leukerbad** ⓫ is famous for thermal baths. They are open year-round, both indoors and out in the open, at their natural 50°C (122°F) or cooled in pools down to a more tolerable 25°C (77°F). Refreshing, to say the least – particularly when you take the treatment which alternates steam, hot water and ice-cold water. The springs not only nourish the expensively furnished bath-houses, but also keep the steep part of the street near the church completely free of snow and ice in winter, thanks to a system of pipes laid under the road surface.

The Lötschental

Branching off to the north near the twin towns of **Gampel-Steg**, east of Leukerbad, is one of the most beautiful and unsophisticated lateral valleys in the whole Valais – the **Lötschental** ⓬. Bordered by a mighty circle of mountains, this valley has managed to preserve not only its villages but also some pre-Christian customs, such as the winter tradition of the *Tschägättä*. With their frightening masks carved from Arolla pine and their shaggy sheepskins, the *Tschägättä* can send quite a shiver up your spine.

Map on page 174

BELOW: soaking in the hot springs of Leukerbad.

The Matterhorn

Perhaps the most instantly recognisable peak on the planet, the Matterhorn – Il Cervino to the Italians – breaks the horizon south of Zermatt like a giant canine tooth. This is the archetypal chocolate-box mountain: it has inspired everyone from the Victorian aesthete and art critic John Ruskin, who called it "the most noble cliff in Europe", to the inventor of pyramidal Toblerone. Its limestone and serpentine mass, 4,478 metres (14,730 ft) high, stands sentinel over a tough Alpine pass that has been used since before Roman times. However, it was not until 1858 that anyone had the temerity to attempt to scale a peak that was feared by some locals as the abode of giants or even the devil, who, in a rage, was wont to hurl rocks down from the heights.

The early attempts all ended in failure, with the result that the Matterhorn became the last of the major 4,000-metre-plus Alpine peaks to remain unconquered: it was

indomitable, the ultimate mountaineering challenge of the day. In the end, it was the British engraver-cum-mountaineer, Edward Whymper (1840– 1911), and six comrades (three fellow Brits; the Chamonix-born guide Michel Croz; and a father-and-son team of Zermatters, both called Peter Taugwalder), who first reached its summit, on 14 July 1865, narrowly beating a team led by the famous local Italian climber Jean-Antoine Carrel. Triumphalism turned to tragedy, however, on the descent, when four of the victorious party slipped to their deaths, as recounted graphically in Zermatt's Alpine Museum.

Of course, the Matterhorn did host many subsequent feats of heroism: Lucy Walker became the first woman to reach the summit in 1871; the fearsome north face was first scaled in 1931; and, in more recent decades, Jean-Marc Boivin skied down the east face, and then solo-climbed the north face in a mere four hours.

Today, it remains an extremely popular climbing destination. The most straightforward season to climb runs from mid-July to mid-September, depending on snow conditions and, all being well, as many as 200 climbers can reach the summit every day via Whymper's classic Hörnli route, using the fixed ropes up this northeastern ridge (your time at the top will be restricted if it is busy). However, over 400 people have died on the mountain, so do not underestimate the dangers of weather, rockfalls and inexperience. A guide is essential, plus you will need to be in excellent physical shape and to have some prior rock-climbing experience. It is also worth acclimatising by ascending some of the less challenging high peaks in the area.

"The time may come, wrote Edward Whymper, "when the Matterhorn shall have passed away, and nothing, save a heap of shapeless fragments, will mark the spot where the great mountain stood. That time is far distant; and, ages hence, generations unborn will gaze upon its awful precipices, and wonder at its unique form. However exalted may be their ideas, and however exaggerated their expectations, none will come to return disappointed!" ❑

LEFT: a constant stream of visitors is drawn by the awesome outline of the Matterhorn.

A stay in the Lötschental would not be complete without a visit to the local history museum in **Kippel** (15 km/9 miles north of Gampel-Steg), the chapel in nearby **Kühmatt**, or the place of pilgrimage in **Blatten**, with its impressive votive offerings.

Further up the Rhône Valley, you can visit the grave of famous Austrian poet Rainer Maria Rilke (1875–1926). It is next to the south wall of the impressive-looking church in **Raron ⓭**, a few kilometres/miles east of Gampel-Steg. The Burgkirche was built between 1508 and 1517 at the request of Cardinal Matthäus Schiner, and contains the remains of Rainer Maria Rilke, as well as a fresco depicting the Day of Judgement, with devils dressed in the clothing of the notorious Swiss mercenaries of that time.

Zermatt and the Matterhorn

Further east, at Visp, the Visp Valley branches off southwards, and later separates into the Mattertal and the Sasstal at Stalden. Zermatt and Saas Fee compete for tourists' favours at the head of each valley.

Zermatt ⓮ covers a large winter and summer skiing area with its Klein-Matterhorn cable railway, and Saas Fee does much the same with its Metro Alpin. Looming over this busy resort, the **Matterhorn** (4,478 metres/14,692 ft) is the very obvious draw to Zermatt, although at 4,634 metres (15,203 ft) the nearby **Dufourspitze** is the highest peak in Switzerland, named after General Henri Dufour, who made a name for himself in the Swiss Civil War of 1847 (between the old Catholic cantons and the reformed ones). It is the photogenic Matterhorn, however, that is instantly recognisable to most visitors – and, if its crooked peak can be seen (clouds are frequent), it is certainly an impressive,

Map on page 174

A furry model of the mythical Tschägättä.

BELOW: harvesting apricots in the Rhône Valley.

TIP

Near Brig is the mountain village of **Mund**, which is the only remaining place in Switzerland where they still cultivate the saffron plant.

almost unbelievable, sight of sheer rock in perfect proportions. Much of the walking here is scary and challenging, and the climbing – well, that is for serious experts only. Despite – or perhaps because of – its quite remote position, Zermatt is also becoming something of a haven for action-adventure junkies. They sign up with one of the numerous hiking, climbing or biking outfitters, then drink hard in the bars lining Bahnofstrasse before crashing to sleep.

Saas Fee

If Zermatt did not have the most original and thus most famous rock formation in all the Alps, it might have to compete for visitors with **Saas Fee** ⓫ at the end of the adjacent Saastal Valley, accessible by road via Stalden to the north. Another car-free resort, Saas Fee is set in even more splendid surrounding mountains and nearly touched by the icy tongue of the Feegletscher. **The Ice Pavilion**, at the top station of the funicular leading up to the glacier, is well set up for children, with educational exhibits on glacial activity (entrance fee). The town itself has retained much of its sedate village character, especially at night.

Returning north, and back to the east of Visp, **Brig** ⓰, the capital of the German-speaking Valais, is dominated by the **Stockalper Palace** (open May–Oct Tues–Sun for hourly guided tours 9.30 and 10.30am, 1.30, 2.30 and 3.30pm; entrance fee; book through the tourist office: tel: 027 921 60 30), former residence of one Kaspar Jodok von Stockalper, 17th-century merchant whose industrious zeal played a large part in the city's rise to power. The palace is more generously proportioned and more imposing than any other building in the canton. It was purchased from the impoverished Stockalper family in 1948 by a foundation and the municipality of Brig-Glis, and restored at great expense.

BELOW: local Valaisans sharing a rustic meal.

For Stockalper, just as for the French some time later, the **Simplonpass ⑰**, south of Brig – and the connection it provided with Italy – was vital to strategic planning. Under orders from Napoleon, forced-labour convicts upgraded the road between 1801 and 1805. The first crossing of the Alps by aeroplane is also closely associated with the Simplonpass. Jorge Chavez, from Peru, won the competition in 1910 by flying his monoplane over the Alpine pass, which lies 2,000 metres (6,500 ft) above sea level. Unfortunately, he crashed as he landed in Domodossola and was killed.

If you are travelling further east into the **Goms Valley**, it is worth a detour to look at the mighty **Grosser Aletschgletscher ⑱** and the **Aletsch Forest** – a wonderland of ancient pine trees and interesting Alpine vegetation. Get there by taking the cable car from **Mörel**, just east of Brig, up to either the **Riederalp** or the **Bettmeralp**. This mighty river of ice, the largest (surface area: 118 sq. km/45 sq. miles) and the longest (nearly 24 km/15 miles) in Switzerland, which is nearly 800 metres (2,500 ft) thick in places, extends in an elegant arc from the Konkordiaplatz at the foot of the **Aletschhorn** to below the **Riederfurka**. On its northern slopes it has one of the finest forests of Arolla pine in the country, which has been strictly protected since the 1930s.

The Nature Conservation League has renovated the **Villa Kassel**, in Riederalp. This building, in which Sir Winston Churchill used to spend his summers as a boy, now hosts courses in botany and conservation, under expert supervision.

The 16th-century church at Münster, in the Goms Valley.

In the Goms Valley

Three passes – the **Furkapass ⑲**, leading northeast along autoroute 19 into Switzerland's interior and into Graubünden; the tortuous **Grimselpass ⑳**, leading north to Interlaken; and the **Nufenenpass ㉑** leading to the Bedretto Valley in the Ticino – can all be reached by rail or road via the **Goms**. The breadth of this high valley and the villages in the upper part of it – still intact, with their dark wooden houses and famous baroque churches – give the magnificent landscape its distinctive appearance.

Niederwald, one of the small villages in the Goms some 25 km (15 miles) northeast of Brig, was the home of the "king of hoteliers and hotelier to kings", César Ritz. The Valais is rich in ecclesiastical buildings, but the nearby churches at **Ernen** and **Münster** are considered particular jewels.

Many visitors who dislike the hectic pace of life in the larger winter sports resorts are attracted to the northernmost parts of the canton. The carefully tended cross-country ski trail in the Goms, which is nearly 40 km (25 miles) long, is especially popular, while in summer the Goms is considered an absolute paradise for hikers. The passes are open only in the summer. If you have time, driving along them is well worth the trouble, even though an efficient rail-car ferry through the Furka Tunnel between **Oberwald** and **Realp** reduces travelling time between central and eastern Switzerland considerably. Since the Furka-Oberalp-Bahn cut its service, driving through the pass is the only way of getting to know the mighty **Rhône Glacier** – the source of the great river. ❏

Map on page 174

BELOW: Brig's Stockalper Palace.

TICINO

Switzerland's southern region has more than a little flavour and dolce vita of its neighbour Italy; tourists are drawn by the mild climate, beautiful lakes, and atmospheric Mediterranean architecture

Map on page 188

The Italian-speaking canton of **Ticino**, separated from the German regions to the north by the Alpine massif, is a country within a country; a sunny, swaggering province that, superficially at least, is more Italian in most respects than it is Swiss. Travelling by road or train from the north, you disappear into one of the sub-Alpine tunnels that have linked the two regions since the latter part of the 19th century, and emerge into a lake-studded land of pizzerias, stuccoed Catholic churches and erratic drivers. Even the people are obviously different, with Germanic reserve and orthodoxy giving way to typically Italian spontaneity.

The main attraction for visitors, in summer at least, is the sunny, Mediterranean climate. The annual average temperature here is some 3°C (5.5°F) higher than in the north of the country and spring often begins in March; autumn ends later too, with the warm days sometimes extending into November. Which is good news for the Merlot grape, grown in these parts to make popular Ticino red wines.

Many tourists head straight for the chic lakeside riviera towns of Locarno and Lugano, with their medieval piazzas and *gelato* stores. Up in the sparsely populated mountains in northern Ticino, between Airolo and Biasca at almost 1,500 metres (4,900 ft), the winters are harsh. Even in summer, the weather in the valleys in the northern part of Ticino never gets as hot as it does in the south, making it excellent trekking country. This was actually an advantage in the days when people went to mountain health resorts for the summer rather than to the Adriatic: the first hotels in Faido and in the hills of the Val Blenio were built around the beginning of the 20th century for wealthy visitors from Milan and Lugano, who came here looking for an opportunity to cool down and see the thundering waterfalls, a common natural feature in Ticino.

PRECEDING PAGES: Morcote village on Lake Lugano. **LEFT:** view over Lugano from Monte San Salvatore. **BELOW:** the gorge at Ponte Brolla, near Locarno.

Ticino's geography

Ticino is bisected south–north by the Ticino River, which runs south from the Alps around Airolo before draining into Lago Maggiore. The Ticino flows through a valley peppered with traditional settlements and pastoral farming villages, many of them rarely visited by tourists. Romanesque churches and small baroque chapels cling to the high slopes, well beyond the reach of the floodwaters that sometimes cause havoc in the area as a result of spring meltwaters and summer thunderstorms. In October 2000, several people were killed in Ticino when torrential rain led to floods and landslides that washed away whole villages.

At the region's southernmost tip, where a finger of fertile land reaches out to the Italian border, the hills around Mendrisio were once planted with tobacco; there are many unspoiled villages in the area that are never overrun by tourists and are a pleasure to explore. Further south still, the Magadino Plain, which spills over into

northern Italy near the town of Como, used to be swampland before it was drained for agriculture. It remains one of Ticino's few flat and fertile areas of cultivable land.

Quiet valleys

Ticino is, first and foremost, a canton of spectacular lakes and mountains. Its two biggest and most popular lakes are at the foot of the Alps where Ticino borders on Italy. **Lago Maggiore**, broad and majestic, nestles among the southern Alpine foothills, while the contorted **Lago di Lugano** lies between the majestic peaks of Monte Bré, San Salvatore, San Giorgio and Monte Generoso. Away from the lakes, but just a few kilometres from the motorways and railways that have opened up the region to tourism, it's still possible to find wonderfully quiet valleys filled with sunshine and sub-Alpine vegetation, and crisscrossed by idyllic footpaths meandering through the hills to rarely explored villages that have hardly changed in hundreds of years. Here, south of Lago di Lugano, the gentle hills of Mendrisiotto give way to the fertile plain of the Po as you cross into northern Italy.

The Ticino region is well known for its stone architecture, such as this chimney detail.

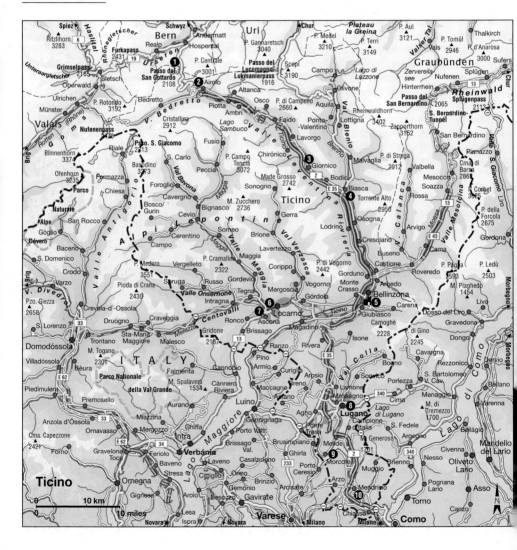

A land of emigrants

Northerners may envy Ticino's sunny climate, but this is a region whose enticing way of life is founded on much more than long days and balmy air. The aspects of the local way of life that foreigners and Swiss-Germans have consistently idealised – the contended simplicity, the rustic cuisine – are characteristics not of a people who have discovered the secret of happiness, but of a people who have often lived a life of poverty and hardship with dignity and decency. For centuries, the hardship of life south of the Alps made Ticino's history one that was characterised by steady emigration.

An initial phase of industrialisation from the mid-19th century onwards, which made German- and French-speaking Switzerland relatively prosperous, bypassed the valleys of Ticino, and when a comparatively modest tobacco and silk industry was established towards the end of the 19th century it was mainly because the area had such a large pool of cheap labour. Even the construction of the 15-km (9-mile) Gotthard railway tunnel in 1882 did little to change things in the early years (though it did gradually turn Lugano and Locarno into tourist resorts).

For most of the population, nothing really changed for the better. Between 1881 and 1930 alone, a total of 25,300 inhabitants emigrated abroad. Right up until the 1950s, a trip to Ticino was still considered to be a trip back into a different era.

Now all that has radically changed. The villages in the valleys are still there – romantic and sleepy – but many of their former inhabitants have emigrated to the overcrowded industrial areas around Lugano, Locarno, Bellinzona and Mendrisio-Chiasso. Four-fifths of the population of 300,000 and 90 percent of the available jobs are crammed into approximately 14 percent of the canton, within easy reach of the main traffic arteries.

Map on page 188

The rail journey through the Gotthard Tunnel is one of the most visually memorable. This stretch of track is one of the country's busiest.

BELOW: the attractive lakefront at Ascona on Lago Maggiore.

Meanwhile Swiss-Germans, Germans and other strangers to the area are venturing into the mountain villages and *rustici* in the valleys, and are converting the deserted houses and former stables into smart holiday homes – which, of course, are only ever used for a few weeks in the year. If you include the buildings constructed since the 1970s, then every fourth house in Ticino turns out to be a holiday home. As a result, locals find it increasingly difficult to secure inexpensive homes because of the demand for property and the massive rise in the cost of land.

A trip from Zürich to Lugano on the Trans-Europa Express passes through the Gotthard railway tunnel. Alternatively, visitors can take the train from Basel to Lugano, which also goes through the tunnel.

Forging an identity

Other changes have affected the area, but not all of them depressing. Many factors have transformed Ticino into a centre of finance and services, including radically improved transport facilities, such as the international airport at Lugano and the direct motorway connection with the rest of Switzerland and Milan, Italy. Manpower in the canton is still relatively cheap and the Italians willingly commute across the border to work here. Do not forget, either, Swiss reliability, Ticino's long tradition of producing the bulk of the country's lawyers, and the flood of capital into Switzerland in the 1960s as a result of social unrest in other countries.

Thus, in only 15 years, Lugano saw its very own banking quarter spring up. Storehouses, lawyers' offices, banks, insurance companies and an ever-growing number of filling stations (Ticino comes second only to Geneva in the number of cars it contains) employ some 56 percent of the canton's workforce, half of which is made up of frontier commuters and foreigners who live here.

This rapid development, combined with a vague feeling among the people of becoming more dependent on Zürich and Milan, has led to disputes about Ticino's actual identity. One response to the threat of cultural colonisation – and the most

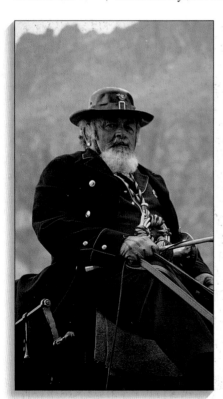

BELOW: a carriage driver on the St Gotthard Pass.

visible one too – has been the emergence of a unique form of Ticino architecture, which has even become something of an export commodity. The movement sprang from architect Mario Botta, who was commissioned to rebuild the 17th-century chapel in Mogno in the hills of northern Ticino when it was destroyed by an avalanche in 1986. What he built in its stead was a futuristic granite and marble structure, topped with a glass roof. It caused apoplexy among the local gentry, but the people of Ticino have come to see it as being in perfect harmony with the traditional buildings and the Alpine landscape. Botta's home town, Lugano, has become a virtual showcase for his work. Luigi Snozzi performed similar wonders restoring a former convent in the village of Monte Carasso near Bellinzona. Beautiful traditional buildings remain, of course, such as the spectacular Villa Favorita, just outside Lugano, home of Baron Thyssen-Bornemisza *(see page 200).*

Rugged mountain town

One of the most dramatic entrances to the Ticino area is through the northwestern **Passo del San Gottardo** ❶ (St Gotthard Pass). One of the best-known Alpine journeys, the pass runs 2,108 metres (6,916 ft) along the route through the lush valley, offering wonderful views of the mountainous countryside and lakes.

The town of **Airolo** ❷, once the staging-post where travellers took a rest and changed horses after the rigours of crossing the St Gotthard Pass, and today the place where drivers emerge into the fresh air after 17 km (10 miles) inside the Gotthard road tunnel, is an example of the rugged side of Ticino, and of the tough living conditions still faced by many of its inhabitants even today. One can also reach Airolo by taking the visually rewarding route over the pass, along well-surfaced roads, and pay a visit to the **Museo Nazionale del San Gottardo** (St Gotthard Museum; open daily June–Oct 9am–6pm; entrance fee), housed in an old hospice building at the top of the pass. The museum contains a collection of historical documents and models which plot the history of the pass and the tunnel construction.

A monument by Ticino sculptor Vincenzo Vela erected near the railway station in Airolo is a reminder of the 177 people who lost their lives while the Gotthard rail tunnel was being built. In winter the snow here can be as deep as a metre (3 ft) or more; the devastating winter of 1951–52, when avalanches caused death and destruction, is still remembered today.

To guard against damage by storms and floods the villages are built high up on the slopes of the valley of the Ticino River, or huddled against the mountainside: **Quinto**, **Rodi Fiesso**, **Ambri** and **Piotta** and, further down, **Faido** and **Bodio** are all examples of villages deliberately built away from the threat of natural disasters. One level higher up are the farming villages, often consisting of only a handful of houses and a church, some free from ornamentation, and some richly decorated like the one at **Rossura**.

Today, all these villages are connected by the **Strada Alta**, a hiking trail (with modest overnight accommodation) that leads from Airolo high above the valley to Biasca. Unfortunately, some of the mountain trails and paths along it have been asphalted over. A somewhat more attractive prospect is the path that runs

Map on page 188

There are many colourful exhibits at the Museo Nazionale del San Gottardo.

BELOW: the museum at Olivone, near Biasca.

along the top of the right-hand side of the valley (one can be transported to exactly the right height via cable car from Airolo). The route has no real gradients, passes through extensive woods, and takes in the unspoilt villages of **Prato** and **Dalpe** near Faido and also **Chironico**, near Giornico, with its remarkable church.

Steeped in history

The centre of the **Valle Leventina**, the second-highest valley in Ticino (the **Val Bedretto**, which connects Ticino with the Valais via the Nufenen Pass is the highest accessible pass in Switzerland), is picturesque **Giornico ❸**; it is here that the canton's history is most comprehensively illustrated. High up among the ruins of a Milanese castle that was destroyed in 1518 stands the 12th-century **Chiesa di Santa Maria di Castello**, with its frescoes dating from 1448.

Only a few steps away from the church lies another, and what is probably the most important – and moreover practically unaltered – Romanesque building in Ticino: the **Chiesa di San Nicolao**. Built in the first half of the 12th century, the church has a baptismal font dating from the same period and an impressive series of frescoes from 1478. It was in Giornico that the Swiss gained their first decisive victory over the Milanese, and thus began to establish a lasting grip on Ticino. A monument in the town serves as a reminder of the successful battle.

Up until the capture of Bellinzona in 1503, the *balivo* (lord) of the Leventina had his seat here, in the **Casa Stanga**, now the **Museo di Leventina** (open April–Oct Tues–Sun 2–5pm; entrance fee). The coats-of-arms on the outer wall remind us of the famous visitors who stopped here on their way over the St Gotthard Pass.

Further southeast in **Biasca ❹** is an old church which is just as important as those of Giornico from the point of view of art history. The **Chiesa di San**

Visitors touring Biasca may want to look around inside the beautiful Chiesa di San Pietro e Paolo. Ask for the key at one of the nearby houses or at the parsonage in the village below.

BELOW: the Castello di Montebello in Bellinzona.

Map on page 188

Pietro e Paolo was built between the 11th and 12th centuries at a safe height above the village, and for a long period was the mother church of the whole of upper Ticino. The frescoes (12th–17th century) inside the building are particularly fine. If you want to visit the church you should ask for the key from a house nearby – check at the parsonage in the village.

Biasca is positioned defensively at the entrance to the **Val Blenio**, to the north, and thus also to the **Passo del Lucomagno** (Lukmanier Pass), which along with the St Gotthard is one of the most important north–south routes across the Alps. A northern excursion from Biasca provides good opportunities for country hikes through the unspoilt valley. Though still a rural haven, Val Blenio has seen some homes converted into holiday cottages.

There are many reminders of the strategic importance of this traffic route including the ruins of the once-mighty **Castello di Serravalle** at **Semione**. In **Lottigna** the Swiss showed the right instincts when they erected their lords' seat high above the valley. The building, richly decorated with coats-of-arms, houses a museum of local history and an important weapon collection.

In fact, a whole series of fine churches more than justifies an extended stop-over in the Val Blenio: **San Martino** in **Malvaglia**, **San Remigio** near **Dongio**, **San Martino** in **Olivone**, and above all the remote Romanesque church of **San Carlo** in **Negrentino** near **Prugiasco**, with its extraordinary and very well-preserved frescoes and wall paintings dating from the 11th–16th century.

Today, the valley is a popular holiday, recreation and skiing area. The mighty heap of rubble at the entrance to the valley is the only reminder of the enormous landslide in 1512 which dammed up the **Biaschina**, creating a lake that, upon bursting the following year, caused a flood that extended as far as Lago Maggiore.

Castelgrande at Bellinzona has a lift built into the rock.

BELOW: view from Monte Brè towards Lugano and San Salvatore.

A medieval barrier

South of Biasca is the town of **Bellinzona ⑤**, which has been the canton's official capital only since 1878; before then, the job and its responsibilities were alternated every six years between Bellinzona, Lugano and Locarno. Bellinzona is not only the ideal capital because of its geographical position – important Alpine passes near here include the San Gottardo (St Gotthard), the Lucomagno (Lukmanier), the San Bernadino and the Nufenen – but the town has been a centre of authority for centuries, and was the starting-point for settlement of Ticino's Alpine valleys.

There is evidence to prove that the castle mound known as the **Castelgrande** (open daily 10am–6pm; entrance fee; tel: 091 825 81 45) – in the 14th century known as Castel Magnum, in the 17th century as Burg Uri, and in the early 19th century as San Michele – was settled as early as 5200 BC by small groups of farmers – at a time when only hunters and gatherers were believed to be roaming the forests of German-speaking Switzerland. From then on, it is assumed, more Neolithic settlers, followed by Celts, Romans, Lombards, Franks and native chieftains, occupied the safe position.

This strategically important site was then furnished with a fortress extending right across the marshy valley and secured by several extra fortifications of generous dimensions – the castles of **Montebello** and **Sasso Cor-**

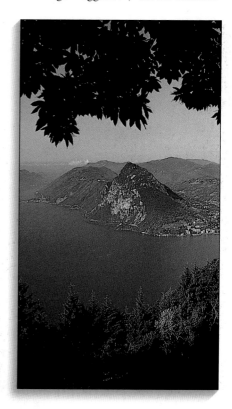

baro, alongside Castelgrande. Milanese dukes, Visconti and Sforza, who in the 13th century extended their dominion over the whole of Ticino, were responsible for the construction. The Castello di Montebello, originally based on a keep, is a particularly interesting example of fortification. In the long run, however, the fortress could not stand up to the repeated attacks from the Swiss, and in 1503 they succeeded in capturing Bellinzona. The three inner provinces of Uri, Schwyz and Unterwalden set up their lords' seats in each of the three castles, thereby ensuring that this most impressive example of medieval fortifications has remained largely intact.

Further edifices of note, both inside and outside the confines of what has since become a rather sleepy and sober-looking town full of civil servants, include three remarkable churches. **Chiesa di San Biagio** in **Ravecchia**, **Chiesa di San Bernardo** on **Monte Carasso**, which can only be reached on foot and, in Bellinzona itself, the former Franciscan **Chiesa di Santa Maria delle Grazie**. The latter has noteworthy Renaissance paintings – including a picture of the Crucifixion – and one of the few rood screens still in existence in the country, making it one of the most valuable churches in south Switzerland.

Proceeding further south, travellers have a choice between the Locarnese on one side of Bellinzona and the Luganese on the other, for **Monte Ceneri** divides the southern part of the canton into two sections. Their inhabitants live in two different worlds – and not just in the geographical sense.

In the Luganese, people prefer to read the *Corriere della Sera* in addition to the local papers, and are culturally oriented towards Milan and Lombardy; in the Locarnese, *La Stampa* from Turin is the most widely read Italian newspaper, and here one feels a great deal closer to Piedmont, Novara and Turin. One explanation for this cultural division could be the historic transport route across Lago

BELOW: the Grand Hotel, Locarno.

Maggiore: the narrow-gauge railway leads from Locarno through the **Centovalli** to **Domodossola** and then into Piedmont.

Locarno

Locarno, Ascona and the numerous small villages on the banks of Lago Maggiore can claim to enjoy the mildest climate in Ticino. This has encouraged tourism, and led to large numbers of Germans and Swiss-Germans coming to build second homes or retirement homes here, in many cases renovating *rustici*.

It has also led to the campsite at Locarno being booked solid throughout the summer months and a perpetual coming and going, year in, year out, around the lake area. The consequences of this increase in traffic have become almost unbearable, leading to a whole series of housing estates blighting the slopes by the lake and second homes standing empty through the winter months. There are closed hotels off-season and it is now almost impossible to come across any real locals with whom one can exchange even a few words in Italian.

Southwest of Bellinzona is **Locarno ❻**, a lakeside town with pretty piazzas and colourful gardens. Here you will find the remains of the 14th-century **Castello Visconteo**, which belonged to the Visconti Dukes of Milan and was largely destroyed in 1518. The *castello* is still intact and houses the **Museo Civico** and the **Museo Archeologico** (open Apr–Oct Tues–Sun 10am–6pm; entrance fee).

Perched on a crag above Locarno is the **Chiesa della Madonna del Sasso** and its attendant Capuchin monastery, an important stop on the pilgrimage route. Founded in 1480, it was rebuilt in the early 17th century and renovated in both the 19th and 20th centuries. It contains Bramantino's *Flight into Egypt* (1536) and an entombment by Ciseri (1865).

Map on page 188

TIP

Visitors in town for the Locarno International Film Festival (August) can buy a universal festival pass which allows access to almost all film screenings. Contact the Festival internazionale del film Locarno (tel: 091 756 21 21, www.pardo.ch).

BELOW: Switzerland-in-miniature at Melide.

Other church buildings of merit include the former **Monastery** and **Chiesa di San Francesco** (1528–72), west of Castello Visconteo, which serves the German-speaking Catholics of the town. The **Collegiate Church of San Vittore** in nearby **Muralto**, east of the station, along with San Nicolao in Giornico, numbers among the most important Romanesque churches in the whole of Ticino. Ecclesiastical splendour apart, Locarno's main claim to fame is its International Film Festival. Held over 10 days in early August the festival claims to be among the top five in the world. Some of the new films are displayed on a large screen set up in the main square, the Piazza Grande, where thousands of people enjoy the open-air shows. Alternatively, catch other festival hopefuls in any of the local cinemas.

If you are looking for a refreshing change of scene after sightseeing, your best bet is to visit the town's open-air swimming pool. It is one of the best laid-out swimming complexes in the whole of the canton.

Interior ceiling detail at the Church of Madonna del Sasso.

A trip into the valleys

As well as being a thriving tourist centre, Locarno is one of the busiest postbus terminals in Ticino. From here, travellers can reach the three main valleys and some 12 lateral valleys, which make up a third of the canton. For many people these valleys epitomise Ticino: stone-roofed houses huddled closely together in narrow village streets; picturesque slopes populated by goats and haystacks; forests of chestnut trees; and narrow little bridges spanning wild mountain streams of crystal-clear water.

Of course, the locals in the **Val Verzasca**, **Valle Maggia**, **Valle Onsernone**, **Val di Vergeletto** and all the surrounding villages have seen things very differently over the centuries: poverty, need and, not infrequently, natural catastrophe forced the menfolk to work in Milan, Venice and Turin where they would hire themselves out as chimney-sweeps or builders, often not returning home again for years at a time. Also, the people of these valleys – including the Val Blenio – made up the bulk of emigrants to Australia and California in the US. The few rich people living in the valleys capitalised on this trend. Accepting land as security, they lent the migrants money for their journeys; very few emigrants were able to repay the loans, and invariably their houses and estates fell into the hands of the moneylenders sooner or later.

This – and the fact that some local people who managed to make their fortunes abroad eventually returned to their villages and valleys – explains why even in the smallest, most remote villages there are buildings that are large and even majestic, and why churches are often of a size and splendour quite unexpected in this region. This is certainly the case in the group of 17th-century **Franzoni Houses** in **Cevio**, and the **Casa Respini**, which used to be the seat of the Swiss lords in the Valle Maggia, in the same village.

It also applies to the fine **Parish Church of San Maurizio** in **Maggia** itself and to the chapel of **Santa Maria delle Grazie** in **Campagna**, to the church at **Intragna**, the church in **Brione/Verzasca** and to the baroque **Castello Marcacci**, also in Brione/Verzasca.

BELOW:
the lakeside at Ascona.

West to Ascona

Leave Locarno and head 3 km (2 miles) southwest, and not far from the lovely **Centovalli** region, with its rolling hills and Alpine streams, is **Ascona** , where one or two narrow alleyways in the old part of the town still hint that this was once one of the most ancient settlements on Lago Maggiore. The houses along the promenade, too, are a reminder – from afar, at least – that fishermen once lived there.

The church of **Santa Maria della Misericordia** (1399–1442) contains one of the most extensive late-Gothic fresco cycles in Switzerland. The **Collegio Papio** surrounds Switzerland's finest Renaissance courtyard, and the **Casa Serodine** features the most richly decorated stucco facade on a secular building that Switzerland has to offer.

Finally, **Monte Verità** used to be a place of pilgrimage for vegetarians and nudists. From 1901 to 1920 it attracted a steady stream of people interested in alternative lifestyles and became a centre for natural healing. It was also a meeting place for artists and writers (Hans Arp and Hermann Hesse among them) and later became an oasis of tranquillity for those in search of rest. However, the hotel here was taken over by the Swiss Technical College.

Among the distant ramifications of the valleys beyond Locarno towards the northwest, at the end of a lateral valley of the Valle Maggia, lies the small village of **Bosco/Gurin**. Here, unlike in the rest of Ticino, German has been spoken for centuries. Its unusual and very traditional form is explained by the fact that the inhabitants of Bosco (Italian) and Gurin (German) moved here in the 14th century from the German-speaking upper Valais, probably after taking a roundabout route via the Livinen Valley. They settled in Ticino much in the same way that other Valaisans settled in various valleys of Graubünden.

The Casa Anatta Museum on Monte Verità explores the development and the history of the alternative lifestyles that earned the area its utopian reputation. The museum is open Apr–Oct Tues–Sat; entrance fee.

BELOW: on Monte Verità near Ascona.

South to Lugano

The Luganese were sucked into Switzerland's political whirlpool much later than the Locarnese. For a long time, the region between Monte Ceneri and the Italian border at **Chiasso** was a lawless kind of appendage of Switzerland. While officially a part of the canton, the **Mendrisiotto**, at its southern tip, was vaguely considered to be Italian anyway, even though its inhabitants had clearly declared their Swiss allegiance in 1803 with the slogan *Liberi e Svizzeri* (Free and Swiss).

Political developments in neighbouring Italy were frequently felt by Mendrisiotto's inhabitants. The local liberals and conservatives fought each other so fiercely that on a number of occasions they nearly resorted to using arms – methods which, even then, as far as the rest of Switzerland was concerned, were considered Italian rather than Swiss. As late as the 19th century it was even possible for travellers to be attacked and robbed by brigands on the heights of the Ceneri. It was only when the railway was built across Lago di Lugano between Melide and Bissone that the Mendrisiotto was brought closer to the canton, and a long-lasting bond was established.

Since the Gotthard railway tunnel was opened in 1882, **Lugano ❽**, frequently described as "the pearl of Lake Lugano", has been deluged with tourists from all over the world. Unlike the flat and rather unexciting landscape around Locarno, the bay of Lugano, between the two mountains of **Monte Brè** and **Monte San Salvatore**, can almost compete with Rio de Janeiro and its famous Sugar Loaf in terms of grandeur. Both Monte Brè and Monte San Salvatore can be scaled by funicular. From their summits, in fine weather, one can see the plain of the Po all the way to Milan in one direction, while enjoying a panoramic view of the whole of the Bernese and Valais Alps in the other.

There is a thriving cigar-making industry in Brissago, a little island off Lago Maggiore.

BELOW: harvesting grapes near Lago Maggiore.

WINE COUNTRY

Swiss wine is such a well-guarded secret that little is known about it beyond the country's borders. The home-grown varieties produced from grapes grown in the beautiful vineyards of the main wine regions such as Valais, Vaud, Neuchâtel, around Lake Geneva, eastern Switzerland and Ticino are not to be sniffed at.

Though not in one of Switzerland's main wine-producing areas, the small Ticino vineyards which dot the southern landscape cover more than 900 hectares (2,220 acres) and have developed a healthy wine industry known for its Merlot. The mild climate combined with just enough rainfall contribute to a fruitful annual harvest of the Merlot grape, introduced from Bordeaux, France, in 1907. Today it has become something of a trademark of the canton. The grape is used to produce a full-bodied red wine, and also rosé wine and a white Merlot.

In the early 20th century Ticino was home to more than 7,000 hectares (17,300 acres) of vine, but disease and pests ruined many of the indigenous grape varieties.

Look out for sNostrano – a table wine made from a combination of grape varieties, and also for Gordola. Grapes used to make white wine, such as Chasselas, Sauvignon and Sémillon, are also grown in Ticino.

Understandably, this lake region has long been used as a trade route; traces of the Etruscans and Gauls as well as the Romans, Franks and Lombards have all been found around Lake Lugano.

Modern Lugano has been greatly influenced by the many big banks based in the city. The imposing-looking buildings housing the prestigious financial institutions seem to compete with one another in terms of splendour. Ticino architect Mario Botta set the pace with two buildings, the **Banca del Gottardo** and the **Palazzo Ransila**.

Rapid construction in the town has spared many of its arcaded alleyways. Two of Lugano's finest traditional restaurants, the Bianchi and l'Orologio, have also bravely resisted development. Another building to survive modernisation is the **Cattedrale di San Lorenzo Ⓐ**, situated on a steep slope between the railway station and the lower part of the town. Originally Romanesque, it was enlarged in the 14th century and renovated in the 17th and 18th centuries. A notable feature is its facade, a masterpiece of the Lombardy Renaissance.

The church of a former Franciscan monastery, **Chiesa di Santa Maria degli Angioli Ⓑ**, built in 1499 and jammed between two houses on the lake promenade, not only possesses a rood screen that is still intact but also contains the most famous Renaissance wall-painting in Switzerland: the grandiose depiction of the *Passion of Christ* by Bernardino Luini (1529).

The **Piazza della Riforma Ⓒ**, next to the Municipio, a generously proportioned square right beside the lake, offers outstanding views. This is the place to laze in the sun or relax in one of the very convivial cafés.

With its clutch of museums Lugano has made a name for itself as a city of the arts. Just east of Piazza della Riforma is the **Museo Cantonale d'Arte Ⓓ** (open

Maps:
Area 188
City 197

The casino near Lugano is in Campione d'Italia, a little piece of Italy within Swiss territory.

BELOW:
the *cantina* (wine cellar) in Mendrisio.

Maps:
Area 188
City 197

TIP

The Alprose Chocolate Museum and factory, on Via Rompada, allows visitors to see how chocolate is made. Open Mon–Fri 9am–8pm, Sat and Sun 9am–5pm; entrance fee; tel: 091 611 88 56.

BELOW:
Palazzo Ransila.
RIGHT:
tropical garden on Isla Brissago, Lago Maggiore.

Tues 2–5pm, Wed–Sun 10am–5pm; entrance fee), where modern art exhibitions can be seen, in the Villa Malpensata. A short stroll along the lake leads to Parco Civico, a small park with pretty gardens and a deer enclosure, and also the **Museo Civico di Belle Arti** ❺ (open Tues–Sun 10am–noon, 2–6pm; entrance fee) in Villa Ciani. The art collection includes the work of Impressionist and Modernist painters such as Henri Rousseau. In the south of town past the Chiesa di Santa Maria degli Angioli is the **Museo d'Arte Moderna** ❻ (open Tues–Sun 9am–7pm; entrance fee), on Riva Caccia, near the banks of Lago di Lugano. The museum hosts a series of contemporary art exhibitions.

One of the chief attractions for art lovers is the **Villa Favorita** ❼ (open Easter–Oct Fri–Sun 10am–5pm; entrance fee), on Viale Castagnola, which contains paintings from the collection of Baron Heinrich Thyssen-Bornemisza. Since 1993, when a large part of the magnificent old-master collection went to Madrid's Palacio de Villa Hermosa, works of American and European artists from the 19th and 20th centuries have been on show at the Favorita.

East of Lugano is the delightful little **Museo delle Dogane Svizzere** (Customs Museum; open Apr–Oct daily 1.30–5.30pm; free) in **Gandria**, which can only be reached by boat. The museum documents the ingenious schemes of whole generations of smugglers. Gandria itself is a delightful village clinging to a steep slope rising from the lake. With its baroque church, narrow alleyways and terraced vineyards, the village is a joy to visit for the day.

Away from the city centres

Anyone keen to venture out of the cities and towns and get to know a genuine piece of Ticino at first hand is sure to appreciate the **Val Colla**, northeast of Lugano, with its villages of **Tesserete**, **Bigorio**, **Cimadera**, **Sonvico** and **Dino**. To the northwest there is also the **Malcantone**, where picturesque villages such as **Bedigliora**, **Astano** and **Breno** nestle in the hilly landscape.

Undoubtedly, the most popular mountain in Ticino as far as tourists are concerned is **Monte Generoso**. Southeast from Lugano, the mountain can be reached from **Capolago** via a rack railway. It affords magnificent views far across the plain of the Po. Nearby, the narrow, deep **Valle di Muggio** is a wonderful place for hiking.

West of Monte Generoso is **Morcote** ❾, on the Ceresio Peninsula. Once a sleepy fishing village, it is now a popular tourist spot. Visitors come to see the pretty architecture including the **Chiesa di Santa Maria del Sasso** which sits high up in the hills. On the outskirts of the village are walking trails from which to enjoy the scenery and views over the lake.

There are quiet villages southwest of Capolago, which lie among the gentle hills of the Mendrisiotto, named after the area's largest town – **Mendrisio** ❿. This is wine country, where the climate and fertile land have made Mendrisio a major producer. Villages such as **Meride**, where the San Silvestro Church and the Casa Oldelli are official national monuments, have the motorway to thank for the fact that they have been left largely undisturbed by the modern world. ❏

THE SOUTHEAST

*Switzerland's largest canton, Graubünden, is home to the
Swiss National Park and the swish resorts of St Moritz,
Davos and Klosters*

Map
on page
206

The canton of Graubünden (Grisons in French, Grishun in German) is most people's view of Switzerland in microcosm, a picturesque region of rolling valleys, emerald lakes and swish ski resorts such as Davos, St Moritz and Klosters high up in the Bernina Massif. It was here in 1864 that winter sports had their origins as a mass tourism activity in Switzerland when an hotelier seeking extra income during the unprofitable cold months invited some of his more illustrious guests to stay on for free. Today, more than 50 percent of the canton's population is allied to the tourism industry.

A conservative people

Despite the riches brought to Graubünden by tourism – "snow business" in particular – it remains a traditional and conservative area, with its people seen by the rest of the country as the quintessential *konservativ* Swiss. The Bündner (the people of Graubünden) have a reputation for rejecting nearly everything new out of hand. They were the last people in the developed world to forbid cars on their roads: motorised traffic was banned in the canton until 1925. Graubünden was among the last Swiss cantons to continue to deny their women the vote. Some of this resistance to change stems from the traditionalism that still exists among the small pockets of population in many of the canton's isolated valleys. Some neighbouring valleys speak different dialects. This was once a largely Romansch-speaking province, which further set it apart from the rest of the Confederation (which it joined in 1803). German speakers now account for more than 65 percent of the population, with those speaking Romansch down to 16 percent.

Traces of the Roman legacy are evident everywhere in Graubünden. The people of the Engadine still hold their New Year's Day celebration on 1 March, just as the Roman occupiers used to do: on the *Chalanda Marz* (Kalends of March), young people mark the end of winter by cracking whips, singing songs and ringing bells. The Romans were also responsible for giving the canton the foundations of its existing road infrastructure, with many roads in the Graubünden Alps still following old Roman routes.

The canton's capital

Even though the capital of Graubünden, **Chur ❶**, seems rather jammed into one corner of the canton, it is the ideal starting point for any Graubünden holiday because of its excellent road and rail network.

This town, the oldest in Switzerland, was already settled by the Celts 5,000 years ago. You can best see how conveniently situated it is, and thus how valuable strategically, from the cone-shaped **Pizokel**, part

PRECEDING PAGES:
winter coat on
the Julier Pass.
LEFT:
a striking church
spire in Zernez.
BELOW: minding the
herd in the Schams.

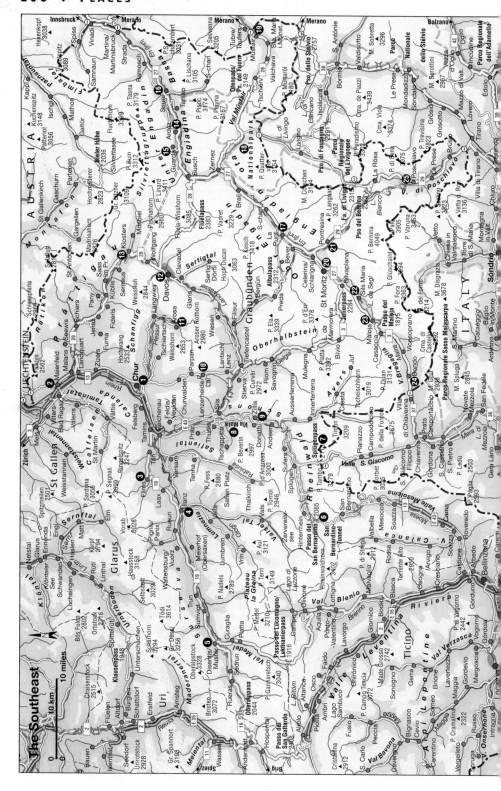

of the local mountain, the **Dreibündenstein**. Those only interested in the view should alight at the Mittelstation of the **Brambrüesch Cable Car** (its valley station is in Welschdörfli).

Map
on page
206

Just a few minutes' cable ride from the bustle on the Postplatz will bring you up to the Alpine meadows at the end of the line, surrounded by the tinkling of cowbells and refreshed by the pure mountain air.

Seen from up here, the concrete wedges driven into the medieval town centre by profit-conscious property developers are all too painfully obvious. There again, all is well for anyone who follows the red and blue markings the tourist office has painted on the streets. They do not lead, as malicious rumour has it, from pub to pub, but from highlight to highlight. You pass the Gothic **Town Hall** and the **Obertor**; the **Arcas**, the town's loveliest square; the **Bishop's Palace**, and the rather squat-looking but nevertheless splendid 12th-century Romanesque **cathedral** (open daily 8am–7pm; tel: 081 252 92 50); it was once referred to by a well-meaning man of letters as a *symphonie sur un air montagnard* and contains a magnificent late-Gothic carved High Altar by Jakob Russ.

The stained glass window of Chur Cathedral.

The way leads past some very imposing-looking mansions – most of them financed by soldiers' pay from foreign wars; massive grey blocks with whitewashed vaults and spacious stairways. Two in particular are worth a visit: one of them, situated on Reichsgasse, houses the local government, and the other, on Poststrasse, the law courts. The city's **Fine Arts Museum** (open Tues–Sun 10am–noon and 2–5pm until 8pm Thurs; entrance fee; tel: 081 257 28 68), on Postplatz, is worth a visit, with work by such artists as the Giacometti family, Angelika Kaufmann, and the local Giovanni Segantini.

Chur cannot really be described as a charming town but the old part of it is

BELOW: the cathedral in Chur.

THE FATE OF THE PASSES

Graubünden's Alps contain no fewer than 14 different passes, all very close to each other, but this was far more of a curse than a blessing for the inhabitants of Graubünden over the millennia since the Romans marched through the Julier Pass in 15 BC.

Half of Europe fought over the most important throughroutes across their territory, dividing the population's loyalties on several occasions. During the Thirty Years' War it found itself at the heart of bitter wranglings between the supporters of France and the Habsburgs. Even when calm finally descended on the European political scene, and Graubünden had joined the Confederation – albeit as late as 1803 – and begun their 100-year-long task of transforming the medieval gravel-covered mountain tracks into thousands of kilometres of navigable road, the region's luck failed to change: the new Austro-Italian Brenner railway and the Swiss St Gotthard railway snatched away the entire north-south traffic.

With this, the classic pass region of Graubünden was relegated to the status of a poor border region almost overnight. Whole valleys of people who had lived off the north-south traffic for centuries suddenly emigrated to California and Australia.

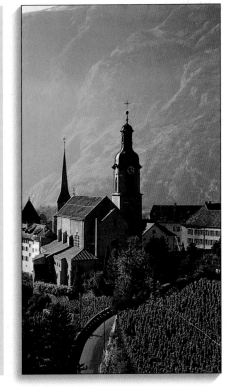

Romansch

Unterländer (the name the people of Graubünden readily give to anyone in Switzerland who does not live "up" in Graubünden) and foreign visitors who are interested in the Romansch language – which is still spoken by around 100,000 people in Switzerland – are faced with a confusion of languages worthy of Babel.

Romansch (the general term applied to the Rhaeto-Romanic dialects) is a mixture of the language spoken by the original Rhaetish inhabitants of Graubünden and the Latin spoken by the Roman conquerors.

Because of the region's topography, however, five main dialects developed over the centuries in what used to be Rhaetia. The *Bündner Oberländer*, the largest group, speak *Sursilvan* (from *Surselva*, meaning "above the wood"). In the Lower Engadine they speak *Vallader* and in the Upper Engadine *Puter* (the two are also known collectively as *Ladin*). In the Oberhalbstein and Albula valleys, as well

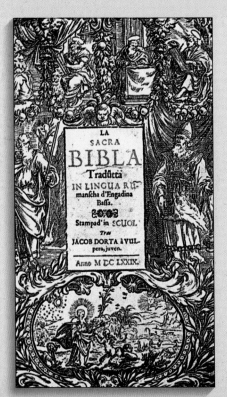

as in parts of central Graubünden, they speak *Surmiran*. In the rest of central Graubünden, *Sutsilvan* (from *Sutselva*, meaning "below the wood") is spoken.

All five dialects are considered standard Romansch languages; in addition to these five there are also dozens of local dialects which make the Romansch region an area of extreme linguistic confusion. In the Upper Engadine, for example, the inhabitants of some neighbouring villages can be recognised from the way they pronounce the letter "e". In Zuoz, the word for bread is *pem*, while in Samedan it is *päm* (and, when written, *paun*). In the Lower Engadine, the word, both written and spoken, is *pan* – but that belongs to another dialect altogether, *Vallader*.

The shadowy origins of the first Rhaetians might shed some light on these linguistic oddities. According to the latest research, the Rhaetians – who also include the early inhabitants of the south Tyrol and of Friuli, where Rhaeto-Romanic dialects also exist – are, in essence, not Indo-Germanic. One thing is certain: Etruscans living in the Po Valley influenced the Rhaetian language.

The Celts, too, an Indo-Germanic tribe from middle and western Europe, left their mark on pre-Roman Rhaetia. Research also indicates Semitic origins, which would mean that the mysterious original language was related to Arabic, Hebrew and Accadian.

To begin with, around the year 300, the Emperor Diocletian divided the province of Rhaetia into *Raetia prima* (with Chur as its capital) and *Raetia secunda* (Augsburg being its capital), both of which fell into the hands of the Teutons at some point during the 5th century. Later, in the Middle Ages, the economic problems of the mountain valleys forced many young neo-Latins to emigrate. Then the tourists finally arrived.

Step by step, Romansch was pushed aside. The flowering of Rhaeto-Romanic literature, which began in the 19th century, hardly provoked a Romansch linguistic renaissance. Whether the standard language *Rumantsch grischun* developed by Romansch scholar Heinrich Schmid will survive, or prompt a new surge of interest, is doubtful. ❑

LEFT: the Bible, first translated into Lower Engadine Romansch between 1678 and 1679.

Map on page 206

exceptionally beautiful when snow lies on its mighty roofs, and the grey squared-stone masonry of the houses seems more intense and powerful than ever. In the autumn, by way of contrast, when the *Föhn* wind whips south and colours the sky Prussian blue, the smell of new wine forces its way out of the few remaining wine-presses in towns like **Lürlibad**, and every restaurant in town serves venison from the hunt.

On mild summer evenings people sit out of doors in Chur's old quarter, enjoying the warmth of the day radiating from the walls of the houses. On nights like these, Chur becomes the most Italian town north of the Alps.

Walking tours

Most visitors treat Chur as an obstacle on the way to their destination resort, but it is worth taking time to look around. Here is a mini-programme for people in a hurry; it can be covered in a couple of hours.

Take a leisurely stroll up the old Reichsgasse to the Hofkellerei, a convivial inn, inside the **Gate Tower**, before carrying on to the so-called **Hof**, the heart of the old town, where you will find the Romanesque and Gothic cathedral, the Gothic bishop's palace, the priests' seminary and the former monastery church of St Luzius with its round Carolingian crypt.

The speciality of the Hofkellerei is *Capuns*: noodles wrapped in beet leaves and boiled in stock, a traditional and very filling Graubünden dish. It is also a good idea to take a seat at the wood-panelled, Gothic bar and order a glass of *Schiller* wine from the episcopal vineyards just below the Hof. It looks harmless, but you'll feel its potency when you stand up, which few of the guests are in much of a hurry to do.

TIP

A hearty dish traditionally served in Chur's restaurants in the winter is the accurately named *Beinwurst*, a bone-shaped pork sausage, which actually contains a bone.

BELOW: the Rhätische Bahn railway crossing the Landwasser Viaduct.

Then how about following the people of Chur on one of their typical outings? In autumn, take the route into the **Bündner Herrschaft**, 15 minutes north of Chur by rail, to **Maienfeld ❷**, the third town on the Rhein. There's a tranquil walk 5 km (3 miles) southeast to **Malans** on the itinerary too. This hiking route – which is completely flat – is also called *Kistenpass*, because quite a few people end up in a *kiste* (the Swiss word for drunken stupor) while walking along it. This walk is ideal for those interested in enjoying a quick tipple. Without stops, it takes an hour, but temptations are there every step of the way and few people manage it in less than 2 ½ hours.

Excavations of Roman remains at Welschdorfli near Curia have even revealed oyster shells imported from Burgundy, suggesting that life for some of the imperial forces was far from harsh.

If you fancy a cultural interlude during the trail, take a look at the massive mansions here in Maienfeld – and then hike, following the red markers, to **Unterrofels** from the Städtliplatz, and to the **Heidi-Dörf** and the *Heidi-Hüsli*, where the heroine of Johanna Spyri's famous novel *Heidi* is said to have lived. Since 1999 the house has been a **museum** (open Mar–Nov daily 10am–5pm; entrance fee; tel: 081 330 19 12) with an outside area set aside for farm animals.

A route even less travelled, but just as comfortable and almost as beautiful as the Maienfeld trip, is the 42-km (26-mile) route from Thusis via Chur to Fläsch, which goes right to the heart of the Bündner Herrschaft wine region.

The Bündner Oberland

Much originality – alongside a few concessions to modernity – is provided west of Chur by the **Surselva**, which was discovered by tourism only a short while ago. It is here that you can find those white-bearded individuals so loved by photographers, and houses burned dark by the sun, and bread is still baked in some of the public ovens in the village squares. A particularly fine example can be found in **Luven** above Ilanz, decorated with the rather apt saying: *Nies paun da mintg gi* (our daily bread).

Tourism has still only reached the entrance to the Surselva and the **Vorderrhein** 20 km (12 miles) west of Chur – above all at Flims and Laax. In the summertime white-water enthusiasts go river-rafting here, down into the ravine of the wildly foaming Rhein. However, the Rhein is developing into more of a thin trickle than a torrent since Graubünden allowed itself to be done out of its water rights – for a pittance – by lowland power stations. River-rafters on the River Innen in the Lower Engadine (Unterengadin) are also familiar with this problem.

Flims ❸ (a postbus stop on the road from Chur, thus more built-up) and **Laax** (a somewhat quieter, more rustic town) have long since turned their attention to wooing skiers: within the so-called "**White Arena**", the brainchild of a master butcher from Flims, which covers an area of 140 sq. km (85 sq. miles), even the most energetic skier cannot hope to cover all the descents in a single day. Unfortunately, the ski-lift reaching the summer ski resort on the glacier is no longer in regular operation, but other offerings have taken up the touristic slack. A young backpacker set is thronging here for the spectacular hiking, biking and snowboarding.

At the very top of the valley, too, near the source of the Rhein at the **Tomasee** (incidentally, there is a very attractive walk which can be taken along its banks), the locals are trying to attract as many tourists as possible. Some 40 km (25 miles) west of Ilanz in **Sedrun** – on the **Oberalp Pass**, which leads onward to Andermatt in the canton of Uri – snowfall is reliable, even when other health-spa managers are wringing their hands in despair.

It is also worth pointing out that no other valley in Switzerland contains quite so many baroque churches and chapels. Many of them were built at the time of the ravages of the Plague, when people were frightened of being infected in the bigger churches. The finest examples – some of them Gothic – can be found in **Falera** outside Laax (the Church of St Remigius), **Sevgein** (just southeast of Ilanz), Ilanz (St Margarethen) and **Waltensburg**, 8 km (5miles) west of Ilanz off the main road (the Reformed church).

The wild **Safiental** can only be reached via 365 hairpin bends; head 10 km/ 6 miles east from Ilanz, then turn south at Versam. In the **Valser Tal**, due south of Ilanz, you can drink the mineral water of the same name and swim in it too, in open-air thermal baths (at the Hotel Therme – open to non-residents).

Map on page 206

Smooth roads but hair-raising bends through the Safiental.

The Surselva's faith and politics

In no part of Graubünden are politics so closely tied to the church as they are in this Surselva region: when votes are taken on Sundays, the ballot boxes stand in front of church doorways. The priests' sermons tend to be far more political than they are in other parts of the country. It is not only ethical issues – such as refugee problems or abortion – which concern the priests; even such seemingly secular matters as proposed nuclear power stations and highway construction projects are likely to come under fire from the pulpit.

Centuries of religious apartheid and conflict between Catholics and Protestants have certainly left their traces in the region. The differences are already evident in the language itself. In the Romansch-speaking Surselva, one confession writes *de (of)* while the other uses *da* in preference – this is still a consequence of the Reformation, when anything that had been written or printed in the heretical neigh-bouring valleys was totally ignored. It was only very gradually that the barriers between the Catholic and Protestant areas crumbled.

Today things have progressed so far that, when the expression "mixed marriage" is mentioned in con-versation, the first thing that crosses most people's minds is not their religion but the language that the couple speak.

For art and nature lovers, **Ilanz ❹** – some 30 km (20 miles) west of Chur along the Rhein, beyond Laax – is the best base to choose: everywhere is within easy reach – by car, on foot, or by postbus. In the lateral valleys of the Surselva, far from the through-routes and their filling stations, it is possible to take a jour-ney back 100 years into the past.

Farther west still, past Trun and just east of Sedrun, is **Disentis ❺** (in Romansch: Mustér) – with its **Bene-dictine Monastery**, the finest baroque edifice in

BELOW: riding the St Bernard Express, at Orsières.

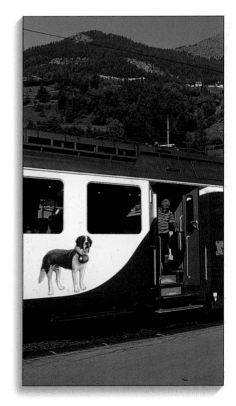

Graubünden. Its reputation now rests on its lawn tennis courts, facilities which have inspired the tourist office to label it the "Wimbledon of the Alps".

Magnificent passes

It is thought that the Passo del San Bernardino has been in use since Bronze Age Times.

Everyone who wants to cross the passes in Graubünden these days has to take the route used 2,000 years ago: through the narrow gap formed by the Bündner Herrschaft and Chur. For real pass enthusiasts, here are two particularly attractive routes.

The first is ideal for motorists with relatively little pass experience: it leads from Chur (via Lenzerheide and Tiefencastel or via Landquart and Klosters) to Davos, and then on over the **Flüelapass** – which has a barren landscape of stone and water – to **Susch**.

Passo del San Bernardino

Another trip into the southern part of Graubünden provides the possibility of going over a pass on the journey there and travelling back via a road tunnel. This is the **Passo del San Bernardino ❻**, the alternative to the St Gotthard for road traffic travelling through Switzerland. The pass is named after the 15th-century San Bernardino of Siena, who used to preach here. The tunnel, at 6.6 km (4 miles) long, is only about half as long as the road over this ancient pass, if you are in a hurry. If you do opt for the tunnel, you will be missing some excellent views from the road over the Rheinwald Valley and its northern peaks – although negotiating the 18 hairpin bends will demand most drivers' attention.

BELOW: looking up the Albula Pass.

It is worth taking this route if only to make a reconnaissance of the **Misox Valley** (or Valle Mesolcina as it appears on most maps): the way leads from Chur

Map on page 206

through the valley of the Hinterrhein, then up over the pass (which is dotted with Alpine roses in the summertime) to the mountain resort of **San Bernardino**, just beyond the southern entrance to the tunnel, a popular base for local hiking and cross-country skiing activities.

The main village in the region, though, is **Mesocco**, with a solid-looking cluster of stone houses. The ruins of the **Castello di Mesocco**, dating from the late 15th century, dominate the valley from the heights of its rocky ridge below the village. By following a route through the villages in preference to the *Autobahn*, you will see the picturesque stables built from rubble dotting the fields outside the villages, and you will not miss **Roveredo** either, where the road branches off towards the **Val Calanca**, high in the mountains. The entry to it is guarded by a 13th-century pentagonal tower and the lavishly decorated **Church of Santa Maria Assunta** (17th-century) in **Santa Maria di Calanca**.

Then there is a whole series of tiny villages nestling in a delightful landscape. Many of these look almost deserted, and not without reason: people have emigrated from this high valley since the 16th century. The able-bodied men have traditionally gone off to seek their fortunes in Italian cities, first as master builders and as artists, then later as chimney-sweeps.

Anyone who finds these pass routes a little too tame should take another, third variation, which has been known to send a shiver up the spine of even pass-hardened travellers. This particular tour starts in Chur, then continues via **Thusis** along highway 13 on to Splügen, then detours south over that classic north-south pass, the **Splügenpass** ❼, and down several wildly romantic hairpins across the border and into the Italian town of **Chiavenna**. Then it goes back into Switzerland via the Bergell. The mountains here are so high that some

BELOW: the village of Splügen, in the Hinterrhein Valley.

Detail of the church ceiling in Zillis.

BELOW: cable-car station in the Davos-Parsenn skiing area.

villages remain without sunshine for months at a time. It continues over the **Maloja Pass** into the Engadine and then back to Chur via the Julier; and the Julier, a route once used by the Romans, is child's play compared with the route covered so far. If you would rather let others do the driving, you can do the whole round trip on comfortable postbuses (with changes in Splügen, Chiavenna and Silvaplana).

Into the abyss

If you are driving south, ease off the accelerator in **Thusis**, resist being sucked down into the new, multi-lane motorway and take the old road instead – the aptly named **Via Mala** (Bad Road) ❽. This winds its way along the mountainside, leading through tunnels that are still crudely hewn. The sensation is similar to being on a particularly scary ghost train; you can even feel the moist air wafting up from down below. Black and forbidding, the crumpled-looking layers of slate, 300 metres (985 ft) high, tower to left and right.

In Roman times there was no road, only a narrow trail. The first road was built in 1473, but the first time it was mentioned as being completed was 1723. About half way along the Via Mala you can stop at the well-signposted **Via Mala Gorge**, walking down 321 steps to the thundering river. Walk across the small bridge and through a tunnel and you'll reach a viewing platform with spectacular views of the wider, southern end of the gorge. The gorge is 1,000 metres (3,300 ft) long, but what makes it so impressive is that it has a number of sections that are only a metre wide. When meltwater rushes through in spring, it's a memorable sight.

Looking up you can see the famous **Via Mala Bridge** high above, looking

Map on page 206

exactly as it did when Goethe sketched it in 1788. It also appears in several plays, and books such as John Knittel's *Via Mala*, which has been filmed several times, and which the local inhabitants still have not forgiven him for writing: he turned them into a group of drunkards and rowdies. He may also have drawn inspiration from the fact that the Romansch language contains more expressions for fighting and brawling than any other in the world.

Lingering idyll

Emerging from the gorge, the Schams Valley greets you as delightfully as a ray of sunshine after a thunderstorm. Out here, the sun still sets behind mountains rather than *Aparthotels*. Not a single ski-lift mars the slopes, and the gardens in the villages have not been asphalted over. No other Protestant area contains so many churches serving so few inhabitants as Schams. They are not situated, as many are, in the middle of the villages, but perched on projecting sections of mountainside or wall, facing down into the valley below in a cheerful, friendly manner, like children on tiptoe.

Leaving your car or postbus in Zillis, you can spend a few hours wandering up to the ruined castle of **Cagliatscha**, then across the old wooden bridge to Andeer, just 5 km (3 miles) south of Zillis, and return to Zillis either on foot or by postbus again. You will be rewarded by church interiors of touching simplicity (the one at **Clugin**, for example, is particularly moving) and by villages which, thanks to strict building laws, still look the same as they did 100 years ago, unspoilt by clusters of holiday homes. The finest church of all, however, lies practically on the main road: the Romanesque church in **Zillis ⑨**, which contains the oldest completely painted and preserved wooden ceiling in the West, constructed around 1150. No one knows who the artist was, but it is thought that the masterpiece was probably intended to commemmorate a successful crossing of the Via Mala. It clearly shows the influence of book illuminations in Bavaria and northern Italy. The life of Jesus Christ and several scenes from the life of St Martin are depicted on 153 painted panels. With the help of the hand-mirrors provided these can easily be inspected. The border panels depict mysterious monsters and strange, nightmarish-looking sea-creatures.

Offering a quiet idyll in overrun, over-visited Europe, the Schams may well tempt you to stay for a while. If you have the time to linger in **Andeer**, it is worth exploring this quiet backwater. Take a leisurely look at the **Haus Pedrun**, covered in *sgraffiti* from the 16th century.

Away from the bustle

Alongside the two brightest stars in the Graubünden holiday firmament, St Moritz and Davos, its less dazzling resorts have quite a hard time of it. Approximately 16 km (10 miles) south of Chur, on the Julier Pass route, **Lenzerheide ⑩** prides itself on being a family resort, while **Parpan** and **Churwalden** en route are said to have introduced Graubünden *Bindenfleisch*, air-dried beef. The dish is known all over Switzerland by its local name, *Bündnerfleisch*. Gourmets, and people who are in search of some

TIP

A grand old hotel in the Schams Valley is the Hotel Fravi in Andeer, where various crowned heads of state, as well as Karl Marx, have stayed (see Where to Stay, Travel Tips, page 332).

BELOW: the Romanesque church at Zillis.

peace and quiet, are liable to feel a lot more at home in such places than avid downhill skiers and celebrity-spotters.

Isolated Arosa

Another place almost isolated from the outside world is **Arosa** , a classic Graubünden holiday resort, which has extensive sports facilities and is especially well equipped to deal with families. The resort – best known for its moderately difficult downhill skiing, but also for ice-skating on the local lake, and the sort of pleasure that comes from being far removed from (most of) civilisation – can be reached from Chur in an hour, via a very scenic narrow-gauge railway or a twisting, 30-km (20-mile) road. It is a romantic trip which is at its most attractive in the summer. In good weather, the Arosa train also has a special observation car. With no roof overhead and the wind in their hair, passengers travel over deep ravines, through quiet forests and finally over the famed viaduct at Langwies.

It is a wonderful journey, though the town may not quite live up to expectations of an idyllic village. At least the views – not to mention the skiing, snow-shoeing, walking, cable-car rides and crisp air (there is a paragliding school here if you fancy it) – are splendid.

One major highlight, once you have reached the end of the railway line to Arosa, is a hike up to the famous **Innerarosa Church** (open June–Oct for guided tours only at 2.30pm; free), with its wood-planked tower. Visitors from the US who look at its two bells may be in for a surprise: according to the inscription the bells were cast in 1492, the year Christopher Columbus reached America.

TIP

Arosa is divided into two parts: Ausserarosa has the main resort facilities, based around the train station by the shores of the Obersee lake, and Innerarosa is the older part of town.

BELOW:

checking the goods at Andeer's cattle market.

Magic mountain

The **Prättigau**, running southeast from Landquart, shares the same fate as many other valleys with famous resorts at the end of them, in this case **Davos** and **Klosters**: it is treated as merely an access route and most visitors drive through it quickly, sparing no time for a closer look. In the autumn, though, the magnificence of the huge beech woods here can be captivating, and the region's Romansch villages are renowned for their festivals.

It was through the Prättigau in 1889 that the Rhätische Bahn (Rhaetian Railway) transported the first tuberculosis patients to the sanatoria of **Davos** ⓬, which today publicises itself with the slogan "Davos – famos". With a resident population of over 10,000, it is a town that pulsates with life all year round. The mountain air was thought to be particularly beneficial to people with lung complaints. The forbidding buildings of former days have long since become five-star hotels, one example being today's Steigenberger Hotel Belvedere, on which Thomas Mann based his *Magic Mountain* sanatorium.

It is the **Parsenn Mountains** that have made Davos famous: 200 km (125 miles) of the Davos' 320 km (200 miles) of piste lead down from it into the valley below. The slopes here are so gentle that they do not even worry beginners. Anyone keen on avoiding waiting time at the crowded ski lifts on weekends and public holidays should do as the natives do and take the **Schatzalp-Strelabahn** to the top of the slopes. At night, there are plenty of clubs (though some are dear and clique-ish) in which to drink your cares away with the jet set. In summer, there is just as much – probably more – to do in the area, including inexpensive luge runs (they operate year-round) and some testing mountain biking and hiking up into the surrounding mountains.

Map on page 206

The Protestant villages of the Prättigau are noted for their belief of superstitions – most have a local healer or a clairvoyant.

BELOW: rafting down the Vorderrhein.

Window in Tarasp Castle, depicting Hans Ort of Einsiedeln, dated 1517.

Klosters

Some visitors, however (including, traditionally, the British royal family), prefer quieter **Klosters** next door, sharing the same ski slopes but a more authentic Alpine charm. A rail tunnel has opened up Klosters to the north, allowing quicker passage from Landquart and Chur. Once here, you could hit the slopes with skis or, increasingly popular, a snowboard; in addition to some world-class half-pipe on **Jacobshorn**, there are several recently opened snowboard-theme hotels around town as well. However, these are definitely *not* the places to go to for peace and quiet.

Another option from Klosters is to take a pricey mountain-railway ride up the **Gotschna** for views back down into the valley, or up the **Madrisa** to begin a hike. Locals also recommend hikes in the Jöri lakes – you get there from Berghaus, a postbus ride away from town. Still another fine idea, if you have the time, is to take a leisurely walk into the two quieter adjacent valleys to the southeast, the **Sertigtal** and the **Dischmatal**. The German Expressionist painter Ernst Ludwig Kirchner used these landscapes in many of his works. The artist lived here from 1917 to 1938. His house in Davos-Frauenkirch is privately owned and so cannot be visited, but there is the **Kirchner Museum**, containing oil-paintings, sketches and assorted documents, in the old post-office building.

The Lower Engadine Valley

BELOW: the Swiss National Park is preserved in its natural state.

The **Unter Engadin** is particularly conscious of its ancestral heritage. The village of **Ardez** , for instance, 35 km (20 miles) east of Davos via highways 27 and 28, was chosen as a model municipality in Europe's year of preservation; the "Fall" depicted on the double-oriel facade of the **Haus Claglüna**, the most richly decorated house in the whole of the Engadine, is worth stopping to admire.

From Ardez a small road, which is also good for hiking, leads 5 km (3 miles) up to **Guarda**, which clings dramatically to the sunny slope; it has been painstakingly renovated with the help of national funds. The village's houses and inns are typical of a style prevalent in the Lower Engadine since the 14th century, combining living quarters and stables under one roof. The window openings slope inwards and many of the houses feature the elaborate *sgraffiti* which originated in Italy.

You will discover a way of life that is still largely unspoilt in the nearby municipality of **Sent**, 15 km (9 miles) back east on highway 27, with its decorated gables, as well as on the **Panorama High Path**, lying on the former route through the Lower Engadine. En route, the hamlet of **Ftan** has recently gained a reputation as a centre for excellent food.

The best starting point in the Engadine is **Scuol** (Schuls in German), a romantic and pretty spa town nestling down in the valley below, whose attractions include an 11th-century **castle** and a picturesque old quarter, featuring cobbled alleys, bubbling fountains and old bakery ovens. The local **museum** gives an insight into Romansch culture (open Apr–Oct

Tues–Fri 10–11.30am and 3–5pm, Nov–Mar tours Tues and Thurs at 5pm; tel: 081 864 82 21). Scuol's mineral water, known as the "champagne of the Alps", can be drunk from the village fountain or soaked in; thermal baths are available, offering a wide range of steamy therapeutic indulgences. You might appreciate these if you are here for the town's livelier activities: it also has the oldest established snowboarding school in Europe, offering a wide range of courses for all ages and abilities (Element Swiss Snowboard School, 7550 Scuol; tel: 081 860 07 77; www.element.scuol.ch).

On an architectural note, most of the town's older houses feature a *balcun tort*, an oriel window from which the street can be observed from both sides. Oriel windows of this type are not found anywhere else in Switzerland; they were a means by which members of the community kept a careful eye on each other.

Population drift

Such close supervision has made life in Graubünden too claustrophobic for many of its inhabitants and the town has witnessed a steady stream of emigration over the centuries. It was often the brightest who upped and left; philosophers and idealists never really felt much at home under the watchful gaze of their neighbours in Graubünden.

Architects who had built such castles as **Schloss Tarasp** (just to the south of Scuol; open for tours June–mid-July daily 2.30pm, mid-July–mid-Aug daily 11am–4.30pm, mid-Aug–mid-Oct daily 2.30–3.30pm; entrance fee; tel: 081 864 93 68) were also attracted abroad. The Bavarian castles of Nymphenburg and Schleissheim were built by Graubünden architects from Roveredo. Powerful Graubünden merchants traded in Italy, Russia and Spain, and ran the

Map on page 206

TIP

Scuol holds large festivals in February and March, dating back to Roman times, when the end of the winter and the start of the New Year (1 March) was celebrated.

BELOW: view over Tarasp.

most famous cake shops in Venice. Meanwhile, the vacancies they left at home were filled by foreigners: the German Hennings and the Dutchman Holsboer planned the most difficult stretches of the Rhätische Bahn; the German doctor Alexander Spengler turned the Davos area into the international health spa that it is today. The annual "Spengler Cup" ice-hockey tournament is named after him.

If you are after more tranquil outdoor pursuits, however, you can find more room to move and as much wild and romantic natural scenery in the **Val Scharl**, which can be reached easily from Scuol either on foot, by car or by postbus heading due south. There are no hotels here, but it is a popular area with hikers, with good summer walking as far as the Ofenpass and the Val Müstair.

Riding on the Glacier Express between St Moritz and Zermatt.

The Swiss National Park

Those after more gentle scenery choose a different road – beyond Tiefencastel – that goes 40 km (25 miles) east via **Bergün** and the **Albulapass** (open to cars only in the summer). It features exceptionally attractive vegetation – and less stony desolation – but the road is very narrow, and so driving carefully is a good idea. Then again, there is a lot less traffic as a result. Taking this route, you end up in **La Punt ⑰**, where there is the impressive Engadine memorial, the **Chesa Mereda**, which has a striking battlemented gable dating from 1642.

Continuing north up highway 27, you soon come to **Zernez**, useful chiefly as a gateway to the **Swiss National Park ⑱** nearby. Here, in a rugged mountainous area covering 1,700 sq. km (650 sq. miles), nature has been left to itself since the park was founded in 1914. The park is indeed a place of some wildness today and conditions of its protection have remained strict; visitors may only access certain areas in limited ways; campfires and flower-picking are punishable by large fines levied by unsmiling rangers. Visitor information is provided at the **Nationalparkhaus** (open June–Oct daily 8.30am–6pm, until 10pm Tues; entrance fee for museum; tel: 081 856 13 78; www.nationalpark.ch), where a slide-show exhibition prepares you for the experience ahead.

BELOW: keeping warm at the start of the Engadine skiing marathon.

The park is cut through by the **Val Müstair**, which you can follow to the southeast along highway 28 over the **Ofenpass**, and up to the village of Santa Maria, where there is a north-south fork in the road. The north fork leads, after a short distance, to the staunchly Romansch village of **Müstair ⑲** on the Italian border, and from there on to Glurns/Glorenza in the Trentino Alto region of Italy. If you take the southern fork, the road leads on over the Umbrailpass (open only between June and October) and the sinuous Stilfser Joch/Passo di Stelvio into northern Italy's enormous national park of the same name.

The big attraction in Müstair, however – unmissable even for those in a real hurry – is the **Carolingian convent** of St John the Baptist, dating from the 8th century; it contains the best-preserved and most extensive collection of Carolingian wall paintings in the Alps. The convent is closed to the public but the church opens daily 8am–7pm, and a museum with guided tours tells the history of the convent (open daily 9am–5pm; entrance fee).

Map on page 206

A world apart

The Unter Engadin and the **Ober Engadin** (Upper and Lower Engadine) valleys are not divided by any visible border, but are worlds apart when it comes to attitude. In the Unter Engadin, tradition is still considered a private, local affair. In the Ober Engadin, it has blatantly been adapted to meet the demands of tourism. For example, the *Schlitteda*, the traditional winter sledge outing of the village youth, uses horse-drawn buggies in summer to oblige visitors. In the Unter Engadin, valuable Romansch artefacts stand unobtrusively in parlours. In the Ober Engadin, they are more likely to be found prominently displayed in chic establishments such as the Chesa Veglia in St Moritz.

St Moritz ⑳ then, is the Ober Engadin's winter resort *par excellence*, and, though it costs a pretty penny to eat and stay here, it undeniably makes an excellent base for outdoor sporting; the place claims to be the oldest winter resort in the world, after all, and once hosted the Winter Olympic Games.

It all began in 1864, when Johannes Badrutt, who built St Moritz's Kulm Hotel, invited some English summer guests to spend the winter here, promising that they would be able to sit outside in their shirtsleeves in December. Various other St Moritz premières followed: in 1880, Europe's first curling tournament took place in the town, and in 1884 the first toboggan run was built here. In the case of the latter, the daring participants plunged down the run, reaching speeds of up to 140 kph (85 mph). It was also in St Moritz that the bobsleigh was "invented" in 1891. Occasionally, a visitor to St Moritz will pluck up the courage to go down the famous bobsleigh-run – albeit usually in the passenger seat.

The Ober Engadin lives up to every cliché you hear about it. Here we see the jetset stepping out of Rolls-Royces, and members of Europe's aristocracy at

BELOW: the deceptively bland lakefront of St Moritz, playground of Europe's elite.

play. There is always something astonishing going on – beautiful women draped in fur coats and being transported in a sledge pulled by dogs the size of calves are reality, not fantasy. Up on the sun terrace on **Corviglia**, St Moritz's local mountain, which can be comfortably reached via cable railway, VIPs and would-be VIPs greet one another like castaways who have just been rescued. After several *Kaffee Grischas* in the "Alpina" skiclub the welcoming kisses tend to be aimed rather less accurately: the four different kinds of schnapps in the solid-looking Arolla pine bowl being passed around have a pretty powerful kick.

Fun and games

This is when the fun really starts. Bolstered by schnapps and feeling positively foolhardy, revellers are suddenly willing to participate in the most dangerous sports. One of the most popular activities is hang-gliding down to the **St Moritzer See**, where the range of sports on offer seems to multiply every year: golf and polo in the snow (using red balls) are both popular. In the evening, the bars are full of tourists sporting injuries: tobogganists with plaster casts and skijoring gladiators whose chests are covered in livid bruises (caused by the lumps of ice flying off the horses' hooves). As Art Buchwald said of St Moritz in *I Chose Caviar*, it is "the heart of the broken-limb country, where a man must prove himself first on skis and then on a stretcher".

No one can dodge the bustle in St Moritz or avoid all the frantic activity. That is why there should be somewhere in the resort where you can retire. Luckily, the Upper Engadine is just like all other "in" places frequented by the rich and fashionable: take only a few steps off the beaten track and the roar of Ferrari exhausts and the cloying scent of perfumes and aftershaves fade away.

BELOW:
dogsledding
near St Moritz.

Only then can the visitor get a glimpse of the Upper Engadine as the Austrian poet Rainer Maria Rilke described it in 1919: "How demanding these lakes and mountains are, there is a strange abundance about them, the moments they provide are far from simple. The astonishment of our grandfathers and great-grandfathers seems to have had much to do with this place: they travelled here from their own countries which apparently had 'nothing', while here there was 'everything' in plenty. Nature with its ups and downs, full of abundance, full of increase, its outlines starkly emphasised."

However, tourism has arrived in full force to see this grandeur and the results have not always been good. Parts of the town resemble city blocks of ugly concrete-box hotels, and in recent years St Moritz has even been compelled to hold its village festival on the roof of its multistorey car park because all the other open areas have now been built up.

Evening delights

What about evenings in the Engadine? Shortly before dinner is the best time in the day to catch a glimpse of the rich and famous. However, anybody who is anybody tends to prefer cocktail hour in the privacy of his or her own villa on the **Suvrettahang**. This area sloping to the west of St Moritz is the most exclusive part of the town. A tabloid newspaper once made the exaggerated claim that it contained some 50 multimillionaires.

A large herd of ibex lives high above the Val Bernina.

A more rewarding way of spending the twilight hours is to travel via cable car from Punt Muragl (a short ride to the north of Pontresina) to **Muottas Muragl**: from no other observation point is the sheer breadth of the Upper Engadine lake landscape so impressive as when the silvery light starts to build up on the mountainside towards evening. Anyone who has experienced it once is always drawn back to this spot: it permeates the broad expanse of the plateau until both earth and heaven become a single supernatural shimmer – and then, suddenly, dusk falls.

BELOW: fresco of St Christopher on the church in Waltensburg.

If you are looking for a less exclusive crowd (or just less of a crowd), take the narrow-gauge trains or one of the postbus fleet to the surrounding towns, most of them quieter than St Moritz. If you cannot tear yourself away from the St Moritz party scene, at least make time for a day trip into the hills – via one of the many cable cars ascending Piz Nair, Diavolezza and other peaks and ski slopes – for a look or a stroll.

The Morteratsch Glacier

To the east of St Moritz, and branching south off the **Val Bernina** are the two valleys of **Val Roseg** (accessible from the station in **Pontresina ㉑**, where horse-drawn sledges can be hired) and **Val Morteratsch** (which can be reached from the railway station of the same name), both of which are equally pretty in summer or winter. The footpaths here are not steep, and if you walk quietly enough you might just see some young and fearless ibex on the mountain slopes, or a few chamois rooting about in the snow for grass; and in summer maybe even a herd of deer. If you are lucky, the wind might part the clouds suddenly and – for a few glorious minutes only – reveal the **Morteratsch**

TIP

Celerina, just to the north of St Moritz, and sharing the same ski slopes, offers a more homely winter resort, plus the chance to cruise down an old-fashioned bobsleigh run in winter (quite expensive but a thrilling experience).

BELOW: nursery slopes near Laax.

Glacier lying ahead, covered in fresh snow and bathed in sunlight, and the **Bernina Massif**, towering more than 4,000 metres (13,000 ft). The Morteratsch Glacier provides skiers with pretty demanding and varied downhill runs from the **Passo del Diavolezza**, and can be reached from the Bernina Pass road via cable car; through binoculars from here, you can see the mountaineers on the Piz Palü, the Bianco Ridge or the Bernina, whatever the time of year.

Pontresina also offers the option of horse-drawn carriage rides up the Bernina Valley, and is another potential jumping-off point for the spectacular Bernina Express train-and-bus ride into Italy or the Glacier Express west all the way to Zermatt. Alternatively, for those who crave a two-wheeled experience, without doubt the finest cycle route in the canton is a 60-km (37-mile) stretch in the Upper Engadine, where every holiday resort is directly connected to the cycle route network. The way leads along the edge of the **Oberengadiner See**, through forests and across broad meadows.

Lakes Silvaplauna and Segl

Another spectacular region to find natural tranquillity is to the southwest of St Moritz where a string of lakes forms the final link in the Ice-Age chain of glacial erosion. The route down the right-hand side of the valley from St Moritz is not too busy. It leads perhaps 20 km (12 miles) southwest across wooded, sheltered slopes, past bog lakes and special stands containing food for the deer, through an idyllic landscape with wonderful views over **Lej da Silvaplauna** below; continue past the foot of the **Corvatsch**, considered by many to be the best mountain for skiing in the world. It is shady and cool here in the summer, and in winter the cross-country skiing routes are prepared and freshened up

Map on page 206

every day. These are particularly recommended for people wishing to avoid the thick columns of cross-country skiers on the frozen lakes and who want a bit more excitement and exercise.

Beyond Lake Silvaplauna, linked by the town of Sils Maria (Segl in Romansch) is **Lej da Segl**. Nietzsche wrote his *Zarathustra* in **Sils Maria** ㉒ in 1888. Plagued by almost unbearable migraines, his eyes aching, and totally exhausted, he felt transported by nature on this plateau "which has piled itself up fearlessly close to the terrors of the eternal snows, here, where Italy and Finland form a pact with one another and seem to play host to every silvery colour nature possesses – happy is he who can say: 'Nature certainly has bigger and better things to offer, but this is something truly close to my heart'."

Nietzsche Haus (open mid-June–mid-Oct and Jan–mid-Apr Tues–Sun 3–6pm; entrance fee), where Nietzsche lived in the summers from 1881 to 1888, is now a museum, although the exhibits are all captioned in German, but it has some interesting photographs of the man throughout his life.

From the village square of Sils Maria, you can climb aboard a horse-drawn sledge and travel due south into the car-free **Val Fex**. With luck, there may be just enough daylight left to visit the pretty little church in **Crasta** in the valley and admire its wall paintings, dating from 1500. They have only recently been uncovered, but they look almost as good as new.

Val Bregaglia villages

Reaching Maloja is like reaching the edge of the world: the pass road plunges 300 metres (1,000 ft) into the depths, in 12 steep curves. The villages in Val Bregaglia are agreeably intact; the valley is mainly attractive to mountaineers (the Sciora and Bondasca ranges to the southeast are particularly popular), and hikers, too. The hamlet of **Grevasalvas**, situated high above the **Lej da Segl** up a mountain track just east of the Maloja Pass on the northern side of the lake, can be reached on foot only in summer months, from Maloja.

Thanks to the enterprising spa director of St Moritz, large numbers of tourists have been making the pilgrimage to this unspoilt Alpine hamlet for some years now. Impressed by the number of foreign tourists in St Moritz asking about Heidi – heroine of Johanna Spyri's children's book (who inconveniently had her home in Maienfeld, way to the north of the canton) – he took advantage of the fact that one of the innumerable Heidi films had been shot in Grevasalvas and declared the whole of the Engadine "Heidiland".

Maloja ㉓ itself is extremely small, quiet and Italian-flavoured – a wonderful antidote to the excesses of its famous neighbours Davos and St Moritz – and the stroll to Silvaplana is breathtaking.

The Val Bregaglia has produced at least one famous artistic family: the village of **Stampa**, further down highway 3 towards the Italian border was the home of the Giacometti family: glass painter Augusto, his cousin Giovanni, the Impressionist, and last but not least Giovanni's son Alberto, whose sculptures can be found in the world's top museums.

In **Bondo** ㉔, 25 km (15 miles) southwest on high-

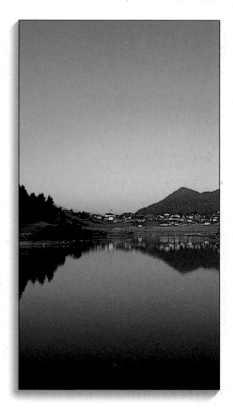

BELOW: lakeland reflection in the Bündner Oberland.

The Val Bregaglia churches are richly decorated with Romanesque murals.

BELOW: the chain of lakes in the Upper Engadine.

way 3, visit the **Valley Museum** inside the Ciäsa Granda, built in 1581. Further west, on a terrace above the valley, lies **Soglio**, which can be reached via a journey through the largest chestnut forest in Europe, which extends as far as the Italian border at **Castasegna**. Here, the three **palaces** belonging to the renowned patrician family of Salis-Soglio dominate the scenery; one of them is now a hotel.

Spectacular rail journeys

In the aftermath of World War I, when Graubünden picked itself up out of the dust by spending 26 years building its very own 375-km (235-mile) narrow-gauge railway network, the railway was used to transport not the wealthy nobility they had expected but war refugees instead. The first-class carriages went quietly rusty. Today the Rhätische Bahn plays on people's nostalgia. The old trains are being made railworthy once again. They rock their passengers to and fro on velvet cushions, through 115 tunnels and across 485 bridges. A train such as the Glacier Express takes 7 ½ hours to reach Zermatt in the Valais from St Moritz.

Most of the tourists on these trains are so preoccupied by their own enjoyment that they do not realise that the little red train and the delightful stations are not laid on by the tourist board but have their own day-to-day, normal working routines. No other railway in the world alternates between such extremes. Even when the champagne is bubbling and the caviar is being spread on the bread in the walnut-panelled, lavishly upholstered restaurant car with its shiny brass fittings, three carriages further down the farmers are travelling to market, and the children to school.

Indeed, between Christmas and the New Year every single seat is occupied, and even the most dilapidated-looking wooden carriages groan over the rails, transporting passengers to the skiing resorts. In May and November, on the other hand, the carriages are often almost empty.

Map on page 206

The Bernina Pass

The "showpiece" stretch of the Rhätische Bahn winds its circuitous way south-east from Chur, through gorges, over the famous Landwasser Viaduct, north of Bergün – 130 metres (420 ft) long, 65 metres (200 ft) high – and on to Tirano on the Italian border, which it reaches roughly 4 hours later. The most daring stretch of rail awaits the passenger at the **Passo del Bernina**, where in winter and spring the Bernina Express locomotive track, at a height of 2,257 metres (7,400 ft) above sea level, and flanked on all sides by mountains over 4,000 metres (13,000 ft) high, ploughs its way through metre-high snow, before coming to a halt some time later among palm trees and magnolia. The gradient achieved in the first part of the journey is about 7 percent, which makes it one of the steepest conventional rail routes in the world.

Railway enthusiasts will enjoy the stretch between **Bergün** and **Preda**. In order to gain height, the railway line performs a series of five loops and two tunnels through the mountainside, thus avoiding the more typical Alpine cogwheel system. In this section alone, the line climbs 416 metres (1,365 ft) over a distance of only 12.6 km (8 miles), and goes through the **Albula Tunnel**, at 1,820 metres (5,970 ft), the highest rail tunnel in Europe. In winter, the trip can also be done by sledge. Then the 5-km (3-mile) stretch of road between Preda and Bergün is closed to cars, and turned into the most popular sledge run in the whole Graubünden Alps. Sledges can be hired from a shop at the station in Preda; a ride through the snow during a full moon is particularly recommended. The train shuttles the sledge parties from Bergün back to their starting point until 1.30 in the morning.

The Rhätische Bahn runs several tourist trains on this route throughout the year, all equipped with modern comforts and panoramic observation carriages (tel: 081 288 61 04; fax: 081 288 61 05; www.rhb.ch).

Beyond the Passo del Bernina, at the heart of Val Poschiavo is the picturesque town of **Poschiavo ㉕**, where, alongside several remarkable churches, the *quartiere spagnolo*, with its colourful and richly ornamented facades, is certainly worth a visit: it was built around 1830 by emigrants returning from Spain.

In November 1999, the Vereina railway tunnel opened. The new railway line goes from Landquart near Chur to the Unter Engadin. It was built to allow travel to the Engadine all year round, as the Flüelapass between Davos and the Unter Engadin was often closed in winter and a detour had to be made.

For the even more athletic, the Bahn also offers a very unbureaucratic bicycle service. If you book two days in advance you can pick up your hired bike from any station on the Rhätische Bahn, ride off on it, and hand it in at the station of your choice once your tour is over. There are bicycles for rent – as well as mountain bikes – at most local tourist offices too. ❏

TIP

As a revival of an old custom, the Val Poschiavo is running guided winter walks on snowshoes. Contact the Poschiavo Tourist Office for more details (tel: 081 844 05 71; fax: 081 844 10 27; e-mail: info@valposchiavo.ch)

BELOW: the chestnut harvest in the Val Bregaglia.

TOURING THE SWISS LANDSCAPE

Switzerland's tourist industry has an enviable reputation for excellent facilities, reliability and cleanliness. But it was not always so…

Until relatively modern times, travellers shunned the Alps, regarding them as dangerous and inhospitable, and as little more than "considerable protruberances", thinly populated by suspicious and hostile mountain peasants. Hotels were non-existent and inns dirty and flea-ridden. Yet by the late 18th century peaks and glaciers were being explored and studied, less for their beauty than for their scientific interest. Then came the Romantic movement's cult of wild Nature, which endowed the mountains with a quasi-religious, near-mystical meaning, appealing to the upper-middle classes of Victorian Britain. Professional people flocked to the Alps, some to boldly scale the summits. The first climbers had been Swiss, but most peaks were conquered by Britons, notably the Matterhorn by Edward Whymper in 1865. Huts were built high up for climbers, and grand hotels and modest pensions at lower altitudes for an increasing number of ordinary tourists, some of them brought here on Thomas Cook's pioneering tours.

TOURIST CHIC

By the early 20th century a stay in an elegant Swiss resort such as Interlaken or St Moritz was the ultimate in chic. Few tourists came to an isolated Switzerland during the two world wars (1914–18 and 1939–45), but postwar affluence opened the country to a wider public. Today more visitors come here than ever before, staying in anything from a self-catering chalet to a luxury hotel.

△ **THE MATTERHORN**
Most visitors travel to Zermat for spectacular panoramic views of the majestic Matterhorn, but in fact the firs good sighting of the mountair can be had at Gornergrat.

▷ **MOUNTAIN RESORT**
The small village of Arosa, in a valley southeast of Chur, has developed into a popular winter and summer sports resort.

◁ **SUMMER WALKS**
A hiker takes a break and a little liquid refreshment at Allmenalp, above Kandersteg The scenery and a good choice of interesting trails attract hikers in the summer.

◁ **ON THE PASS**
Walkers on the cliff face of the Gemmipass, northeast of Sierre and several popular Valais holiday resorts and pretty hamlets.

△ **AT THE FOOT OF THE PEAK**
The village of Mürren is only accessible by cable car. Leave your vehicle in the valley below and enjoy the place in the shadow of the Eiger.

SWITZERLAND ON FOOT

A glance at a large-scale map of any part of Switzerland, lowlands or Alps, will reveal a dense mesh of footpaths, a paradise for walkers. The country's paths are not only comprehensively mapped, but they are impeccably waymarked, with signs indicating destinations and the approximate time necessary to reach them. One important distinction, clearly shown on the signs, is between an ordinary footpath, *Wanderweg* in German, and a mountain path, a *Bergweg*. Ordinary footpaths can be attempted by anyone, while a mountain path may involve crossing a high pass or rough surfaces, and is only for experienced, properly shod and equipped walkers. Many visitors content themselves with day walks, but it can be great fun to ramble from place to place. Staying overnight in alpine huts makes it possible to cover long distances at high altitude. Enthusiasts could try one of the great cross-country walks, like the historic Gotthard route, which traverses Switzerland from Basel on the Rhein via the St Gotthard Pass to Lake Lugano in Ticino.

▷ **SWISS SKIING**
Kleine Scheidegg is little more than a train terminal, yet it lies below the north face of the Eiger and above Wengen, a popular ski resort.

▽ **MOUNT PILATUS BY RAIL**
Visitors are transported around on an incomparable system of railways, including the steepest rack railway which runs from Alpnachstad to the summit of Pilatus.

◁ **TOURISM PIONEER**
Thomas Cook (1808–92), British founder of the travel company led the first group holidays to Switzerland.

ZÜRICH

Maps:
City 234
Area 241

Best known for its bankers and financers, Switzerland's pecuniary capital also has a thriving cultural life, with fine museums, art galleries and concert halls

Visitors to Zürich may sometimes get the feeling that the city is Switzerland itself, and that everything else – Lake Constance (Bodensee), the snow, the mountains and glaciers all the way to Lake Geneva (Lac Léman) – is no more than a picturesque wrapping, a recreation area for the hard-working inhabitants of the city's rich. Zürich is seen, especially by the people who live there, as the pulsating heart that gives life to the entire country.

The city does have some claims to dominance. Zürich's own form of Swiss-German – Züridütsch – has a somewhat wider audience than the other regional dialects. It is spoken by the announcers on Switzerland's radio programmes, most of which are produced in Zürich. Not only do the country's language and radio come from Zürich, its television, too, is based here, and films made for television are shot either in or around the city. What happens in Zürich is soon imitated in other parts of the country.

PRECEDING PAGES: an alleyway off the Oberdorfstrasse. **LEFT:** a warm autumn day on the Limmatquai. **BELOW:** one of Zürich's banks.

Arrival in Zürich

Travellers who approach the city by air will land at **Zürich Airport**, which is the largest in Switzerland – everything Swiss, apart from the mountains, is bigger in Zürich. To reach the centre many visitors board one of the efficient trains (four to six every hour) that run from the airport into the city.

One possible starting point is known as "Dörfli", in **Niederdorf**, which is at its best towards the evening. This narrow street in the old town, intersected by over 30 other streets, is traffic-free and lined with narrow Gothic houses, some perennially dingy, occupied by bakeries, delicatessens, tobacconists, second-hand bookshops and antiques shops. It is also a thriving residential area populated by some 5,000 people: some young and fashionable who have injected new life into the heart of the city; others, older people who were born here and who have chosen to stay, keep their original "village spirit" alive for as long as they can.

Niederdorf is also Zürich's oldest entertainment district, with many people attracted here by its nightlife. The place does not really pick up momentum until about eight in the evening; until then there are still empty tables in the restaurants and at the pavement cafés; the street musicians are busy tuning up, the prostitutes and club dancers are drinking coffee at the bar. Soon, however, everything is in full swing; the crowds fill the streets, the beer flows Munich-style, and the bars throb with music. Most of the activity stops at around midnight, but it continues on a smaller scale until at least 2 o'clock in the morning in a number of select nightclubs.

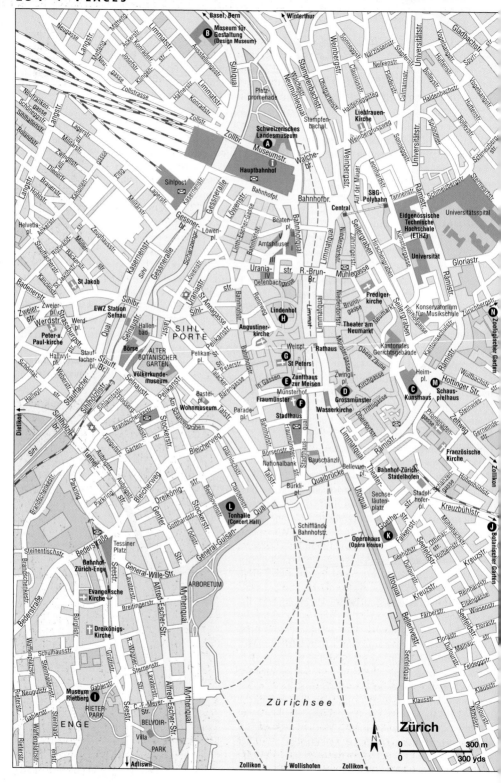

Zürich

0 _____ 300 m
0 _____ 300 yds

The busiest place in Zürich every morning is the **Hauptbahnhof** (main station). A sea of office workers – businessmen, secretaries, clerks and managers – flows into the city from the suburbs, which are continuing to eat their way further into the green and hilly outlying areas to the west, north and east. Whatever residents of Bern or Geneva might say, Zürich remains Switzerland's main commercial and cultural centre. It has also been voted the city with the best quality of life in the world. No wonder so many want to live and work here.

It was here, outside the old town on the former Schützenplatz, that Zürich first began to improve its links with the rest of Europe. The large, bright railway station hall was considered an architectural achievement of European significance in its time (built 1865–71). Since then, it has been the subject of extensive renovation, most recently in the mid-1990s.

Just behind the station, on Museumstrasse, is the excellent **Schweizerisches Landesmuseum** ⓐ (Swiss National Museum; open daily except Mon, 10am–5pm; free; tel: 01 218 65 11) , a castellated building erected in 1893. Inside, you will notice the enormous fresco by Ferdinand Hodler, showing the defeat of the Swiss Army by the French at Marignano in 1515. The fresco caused a nationwide uproar and gained Hodler international acclaim. This labyrinthine building comprises a collection of art work and exhibits in over 100 different rooms. There are archaeological finds, Roman relics, cultural artefacts dating from the Middle Ages, heraldic shields and a whole series of rooms and halls furnished in the styles of the 15th–18th century.

Also worth visiting is the **Museum für Gestaltung** ⓑ (Design Museum; open Tues–Thur 10am–8pm, Fri–Sun 11am–6pm; entrance fee; tel: 01 446 22 11), nearby at Ausstellungstrasse 60, with dynamic and cutting-edge temporary exhibits ranging from graphic design to poster art and photography.

Bahnhofstrasse and beyond

Bahnhofstrasse lies at the economic centre of the city. Some call it the finest street in Europe, and, though other cities possess their own special streets, the people of Zürich are particularly proud of this one. It extends from the Hauptbahnhof to the lake, bending slightly on the way. Along its length is an impressive display of wealth: the dazzling consumer temples of Globus and Jelmoli; the head offices of the "Gnomes of Zürich" (the five largest banks in Switzerland) and, in a shopping enclave bordered by Bahnofstrasse, **Storchengasse** and the **Limmat River**, every sort of fancy handbag, clothing or jewellery store even the most ardent shopper could hope for. This is the centre of Switzerland's opulence, as luxurious as anything you will find in Tokyo, London or New York.

An embodiment of everything Swiss, Bahnhofstrasse has all the typical virtues of order, cleanliness and punctuality. An everyday pair of trousers or a simple shirt is displayed in the shop windows like a masterpiece at the Louvre. Everything you can never afford to buy can be found here. The necessary loose change for such purchases can be obtained from the UBS – biggest of the famous Swiss banks – off **Paradeplatz**, the little square near the lower end of the street.

Alfred Escher, 19th-century councillor whose statue stands on Bahnhofstrasse.

BELOW: the bustling Bahnhofstrasse.

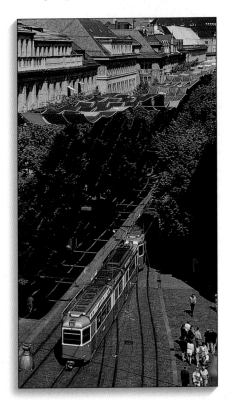

Map on page 234

Riverside treasures

The architecture on Bahnhofstrasse is also worth closer inspection: in particular the Art Nouveau facades of the department stores of Manor and St Annahof; the early iron construction of Jelmoli (Zürich's first glass palace, dating from the 1660s); the **Bank Julius Bär**, modelled on an Italian palazzo, and the head office of the **Credit Suisse Bank**, which takes up one whole side of the **Paradeplatz**.

Bahnhofstrasse has always been famous for its pristine condition: James Joyce once said that you could eat minestrone off the street without even needing a plate.

At the south end of Bahnhofstrasse, modern architect Arnold Bürkli used the excavated material from the city's many new building sites to fill in the large quay area at **Bürkliplatz** by the lake. Here is unquestionably the finest **post office** building in all Switzerland, and beside it the Renaissance *palazzo* of the **Fraumünsterpost** and the Renaissance-style **Stadthaus**. The area is also home to some of the city's most luxurious hotels. While strolling here, have a look at the guild buildings: Zunfthaus zur Saffran and Zunfthaus zur Zimmerleuten, and the Zunfthaus zum Rüden, which are all now expensive restaurants.

You should not, however, burden yourself with too many shopping bags before crossing one of the bridges to the east bank of the Limmat. Here in Niederdorf – an area which stretches along the riverbank for a kilometre or so, between Limmatquai and Niederdorfstrasse – under the roller blinds of the south-facing facades of the old houses, beside the quiet river and the contrasting loud roar of the traffic, Zürich has an almost Mediterranean feel to it. Between Bellevue and Central squares there is more than enough room to eat outside on summer evenings and, moreover, to see and be seen while consuming *coupes* (ice cream) and *Cüplis* (glasses of champagne). An afternoon passes by like a flash in the **Kunsthaus** ❻ (open Tues–Thur 10am–9pm, Fri–Sun 10am–5pm; entrance fee;

BELOW: a bank off Paradeplatz, the heart of the city's financial empire.

ANONYMOUS BANKING BUSINESS

Zürich has the third-largest stock exchange in the world after Tokyo and New York; above all, gold and silver are traded and stockpiled here and this is also the city where their international prices are fixed. Yet just which potentates from the east and the west are either laundering or accumulating money here is shrouded in secrecy – Swiss banking secrecy. Revelations about the secret Swiss possession of Nazi accounts and assets has heaped even more controversy than perhaps even the stoic Swiss are keen to endure.

The "Gnomes of Zürich" is an expression coined in the 1970s by a British Foreign Secretary who needed a quick explanation, and preferably also a scapegoat, for chaos in international money markets. The insinuation was of sinister manipulations behind a screen of state-sanctioned secrecy, and it reinforced the idea of the numbered Swiss bank account as the haven of drug dealers, terrorists, tyrants and shady tycoons generally.

As the history section of this book shows, the origin of Switzerland's wealth was plainly and simply booty: the haul of centuries of European wars, in which the legendary position of Swiss neutrality was in reality aimed more towards profit than pacifism.

tel: 01 253 84 84) on **Heimplatz**. Here you can race through two millennia of European art history in the best gallery in the country. The basic collection was founded in 1787 and has been further extended by purchases as well as generous endowments by private collectors. Now it offers a remarkably comprehensive documentation of both Swiss and other European art.

Nightlife

Zürich's nightlife has had a reputation as being rather Swiss: conservative and safe. If that was the case it's not any more. In recent years Zürich has loosened its shackles and dozens of chic new bars, cocktail lounges, restaurants and clubs have opened. Many of the more traditional places – Teutonic pubs serving frothy Pilsner and smoky little cellar bars – have remained, resulting in more than enough choice if you're planning a night on the town. A good place to start the evening is Niederdorf, where you can wander from café to café before choosing a restaurant for dinner. After dinner take a stroll along Langstrasse, the once seedy, now hip, red-light street.

The city's nightlife reflects its cosmopolitan nature, with bars and restaurants that take their inspiration from Morocco, Brazil and Vietnam. Sit sipping a Mai-Tai in a bar like Acapulco in trendy Neugasse and you'll forget you're in Zürich at all. Some of Zürich's uber-chic nightlife is expensive, but a good night out doesn't have to bankrupt you. In the increasingly fashionable district tucked away behind the Hauptbahnhof there are eastern European restaurants serving goulash and local bars where you can drink alongside budget-conscious students.

If you're not in the mood for nightlife of this sort, take a walk after dark (or if that's too much, a short trip on the Polybahn funicular from Central) to the so-

Map on page 234

TIP

Highlights of the **Kunsthaus** include Rodin's sculpture *The Gates of Hell*, as well as the largest set of works by painter Edvard Munch outside Scandinavia.

BELOW: the bustling cafés and bars of Niederdorf.

One of five stained-glass windows in the Fraumünster by Marc Chagall, which he completed in 1970 after three years' work, aged 83.

BELOW:
Zürich's Rathaus
(Town Hall).

called **Polyterrasse**, a terrace lookout point next to the city's polytechnic university. Here you will see Zürich nestling below you, its brightly lit landmarks towering out of the sea of lights. The **Predigerkirche**, a Gothic church, is in the foreground; behind it is the Romanesque-Gothic **Grossmünster** , with its twin towers, cut down to size somewhat after an 18th-century fire. Back on the west bank of the Limmat, the rococo **Zunfthaus zur Meisen** , a jewel-box of a building, contains a ceramics collection from the National Museum, highlights of which include faïence-style ceramic stoves. Alongside is the slim Gothic grandeur of the **Fraumünster** , once part of a convent; its stained-glass windows were created by Russian-born artist Marc Chagall (1887–1985). Also nearby is the tower of **St Peters-Kirche** , with its eye-catching clock face, which, at 8.7 metres (28 ft in diameter), is Europe's largest.

Architectural history

If you want to view some more interesting architecture, begin another jaunt on the **Lindenhof** , a small hill on the left bank of the Limmat with a fine view of the Limmatquai, the ETHZ (Federal Institute of Technology), and the university in the distance. It was on the Lindenhof that remains of the Roman "Turicum" were found: a customs post and a late Roman settlement in a fort.

Nestling around the Lindenhof, on various levels, is the most ancient part of the medieval town. The small streets are lined with high, very narrow houses. The city walls were moved several times to accommodate the growing settlement, and in 1642, within the span of a single generation, vast entrenchments were constructed.

As early as the baroque and rococo periods – several buildings in the Stadel-

Map
on page
234

hoferstrasse, the Haus zum Kiel and the Haus zum Rechberg in Hirschengraben date from this time – a new wealthy class of textile merchants and industrialists built themselves country seats in the nearby rural area, or even further afield out on the banks of the Zürichsee, away from the eyes of city society. Fine examples include the **Muraltengut** (Muralten Estate), the **Schlossgut** palace on the Au Peninsula, and the country seat of Schipf in Herrliberg. It was only when the entrenchments eventually disappeared in 1833 that Zürich began to develop into the Swiss-German metropolis it is today.

Around the Zürichsee

Zürich's lakeside is close to the city centre and can be reached from Bürkliplatz via a few shady walks – first following General-Guisan-Quai and Mythenquai, then crossing Belvoir Park – until one reaches **Villa Wesendonck**, situated on a small rise in **Rieterpark**.

It was here that the composer Richard Wagner set his famous *Wesendonck Lieder* to the words written by his beloved Mathilde. Not only Wagner, but also Franz Liszt, Gottfried Semper, Johannes Brahms and the Swiss poet Conrad Ferdinand Meyer were guests at this villa, which today houses the **Museum Rietberg** ❶ (open Tues–Sun 10am–5pm; entrance fee; tel: 01 202 45 28). It contains more than 2,000 cultural artefacts from faraway countries, which make you forget Zürich completely.

Equally exotic is the **Succulents Collection**, situated on the nearby Mythenquai, with over 5,000 magnificent plant specimens from Africa, South and Central America. Nature lovers might also like to visit the city's **Botanischer Garten** ❷ (Botanical Garden; open daily all year; entrance fee), at Zolliker-

"The bustling metropolis of swiftly gliding trams... of cosmopolitan restaurants on the great stone banks of the swiftly gliding snot-green... Limmat River, of jewelled escarpments and refugees of all kinds".

– TOM STOPPARD (1975)

BELOW: the PTT telecoms centre in Zürich-Altstetten.

strasse 107. Its greenhouses and the university's herbarium housing 1.5 million plants offer a real oasis of tranquillity after an eventful day.

Classical music and opera

Two buildings are worth visiting even if there is no performance that you want to see: the **Opernhaus**  (Opera House) at Bellevue on Sechseläutenplatz, restored at a cost of over 60 million francs, and the **Tonhalle**  (Concert Hall), in Gotthardstrasse, with its magnificent organ and unusually clear acoustics. Both buildings contain so much stucco and painting that the eye can happily take over from the ear during any boring stretches of a musical performance. No criticism of Zürich's two orchestras is intended, however; both of them are so generously supported by public funding that quality is assured. The operas are world-renowned, with a number of new productions each season.

Zürich's thriving alternative arts scene can be found at the **Rote Fabrik** (a former factory, now a music performance venue with everything from pop to dance music), the **Reithalle Gessnerallee** (once an army barracks) and the **Kanzlei-schulhaus**, previously a school and deprived of further funding from the public purse as an arts venue after a vote was taken in the autumn of 1990.

The highlight of musical and theatrical life for many people is the 10-day Theaterspektakel which takes place in August and September, when the very best in experimental productions from all over the world can be seen at the alternative culture venues. Others consider the peak of the season to be the Internationale Junifest Wochen held every June, under the patronage of the city's president. A cultural theme is given wide-ranging treatment and its various aspects, from painting to theatre, can be experienced in the city's tradi-

A polite welcome from a Zürich hotel doorman.

BELOW: the Münster-Brücke and Quai-Brücke, over Zürich's River Limmat.

tional cultural centres. Highlight number three in the arts calendar is the jazz festival, held at the end of October.

Rock music and cinema

Pop and jazz concerts are usually staged in the rather gloomy Volkshaus, Rote Fabrik or the sterile Kongresshaus, annexed to the Tonhalle. Or try one of the occasional music festivals that take place in the restored and very militaristic **Schützenhaus Albisgüetli**, an extravagantly laid-out, wooden Valhalla with its own tower and other wartime paraphernalia. It is also a congress and concert hall and contains a couple of restaurants. The huge rock concerts that are held in the **Hallenstadion** attract coachloads of fans, many travelling from Germany and Austria.

Then there are the discos. Once they were staid, but everything has changed in blazing fashion: Zürich now counts itself among a handful of cities in the world at the centre of the house, techno and trance music scene. Whether or not the throbbing bass lines and endlessly repetitive synthesised beats are to your taste, they have brought an unprecedented surge of youthful energy to the city. All-night rave parties are the norm, nightclubs are popping up everywhere, and the annual Street Parade is truly wild – particularly set against this buttoned-down town. Each August, some half a million Euro-youths descend upon the city for an afternoon parade and an all-night dance session.

For those who want more sedate diversion there is always the cinema. The most popular are those that show films in the original language, from the latest Hollywood box-office hits to the established classics, all the way to the outermost fringes of the avant-garde. Despite the distinct lack of cinemas, and the fact that nearly every home in Zürich has access to cable television, the city is still

Map on page 234

TIP

If you fancy a breath of fresh air while watching a film, the **Zürichhorn** is the city's open-air lakeside cinema, showing about 30 films, from latest releases to vintage slapstick, from mid-July to mid-August.

BELOW: Zürich's Tonhalle organ.

Dramatic shop window on Bahnhofstrasse.

very much a cinema city, where seeing the latest film is a must if you want to keep up with the cultural and social scene.

The Swiss stage

There is a good deal of theatre to enjoy in the city too, in many styles. In fact, one Zürich cabaret was the site of the first Dada event, an anti-traditional art movement that opened the way for Dalí, Picasso and a host of other artists trying new ideas and forms.

The **Schauspielhaus** , in its time a bastion of anti-fascist resistance, used to produce star-studded premières of Brecht plays, and up to the 1960s was famous for its modern classics by Swiss authors Max Frisch and Friedrich Dürrenmatt. Today the theatre programme ranges from Shakespeare, Schiller and Goethe to contemporary young Swiss playwrights. Beneath the main building, in the **Schauspielhauskeller**, there is also a venue for fringe theatre. This offers a more politically and artistically daring programme. Though the "Keller" is a big success among younger theatre audiences, its economic future is by no means assured. Around this large building a series of small, yet no less significant, theatres are found: the Theater am Neumarkt, Theater an der Winkelwiese, the Theater Heddy Maria Wettstein, and the atmospheric Theater Stok.

Folk festivals

The high point in Zürich's festival calendar is the **Sechseläuten** in April (mostly popular with the younger generation, while the older inhabitants tend to do anything to get away from the city for the duration).

During the Sechseläuten the medieval order of the guilds is celebrated in just

BELOW: the Schauspielhaus.

as exaggeratedly idealistic a manner as it was in the 19th century, when the festival was first celebrated. All the city's notables, dressed in a range of historical costumes representing the various artisans, take part in a procession. On horseback or in carriages, they parade through the crowded streets. The idea is to represent "permanency in change", as the official definition has it. The guilds then ride around a snowman, made of cotton wool, known as "Böögg" – an allegorical symbol of winter. In similar fashion to England's Guy Fawkes, he is perched on a funeral pyre, which is subsequently ignited, symbolising the end of winter.

Much the same is true of the **Knabenschiessen** held in September, when schoolboys and girls take part in a shooting competition, using live ammunition at a range of 300 metres (1,000 ft). The winner of the contest is proclaimed Champion Marksman. However, the main attraction on the Albisgüetli shooting range is a miniature town of booths and sideshows, the largest *chilbli* (fair) in Switzerland. The **Zürich Fasnacht** (carnival) is altogether a more subdued affair and not a patch on the one in Basel. Despite several attempts, it still has not managed to gain a real foothold in puritanical Zürich.

Zürich's many faces

Not all that much remains of the magnificent villas in the Enge, the Weinbergstrasse and the Riesbach quarters of town. Despite this, there is a pleasant walk that leads up from the lakeside to the Art Nouveau **Dolder Grand Hotel**, east of the city centre, and the residential area of middle-class Zürich. Those who live here usually inherit their houses and possess a considerable personal fortune. In the silence that hangs over these town houses and villas you can almost hear the interest and dividends piling up, assuring children and grandchildren of a decent standard of living. Up here on the so-called **Zürichberg** the view stretches for miles into the distance, right across the city. The suburban sprawl will soon extend the entire length of the lake all the way to Rapperswil.

A fun day trip in this area, requiring only a short tram ride from the city, is out to the **Zoologischer Garten** (Zoo; open daily 9am–5pm, until 6pm Mar–Oct; entrance fee; tel: 01 254 25 05) at Zürichbergstrasse 221. On the way to the zoo, take a peek at **James Joyce's gravesite**, which is on the right as you get off the tram. The Irish writer, who made the city his home, died here in January 1941. A statue of Joyce tops the memorial which marks his grave.

The shadier sides of the city face away from the lake. They begin in the former Limmat swamps, on either side of the railway line leading westward from the main station: shabby, gloomy blocks of flats which once provided shelter for the rural immigrants from the Catholic cantons, and later for those from Italy.

No other street in the city is livelier, day or night, than **Langstrasse**. It runs through an ethnically mixed area with a dazzling variety of lifestyles. In the daytime there are Turkish and Italian delicatessens, and Hong Kong second-hand clothes and shoe shops; in the evening there are the restaurants with their exotic specialities, alongside the *Beizen* (traditional inns) and bars.

Far into the small hours, the pimps patrol the narrow streets in their limousines, keeping an eye on a

Map on page 234

TIP

Zürich's Dolder Grand Hotel is an architectural attraction in its own right: a sumptuous 19th-century turreted palace, complete with nine-hole golf course, swimming pool with wave machine, and extensive grounds.

BELOW: the Dolder Grand, one of Zürich's top hotels.

BELOW:
people sunbathing on the banks of Zürich's lake.

host of glittering girls from all over the world and giving the city's right-thinking moralists something to complain about.

Because the teeming life here is so attractive, and because it is so close to the city centre, rents are rocketing, and many foreigners are having to move out while newcomers move in. The latest sign of gentrification in this former workers' district is the nearby **Kunsthalle** exhibition centre, which has made a name for itself with varying international contemporary art shows. The waterfront area known as the **Seefeld** – stretching from the opera house south and west to Mühle Tiefenbrunnen – has become similarly trendy. Here are *Beizen* to be seen eating in, shops to be seen buying clothes in, and the time-honoured, wooden **Utoquai Swimming Baths** – the only place to be seen swimming in (if your scantily clad body is worth seeing at all).

Local issues

Conflicts tend to surface more frequently and violently in Zürich than elsewhere in Switzerland. The housing shortage, noise levels, car-exhaust emissions – whatever is currently bothering the population – is expressed here in its own special way. The "Globus Riot" of 1968, when Zürich's students attempted their own version of the May riots in Paris, and the "Movement" of 1980, when young people hurt by the recession in the 1970s showed a new creativity – these have not been the only major disturbances in this city. Still unsolved, and more urgently in need of solution than ever before, is the drug problem, which has been around since the 1960s. Gone are the days when the police had only to hunt down ordinary pot smokers; today the problem is a tough heroin and crack cocaine scene. Many feel that the police are not up to dealing with the

problems, and level the same criticism at the government, whose response until recently has apparently been to turn a blind eye.

The city's main drug area used to be Platzspitz, which – following official intervention – became a public park, clear of undesirable elements. The dealers and addicts are now to be found in other parts of town. Middle-class society seems to be better at managing money than dealing with the drugs problem.

There is more to see on the outskirts of the city and anyone who has not tired of touring, or shopped till they have dropped, will find what they are looking for in the amazingly varied shopping centres in Spreitenbach.

It is both a residential and a working area: a typical agglomeration stretching to the west to Baden, Brugg and Aarau and – in the opposite direction – as far as Winterthur and beyond. This is where the lower middle classes live out their T-shirted *Gemütlichkeit* (comfortable life) with their families. They are the kind of people that one often meets on holiday, or finds oneself sitting next to on the S-Bahn, and thinks of as the typical Swiss. These concrete housing estates, which were built in the 1960s and 1970s, contain more yodellers, accordion players and wearers of traditional local costume than all of the mountain cantons put together.

TIP

Block 37 in Winterthur is the largest indoor sports park in Europe. Its high-energy facilities include a roller park, volleyball court and a climbing wall. Open daily; entrance fee; tel: 052 204 07 00; www.block.ch

Winterthur: city of art

Typical Swiss countryside – that of the popular image – lies close to Zürich. The American writer F. Scott Fitzgerald commented on this quality in *Tender is the Night*: "In Zürich there was a lot besides Zürich – the roofs upled the eyes to tinkling cow-pastures, which in turn modified hilltops farther up – so life was a perpendicular starting off to a postcard heaven". The citizens of Zürich tend only to dream of the country. They seldom actually go there, and when they do they tend not to stay for long.

BELOW: Zürich's Haus zum oberen Schonenberg.

Not more than a half-hour's drive or express train away from Zürich, the city of **Winterthur ①** makes an easy day trip. Winterthur was founded in 1170 by the Kyburgs, but had its origins in the Gallo-Roman camp of Vitudurum. It has been unlucky more than once in its history: in 1467 the Habsburgs pledged this market town to Zürich, and ever since that time it has been in a state of permanent rivalry with its more powerful neighbour, the canton's capital, which lies only 25 km (15 miles) away, and which has jealously guarded its civic privileges. It was, however, this competition that acted as a catalyst for Winterthur's industrialisation during the 19th century, after protectionist trade barriers had been removed.

It all began with the textile industry – Europe's first textile factory was in Winterthur – which soon extended its sphere of activities to towns in the Zürich Oberland situated beside rivers, using the hydraulic power the water provided. Textile manufacturing then led to the textile machine industry, and diversification followed: Winterthur produced turbines for power stations, ships' propellers and engines, and then locomotives and railway carriages. Paradoxically, it was the planned expansion of the Swiss rail network that ended up isolating Winterthur from the major transport routes so that it was finally beaten by its more successful competitor, industrialised Zürich.

Zürich's gold even finds its way onto gilded window decorations.

Meanwhile, another facet of the early stage of rapid industrial expansion was the need for a lifestyle and a culture appropriate to individuals' personal standing. This manifested itself in various buildings as well as in private patronage in music and the fine arts, something which has formed the basis of Winterthur's reputation as a centre of culture to this day.

The city has several museums including the Dr Oskar Reinhart collection which takes up two whole buildings: the **Römerholz** collection and the **Oskar Reinhart Foundation**, at Haldenstrasse 95 (open Tues–Sun 10am–5pm; entrance fee; tel: 052 269 27 40). The striking thing about both is not only the sheer number of works of art on view but also their quality, ranging from the old masters right through to modern classics. Artists whose work features in the museum include Brueghel the Elder, Rubens, Rembrandt, El Greco and Goya, and several 19th-century French artists.

There are three other well-stocked museums: the **Fotomuseum** (open Tues–Fri noon–6pm, weekends 11am–5pm; entrance fee; tel: 052 233 60 86) at Grüzenstrasse 44 is the only photographic museum in German-speaking Switzerland; the **Gewerbemuseum** (Museum of Applied Arts and Design; open Tues–Sun 10am–5pm, Thur until 8pm; entrance fee; tel: 052 267 51 36) at Kirchplatz 14, which houses the Kellenberger Watch Collection, including the world-famous console watches of the Liechti watch dynasty; and the **Villa Flora** (open Tues–Sat 2–5pm, Sun 11am–3pm; entrance fee; tel: 052 212 99 66) at Tösstalstrasse 44, which has works by 19th- and early 20th-century artists such as Cézanne, Van Gogh, Matisse, Renoir, Rodin, Vallotton and Toulouse-Lautrec.

BELOW: Rapperswil Castle.

One surviving relic of prosperous 19th-century Winterthur, apart from its industry, is the delightful – and still intact – old town, which more than stands up to comparison with that of Zürich. The **Marktgasse**, with its late-Gothic and Baroque town houses, has been turned into a pedestrian precinct, and is so lively in its own provincial way that a gentle shopping trip here can be a lot more enjoyable than one undertaken in its more hectic, neighbouring city.

The surrounding countryside

Reppischtal, the **Türler See**, the **Greifensee**, the **Forch**, the hills of the **Albis**, the **Etzel** and the **Pfannenstil** are popular weekend excursions for Zürich's residents, but you should not be put off by the thought of crowds. They offer excellent hiking opportunities and enthusiasts can try a trip up Zürich's "home" mountain, the **Uetliberg** ❷, for a magnificent panorama of city, lake and Alps. For a longer trek, follow the footpaths across the wooded cliffs, across the *Seedamm* to **Rapperswil** ❸, around 40 km (25 miles) away.

This small country town, once so important that on one occasion it actually went to war against Zürich, is delightful with its striking-looking castle and its quay. Hotels and fish restaurants which have all the charm of establishments on a genuine Italian *piazza* tempt visitors to spend the night. The Stäfner Clevner and other wines produced around Zürichsee are sure to put you in the right frame of mind. The way back into the city leads along Seestrasse – the "Gold Coast", so called because of its high incomes and low tax brackets.

The country towns of Regensdorf, Grüningen and Eglisau are all close by; as are the Roman citadel of Irgenhausen, the Fahr and Kappel monasteries and the wine villages of Marthalen, Oberstammheim and Unterstammheim. No tour of Switzerland would be complete, however; without a walk through the lowlands around Zürich's lake.

Map on page 241

Painters' lake

Zürichsee reaches almost into the heart of the city itself and is therefore considered part of "Zürich Land". With its gentle shores, and the Alps in the distance which tend to look even bigger and closer because of the *Föhn* (a warm southerly wind), it inspired the English artist J.M.W. Turner to paint some of his best skyscapes. Jump aboard one of the lake's nostalgic paddle-steamers, complete with its own restaurant, and take a relaxed ride south to the waterside taverns on the **Au Peninsula ❹** or, further south still, to the romantic island of **Ufenau ❺**. The numerous and very well-maintained fish restaurants at the waterfront are flanked by the motorboats of the rich – and possibly famous.

The excellent Zürcher Verkehrsverbund transport network, as Swissly efficient as ever, enables you to do all of this even during a relatively short stay. It is important, though, to remember to take plenty of small change along with you: manned ticket-offices – apart from those in railway stations – are relatively thin on the ground, especially in the remote spots, and often you will need to buy tickets from an automatic ticket machine. It is also a good idea to keep a plan of the various transport networks handy, because the machines can be difficult to understand.

The Swiss refer to the Glarus valley with fond condescension as the "Zigerschlitz" – with reference to its green Schabziger cheese – one of the oldest-known types of hard cheese in the world (see also Cheese, page 81).

BELOW:
the gentle slopes around Zürichsee.

Undiscovered Glarus

An excursion southeast of Zürich leads to the canton of **Glarus ❻**, its tiny capital of the same name, and some beautiful surrounding valleys. Head out of Zürich on the N3, passing Kilchberg, until Näfels where you can join highway 17. The distance from the city probably makes this excursion more than a day trip, but there is plenty to do along the way. Today known for its winter sport facilities, the canton of Glarus also has a colourful history. The city's uncontrolled hordes managed to defeat a Habsburg army in 1388 and thus secure their independence as part of the Confederation. The valley, almost 40 km (25 miles) long, was a harsh environment for those who settled there – Rhaeto-Romans, then Alemannians.

While times became much easier for the residents of Glarus, they still had to compete with the destructive winds of the *Föhn (see page 92)*. While it occurs in Inner Switzerland, **Graubünden** and elsewhere too, it has set fire to a particularly large number of houses in this canton's 30 villages or so. The city of Glarus was almost completely burned down in 1861 by a fire fanned by the warm winds of the *Föhn*; it was rebuilt to a regular grid-pattern with many fine Neoclassical buildings.

An interesting local tradition still upheld after 700 years, is the Glarus Landsgemeinde. This deeply democratic community meeting is still popular in this

canton situated between the Linth Plain, Walensee and the Tödi, despite all attempts to abolish it. Just as in the half-cantons Appenzell Innerrhoden and Appenzell Ausserrhoden, each citizen of Glarus can sit in the "Ring" – an open air assembly in the town centre, and directly criticise the canton's government, or even table their own motions through a mass show of hands. Glarus Landsgemeinde is held on the first Sunday of May and draws large crowds to the spectacle, which is treated as a day of festivities as well as governance.

Past and present can be viewed at the city's attractive **Kunsthaus** (Art Museum; open Tues–Fri 2–6pm, Sat & Sun 11am–5pm; tel: 055 640 25 35), which has works from Swiss artists dating from the 19th century to the present day. The museum has an excellent reputation for its visiting exhibitions of modern art.

Ski jumping and hiking

Before **Walenseestrasse** had been dug along the bank of the lake, when the mouth of the **River Linth** was an unspoilt natural paradise, the road leading from Mollis over the Kerenzerberg still provided the best opportunity for lowlanders to reach the winter sports resorts in Graubünden. These days, however, **Filzbach** and **Obstalden**, the two villages up here, are largely free of traffic, and because of its remoteness the region is ideal for hikers.

The first ever ski jumping in Alpine winter sport took place in Glarus, whose ski club, founded in 1892, is the oldest in Switzerland. The Pragellauf, a cross-country skiing event that led from the Muota Valley in the canton of Schwyz across to the **Klöntalersee**, a real Alpine gem, and then to the main town of Glarus, was for many years the most popular in Switzerland. In fact, its win-

BELOW: painting by Albert Anker, from Winterthur's Reinhart collection.

Map
on page
241

ter sports and mountain climbing have made Glarus an excellent choice for those in the know. **Elm**, in the Sernftal, is the place where American and Swiss women's downhill skiing teams sometimes train for competitions. Four times a year, on 12 and 13 March, 30 September and 1 October, a natural spectacle occurs in Elm when the sun shines through the Martin Hole, an opening in the side of nearby Mt Tschingelhorner, and onto the village church steeple.

Many years ago, before measures were taken to prevent them, the risk of avalanches was high in the villages of this valley. This was largely because of the vast difference in height between the valley floor (660 metres/2,000 ft above sea level) and the highest mountain, the majestic **Tödi** (3,614 metres/12,000 ft above sea level).

The Tödi seals off the relatively narrow valley. The furthest village inside the valley is Linthal, and high above on the mountain the River Linth has its source; further down, after it has flown out of Zürichsee, it is known as the Limmat. Linthal is a village on a pass, too. The **Klausen Pass**, Switzerland's longest, leads from here over into the Schächen Valley in the canton of **Uri**. It was here that the European Mountain Car Rally Championships were held in 1922 and 1934.

Glarus is also a paradise for hikers, with its gorges, forests, mountains, lakes and over 100 km (62 miles) of continuous hiking and cycling trails. Any local tourist office can point you in the right direction, offer advice and probably supply basic maps of the trails.

Flower nursery on the fertile pastures of the Zürichsee.

Unexpected opulence

It is hard to believe that as recently as the 18th and 19th centuries this canton was the most highly industrialised in Switzerland, as well as one of the most prosperous, along with Zürich and Basel. The history of the local textile industry and of the early phase of industrialisation is well documented in the cantonal museum, situated inside the remarkable **Freuler-Palast** (open Apr–Nov Tues–Sun 10am–noon, 2–5.30pm; entrance fee; tel: 055 612 13 78) in the town of **Näfels**.

It was in the service of the French kings that the Freuler family and their relations made their fortune. This in turn enabled Kaspar Freuler (1590–1651) to construct what has come to be known here modestly as "the big house" in his home town. Many questions remain. Who designed the building? Where did the craftsmen who created the stucco ceilings and the stone staircases come from? Who furnished the rooms so majestically, and what made Kaspar Freuler build a palace on such a scale in Glarus when he was hardly ever there? All these questions remain unanswered.

There are several other treats within the canton of Glarus, such as **Braunwald**, the only pedestrianised spa town in eastern Switzerland, built on various rocky terraces with fine hotels and guesthouses, as well as plenty of places to eat and drink. The resort affords unparalleled views of the area, and the hiking opportunities are excellent; it is the very model of a Swiss Alpine resort. ❏

BELOW:
the village of Elm.

THE NORTHEAST

*The rural northeast is one of Switzerland's best-kept secrets –
visitors can still enjoy tranquil, picturesque medieval settlements
and lush green Alpine valleys; but how long will peace reign?*

Map on page 254

Bern

Switzerland, so the saying goes in Bern, Zürich, Basel and Luzern, "ends at Winterthur". What this means is that in the eyes of many Swiss the northern and especially the eastern parts of the country are of little relevance to the way the Confederation sees itself, and if through some bizarre twist of fate the country were ever forced to relinquish any of its territory, the east would be the first part to come under consideration because it is almost in Germany anyway.

In the opinion of the average Swiss citizen, northern and eastern Switzerland are only of secondary importance industrially, culturally and touristically. In short: eastern Switzerland is seen as a border region.

As with most sayings, the vox populi expressed here is, first and foremost, merely an expression of accepted wisdom; northern and eastern Switzerland need not fear either industrial or cultural comparison with other parts of the country. Measured in terms of industrial output alone, the cantons of northeastern Switzerland – not including the two Appenzell half-cantons – occupy a solid mid-field position. The special characteristic of this often-neglected part of the country, however, is its landscape and cultural heritage.

Thurgau, with its meadows, forests, fruit plantations and monasteries, has been spared the excesses of industrial expansion. If one disregards the increasing clusters of detached family houses that have sprung up almost overnight along the motorway to Zürich, many of the small towns and villages in Thurgau still seem draped in history. The weight of the past is instantly felt in Schaffhausen and nearby Stein am Rhein, with their medieval half-timbered houses and fortresses. The monastery town of St Gallen, both baroque and sober-looking, reflects the two faces of the people of eastern Switzerland: traditional and yet gregarious.

The landscape in the two Appenzell half-cantons, with its lush green hills and neat farmhouses set against the imposing backdrop of the Alpine Massif, is delightful. The area around the broad expanse of **Lake Constance** (Bodensee), with its colourful, flowery parks and vine-covered slopes alternating with reeds and marshes, with its fields and orchards, its forests, meadows and historic towns, fishing villages and wine villages, is a scenic oasis on a scale scarcely equalled elsewhere in Switzerland.

Thus, in terms of landscape and history, northern and eastern Switzerland seem able to exist quite happily without the approval of the rest of the country.

There is, however, a grain of truth in the quotation at the beginning of this chapter: a part of the country with a character all its own actually does begin beyond Winterthur. Northeastern Switzerland is a Swiss creation that is not so much oriented towards Zürich or Bern – the industrial and political centres of

PRECEDING PAGES: the abbey library in St Gallen. **LEFT:** the Moors' Fountain in Schaffhausen. **BELOW:** young reveller at Döttingen's wine festival.

Switzerland respectively – as towards the cultural region of Lake Constance with the three countries (Switzerland, Austria and Germany) surrounding it.

The Lake Constance area has very little to do with national borders. Here, in the basin formed by the "Swabian Ocean" (as the lake is popularly referred to), the common Alemannic culture, unique geographical location and strong trading history have contributed to the formation of a region that is occasionally described, perhaps exaggeratedly, as "the cultural heart of western Europe".

Ancient unity

At one time the Alemannic region was unified, and vestiges of this unity survived in central Europe until quite late in history. Eastern Switzerland's city of St Gallen, for instance, had its own policy of alliances, mostly directed towards southern Germany, right into the 14th century. Throughout the 1st millennium AD, the abbey in St Gallen played a leading role in the region; indeed it was among the most important abbeys of the Carolingian and Ottonian empires.

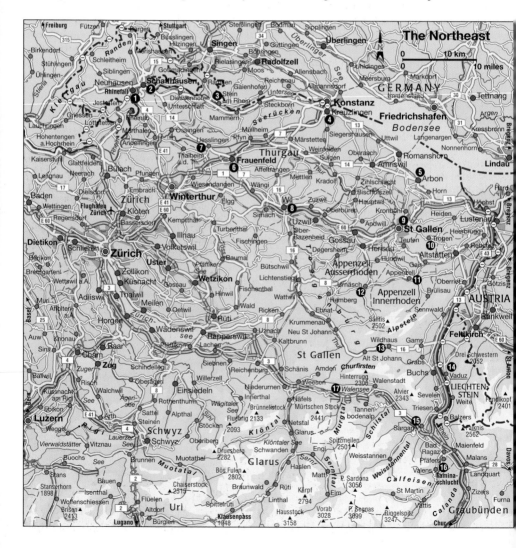

Map on page 254

The regions around the main national borders are closely related, so close in fact that in a referendum in 1919, most of the citizens of Austria's Vorarlberg region declared themselves in favour of annexation with Switzerland. However, the central governments in Vienna and Bern were not eager to comply with their wishes, and so the dream of unification in the Rhein Valley was never fulfilled.

The people of northeastern Switzerland do not mind being seen as peripheral by their fellow Swiss. What really hurts them, however, is a lack of attention to them as far as politics, industry and tourism are concerned. For tourists there are advantages to the region's "separateness". It has steadfastly remained an area apart from the rest of the country, a region off the beaten track that is full of beauty, some of its obvious, some of it hidden away and needing to be discovered.

Around the Rhine

The city of St Gallen, the largest in eastern Switzerland, can be reached quickly and easily from Zürich by motorway on the N1, or by intercity train, but anyone with time to spare would do well to make their way into eastern Swiss territory via either **Rapperswil** on **Lake Zürich**, or the **Toggenburg**. Alternatively go via the **Linth Plain**, **Lake Walenstadt** and the **Rhein Valley**. Yet probably the most appealing route is the one that starts off in the north, following the course of the Rhein, and then describing a huge curve before entering the depths of eastern Switzerland. Travellers choosing this route will become acquainted with the magnificent landscape, and can travel through many historic little towns before the broad basin of Lake Constance finally opens up before them.

The first stop on this route is **Neuhausen**, an industrial suburb of Schaffhausen as well as the starting point for a descent to the **Rhein Falls** ❶,

The Goldenes Schäfli in St Gallen is one of Switzerland's oldest inns (see page 261).

BELOW: the Rhein Falls, near Schaffhausen.

considered to be one of the most spectacular natural sights in the country.

This grand spectacle of crashing water and flying spray can be enjoyed from many different observation points at the foot of the falls. However, anyone who wants a real close-up of the thundering mass of water – at peak times it can reach 1,250 cubic metres/sec (37,500 cubic ft/sec) as it crashes over the 150-metre (500-ft) wide cliffs – can travel by ferry either to the rock in the middle of the falls or to **Wörth Castle**, which used to be the customs house for Rhein shipping.

Just a few kilometres northeast of Neuhausen is **Schaffhausen** ❷, also called the Rheinfallstadt, because of the waterfall, or Munotstadt, because of the Munot Fortress that towers above the city.

A stroll through Schaffhausen reveals that, despite industrialisation (watches, textiles and machinery), it has managed to retain many of its historic buildings. The "old town" is relatively new: a fire almost destroyed the medieval section in 1372, but it is one of the best-preserved townscapes in Switzerland.

The **Haus zum Ritter**, on the corner of Vordergasse and Münstergasse, is worth a visit. On the exterior of the house are copies of frescoes by the Schaffhausen artist Tobias Stimmer. The remains of the original facade, dating from 1570, are preserved at the nearby Museum zu Allerheiligen. The old part of the town is full of Gothic buildings, rows of magnificent residential buildings and guild halls designed in the baroque and rococo styles. Oriels – richly ornamented projecting windows on upper floors – ancient fountains, small squares and sleepy corners can be discovered during a stroll in this pedestrianised quarter.

BELOW: the Munot
Fortress in
Schaffhausen.

South of Vordergasse, on Klosterstrasse, is the reformed **Münster**, which dominates the town centre. Part of the former Benedictine monastery of **Allerheiligen** (All Saints), it is a masterpiece of Romanesque architecture. The monks left the monastery centuries ago during the Reformation, and now the buildings house the **Museum zu Allerheiligen** (open Tues–Sun 11am–5pm; free; tel: 052 633 07 77).

Nearby, south towards the river on Baumgartenstrasse is a former textile factory that has been transformed into the **Hallen für neue Kunst** (New Art Halls; open Tues–Sat 3–5pm, Sun 11am–5pm; entrance fee; tel: 052 625 25 15). This outstanding museum of contemporary art exhibits key works by 12 leading international artists from the 1960s and 70s. Among the artists featured in the 5,500-sq. metre (59,000-sq. ft) space are Bruce Nauman and Joseph Beuys, who is represented by his most famous installation *Kapital*.

A paved path leads up to the **Munot Fortress** (open daily May–Sept 8am–8pm, Oct–Apr 9am–5pm; free). This circular fortress was built between 1564 and 1589 as a bastion against Germany, to defend Schaffhausen, the only estate on the right bank of the Rhein held by the Confederation. It was built according to the principles outlined in Albrecht Dürer's theory of fortification of 1527. The fortress is 49 metres (161 ft) in diameter, with a panoramic view of the town from the battlements; at their foot lies a fragrant rose garden.

Swiss vineyards

There are various excursions from Schaffhausen: to wine villages such as **Wilchingen** to the south, or to the mountains of the **Randen**, the easternmost part of the Jura mountain range, or across the vineyard slopes of the **Klettgau**. This quiet border region of Switzerland is an excellent place for walking tours, and the Klettgau is famed for its wines. Here, around the smart little village of **Hallau**, is the largest continuous wine-growing area in eastern Switzerland, covering nearly 300 hectares (750 acres), and a museum of wine growing. Far more red wine is produced here (Blauburgunder) than white (mostly Rieslings and Sylvaners). Just as delightful as Hallau is Wilchingen, the second-largest wine-growing area in the canton.

The section of river between Schaffhausen and Stein am Rhein is considered one of the finest in Europe: largely unspoilt natural scenery, and historic sites such as the former monastery estate of **Paradies**, or the former monastery of **St Katharinental**, never fail to enchant the eye of the beholder.

Stein am Rhein , at the gateway to the Untersee (one of the western arms of Lake Constance), is another gem of medieval architecture, accessible by road or a 20-km (12-mile) boat trip along the Rhein, east from Schaffhausen. The town's former **Benedictine Abbey of St Georgen** is considered to be one of the best-preserved medieval abbeys in the entire German-speaking region. Inside is the small **Klostermuseum St Georgen**. The reformed **Parish Church of Burg** (first mentioned in a document dated 799) is the oldest church in the Schaffhausen area.

The town's central square, the **Rathausplatz** with its large, 10-cornered fountain, the **Marktbrunnen**, is striking because of the magnificent facades and the sheer quantity of frescoes and oriels on the surrounding buildings. Particularly worthy of note among this wealth of paintings are the frescoes on the **Gasthaus Roter Ochsen**, on the **Haus zur Vorderen Krone** and on the **Haus zum Weissen Adler**, to the left of the Town Hall.

Map on page 254

TIP

The Rhein Falls is the site of a fantastic firework display, part of the Swiss National Day celebrations on 1 August every year.

BELOW:
the wine village of Wilchingen.

Enjoying the cattle market and festival at Urnäsch.

At Rathausplatz, the main street connects with the lower part of the town. Half-timbered houses, a feature of the Lake Constance region, determine the character of the townscape. The heavy oak beams bend beneath the weight of centuries; sometimes entire house facades seem to be on the point of collapse. Continue on to **Untertor**, the ornate gatehouse which once formed part of the medieval fortifications, as did the **Thieves'** or **Witches' Tower** at the lower end of **Choligasse**.

After a stroll past the facades, visit the **Puppenmuseum** (Doll Museum; open Apr–early Jan Wed & Sun 3–5pm; tel: 071 672 4655) in the "culture barn" at Scloss Girsberg – a historic house that also runs a summer theatre and the Zeppelin museum (also in the culture barn; the same opening hours as the Doll Museum), or the **Lindwurm Museum** (open Mar–Oct Wed–Mon 10am–5pm; entrance fee; tek: 052 741 25 12) on Understadt, with its 19th-century agricultural exhibits. Then take a break in one of the town's numerous wine taverns, which radiate *Gemütlichkeit* (a comfortable warmth) with their oriels and Gothic wooden ceilings.

The Bodensee

Observe the landscape from the heights of the **Seerücken** on an autumn day when the light is fading and the Untersee has turned a dull and tired-looking grey: water and sky blend into one another perfectly. The **Höri Peninsula** takes on the appearance of a smudged pencil drawing, and the island of **Reichenau**, with its Benedictine monastery founded by St Pirmin in 723, can just be made out in the distance. The sights of the Untersee are not confined to culture and history; the villages on the Untersee also exude tranquillity: **Mammern**, **Steckborn**, **Berlingen**, **Mannenbach** and **Ermatingen**.

On the gentle slopes surrounding the lake the traveller is greeted by imposing country houses steeped in history. Surrounding the quiet bay in Mammern is the huge park (90,000 sq. metres/295,000 sq. ft) belonging to **Schloss Mammern**, where knights, and later the abbots of Rheinau, once resided. Also forming part of the castle, which today houses a clinic, is a **baroque chapel** dating from 1749 that contains noteworthy frescoes.

Salenstein, with its medieval core, rises high above Mannenbach. Further on, on the way to Ermatingen and at one of the finest points of the Untersee, **Schloss Arenenberg**, partially hidden by trees, can be seen at the top of a steep hill. The modest exterior belies its historical importance, particularly in the 19th century. After Bonaparte's downfall Hortense de Beauharnais lived here with her son, who was later to become the Emperor Napoleon III. After the latter's abdication, the fêted Empress Eugenie spent time at this country seat. The grand furnishings at Arenenberg include royal relics, such as a marble statue of Napoleon, furniture obviously influenced by the Egyptian campaign, and court portraits featuring all the finery of the Deuxième Empire.

In contrast, there are simple farming hamlets on the Seerücken, and villages down by the lake, where fishing is still a favourite local pursuit. Many restaurants pride themselves on their distinguished past. The **Hotel Adler** in Ermatingen – an imposing-looking half-timbered building – is the oldest hotel in the canton of Thurgau; Alexandre Dumas, Ernst Jünger, Thomas

BELOW: oriel windows and painted facades in Stein am Rhein.

Mann, Graf Zeppelin, Hermann Hesse and Henri Guisan, the general in command of the Swiss Army during World War II, all dined here.

The "Swabian Ocean" continues along its shore, and a small detour can be made to the German island of Reichenau. Back on the mainland head east to **Kreuzlingen** ❹, a suburb of German Konstanz, where the lake widens, the banks slope more gently, the landscape loses something of its charm and industrialisation increases. Continue southeast to the small town of **Arbon** ❺, or Arbor Felix as it was known in the ancient world, with its 16th-century fort **Schloss Arbon**, which houses a **History Museum** (open May–Sept daily 2–5pm, Oct–Nov & Mar–Apr Sun 2–5pm; entrance fee; tel: 071 446 10 58) displaying finds from Neolithic and Bronze Age lake dwellings as well as from Roman times. The promenade here is an ideal place for a stroll. Southeast is **Rebstein** which has a small castle.

Kretzer or Egli, (lake fish) fried in butter or baked in oil, and accompanied by a fruity Riesling or Sylvaner from the region, is a typical speciality.

Carthusian monastery

By branching off to the south of the Untersee and crossing the ridge above the lake, visitors can reach the **River Thur** and **Frauenfeld** ❻, by means of footpaths. The old town of the capital of the canton of Thurgau is dominated by buildings from the period after the fires of 1771 and 1778, which reduced the number of medieval houses in the town to those between the **Town Hall** and the Reformed church. Another relic of medieval times is the **castle**, which stands on a sandstone rock above the banks of the **Murg**. From Frauenfeld, in the centre of the canton, it is a short detour north to one of the finest and best-preserved monastic complexes of northeastern Switzerland.

In **Uesslingen** ❼, set into the hilly landscape, lies the former **Carthusian Monastery of Ittingen**. Founded in 1152 as an Augustinian priory and rebuilt in several stages from the mid-16th century, the monastery is a unique mixture of styles. Since 1982 it has been used as a conference and cultural centre, and the restored buildings house a **Carthusian Museum** (open Apr–Sept Mon–Fri 2–6pm, Sat & Sun 11am–6pm, Oct–Mar Mon–Fri 2–5pm, Sat & Sun 11am–5pm; entrance fee; tel: 052 748 41 20) and the Thurgau canton **Museum of Art** (which also features a collection of naïve art; open Mon–Fri 2–5pm, Sat & Sun 11–5pm, May–Sept until 6pm; entrance fee; tel: 052 748 41 20).

Head southeast from Frauenfeld to reach **Wil** ❽, which lies halfway between St Gallen and Winterthur. It is an ordinary little town, with next to no tourism, offering visitors the chance to experience genuine Swiss daily life. Wil possesses a faceless agglomeration of houses, and streets that are totally devoid of people the moment the shops have shut. The old town, in contrast, lies on a hill at the bottom of the valley, and is remarkably unspoilt. The Catholic **Parish Church of St Nicholas** can be admired here, as can the **Dominican convent** and also the **Baronenhaus**, the most important neoclassical residence in the canton of St Gallen.

St Gallen

According to local history books, the "decisive factor in the founding of St Gallen… was the finger of God." This refers to the saga in which the Irish monk Gall, in the year 612, was wandering through the "wild valley

BELOW: regatta on Bodensee (Lake Constance).

TIP

North of St Gallen Cathedral on Museumstrasse are a group of museums definitely worth a visit: the Kirchhoferhaus Museum, the Museum of Art and Natural History and the Historical Museum (Neues Museum).

BELOW:
half-timbered house in Thurgau.

of the Steinach" and fell into a thorn bush; he interpreted this as an invitation to stay. A bear helped Gall to build the monastery he founded, and the bear thus became the heraldic animal of the city of **St Gallen ❾**.

There are no external conditions whatsoever to justify the founding of the city. St Gallen does not lie on a river (if one disregards the Steinach, which is little more than a stream); in fact St Gallen, the economic centre of eastern Switzerland, lies somewhere in the middle of a no-man's-land, jammed between the Rosenberg hills and the beginnings of the Alps sloping up towards the Appenzell district. Indeed, had an Irish monk not stumbled into the thorn bush, it is hard to imagine how else St Gallen could justify its presence today.

St Gallen's cultural significance lies in the sacred art of the type to be found in the **cathedral** (formerly the Collegiate Church) and the **Abbey Library** (Stiftsbibliothek). The library hall built in 1763 is a fine example of rococo architecture and it contains rare treasures too.

In the 15th century a ring of houses was erected around the newly built monastery precinct after a fire. The town, now famous for its textiles, developed from this centre, dominated by the baroque church, in a northwesterly direction. St Gallen also contains a series of exceptional baroque facades; notably the **Zum Greif** house (22 Gallusstrasse) has a carved baroque oriel with scenes from the Old Testament. Also view the house at **7 Bankgasse**, the **Haus zum Pelikan** (Schmiedgasse 15) and the **Schlössli** (Spisergasse 42).

From the 15th century onwards, St Gallen developed into a prosperous centre of the linen trade, and then of cotton and embroidery, before facing almost total industrial collapse during a world economic crisis. The textile industry may be past its prime now, but many medium-sized firms serve to maintain the

region's wealth. West of the cathedral is the small **Textilemuseum** on Vadianstrasse (open Mon–Sat 10am–noon and 2–5pm; entrance fee), which displays examples of local embroidery and lace dating back to the 14th century.

St Gallen, especially its old town, is an ideal place for a walking tour and it does have its charms – even if many of them are hidden. The town centre has been largely turned into a shopping precinct with innumerable shops and boutiques concealed behind historic facades. As well as possessing many aesthetically pleasing sights, St Gallen also has a few buildings of no architectural merit at all, such as the Town Hall next to the railway station. A more successful modern architectural symbol of the town lies in its northern outskirts, the Hochschule für Wirtschafts-und Sozialwissenschaften on the Rosenberg, one of Europe's best-known institutions for the training of upper management.

To get a real sense of St Gallen try one of the wine taverns on the first floors of the buildings in the old town: in the **Bäumli**, the **Neubädli** or the **Goldenes Schäfli**, the only guild building to have survived. With its sloping floor and its late-Gothic beamed ceiling, the "Schäfli" is one of the oldest taverns in Switzerland.

Appenzell and the Appenzellers

The journey south from St Gallen into the canton of **Appenzell** means leaving the lowlands behind and climbing up into a landscape with idyllic mountain scenery: the hills spread out like a green carpet, all the way up to the **Säntis** (2,502 metres/6,732 ft) mountain peak. Small farms are characteristic of the area. The villages here grew up around the churches, a large number of which were built by members of the Grubenmann family of master builders.

Map on page 254

The nave and rotunda of the St Gallen Abbey were built in 1755 by Peter Thumb, while the choir with the twin-towered facade was added in 1761 under the supervision of Johann Michael Beer von Bildstein.

BELOW: the "Silvester-klaüse" New Year celebrations in Urnäsch.

Art on display at the Textilemuseum in St Gallen.

BELOW: driving the cattle down from Alpine pastures in Appenzell.

This region is famous for its traditional arts and crafts: men and women, using brushes and paints, scissors, looms and embroidery frames, have been creating small masterpieces for years on their remote farms, masterpieces which today are much sought after by museums and collectors alike. It was here, in this pastoral landscape *par excellence*, that the original and unmistakable art form known as *Senntumsmalerei*, or "herd painting", a variation of farm painting, was able to flourish around the middle of the 18th century *(see page 265)*.

Appenzell, the capital of the Catholic half-canton of Innerrhoden, is really little more than a village. The main town in Ausserrhoden, **Herisau**, is also a village, albeit a slightly larger one. Yet no Appenzeller likes to see himself that way; he is either a *Vorderländer* from **Heiden**, a *Mittelländer* from **Teufen** or just a *Hinterländer* from **Herisau**. The most likely place for Appenzellers to meet is St Gallen – though they do not actually care for St Gallen all that much. Appenzellers have a reputation for welcoming strangers as long as they bring in the money, and also for a certain obstinacy. But reputations are nothing if not proven and the people here, with their odd nasal dialect and pragmatic minds, are as varied in character as the landscape that has shaped them.

They are also a people with unique customs; customs that have risen from a rich and ancient peasant culture which ranges from music for strings to herd painting. These established roots have served to keep the Appenzellers happily immune from contemporary fads.

Anyone visiting Appenzell country would do well to drive along the winding minor roads, or, better still, hike along the simple footpaths of the region. Trogen, Heiden, Gais, Urnäsch and Appenzell are all equally representative of Appenzeller culture in their different ways.

Fine village squares

Trogen lies southeast of St Gallen. Like its southern neighbour, Gais, Trogen has won "best-kept village" awards, and prides itself on its main square like many other villages in the canton. Until the process was abolished in 1997 – and alternating every two years with the village of Hundwil – the men of the canton visited Trogen square to vote and to help decide on cantonal affairs. For hundreds of years, it had been the rule for men to wear a traditional sabre to the event (an army bayonet was also accepted). In 1990, however, the women of Ausserrhoden were finally allowed to take part – and from then on a voting card replaced the sabre as means of entry. The women of Innerrhoden were granted the right to vote a year later, after they took their case to the Federal Court, and won.

Not to be missed in the square is the **Reformed church**, by Hans Ulrich Grubenmann. It forms a fine backdrop on the last Sunday in April for the administrative council meetings. Other sights include the **Zellweger-Haus** at the entrance to the square, the neoclassical **Town Hall** and house number 43, the oldest in the square. South of Trogen is the **Pestalozzi's Children's Village**, where war orphans of all nationalities have found refuge over the past 50 years.

Continuing south on the trip through Appenzell country, try not to miss Appenzell ⓫, the small main town of **Innerrhoden**. Restored at great expense, the town contains delightful, brightly painted patrician houses, as well as a finely preserved village square. The **Alpstein Massif**, a popular hiking area with its soft Alpine pastures, emerald-green lakes and numerous peaks, is very close. Beyond Herisau to the northwest, the landscape climbs over wooded hills all the way up to the limestone mountain range.

Primeval hunters used to seek refuge from bad weather in the prehistoric settlement in the **Wildkirchli Cavern** along its flanks; a **meteorological observatory** has been in operation on top of the Säntis since 1887. Less enthusiastic climbers can take a cable car here, and on the **Hohen Kasten**, the **Ebenalp** and the **Kronberg** as well.

Urnäsch ⓬, 10 km (6 miles) west of Appenzell, has a village square that is lined with fine-looking timbered buildings. It is famous throughout the region for its New Year processions which still take place according to the Gregorian calendar. On 13 January, the "ugly" and the "handsome" *Silvesterkläuse* (hobgoblins) march through the streets. Scenes from everyday rural life are depicted in artistically carved miniatures on their headdresses, which can sometimes be as large as a wagon wheel.

The sheer number of taverns in Urnäsch is astounding – one per hundred inhabitants – and it is here that the Appenzellers like to sit around and drink cider, or coffee with schnapps. The town also has a local history museum – **Appenzeller Brauchtums Museum** (Apr–Oct daily 1.30–5pm and select days in Jan; entrance fee; tel: 071 364 23 22), while a more modern and extensive museum can be admired two villages away in **Stein**. The **Appenzeller Volkskunde Museum** (Folk Museum; open Tues–Sun 10am–5pm; April–Oct afternoon weaving demonstrations; entrance fee; tel: 071 368 50 56) has a fine collection of folk art

Map on page 254

TIP

A special treat for any visitor to St Gallen is a real St Galler *Bratwurst*, sausage with onions and *Rösti*. The *Bratwurst* they make here is nearly as famous beyond the canton's borders as the lace for which the city is internationally renowned.

BELOW: a decorative street corner in Appenzell.

**Map
on page
254**

*A painting of a
farmer and his
animals on display
in the Folk Museum,
Appenzell.*

BELOW:
rolling countryside
of the Trogen area.

dating back to the 19th century. Incorporated into the museum is a *Schaukäserei* (cheese exhibition), which demonstrates how Appenzell cheese is produced.

Lake Walen to Liechtenstein

The canton of St Gallen, including the Appenzell region, stretches across the Rhein Valley and the Toggenburg up to Lake Walen.

Between the lake and the edge of the Alps are many different regions. The **Toggenburg**, like the Appenzell region, is a popular area for hiking, especially **Wildhaus ⓭**, **Unterwasser** and **Alt St Johann**; in wintertime it is a popular destination for skiers. Wildhaus also features the **Zwinglihaus**, birthplace of the famous reformer Zwingli, and one of the oldest wooden houses in Switzerland.

In the **Rhein Valley**, wine villages such as **Berneck** and **Balgach** can be found off the main road, then the journey continues southwards along the Rhein to **Werdenberg** with its castle, as well as the oldest wooden housing settlement in Switzerland. To the east is an entirely different country: the **Principality of Liechtenstein**.

This small state, which joined the UN in 1990, has made a name for itself over the past few decades as a domicile with low tax liability for numerous firms, many of which exist only on paper.

The capital, **Vaduz ⓮**, where the reigning prince's family has lived since 1939 in the castle of the same name, contains the **Liechtenstein Museum of Art**, (open Fri–Mon 10am–5pm; entrance fee; tel: 319 57 67 252) which was presented to the state by the present prince's grandfather. It contains several remarkable works of art from the Dutch, Flemish and English schools. For those interested in philately there is also the **Postmuseum** (Post Office Museum; open daily 10am–noon, 1–5pm; free; tel: 423 239 68 46), situated in the so-called Engländerbau (English building) at Städtle 37. The same building also holds art exhibitions and performances at the second floor Kunstraum (Art Space; open Tues–Thur 1–8pm, Wed & Fri 1–5pm, Sat & Sun 11am–5pm; free; tel: 423 2 333 111).

Heading south to **Sargans ⓯**, bordering the south of the principality, there is a defiant-looking **Castle** marking the end of the St Gallen part of the Rhein Valley. Today it houses a youth hostel as well as the **Sargans Museum**.

From Sargans, you can also reach the international spa town of **Bad Ragaz**, and **Pfäfers**, where Paracelsus was the first-ever spa doctor, and where the reformer Zwingli used to go to cure the rheumatism and gout he contracted on military campaigns. Travellers may dare to venture into the wild depths of the **Tamina-schlucht ⓰** (open May–Oct daily 10am–6pm; entrance fee). Before the water was piped to the spa, visitors to this famous gorge and health resort used to be lowered in baskets hundreds of metres below into its healing mineral waters, which rise to temperatures up to 37°C (98°F).

The tour continues to **Walensee ⓱** (Lake Walen), via **Walenstadt** to **Weesen**, or to **Quinten**. Here is the gateway to the sunny south; in Quinten one can find kiwi fruit growing, as well as persimmons and figs, and almond, acacia and sweet chestnut trees even flourish in the more sheltered areas. ❑

Herd painting

Senntumsmalerei, or herd painting, occupies a very special place in Swiss folk art. The folk art of Europe has nothing comparable to it. The special quality of this culture of Alpine farmers has its roots in Switzerland's historical structure: its topography, its natural features and its climate made the lowlands ideal for farming. The cow did not rank very highly here, and providing for it was left to the women and children exclusively. The *Bergbauer*, or mountain farmer, on the other hand, from the high valleys, was engaged in a constant struggle for survival and had to produce everything himself. Yet, although for him the cow was more important than it was for the lowlanders, "das Hirten" was also considered women's work.

In between these two extremes lie the grass-covered, pasture-farming and Alpine farming areas: the eastern and western foothills of the Alps as well as the Bernese Oberland, Urschweiz (Uri, Schwyz, Obwalden and Nidwalden), Glarus, and the St Gallen Oberland. The people here have made a living from cattle breeding and cheese production from time immemorial; economic thinking, as well as manners and customs, have all revolved around the cow. Other regions had more firmly rooted co-operative agricultural traditions, but every farmer from the Appenzell or Toggenburg areas, which have extremely high numbers of individual farmsteads, was seen as his own lord and master looking after cattle breeding and cheese making all alone. Alpine dairy farming here is definitely a man's business; the women tend to earn cash from domestic crafts.

Farming tools were being decorated as early as the 18th century, mostly through carving. At the beginning of the 19th century, *Fahreimer* (wooden pails carried on the way up the Alp by the two foremost herdsmen) began to have their bases decorated by means of a colourfully painted circular piece of wood which fitted into the bottom of the pail. These *Fahreimerbödeli* were only ever used on trips up the Alp, and were otherwise very carefully preserved. They usually bore the names of at least one herdsman and one cow, as well as the owner's name and the year in which they were made. There is also the *Sennenstreifen*: a long board, or a long strip of paper, depicting a cattle drive to Alpine pastures, which hung either above the door to the cowshed or in the living room. A third early form was the so-called *Wächterbild*, an enormous portrait of a herdsman painted on the outside of window shutters.

Senntum-Tafelbilder, small paintings usually done on either card or paper, play a major part in eastern Swiss herd painting. Themes include cows, herdsmen, farm hands, buildings and landscapes. The cattle drive up the Alp is another favourite. There are also many pictures of farmsteads, and often of country inns too, and scenes of cattle markets and herdsmen playing card games keep turning up. Dozens of men and women made a name for themselves from this art form, from the mid-19th century up to World War II. Many examples of their work can be seen in museums all over Switzerland today. ❏

RIGHT: demonstrating *Senntumsmalerei* in the Appenzell Museum.

BASEL

This ancient city on the Rhein, nestled up against the German and French borders, is best known for its year-round calendar of festivals and carnivals, crowned by the festive Fasnacht

Map on page 282

Basel, Switzerland's second-largest city, is located in the middle of some of Europe's greatest vineyards. The grape-rich areas of Alsace and Baden, and the wine regions of Lac Léman/Lake Geneva, the Valais, Ticino and eastern Switzerland, form a garland around the "knee" of the Rhein – yet the *Basler*, as a rule, prefers to drink beer.

Kleinbasel, or Little Basel – the industrial quarter of the city – first came into being after the river was bridged in the 13th century. The advent of industry brought workers' tenements along with it. People's faces are far more colourful here in every sense, as are the *Beizen*, the restaurants typical of the area. The nightlife here in Kleinbasel, and all it entails, is upbeat by Swiss standards.

Where three countries meet

On a fine day, far beyond Kleinbasel to the northwest, it's possible to make out the distinctive rugged outlines of the Vosges Mountains, which are steeped in history and today divide Alsace from Lorraine. To the east you can make out the first friendly ridges of Germany's Black Forest. If Gross-Basel were not inconveniently blocking the view, the heights of the Jura Mountains would also be visible.

Long ago, the Celts determined certain points in the Jura, the Vosges and the Black Forest and defined an astronomical triangle. Standing near today's city Münster, you will be right at the centre of it. This is the place that made **Basel ❶** what it is today.

Because of this, individuals undergoing some kind of spiritual exile have always felt very much at home in Basel, from Erasmus of Rotterdam to Karl Jaspers, from Hans Holbein to Rolf Hochhuth. The city's wealth of culture, its well-stocked museums, its archives and its antiquarian book shops make it a more than desirable place for a stranger to put down roots. From 1521 on it was the principal centre of humanism and attracted distinguished scholars and teachers from diverse backgrounds.

The *Basler* is an unusual and unique mixture, a relic of history. Situated as he is on the "knee" of the river, he looks across at the plateau of the Upper Rhein, his cultural breeding ground, to which he has not belonged politically since 1501. Adding to Basel's international atmosphere are the many available ways of getting to the city as well as leaving it – it has a tri-national airport (actually located outside Mulhouse, France, about 5 km/3 miles away), as well as two enormous train stations, covering all three adjoining countries: one main one (**Basel SBB**) serving France, and another (**Basel Bad**), for trains from Germany, both with their own passport controls.

PRECEDING PAGES: a parade of pipers at the Fasnacht. **LEFT:** Basel Town Hall (Rathaus). **BELOW:** Basel's Spalentor, gateway to the old town.

A novel form of sunscreen at one of Basel's street cafés.

Touring the city centre

Before you take on Basel's main highlights, the best place for an extensive view of the city centre is the **Pfalz**, an ancient, tree-lined, stone terrace on a bastion overlooking Basel Münster. There are two ways to get to it. The fun way is to walk down Oberer Rheinweg, a pleasant tree-lined stretch of embankment on the north bank of the river. In a few minutes you come to the *Leu*, one of four quaint wooden ferry boats that cross the Rhein, moored opposite the cathedral. For a modest sum, you are transported shakily but safely to the other side of the river, the current struggling against the steel overhead cable.

The next bit is more strenuous – just over 100 steps leading up to the Pfalz. From up here, Basel is almost indecently exposed to view, though what you see is mainly the area of **Kleinbasel** (Little Basel), the industrial area. Apparently there are inhabitants of **Grossbasel** (Great Basel) who have never been to this section of the city in their entire lives. However, Basel is full of such stories, and it tends to thrive on them.

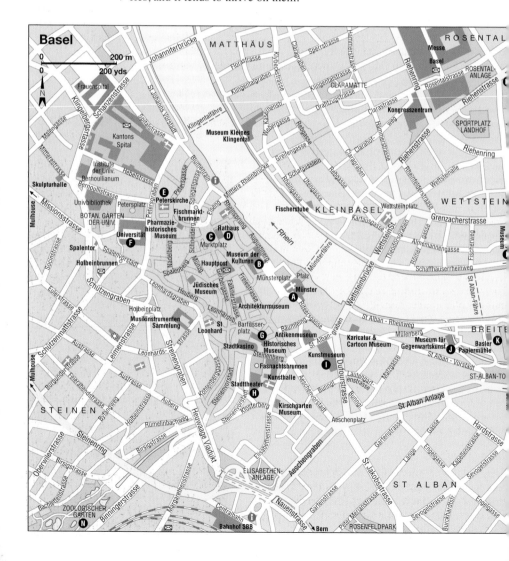

You can also see the Rhein from the Pfalz, forming a long, drawn-out loop, with both ends fading away into the distant horizon. It is here that the river forms its great right-angled bend, or "knee", before it wanders off northwards for good. Often, just as you are feeling like getting your camera ready for a picture up here, you hear the dull thud of a ship's diesel, and a freighter, loaded to the gunwales, pushes its way upriver against the current and squeezes itself underneath one of the low arches of the **Mittlere Rheinbrücke**, the main bridge over the Rhein (and the city's first, built in 1225).

The Münster

Tram number 1 or 8 will take you from the main railway station (Basel SBB) to Schifflände, via the Mittlere Rheinbrücke. From there, you walk up Rheinsprung, a narrow street lined with local-authority offices and quaint 15th- and 16th-century houses, to the **Münster** (open Easter–mid-Oct Mon–Fri 10am–5pm, Sat 10am–4pm, Sun 1–5pm; mid-Oct–Easter Mon–Sat 11am–4pm, Sun 2–4pm), the striking red sandstone cathedral, dating from the 13th century but rebuilt in 1356 after a devastating earthquake. Inside, you will find the tomb of the Dutch humanist writer and thinker Erasmus, a leading light of the Renaissance. Other highlights include the St Vincent relief panel, describing the martyr's macabre story; an intricately carved pulpit and tombs of lesser-known distinguished *Baslers*.

If you feel like a rest now, there is plenty of shade in the square (Münsterplatz) from the 34 evenly spaced chestnut trees. Or you can head straight for the enormous complex in Augustinergasse, housing both the **Museum der Kulturen** (open Tues–Sun 10am–5pm; entrance fee; tel: 061 266 55 00), with an extensive collection of cultural artefacts, largely from Oceania and Melanesia, and the attached **Naturhistoriches Museum** (open Tues–Sun 10am–5pm; entrance fee but free Sundays; tel: 061 266 55 00), covering geology in general, with particular focus on the fossils and minerals of the Alps and Jura regions.

After an initial tour of the main sights of this port city upon the Rhein, you might feel that you deserve a break; that you have heard enough about this city of humanists and Nobel prize-winning scientists, about Nietzsche's lectureship at the university, about the cultural philosopher Burckhardt, about the painters Holbein and Böcklin, about the mathematicians Bernoulli and Euler, and about Hermann Hesse, who wrote his *Steppenwolf* here.

You may also have had enough of admiring the cityscape and the spacious 18th-century architecture, such as the **Wildtsche Haus** on **Petersplatz**, perhaps, or the **Haus zum Kirschgarten** which forms part of the Historical Museum. It may be time to adjourn for a beer or a glass of wine.

Joie de vivre

The *Baslers* may speak German, but their enthusiasm for food, drink, nightlife and fashionable dress is thoroughly French. Fully refreshed, you might want to take advantage of some of Basel's excellent shops, clubs, bars and fine eateries.

Map on page 270

TIP

The **Fischerstube** brewery, which is one of the smallest in Switzerland, serves its beer in a little tavern on Rheingasse 45, in Kleinbasel; its popular beer garden is always full in the evenings.

BELOW: the Town Hall and Marktplatz.

*Basel's massive exhibition centre is the **Messe Basel**, on Messeplatz, near the Bad train station. Trade fairs have been held on the site since the Middle Ages, and during the fair season in spring and autumn it is very hard to get a hotel room in the city.*

First, head for the **Marktplatz** Ⓒ (marketplace), where stallholders rub their hands behind heavily laden stands, extolling the merits of their flowers, fruit, vegetables, bread and cheese, where the red of the apples merges into the colour of the splendid **Rathaus** Ⓓ (Town Hall) and swarms of pigeons flutter everywhere. The main wing of this remarkable building is in late-Burgundian Gothic style. The notable clock (1511–12) is the work of a local craftsman; the Basel craftsman's guild built the entire thing, in fact, possibly as an impudent thumb of the nose at the ruling class; they were secure enough to get away with it, too, and even once locked visiting officials inside while staging a party outside on the streets. The wing on the left-hand side and the tower on the right are both 19th-century additions. Venture inside, and you'll find another surprise – more frescoes (a 16th-century feature still seen all around the city).

On the corner of Marktplatz and **Freie Strasse** is the guild house of the wine merchants, the Renaissance-style **Geltenzunfthaus** (1578), and at No. 25 is the guild house of the locksmiths, dating from 1488 but decorated in baroque style in 1733.

City squares

Take a detour up the Totengässlein stairs for a quiet break in **Petersplatz**. This pretty park is marked off on one side by **Peterskirche** Ⓔ, an impressive Gothic church, and on another by the city's university, the **Universität** Ⓕ, home to thousands of young people who give the street scene such vitality each night.

The area between Marktplatz and **Barfüsserplatz** contains the city's best shops, chic designer boutiques and exclusive department stores. Since most of the narrow streets are closed to cars, this is a pleasant and safe place to walk around. By night, out come the chairs and tables of numerous good (if pricey)

BELOW: ferry across the Rhein, with Basel Münster in the background.

Map on page 270

restaurants and outdoor bars, all well attended by a youngish set that seems to thrive on dressing up, drinking the light local beer, then dancing the night away at discos.

In Barfüsserplatz itself, you will find the 14th-century **Barfüsserkirche** (Church of the Barefoot Friars), now successfully converted into the **Historisches Museum G** (open Wed–Mon 10am–5pm; entrance fee; tel: 061 205 86 00). This historical museum contains an interesting collection of exhibits relating to the history of central European culture. Among the more notable exhibits are the late-Gothic tapestries and the so-called "Lällenkönig" (Babbling King), a crowned head with movable tongue and eyes.

Just a stone's throw from Barfüsserplatz is one of the city's cultural highlights, the Museum of Art *(see next page)*. On the way there, you pass the whimsical **Fasnachtsbrunnen** (Carnival Fountain), with continually changing sprays of water, which was created in 1977 by the late Jean Tinguely, one of Switzerland's best-known sculptor/artists, whose career began here in Basel. Behind the fountain, the modern **Stadttheater H** (Municipal Theatre), every side of which looks like the back, pushes its way aggressively into view.

Holbein portrait in Basel's superb Kunstmuseum.

Museums and galleries

Basel offers a choice of three dozen museums, whose range of exhibits caters for every possible taste. This is partly due to the fact that the Basel area established its own special form of patronage, and the people from the wealthy aristocracy, the so-called *Daig* (from the word *Teig*, meaning dough), discreetly supplied the exhibition rooms at regular intervals. Sometimes a particularly wealthy benefactor would commission an entirely new museum.

BELOW: the Wildtsche Haus, on Petersplatz.

BELOW: Tinguely's
Carnival Fountain,
on Barfüsserplatz.

The **Kunstmuseum ❶** (Museum of Art; open Tues–Sun 10am–5pm; entrance fee; tel: 061 206 62 62) lies five minutes' walk from the theatre, at 16 St Alban-Graben. Auguste Rodin's *Les Bourgeois de Calais* welcomes visitors to the oldest art collection in the world. Originally based on the private exhibition rooms belonging to Basilius Amerbach, it includes the most extensive collection of works by Konrad Witz and Hans Holbein the Younger (1497–1543), as well as several paintings by Picasso. Part of its collection was purchased with city funds after the people of Basel took a democratic vote on what to buy for the museum and obtained a loan to do it. Picasso was so touched by their admiration that he donated several more.

Besides these, the museum houses an outstanding collection of 19th- and 20th-century art, including work by Gauguin, Van Gogh, Chagall, Klee, Ernst and Kandinsky, as well as paintings by local artist Arnold Bocklein. Dostoyevsky and Lenin are both reputed to have spent hours in front of Holbein's painting *The Body of Christ* during their visits to the museum.

The **Museum für Gegenwartskunst ❶** (open Tues–Sun 10am–5pm; entrance fee; tel: 061 206 62 62), at St Alban-Rheinweg 60, is well worth a visit while walking about the old town. This Museum of Contemporary Art was built in 1980 with a donation from local philanthropist Maya Sacher, at that time the richest woman in Switzerland. Its collection includes works by Swiss artists Giacometti, Klee and Tinguely, and others by Di Chirico, Braque, Dalí, Chagall and Mondrian.

Practically next to the art museum, and on the river at St Alban-Tal 35–37, the **Basler Papiermühle ❸** (Paper Mill and Museum; open Tues–Sun 2–5pm; entrance fee; tel: 061 272 96 52) is another worthwhile attraction. Basel has a

FASNACHT

Basel's three-day Lenten festival is the best chance, albeit rather a strenuous one, for visitors to get a whiff of the real city and its inhabitants.

Beginning on the Monday following Ash Wednesday, at exactly four in the morning, all lights in the city centre are switched off; tens of thousands of people, the *Fasnachtler*, organised into small groups, begin beating drums and playing pipes, their masked faces glowing eerily in the light from their lanterns. Spectators fill the streets to witness the huge, but orderly, procession, which begins a three-day spectacle of music, dancing and chanting of satirical songs. The high, piercing sound of the piccolos, blending with the threatening rumble of the heavy Basel drums, evokes the days when Switzerland was one of Europe's great military powers.

Like all Lenten celebrations in Christian cultures, the roots of the *Fasnacht* are pagan. In its earliest days, the festival was a popular protest, a rebellion against those who did not need to go out into the streets to demonstrate their power and influence; but after the Reformation all such festivals in Basel were banned. *Fasnacht* in its current form has been going for only about 60 years, though many people claim the custom is well over a century old.

long tradition of manufacturing high-grade paper – that is why thinkers like Erasmus turned up here: they knew they could spread their ideas – and the museum does a good job explaining it all. The attached café is a popular and inexpensive outdoor lunch spot.

Map on page 270

Tinguely Museum

Continuing further east, and crossing the Rhein on the Schwarzwaldbrucke, brings you to the **Jean Tinguely Museum** ❶ (open Tues–Sun 11am–7pm; entrance fee; tel: 061 681 93 20), at Grenzacherstrasse 210 (Paul Sacher-Anlage 1), which makes a fitting conclusion to a riverside jaunt. This diverse collection of the sculptor's works is suitable for both adults and children; exhibits range from the very strange (such as the 1986 *Mengele Death Dance*) to the very playful, all testament to Tinguely's fertile mind and his ability to put the oddest of odds and ends – including bike wheels, old socks and engine cogs – into thought-provoking art.

If you can make it across the river on the No. 6 tram out to the **Fondation Beyeler** ⓜ (open daily 10am–6pm; entrance fee; tel: 061 645 97 00), at Baselstrasse 77 in Riehen, near the German railway station, you will be well rewarded: though distant, it is the city's second-finest art gallery (and would be the first in some cities), a dazzling private collection containing important Cubist and Impressionist works from the likes of Klee, Cézanne, Matisse and Picasso.

Finally, a few blocks behind the railway station at Binningerstrasse 40, is Basel's lush, renowned **Zoologischer Garten** ⓝ (open daily 8am–6pm; entrance fee; tel: 061 295 35 35), one of the country's best zoos. Besides an impressive array of some of the world's most endangered species, there is a children's area, with pony rides and the usual cuddly animals to stroke.

A morbid but factual piece of local history is that Basel's famous zoo is built on the site of the city's last public executions.

BELOW: the Haus Zum Kirschgarten, Basel's museum of domestic life, arts and crafts.

Map on page 282

Roman remains at Augusta Raurica.

BELOW: inn sign at the country town of Liestal.
RIGHT: verdant pastures.

Excursions outside Basel

If you want to get away from the city for a while, Basel's location at the junction of three nations puts it within striking distance of several tempting destinations. A day trip from Basel could take in a number of interesting towns in Switzerland, as well as the delightful surrounding countryside – at its most glorious when the cherry blossom is out in April, and again in autumn when days are often clear and trees golden. Particular towns worth mentioning are **Riehen** (just northeast), **Münchenstein** (just south), and the suburbs of **Bottmingen** and **Binningen** with their country seats and mansions; not forgetting castles such as those at **Pfeffingen**, **Waldenburg** and **Dorneck**; and, finally, delightful little towns and villages such as **Liestal**, **Gelterkinden** or **Pratteln**, all a short journey to the southeast of the city.

You could start by taking a trip back in time by driving or taking a river cruise to **Augusta Raurica** ❷, site of some extremely well-preserved Roman ruins just up the Rhein. The lovely boat ride (tel: 061 639 95 00) takes 1½ hours each way, the drive not longer than 10 minutes. Once there, you will find part of a reconstructed Roman town, including an amphitheatre that sometimes hosts concerts, some temples and a Roman brothel dating from the time of the occupation. The **Römermuseum** (open Mar–Oct daily 10am–5pm, Mon 1–5pm; entrance fee; tel: 061 816 22 22) at Giebenacherstrasse 17, explains the 2,000-year-old settlement and lays out some exquisite silver items cached by the retreating Romans more than 1,600 years ago.

Rheinfelden ❸, founded by the Zähringen family, can be reached by steamer, a journey taking 2½ hours, with boats departing May–Oct from the Mittlere Rheinbrücke in the centre of Basel (or by train, which takes 15 minutes). A

relaxed, small-town atmosphere, set against a delightful backdrop, awaits the visitor. The town has its own Rathaus, decorated with ornate frescoes, several churches and museums, and a good range of restaurants. Most day trippers take a leisurely stroll through the town and then take in the river side. Rheinfelden is also a spa, claiming some of the saltiest water in Europe with a couple of indoor saltwater baths; the local water is drunk as a medicinal remedy.

Dornach ❹, a 20-minute train ride from Basel, is home to the Goetheanum headquarters of the anthroposophian movement – a Goethe memorial (open daily 8.30am–6pm; tel: 061 706 42 42; with a restaurant on the premises, the Spiesehaus). The town is also world-famous for its Waldorf and Steiner schools.

If you have more time, you could make a tour of the wine villages of Alsace, France, just across the border and north; they lie within an hour's driving time. Without a car, you could make the 45-minute train ride to the lovely cobblestone town of **Colmar**. Alternately, the Black Forest's country customs and dark gorges are easily reachable by car or train, as well, just across the German border. **Freiburg im Breisau**, the capital of the region – and an interesting, quite left-leaning university town – is a short ride from Basel Bad's German station, which is connected to the downtown Swiss station by frequent trains and buses. ❏

THE JURA

This mountain range, forming a natural border with France, and comprising the Jura, Vaud and Neuchâtel cantons, offers a rich mix of attractions, from Roman remains to vast, unspoilt forests

Map on page 282

Bern

According to geologists, the Jura Mountains – a mighty system stretching some 780 km (500 miles) long – are among the youngest on the planet. Some 150 million years ago the Jura, an unusually complex mountain range, rose like a reef from the endless sea, much like the neighbouring Alps. Ferns, conifers and ginkgo trees carpeted the slopes of the new land, and the first of the flying reptiles circled above its peaks; then came the first birds, small carnivores and other mammals; the seas teemed with giant dinosaurs, fish, snails, ammonites and innumerable tiny life forms. Fossils, the petrified proof of these creatures' existence, can be seen today in their tens of thousands in the numerous village museum collections of local history.

In the eyes of the average Swiss citizen, the Jura is known as the Confederation's 26th and most recent member (born on 24 September 1978). Much has been written about the labour pains involved; this region in the northwest of Switzerland, which possesses three lakes, has always been – and most likely will continue to be – politically divided. The variations of the landscape are reflected in the diversity of the region's inhabitants.

PRECEDING PAGES: the rolling slopes of the Jura mountains. **LEFT:** the Vue des Alpes chapel. **BELOW:** Neuchâtel Collegiate Church.

A diverse people

Historians would like to know more about the Raurici, those ancient warriors and heroes who long ago populated the forests and valleys of the Jura. The Celtic tribe had moved southward through Europe with the Helvetii but in 58 BC had been intercepted by Roman legions at Bibracte. The defeated hordes were sent back north and forced to resettle the regions which they had previously put to the torch. Now the very active Society of Friends of Raurician History from the German-speaking region keeps this Celtic heritage alive.

Others also followed the Raurici, and the Jura's population is surprisingly varied today: mountain dwellers, with and without bushy beards, who alternate between speaking German and French; artists, many of whom have taken over farms in the region; city dwellers escaping from the stress of everyday life; dropouts; alternative farmers; and many others, all of them in search of a better quality of life.

Switzerland and France both have a share of the Jura mountain range, after all. To the French, as for the Swiss, it is known simply as *Le Jura*; neither has made any effort to distinguish between the two parts by name. Anyone after a more accurate idea should not overlook the fact that these limestone mountains actually extend right across the canton of Schaffhausen and as far as the Franconian Jura in Germany, an area known as "Little Switzerland".

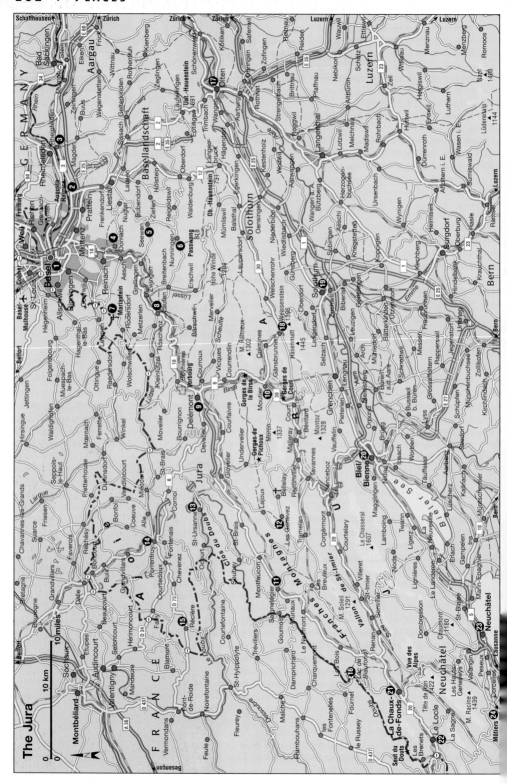

Looking across this range of gentle peaks you can understand why the Jura are often called the "blue mountains". There is no better place to begin a journey here than the River Blauenberg, which separates the rift valley of the Rhein from the Tertiary basin of Laufen. It extends westwards from the gorge at **Angenstein** in the **Birs Valley** to the **Lüssel Valley**, 18 km (11 miles) away, where it leaves Switzerland for France.

A counterpart to the Blauenberg is the **Gempen Plateau** to the east; the Birs runs through much of this, too. Several delightful villages can be found on its ridges, including **Seewen ❺**, 10 km (6 miles) east of Zwingen, with its well-known **Museum für Musikautomaten** (open Tues–Sun 11am–6pm; entrance fee; tel: 061 915 98 80), holding the largest collection of music boxes and related mechanical musical instruments found anywhere in Europe. More than 300 displays serve as a reminder that the indefatigable Swiss once dominated the music-box business, proving once again they build precision machines like few others.

The plateau forms part of the area beyond the mountains known as **Schwarzbubenland**, in the canton of Solothurn. The largest town in the area is **Breitenbach**, down in the Lüssel Valley on the **Passwangstrasse**, a magnificent panoramic route running between Laufen and Balsthal, with a view of the **Hohe Winde** (1,204 metres/3,950 ft), the highest point in the Schwarzbubenland. The ancient capital of the region, however, is **Nunningen ❻**, 10 km (6 miles) southeast of Breitenbach, where the local lords from Solothurn used to rule from **Gilgenberg Castle**, taking advantage of its commanding location in the landscape. Another impressive ruin, **Neu-Thierstein**, lies down in the Lüssel Valley, on a rocky outcrop above the Passwangstrasse: it was once the seat of the rulers of the lower and middle Birse Valley.

Signposts guide you around the network of paths over the Jura Mountains.

The Lüssel River hurries down from the Passwang to join the Birse. Another interesting stream, coming from the Pleigne Plateau, flows towards Laufen and into the broad Laufen basin where it joins the Lüssel. **Lüssel Abbey**, a Cistercian monastery once famous the world over, used to stand on its banks, in the narrow but highly picturesque Lüssel Valley. Now only a few remains of the monastery walls prove that it stood there at all. Another clue to its existence is the nearby small lake, the **Etang de Lüssel**, which used to serve as the monastery's carp pond.

BELOW: cherry blossom in the Passwang region.

We can already see the broad plateau of **Maria-stein**, the second most important pilgrimage shrine in Switzerland (the most important being Einsiedeln). The Jura rises up, right next to the French frontier, and forms the **Landskronkette**. One of the most curious sites hereabouts is the **Benedictine Monastery of Mariastein ❼**, some 7 km (4½ miles) north of Laufen. The monastery was built in late-Gothic style in 1648, a time when that style of architecture had long since been supplanted by the Renaissance. The facade, however, is neoclassical, and the interior neo-baroque. The monastery is an instructive place for anyone wanting a crash course in the history of European church building. The main attraction, however, is the Gnadenkapelle, a chapel built into a cave below the church.

Vital passes to the "French-Swiss" Jura

Besides the Raurici, the Romans also influenced the area, seeing it as of vital strategic importance. It was they who fortified the crossings from the Belfort Gap into the Alps, vital mountain passes which, centuries later, the Habsburgs of Austria and the bishops of Basel were equally keen to protect. Castles were built along the length of the passes at great expense: Alt Biederthal, today simply known as "Burg", Blauenstein, Pfeffingen, Frohberg and Angenstein, most of them now in ruins.

In the old days, anyone wanting to go through the mountains followed the course of rivers – the Birse; the Sorne, the Suze, the Alleine and the Doubs. These days, the express train from Basel to **Laufen** ❽, the main town in the German-speaking Laufental, takes 18 minutes. On the way, it passes the odd-looking **castle** near **Zwingen**. Laufen – its name comes from the word *Lauffen*, meaning waterfall – has a very neat and tidy appearance, and is an efficiently run industrialised town. The town is also the starting point for a series of well-marked walking trails into the surrounding countryside.

One remarkable feature of this region is the "international route", which passes through mountain country belonging to Bern, Solothurn and France and then leads over to Porrentruy, in the Ajoie.

Of course, it is not only the language that makes the difference between here and adjoining areas so noticeable: the whole atmosphere has a definite "French-Swiss" flavour, which is shaped at least in part by the town of **Delémont** ❾, the capital of the republic and canton of Jura. The Grand-Rue, without a doubt the finest street in Delémont, makes it obvious why the bishops of Basel elected to build a château here, around 1716, as their summer residence. The old town

BELOW: farmhouse in the Franches-Montagnes.

remains attractive, with two ancient city gates, a convent dating from 1699 and several interesting churches. The people of the Jura have always held their public gatherings in front of the **Maison Bennot**, which today houses the excellent **Musée Jurassien** (Jura Museum of Art and History, Rue du 23 Juin 52; open Tues–Sun 2–5pm; entrance fee; tel: 032 422 80 77).

Just outside Delémont, at the entrance to one of the numerous gorges of the River Birse, is **Vorbourg**, a ruined castle situated on a rocky spur, which also has an important pilgrimage chapel (open to the public; tel: 032 422 21 41).

The Birse curves around the capital, and Delémont itself lies at the mouth of two rivers: the **Scheulte**, which flows down from the **Scheulte Pass** connecting the **Gulden Valley** in the canton of Solothurn with the Delémont basin, and the **Sorne**, which flows down from Bellelay. It was not that long ago that countless watermills, ironworks and sawmills were still in operation on their banks. The hill on which the Vorbourg stands affords a magnificent view. The capital – a blend of the old and the new – lies at your feet. Beyond it, in the distance, it is possible to make out the wild and jagged-looking series of ravines at Moutier, the **Gorges de la Birse**, and the quiet villages dotted across the Delémont Valley.

Industry in the southern Jura

A short distance south of Delémont the Birse becomes fully Bernese – as it was in the Laufental – and remains so right up to its source, for here the river flows on through the **Moutier** region, one of the three regions that stayed under the jurisdiction of the "old canton", namely Bern, following the country-wide plebiscite that gave the Jura autonomy as the 26th federal state of Switzerland – the first change of cantonal boundaries in 163 years.

Map on page 282

Simon Nicolas de Montjoie, prince bishop of Basel (1693–1775).

BELOW: market day in Laufen.

Access can be gained to the Upper Birse Valley (it is also sometimes called Grandval), via the Gorges de la Birse – here, you are confronted with magnificent natural scenery. The regional capital of **Moutier** ❿, however, could not be more of a contrast. Over the past 100 years this neat and tidy little town has developed into the industrial centre of the Jura (machines, appliances, watches) – a consequence of the tunnel that was built through the Grenchenberg.

The valley basin of Moutier was already an important cultural centre in medieval times. The **Moutier-Grandval Monastery** stood here, and had its heyday in the second half of the 9th century, when great scholars used to teach there. The *Great Bible of Moutier-Grandval,* now in the British Museum in London, still testifies to the enormous influence this monastery must have had as a centre of learning.

The gorge is complemented by the one at **Court**, 5 km (3 miles) southwest. Both are natural traffic hindrances, and their military significance was known in Roman times. The gorge at Court separates the Delémont basin from the Vallée de Tavannes, which is situated between the mountain ranges of Moron (1,337 metres/4,386 ft) and Montoz (1,328 metres/4,357 ft). These mountains are ideal for walkers and mushroom pickers, but the valley itself, heavily industrialised, has a sober, almost strict atmosphere about it.

Horsing about in Franches-Montagnes

The people of the Jura love horses. Since horses particularly like to find footing on ground that is not too hard, the plateau of **Franches-Montagnes**, 1,000 metres (3,300 ft) above sea level, is considered ideal horse country.

As if this still needed to be proved, the **Marché-Concours**, Switzerland's largest horse show, has been held in **Saignelégier** ⓫ on the second weekend in

The botanical wealth of mushrooms (including many edible varieties) to be found in the Franches-Montagnes countryside is much appreciated by connoisseurs of ceps.

BELOW: the Marché-Concours horse show in Saignelégier.

August every year since 1897. With its races and equestrian games, it has become a national attraction. The main town in the region, Saignelégier, has a leisure centre, complete with swimming pool, sauna and skating rink. Alternatively, you can take a stroll into the surrounding countryside, where a series of ponds and bogs lie amid suitably unusual vegetation, echoing landscapes much further north – Ireland, Scandinavia and even northern Canada.

The Franches-Montagnes region extends from the Delémont basin all the way to La Chaux-de-Fonds in the canton of Neuchâtel. The air up here is more noticeably bracing, the landscape starker and more barren. Delightful meadows alternate with dark forests of fir trees and with small villages, some of them still very secluded, whose characteristic farmhouses have broad, only very slightly sloping roofs. Particularly fine examples of these can be found in La Bosse, Lajoux, **Muriaux** (which has a motor museum), Le Noirmont, Les Prailats and Les Bois.

One peculiarity of the region, however, is its lack of any famous river: the rain instantly seeps away into the soil. It is on its eastern border, where the former **Abbey of Bellelay** stands (once just as much a centre of learning in the Jura as Moutier), that the River Sorne, which leads down into the Birse, has its source; it flows through the wild and romantic **Gorges du Pichoux**, to the west of Moutier, whose waterfalls were a great favourite with landscape painters of the 18th and 19th centuries. **Bellelay**, located in the mountains 25 km (15 miles) east of Saignelégier, was founded in 1136 and rebuilt in the baroque style during the 17th and 18th centuries. Also worth a visit is **Les Genevez ⓬**, 4 km (2½ miles) west of Bellelay, where the delightful **Musée Rural Jurassien** (open all year on demand; entrance fee; tel: 032 484 00 80) has a collection of farm machinery and implements plus good meals too.

This is also an excellent area for hiking, and a well-developed network of footpaths guides the visitor to places of natural beauty that are still largely intact, despite human intrusion. Efforts have been made recently to increase the popularity of the Franches-Montagnes in winter, too, as a local recreation area for cross-country skiers, dogsleds and the like. Very characteristic of the Franches-Montagnes region are its many high moors. The most famous of these is probably the **Etang de la Gruère**, 10 km (6 miles) south-east, below Saignelégier. Formerly a millpond, today it is a moor lake of incomparable beauty, and is one particularly good area for picturesque country walks.

Dark beauty

Far away to the west, in France, the **River Doubs** has its source. It enters Switzerland at Les Brenets in the canton of Neuchâtel, and then forms a natural border with France that extends for 45 km (30 miles). It has cut a deep bed, almost a canyon in fact. Many of the municipalities of the Franches-Montagnes region have land that extends down to its lonely banks. The river is of opalesque beauty, flowing darkly onwards and seldom interrupted by weirs. The only important village lying on the Doubs itself in this dark valley is **Goumois**, a border crossing 9 km (5 miles) due west of Saignelégier.

Map on page 282

TIP

Saignelégier's tourist office can provide you with some useful information on a variety of walks in the local countryside (tel: 032 952 19 53, www.juratourisme.ch).

BELOW: for once, Swiss cows are upstaged by horses in Saignelégier.

The ubiquitous, geranium-filled Swiss window box.

At **Soubey**, however, where anglers can be found in their hundreds at weekends, the landscape starts to open up again, and soon the river changes course, no longer heading for the Rhein but for the Saône. Nestled up to a curve in the river is **St Ursanne** ⓭, a historic town with an ancient stone bridge connecting it with the Clos du Doubs, a tongue of land stretching up to the French border. St Ursanne, just 16 km (10 miles) west of Delémont, is one of the few medieval towns with three intact town gates. It also has the rather well-preserved Romanesque-Gothic **Collégiale** church, which is one of the most beautiful buildings in this part of Switzerland, with a Romanesque crypt and Merovingian sarcophagi. The town's well-preserved old quarter and pretty surroundings make it a fine off-the-beaten-track fishing or cycling holiday destination.

At **Ocourt**, 6 km (4 miles) to the west, where a distinctive church can be seen standing in the middle of some fields, the Doubs leaves Switzerland at last.

The Ajoie

It takes the local train less than an hour to get from Delémont to Porrentruy, via Courtetelle, Courfaivre, Bassecourt, Glovelier, St Ursanne and Courgenay. The train heads underground for a short time, through the tunnel beneath the pass of **Les Rangiers**, the Rhein-Rhône watershed, 856 metres (2,808 ft) above sea level. Les Rangiers itself is an important traffic artery, with routes leading off towards the Delémont Valley, the Franches-Montagnes region, St Ursanne and the Ajoie.

After passing hilly grazing land, coniferous forest, stretches of almost Alpine-looking grass, and St Ursanne down in the valley basin, the train reaches **Cour-**

BELOW:
the tranquil lake of
Etang de la Gruère.

Map on page 282

genay. Then the broad meadows of the **Ajoie** come into view. Geographically, this "promontory" jutting far into France is not a part of the Jura, because it lies at the foot of the mountains; politically, it belongs to the Swiss canton of Jura. The landscape here is gentle and spacious; not only can you sense the proximity of Burgundy but you can smell it in the air, too.

There is also often a hint of Burgundian blue in the sky above **Porrentruy** ⑭, a small town of some 8,000 inhabitants, which has been the residence of the bishops of Basel since the Reformation in 1528. Seen from the castle tower above it, the centre of Porrentruy is very similar to the old part of Bern. The town received its first real impetus from the freedom charter granted to it in 1283 by Rudolf von Habsburg, and still retains some of the flavour of its past.

You can sense the past most strongly when you stand next to the **Porte de France** and look up in the direction of the spacious **château**. This has been rebuilt several times, largely in Renaissance style. The buildings that once housed the castle guard, the mint and the chapel are sadly no longer preserved – unlike parts of the Episcopal Gardens, and the pavilion of Princess Christine of Saxony (1697). There is also a 13th-century refuge.

Other sights in town include the former **Jesuit College**, the partly Romanesque **Church of St Pierre** in the upper part of the town, the **Town Hall** and also several feudal houses. A surprising number of festivals come through here, as well, including a jazz festival in June and both a rock festival and a folk-music weekend in August. A more local, down-to-earth festival, celebrating St Martin, takes place in November.

The main river in the Ajoie region is the **Allaine**, which splashes its way almost due north towards the Rhône and leaves Switzerland at **Boncourt**. Very close by are the mysterious **Grottes de Milandre**; legend has it that a beautiful maiden emerges from them from time to time. You probably will not see her, as the grottoes are closed to the public, but you can get to the ones at **Réclère** ⑮ (open daily Apr–Nov 10am– noon and 1.30–5pm; entrance fee; tel: 032 476 61 55), on the border formed by the Doubs, and also visit the prehistoric park at the same location (same hours and same fee as Réclère). Finally, situated diametrically opposite are the ponds belonging to the old pottery town of **Bonfol**. This is where to find the best *Dammassine*; a glass of this delicious schnapps will make a fine reward after a hard day's sightseeing.

The foot of the Jura

On the **Lac de Biaufond** ⑯, a lake created in recent times by artificially damming the Doubs on the border of the cantons of Neuchâtel and the Jura, a boundary stone has stood for more than 1,000 years. Hewn into it is a coat-of-arms depicting the three bishoprics of Lausanne, Basel and Besançon (in France). In its day the territory owned by the prince bishops of Basel extended as far as Bieler See. They managed to get the land as much by luck as anything else. King Rudolf III of Burgundy, terrified that the world was going to end on New Year's Day in the year 1000 and keen on securing a place in heaven, gave away large areas of the Jura to the Bishop of Basel.

BELOW: Porrentruy.

Charles the Bold's last stand

The slopes of the Jura above Concise, on the southwest shores of Lac de Neuchâtel, are the scene of the first battle to take place in the Burgundian wars of 1476, which was named after the castle and town nearby: *Grandson*. After Bern had declared war on powerful Charles of Burgundy ("Charles the Bold"), the Confederates defeated his armies of knights at Grandson, then later at Murten and finally at Nancy, where Charles was killed. These events were summed up in a popular saying which states that "Charles lost his *Gut* (possessions) at Grandson, his *Mut* (courage) at Murten, and his *Blut* (blood) at Nancy". The main beneficiary of these victories was the cruel and resourceful King Louis XI of France.

Yet the Burgundian wars were important for Switzerland, too, above all because the way into western Switzerland had been

opened up, and a first step had been taken towards bringing Geneva and the Vaud into the Confederation.

"Grandson was the first battle," wrote the military historian Hans Rudolf Kurz, "to feature the successful tactical use of the long pike, which had become an increasingly common weapon for the Confederate army – the square had given way to the customary wedge shape – and made it almost impossible for the army on horseback to attack the Confederates. The former kept colliding bloodily with the latter's 'hedgehog' formation, protected by the pikes, and was not even able to break up the foot-soldiers in the open field."

The Confederates captured 400 tents, furnished with valuable tapestries as well as gold and silver tableware, 400 pieces of cannon, 10,000 horses, wagons by the hundred, 600 standards, 300 powder kegs, 800 crossbows – quite sizeable booty, which together with the war purse would have been worth several hundred million of today's Swiss francs. The chronicler Diebold Schilling has left a very accurate description of this booty in his *Lucerne Chronicle*, which he wrote in the last quarter of the 15th century.

However, Charles the Bold's defeat at Murten had even more serious consequences for him. When the peace treaty was concluded with Savoy, Bern was given parts of the Savoy Vaud and control over Aigle and Erlach; Murten, Grandson, Orbe and Echallens were all put under the joint administration of Bern and Fribourg. Bern also wanted to occupy the Franche-Comté region of France, but its fellow Confederates were against the idea. The Swiss settled for reparations in the form of cash.

With the Confederates' victory, the glorious history of the lords of Grandson came to an end. The line still lives on in England under the name of Grandison. A countess of Grandson, mistress of King Edward III, was the reason behind the creation of the highest decoration in Britain, the Order of the Garter: she lost her garter at a ball, whereupon the king picked it up, and as he did so uttered the now historic phrase *Honi soit qui mal y pense* (shamed be he who thinks evil of it). ❑

LEFT: the Mauritius Fountain in Solothurn, commemorating the region's military history.

When people from Solothurn talk about "their" Jura, they usually mean the southern foot of the Jura. For various political, geographical and historical reasons, this region begins at the **Unterer Hauenstein**.

Olten ⓱, 50 km (30 miles) southeast of Basel and the largest town in the canton of Solothurn, has some interesting features: the old town, with its wooden bridge built originally in the 13th century, and the splendid twin-towered **Sankt Martin Kirche**, dating from 1908. The **Kunstmuseum** (open Tues–Fri 2–5pm, Thur 2–7pm, special opening times for groups; tel: 062 212 86 76) has works by local artist Martin Disteli (1802–44). The **Historisches Museum** (open Tues–Sat 2–5pm, Sun 10am–5pm; free) covers local archaeological finds from 40,000 years ago as well as military uniforms, weapons, costumes and ceramics. It also shows the development of the railway, which brought industry to the town and made it an important junction of north-south traffic.

The mountain ridges of the Solothurn Jura go their separate ways at the Unterer Hauenstein, the nearest one being the **Weissensteinkette** some 40 km (25 miles) southwest of Olten. This ridge is interrupted by the mighty gorge at Oensingen, with **Neu-Bechburg Castle** towering above it. The ridge is called the **Weissenstein ⓲** because of its white chalk cliffs, and is the most-visited mountain in the area because of its views. It is also very popular for its spa, built in 1827, which has recently been painstakingly restored. Quite a few famous names have spent time here: Napoleon III, Alexandre Dumas, Romain Rolland and Carl Spitteler, awarded the Nobel Prize for his verse composition *Olympic Spring,* in which he made the Weissenstein into a home for gods. The Weissenstein can be reached from **Oberdorf** by chairlift, or by car.

Map on page 282

Wing-eared drinking fountain in Solothurn.

BELOW: Solothurn's main street, with the cathedral in the background.

Solothurn – the French connection

The town of **Solothurn** ⑲, which possesses some of the best-preserved baroque and neoclassical buildings in Switzerland, is unmistakably French in character. Although cut off from the rest of the Catholic federation by the powerful Protestant canton of Bern, it always remained loyal to the Catholic Church and to France; the town even used to maintain an office for recruiting Swiss mercenaries. This formerly rather insignificant place thus grew prosperous, a happy state which the citizens expressed in a zealous fondness for building. Their supreme architectural achievement is the imposing-looking **Altes Zeughaus** (Old Arsenal; open May–Oct Tues–Sun 10am–noon and 2pm–5pm, Nov–Apr Tues–Fri 2–5pm, Sat and Sun 10am–noon and 2–5pm; tel: 032 623 3528; entrance fee), on Zeughausplatz 1, which today contains what is regarded as the most important collection of weaponry and uniforms in Switzerland.

Another impressive site in the town is the **Jesuit church**, built in 1680. The backdrop of patricians' houses is dominated by the neoclassical **St Ursen Cathedral** (open daily 9am–noon and 2–6pm, to 5pm in winter; entrance fee), built in 1762 by the Pisoni family of Ascona and still counted as one of Switzerland's greatest baroque treasures; the interior is even more impressive. The tower provides an exellent vista of the surrounding countryside.

Solothurn is also a good place for museums; most worthy of mention is the excellent and free-admission **Kunstmuseum** (Werkhofstrasse 30, open daily 10am–noon and 2–5pm; free; tel: 032 622 23 07), containing works by Holbein, Buchser and especially Hodler, to name but a few of the artists.

The surrounding countryside has some hidden attractions. In a wooded ravine up on the Weissenstein to the north lies the **Hermitage of St Verena**, steeped in legend and set amid beautiful scenery. The hermitage is not open to the public but you could ask to see its chapel which has a fresco and painted ceiling.

Following the ridgeway leading from the Weissenstein, where there is also a **Botanical Garden**, in the direction of **Grenchenberg**, you will finally end up in the second-largest town in Solothurn, **Grenchen**, which lies on the cantonal border with Bern. This is a rather haphazard collection of houses, dominated by the all-powerful Swiss watch industry.

Contrasts in a small area

In autumn, on the slopes of the **Chasseral** – the highest and southernmost ridge of the **Bernese Jura** region, another 20–30 km (12–20 miles) southwest of Solothurn – grapes slowly ripen in the sun (the vintners of **Bieler See** produce a good sparkling wine). The Chasseral, accessible from the south and the north via various roads, or by the chairlift via Nods, affords unique panoramic views of almost the whole of the Alps. On its southern flank lies the coomb of the **Tessenberg**, a huge sunny terrace. The Tessenberg can also be reached from **Ligerz** (on Bieler See's northern shore) by cable car or on foot through the Twannbach Ravine. Opposite is **St Peter's Insel** – a rather skinny peninsula sticking out into the lake, and a paradise for

Solothurn was the 11th canton to join the Confederation, in 1481, since when 11 has become a key number for the town of the same name: its cathedral even has 11 bells and 11 altars and its staircase is divided into sections of 11 steps each.

BELOW:
in the Taubenloch Gorge near Biel.

Map on page 282

birds and plants; the philosopher Jean-Jacques Rousseau said he spent "the six happiest weeks of my life" here in 1765.

Bieler See is the most northerly of the three Jura lakes (Lac de Morat and Lac de Neuchâtel are the other two), which had their water levels deliberately lowered in the 19th century. The reason for this was twofold: to reclaim land and to act as a preventive measure against malaria and other epidemics which struck in 1868. At the northwest end of the lake lies the only bilingual town in Switzerland, **Biel ⑳** in German, or **Bienne** in French. Its older quarter is most definitely worth a visit, with several well-preserved 16th-century houses and fountains.

The windy **Taubenloch Gorge**, a narrow defile that leads to the pass of Pierre Pertuis, was considered inaccessible until almost the end of the 19th century. Then, in 1890, a path was hewn from rock, and now it is popular with naturelovers. Today, a road connects Biel with **St-Imier**, about 25 km (15 miles) to the west, the self-proclaimed watch capital of the country, whose busy citizens claim an innate ability to make watches.

This valley, dominated by **Mont-Soleil**, used to contain a Benedictine monastery given to the Bishop of Basel as a present in 999. All that is left of it now is the Romanesque **Collegiate church**, but this is worth visiting. In springtime you will find wild daffodils, Alpine violets and gentians, which grow here in their thousands.

There are several ways in which to approach **La Chaux-de-Fonds ㉑**, a relatively modern town 16 km (10 miles) southwest, about 1,000 metres (3,300 ft) above sea level, and metropolis of the Neuchâtel Jura. This watchmaking town, in which the great architect Le Corbusier and the poet Blaise Cendrars

Exhibit from La Chaux-de-Fonds' international watch and clock museum.

BELOW: Swiss watchmaking, big time.

were born, was designed on a drawing board and right angles predominate. The region's main watch museum, **La Musée Internationale d'Horlogerie** (open Tues–Sun 10am–5pm; entrance fee; tel: 032 967 68 61), is situated here, at Rue des Musées, among whose large collection is a huge chiming carillon and a restoration shop.

The other relatively large town in this high valley is only 7 km (4 miles) further away: **Le Locle** ㉒, on the French border. This is where the Swiss watchmaking industry is said to have begun. Most of the original watchmakers were farmers who needed to earn a bit of extra money in the cold winters. Le Locle has its own museum of watches and other mechanical creations, located within the Château des Monts (open May–Oct Tues–Sun 10am–5pm, Nov–Apr 2–5pm; entrance fee). Its other attraction is a 3-km (2-mile) long lake resembling a fjord, **Lac des Brenets**, beyond the cliffs known as the **Col des Roches**. The River Doubs, which enters Swiss territory for the first time here, was dammed up by a prehistoric landslide. The biggest attraction here is the waterfall, the **Saut du Doubs**, which plunges nearly 30 metres (98 ft) into a rocky gorge.

The Neuchâtel Jura

The Haut Jura Neuchâtelois extends a long way, right up to **Les Verrières,** 35 km (20 miles) southwest of Le Locle. **La Brévine**, about halfway between Le Locle and Les Verrières, is also known as the Siberia of Switzerland because temperatures there can drop sometimes even as low as –40°C (–40°F).

Nearby is the quiet **Lac des Taillères**. There are several ways to approach the Neuchâtel Jura, and one of them is from Neuchâtel itself, going north on highway 20 via the **Vue des Alpes Pass** to La Chaux-de-Fonds. The pass was not given its name in vain: the view is magnificent, and extends for many miles.

Neuchâtel ㉓, at the bottom end of the largest lake of the same name, lying wholly on Swiss territory, is a very old town at heart. It was founded in the 11th century by the counts of Neuenburg, who turned the **castle** above the town into a mighty fortress. The **Collegiate church** which Count Ulrich II built next to it in 1147 makes it clear how important this town – which has now developed into a very lively commercial centre – used to be in former days. More proof of this can be found in the town's fine museums. One of the best of these is the **Museum of Art and History** (Esplanade Léopold-Robert; open Tues–Sun 10am–6pm), which has a large collection of old clocks and watches and other antiques.

Tackling the Travers Valley

The Jura should really be tackled in hiking boots. Those who are up to it should gain access to the heights of the Jura from Lac de Neuchâtel by crossing the **Val de Travers**, a lateral valley that made quite a name for itself in the 19th century: on the slopes of the **Creux du Van**, the most impressive limestone cirque in Europe, 1,200 metres (4,000 ft) wide and 2,000 metres (6,500 ft) long, there grows a plant known as wormwood, from which absinthe is derived. In the 19th century the valley developed into quite a lucrative absinthe producer. Absinthe contains *thuja*, which is addictive, and the drink used to be referred to as "La Fée Verte" (the green fairy). Inevitably, the authorities eventually stepped in to stop its manufacture.

Map on page 282

The main town in the valley is **Môtiers** ㉔, 25 km (15 miles) west of Neuchâtel. There are several fine patrician houses to be found here, one of them containing a museum of local history; next door to it, the **Maison Rousseau** – also a small museum (open May–Oct Tues–Thur, Sat and Sun 2–5pm, Nov–Apr on demand; entrance fee; tel: 032 861 13 18) – is a reminder of the famous philosopher and writer, who lived and worked here from 1762 to 1765.

Also of interest are the nearby asphalt mines, in operation until the mid-1980s and now open to visitors.

The Vaud Jura

One of the oldest and most important buildings in all Switzerland can be found at **Romainmôtier**, 16 km (10 miles) southwest of Yverdon-les-Bains on the border between the Neuchâtel and Vaud Jura: the **church** of the former 11th-century **Abbey of St Peter and St Paul**, which has been lovingly restored to an immaculate and historically authentic condition (open daily 7am–6pm; free). Romainmôtier was formerly the centre of the music-box and musical automata industries; nowadays its small **museum** is a reminder of that time, and the concerts held at the abbey on Sunday afternoons through summer help keep the traditional alive today.

The Abbey of St Peter and St Paul in Romainmôtier.

The rest of the southernmost tip of the Jura is covered in this book by the chapter *The West, pages 143–149*, which includes the Vaud region to the south and east of Lac de Neuchâtel as well as the adjacent canton of Fribourg. ❏

BELOW: cross-country skiing in La Brévine.

THE LUZERN LOWLANDS

Maps:
City 300
Area 302

This central region of rounded hillsides and valleys is dominated by the elegant historic city of Luzern, one of Switzerland's first major tourist resorts

The Luzern lowlands, which are made up of several beautiful valleys, extend from Luzern itself in a northwesterly direction towards the canton of Aargau. These valleys have been given their distinctive topography by the ice masses and moraines of the Reuss Glacier. Three great lakes – the Baldeggersee, the Hallwilersee and the Sempachersee – are the legacy of the last period of Ice-Age glaciation more than 10,000 years ago.

In the northern area closest to Aargau these valleys, interspersed by ranges of gentle hills, are used predominantly for arable farming. To the south, where there is more rain, cattle farming dominates. There is a lot to explore in the Luzern lowlands, including the ancient and picturesque towns of Beromünster, Sempach and Willisau. At the region's southern edge, the topography changes again, as it rises towards the pre-Alpine and Alpine regions of Aarau, near Luzern.

Tourist centre

The city of **Luzern ❶** is one of Switzerland's premier tourist destinations, though of far less commercial and financial importance than Basel or Zürich. It is the largest town in Urschweitz and the cultural capital of central Switzerland, but has always been treated as a somewhat separate entity by the rest of the inhabitants of the Lake Luzern area.

Roughly 200 years ago, the poets discovered the beauty of the mountains here, and the verses they penned in celebration provided the first publicity material for promoting tourism in inner Switzerland. Because of its geographical proximity to the Alps, the town of Luzern developed into a convenient base for mountaineering expeditions. It lies 439 metres (1,400 ft) above sea level. Just 10 km (6 miles) away to the southwest is Mt Pilatus, 2,129 metres (6,984 ft) high.

The tourism of that time altered the town's appearance quite considerably. Until the 19th century when sections were razed to the ground, Luzern had managed to retain its medieval city walls. Yet 870 metres (2,800 ft) of the **Museggmauer** (the city wall, built in 1400) still stand and from Easter to September you can walk along the top of the ramparts, which afford a wonderful panorama of the city and its lake. Climb up to them either via the staircase in the outer edge of the wall that you will find just up from the Nölliturm, the most southwesterly of the wall's nine towers, or via the Schirmerturm, one of the central fortifications.

The city's first big hotel was built in 1845. Others soon followed, most of them on the north shore of the lake facing both the sun and the Alps. Then the quay was built, so that locals as well as tourists could take their constitutionals along the bank of Vierwaldstättersee (Lake Luzern) whenever they wished.

PRECEDING PAGES: alphorn player in Luzern. **LEFT:** Luzern and its lake. **BELOW:** water ballet on the Rotsee, near Ebikon.

*One of the figures in
the Bourbaki-
Panorama.*

The heart of Switzerland

For centuries, Luzern, sometimes officially and sometimes unofficially, has been the capital of Switzerland. In the old Confederation, up until the Burgundian Wars (1474–77), Luzern, which had joined in 1332, adopted a kind of "senior" role, and the emissaries of the individual towns often used to meet here. In the 16th century this role was gradually taken over by Zürich, but by then Luzern was the undisputed centre of the Catholic towns. From 1798 to 1799, for a few months only, it became Switzerland's official capital.

When the federal state was formed in 1848, Luzern was not even considered as a potential capital. Not until 1917–18 did the city become the headquarters of the Confederate authorities. Many people consider Luzern to be the secret capital: if Bern is the head, and Zürich the hand, then Luzern can certainly pride itself on being the heart of Switzerland.

As far as culture is concerned, this is certainly the case. There is not just a lot to see, but a lot to hear, too: the dull thud of footsteps crossing what was the oldest roofed wooden bridge in Europe, the **Kapellbrücke** Ⓐ (Chapel Bridge), painstakingly reconstructed after a fire in 1993 destroyed much of it. The bridge has two particularly interesting features: first, the fascinating cycle of pictures in its roof truss, and, second, the famous octagonal water tower (Wasserturm) halfway along, which was a bastion of the 13th-century fortifications and was once used as the town treasury.

Downstream is the **Spreuerbrücke**, a near-contemporary of the original Kapellbrücke, which has survived better than its bigger sister. It is well worth crossing for its series of paintings illustrating the dance of death, executed between 1626 and 1635 by Kaspar Meglinger.

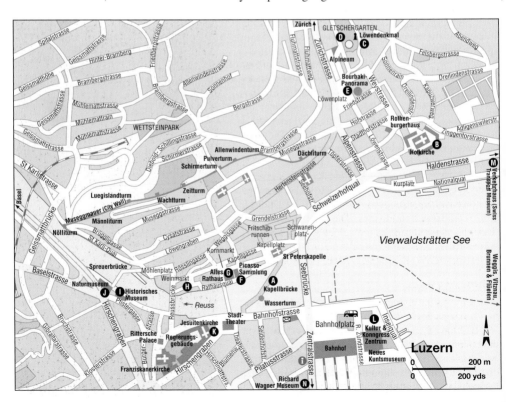

City attractions

On even a short walk through this pedestrian-friendly town you can cover a fair number of interesting sights. Only a few steps from the Nationalquai on the northern lakeshore is the **Hofkirche ❸** (Collegiate church), formerly part of a Benedictine monastery and later a secular canonical foundation. The arcaded churchyard, which is reminiscent of an Italian cemetery, commands a good view of the lake. Take a short detour to see the **Löwendenkmal ❹** (Lion Monument), an exquisite stone memorial, hewn into the living rock. Full of an aching pathos, the lion commemorates the 786 Swiss officers and men who died defending Louis XVI and Marie-Antoinette in the attack on the Tuileries in 1792.

Alongside the Löwendenkmal, at Denkmalstrasse 4, is the **Gletschergarten ❺** (Glacier Garden), with its intriguing potholes, eroded during the Ice Age by glacial meltwater under extreme pressure, and its eclectic museum, which includes a remarkably disorientating mirror maze that was made for the Paris Exhibition of 1896 (open daily Apr–Oct 9am–6pm, Nov–Mar 10am–5pm; entrance fee; tel: 041 410 43 40).

Heading back to the Reuss, you pass Löwenplatz with its **Bourbaki-Panorama ❻** (open daily 9am–6pm; entrance fee; tel: 041 412 30 30), which also merits inspection: it is an enormous circular painting by Edouard Castres, depicting the retreat of the dejected French Army of General Bourbaki into Switzerland in 1871 during the Franco-Prussian War.

The principal site to visit in the delightful medieval core of town is the **Picasso-Sammlung ❼** (Picasso Museum; open daily Apr–Oct 10am–6pm, Nov–Mar 11am–1pm and 2–4pm; entrance fee; tel: 041 410 35 33), in Am-Rhyn Haus, an attractive old Burgher's home on Furrengasse 21, fronting the north bank of the Reuss. It contains a bequest of paintings, but is most interesting for its intimate collection of photographs of the great man during later life.

However, you may simply like to stroll around the centre, window-shopping in its chic boutiques, relaxing in a street-side café, or enjoying the architecture of its squares. On **Hirschenplatz**, several houses have richly painted facades (No. 12, the Göldlinhaus, has an interior courtyard in Renaissance style). Almost adjacent lie two other squares, used in medieval times as marketplaces. On one of these, **Kornmarkt**, you will find the **Altes Rathaus ❽** (Town Hall), built between 1602 and 1606 by Anton Isenmann. Its facade was strongly influenced by the Florentine early-Renaissance style, while the hipped saddleback roof reflects local traditions. The other square, just down Kornmarktgasse, is colourful **Weinmarkt ❾**, whose fountain is a replica of the original, now preserved in the city's Historical Museum *(see below)*.

Top museums

Continuing west, cross the river on Spreuerbrücke to get to the **Historisches Museum ❿** (open Tues–Fri 10am–noon and 2–5pm, Sat and Sun 10am–5pm; entrance fee; tel: 041 228 54 24), on Pfistergasse 24, which counts among its stylishly presented historical exhibits the suit of chainmail that Habsburg Duke Leopold III was wearing at his death in the 1386 Battle

TIP

On 5 December, the town of Kussnacht, in Zug canton, holds a bizarre, candle-lit festival in which men and women parade the streets wearing bishops' mitres.

BELOW: Luzern's historic Kappelbrücke.

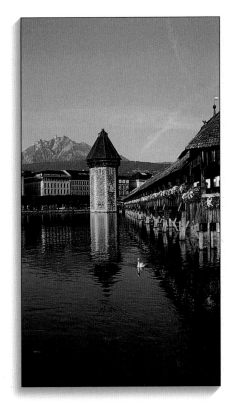

of Sempach *(see page 31)*; and nearby on Kasernenplatz is the **Naturhistorisches Museum** (open Tues–Fri 10am–noon and 2–5pm, Sat and Sun 10am–5pm; entrance fee; tel: 041 228 54 11), which has plenty of "hands-on" exhibits.

Walking along the Reuss in the direction of the lake, you pass the **Jesuitenkirche** (Jesuit Church of St Franz Xaver), Switzerland's oldest large baroque church. Built between 1666 and 1677, it contains the first examples of stucco by the Wessobrunn School. The nearby Franciscan church is also worth visiting.

Cultural attractions

Luzern is also one of the best places to tune into Swiss culture, such as the overpowering din of the Guggenmusik bands during the Fasnacht carnival *(see page 274)*: or the far more harmonious sounds of the International Festival of Music (should you be lucky enough to get a highly sought-after ticket). The festival features orchestras such as the Berlin Philharmonic and takes place in **Kultur und Kongress Zentrum** , the vast, modern Culture and Congress Centre, which dominates the lakeshore in front of the railway station. Opened in 1998, it has some of the best acoustics of any international concert hall.

The **Neues Kunstmuseum** (Fine Arts Museum; open Tues–Sun 10am–5pm, late night Wed and Thurs until 8pm; entrance fee; tel: 041 226 78 00) is housed inside this rather surgical building, which is perhaps more interesting than the collection of contemporary art and 19th-century Swiss landscapes found inside.

Leaving the city centre around the northern side of the lake, you come to the **Verkehrhaus** (The Swiss Transport Museum; open daily 10am–6pm; entrance fee; tel: 041 370 44 44), on Lidostrasse 5, the largest museum of its kind in Europe. It contains exhibits on virtually every conceivable method of

TIP

A range of boat cruises is available on the Vierwaldstättersee, from a short ride to a 6-hour trip to the far end of the lake (tel: 041 367 67 67; www.lakelucerne.ch for details).

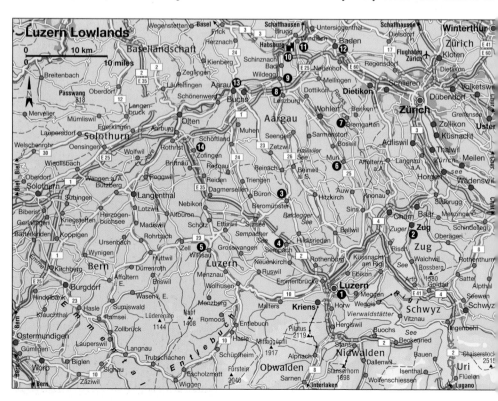

mechanical transport (including space modules and cable cars) and has a commendably interactive ethos that is a delight for adults and kids alike. This vast complex also includes Switzerland's first Imax cinema (great for rainy days; tel: 041 375 75 75) and a ride through a mock-up of the St Gotthard Tunnel, which gives an insight into the tribulations that workers on this pioneering engineering project had to endure. An annexe houses an impressive collection of works by one of Switzerland's greatest 20th-century artists, Hans Erni, and whose star turn is "Panta Rhei" – a series of murals that portrays great philosophers and scientists who have influenced the development of western thought.

In the tranquil villa of Tribschen, on the lake's southern shore, on the outskirts of town, is the **Richard Wagner Museum **, on Richard Wagner Weg 27 (open mid-Mar–Nov Tues–Sun 10am–noon and 2–5pm; entrance fee; tel: 041 360 23 70). In this house, between 1866 and 1872, the great composer wrote his "Siegfried-idyll" in honour of his wife, Cosima. The museum houses a collection of musical instruments and the composer's personal effects.

Maps:
City 300
Area 302

Snow train in Luzern's Swiss Transport Museum.

The Reuss and Aare basins

From Luzern, the Reuss flows in a northerly direction towards the Rhein. To the northeast of the city and the canton of Luzern lies the canton of Zug, one of Switzerland's smallest regions, also bearing traces of the Reuss glacier across its landscape. On the old road from **Küssnacht** to Immensee, which used to connect Lake Luzern and the Zugersee, lies the **Hohle Gasse** (sunken lane) and the **William Tell Chapel**. It was here, in 1307, at the foot of the massif known as the Rigi, that Gessler, the Habsburg bailiff, who had forced Tell to shoot the apple from the head of his son, was killed *(see William Tell, page 27)*.

BELOW: one of Luzern's lake steamers, which depart from the quays in front of the train station.

Travelling 30 km (19 miles) to the northeast of Luzern, you come to **Zug ❷**, on the shores of its lake (Zuger See). This is one of the smallest cantonal capitals in Switzerland, but it nevertheless plays a bustling economic role in the region. The considerable construction work going on here gives a clue to its new-found role as a centre for international businesses but so far there have not been any controversial alterations to the engaging and compact historic centre.

Founded in the 13th century, Zug has a wealth of interesting sites: from the castle (once the residence of the Habsburg governors, today housing a cantonal museum) to the Catholic Church of St Oswald, with its fine choir stalls, and the striking Zytturm (clock tower), with its blue and white painted tiles (the colours of the canton). Ask at the police station next door if you want to visit the church. Also of interest are the imposing mansions on the lakefront and richly decorated 16th-century Brandenberghaus, at St Oswalds-Gasse 17, which houses the **Afrika-Museum** (open Mon–Fri 8.30–11.30am and 2–5.30pm, Sat and Sun on request; free; tel: 041 711 04 17), run by the St Petrus Claver Sodalität sisterhood of nuns. This is a small but interesting collection of stuffed animals and 19th- and 20th-century artefacts from Africa, including a bizarre and rare nail-fetish idol from the Democratic Republic of Congo.

In the restored castle, on Kirchenstrasse 11, is the

A local speciality of Zug is the Zuger Kirschtorte, a rich cherry cake, with a notoriously high alcohol content.

attractively laid-out **Museum in Der Burg** (Cantonal Museum; open Tues–Fri 2–5pm, Sat and Sun 10am–noon and 2–5pm; entrance fee; tel: 041 728 32 97), with some fine religious sculptures and displays on life in Zug through the ages.

Luzern canton

The fact that Luzern and the canton of Luzern are mainly Catholic is something that can be experienced at first hand in **Beromünster** ❸, a neatly kept historical town, just to the west of Baldegger See, which grew up around a monastery founded in 981 by Bero von Lenzburg. Each Ascension Day the impressive "Ascension Ride" takes place: over 100 riders, including the lay canons from the foundation, take part in this church procession on horseback, entering the town in the afternoon. This old ceremony is associated with blessing the fields and checking the boundary markers. Beromünster's needle-spire St Michael's Minster is worth checking out for its wedding-cake rococo interior, composed of dolphin-blue stucco, and the paisley-style heraldic shields of past provosts and canons emblazoned on the whitewashed walls of the portico.

Sempach ❹, northeast of Luzern, reflects a key aspect of Swiss history. The Battle of Sempach *(see page 31)*, on 9 July 1386, when a small Swiss force managed to defeat Duke Leopold III of Austria, is described in every school textbook. The battle site is 4 km (2.5 miles) northeast of town on the road to Hildisrieden and Hochdorf, where you will find a restaurant and a simple chapel with a remarkable fresco of the battle. A commemorative parade in military dress is held in the morning of the first Saturday in July every year. A more contemporary struggle, though, took place in the attempts to restore the formerly heavily

BELOW: masked Fasnacht revellers from Luzern.

Map on page 302

polluted **Sempacher See** (Sempach Lake) to health. Thanks to artificial oxygenation, and much stricter water protection laws, this has largely succeeded – good news for the lakeside **Vogelwarte Sempach** birdwatching area, one of Switzerland's most important bird sanctuaries.

Willisau and Aargau canton

Willisau ❺, a fortified town on the northeastern boundary of the Napf region, is centred on one broad, flag-lined medieval street. It has established itself as the venue for a music festival (running from 31 August to 3 September every year) offering an eclectic mix of everything from jazz to world music and rap. Indeed, members of the local yodelling club have ventured into the realms of jazz improvisation as well. Here at Willisau we are already in the Napf region, which also contains the world-famous cheese production Emmental area (see *The Bernese Oberland, page 123*).

Costumed knight from Sempach's annual historical battle parade.

Most of the region downriver of the Reuss from Luzern belongs to the German-speaking canton of Aargau, the least mountainous region of Switzerland. It is here that the Habsburg family had its origins. There are numerous castles and manor houses dotted along the route here, reminders of the days of chivalry and the life of the landed gentry, or *Junkertum*, in the rococo period. Aargau is now largely reformed, but memories of the Habsburgs also evoke the old Catholicism that still survives in the former Benedictine abbey in **Muri ❻**, a town that lies halfway between Aarau and Zug. Founded in 1027, and one of the great centres of religious art in Switzerland, the monastery was re-modelled in baroque style by Caspar Mosbrugger in 1695. The Loreto Chapel in the north walk of the former cloister has served as a family vault of the Habsburgs.

BELOW: the moated castle at Hallwil.

Due north of Muri, some 9 km (6 miles) as the crow flies, is the delightful little town of **Bremgarten** , which has many medieval and baroque buildings and a covered wooden bridge across the River Reuss. The town received its charter from Rudolf of Habsburg in 1256, and has retained an air of Catholic supremacy for which it was once renowned.

Historic sites and spa waters

The three major rivers of the region – the Aare flowing northeast from Aarau; the Reuss in the middle, streaming north from Luzern; and the Limmat heading northwest from Zürich – converge before running north to the mighty Rhein. Many historical seats of power lie in the triangular area of land found between the Aare and Limmat, whose northern apex is the Wassertor at these two rivers' confluence. The landscape, with its distinctive fields, forests and meadows nestling among rows of hills, is romantically reproduced in pastoral paintings decorating many of the castle walls.

Two of the better-known castles are at **Lenzburg** and **Wildegg** , lying on an imaginary line running roughly northwards from Hallwiler See to Brugg. These castles (both of them museums as well) go to some lengths to give visitors a flavour of their rich history. In some cases the proprietors stage their own attractions. **Schloss Lenzburg** (open Apr–Oct Tues–Sun 10am–5pm; entrance fee; tel: 062 888 48 40) has a son et lumière show of the various wars that raged in the region. The exhibits include a realistic, fire-breathing dragon to scare off visitors. Perched on a hill top and reached via an avenue of beautiful walnut trees, evocative **Schloss Wildegg** (open Tues–Sun 10am–5pm; entrance fee; tel: 062 893 10 33) is an offshoot of the Swiss National Museum. The castle's decorated chambers and halls have been wonderfully restored, with period furniture and exhibits of armour. Outside, you can enjoy the fantastic landscaped baroque-style gardens, which include cultivated plots of rare herbs, fruit and vegetables. There are tomatoes in a star formation and blue potatoes growing alongside flowers. Parts of the castle date back to the 13th century and it originally belonged to the House of Habsburg.

Habsburg Castle (open access), a few kilometres to the southwest of Brugg, is the obvious starting point for understanding the history of this region, and of Europe, come to that. The home of the dynasty of the same name, it has declined like its former owners – it has now become small and unassuming in aspect, and only the western half of it has survived. You should not be disappointed, however: the restaurant alone is worth a visit (restaurant open throughout the year except Mon and Tues during Oct–Apr; tel: 056 441 16 73), for its rich Swiss cuisine and the pleasant, bucolic view.

Known to the Romans as Vindonissa, the town of **Windisch** stands on the Aare close to its confluence with the River Reuss, just to the southeast of Brugg. Here there is a Roman amphitheatre that once had room for 10,000 people; today all that remains is a low, circular wall. **Brugg** itself has a well-endowed Roman museum, the Vindonissa-Museum (open Tues–Sun 10am–noon and 2–5pm; entrance fee; tel: 056 441 21 84). Outside the city walls lies the ele-

BELOW: Alpine meadow in full spring bloom.

gant former 14th-century **Abbey of Königsfelden**, with its magnificent stained glass, dating from the 1320s.

Lying a little further to the southeast, **Baden** , too, can pride itself on its Roman heritage: as Aquae Helveticae it appears in the work of Tacitus. Situated on the left bank of the Limmat above an abrupt bend, this ancient town and spa is now an industrial centre. In the 19th century, however, when spas were the height of fashion in Europe, the town boomed. The prospect of naked female flesh drew Casanova here in 1760, but nowadays visitors are drawn here less for love than for taking the curative treatments in the sulphurous waters.

Visitors not in need of healing should take a stroll through the marvellously intact old town, the ruins of Stein Castle towering impressively above it. The **Landvogtei-schloss**, the bailiff's castle, which dates from 1414 to 1712, houses a historical museum (open Tues–Fri 1–5pm, Sat & Sun 10am–5pm; entrance fee; tel: 056 222 75 74). The town's other major attraction is the **Langmatt Foundation** (open Apr–Oct Tues–Fri 2–5pm, Sat & Sun 11am–5pm; entrance fee; tel: 056 222 58 42), on Römerstrasse 30, which has a marvellous collection of Impressionist and Fauvist art.

Aarau and Zofingen

Standing on the River Aare to the southwest of Baden is **Aarau** , a town with an attractive medieval nucleus of tightly knit lanes and solidly constructed buildings. In 1798, Aarau became the first capital of the new federal "Helvetic Republic", but this honour lasted a mere six months and it had to content itself with being recognised as Aargau's cantonal capital in 1803. However, this status has not always been uncontested: right up until the present day, it has had difficulty in being recognised as the centre of this heterogeneous "patchwork canton", which consists of almost a dozen small towns and several rural regions that were formerly of equal importance. However, Aarau's role as a seat of cantonal government, parliament and administration has definitely contributed greatly to the outward appearance of the town.

The town's most impressive landmark is one of the old city clock-towers: the **Oberer Turm** (mostly 16th-century, but parts of which date from 1270), which has an intriguing Cubist-inspired *Dance of Death* mural on the south side, painted by local artist Felix Hoffmann in 1966.

The last Aargau town before we return to the Luzern lowlands is **Zofingen** , which lies to the southwest of Aarau on the road that leads between Olten and Luzern, via Sempacher See (Lake Sempach). This is a small industrial centre with a remarkably well-preserved historical core, dating back to the high Middle Ages. It was in Habsburg hands from 1251 and its ramparts were besieged by the Bernese in 1415. With its imposing-looking baroque buildings, it also provides a fine example of the numerous towns that were founded here in the high and late Middle Ages and which determined the entire pattern of settlement in Switzerland. Two mosaic floors from a large **Roman Villa** very close to the town are another reminder of earlier inhabitants of this area. ❑

TIP

Near to Aarau, in the town of Schönenwerd, are the headquarters of world-famous Bally shoes, with a Museum of Footwear in the former owner's villa.

BELOW: dramatic portrayal of a drummer boy at Schloss Lenzburg.

INNER SWITZERLAND

The unifying feature of the three otherwise unremarkable cantons of Uri, Schwyz and Unterwalden is the Rütli meadow, historic site of the declaration of the Swiss Confederation in 1291

Historically speaking, a sensible starting point for a journey through Inner Switzerland would be a small meadow known as the **Rütli**, at the northern end of **Urner See** (Lake Uri), the eastern extension of the Vierwaldstätter See (Lake Luzern). Here, on 1 August 1291, three representatives of the regions of Uri, Schwyz and Unterwalden are said to have held a secret meeting at which they solemnly swore to uphold a mutual assistance pact *(see page 29)*. The Rütli meadow, at the centre of so-called Inner Switzerland, is where, according to legend, the liberation of the Swiss Confederation had its origins.

Cradle of the Confederation

The concept of Inner Switzerland conveys no sense of unity, or of any common economic, political or even geographical identity, and the idea of a kind of "Confederate unity" linking Uri, Schwyz, Obwalden and Nidwalden as well as Zug and Luzern is something that will, at best, provoke a smile of sympathy from the inner Swiss peoples.

So what about these "little cantons", as 19th-century travellers called them: Uri, Schwyz, Obwalden and Nidwalden (the latter two known collectively as Unterwalden)? In the final years of the 13th century, they must have comprised an astonishingly lively body politic, as the seeds sown by the formation of the Confederation began to take hold with shifting cantonal alliances, and with the growth of trade boosted by the opening to traffic of the St Gotthard Pass.

A glance at any map reveals that this rather enclosed area was by no means likely to achieve political and enonomic union. Nature, aided by Vierwaldstätter See, had arranged things so that the regions of *Urschweiz* (Inner Switzerland) were not forced to maintain harmonious and lasting relations with one another. The three regions have combined a policy of co-operation towards the other side of the lake – a policy they regard as expedient more than anything else – with a frequent and forthright pursuit of their own interests.

It was thus obvious that Schwyz would start trying to extend its influence, first against Arth, Zug and Küssnacht, then against Einsiedeln and out into the Linth Plain. Until the 19th century, Uri could only be reached from the north by crossing the lake, and was thus only able to extend its influence eastward in the direction of the Urseren Valley, a short way into Glarus, and in the direction of the southern Alpine valleys. Finally, in 1865, work was completed on the Axenstrasse – a narrow road built along the steep eastern shore of the Urnersee from Brunnen, at last linking Uri with the north.

Map on page 312

PRECEDING PAGES:
Einsiedeln Kloster,
Benedictine abbey.
LEFT:
sculpture outside
Ital Reding Hofstatt.
BELOW:
amateur actors
playing William
Tell and his son.

Unterwalden, stuck between the Seelisberg and the Bürgenstock, between the Urner Alps, the lake and the Brünig, never had any real chance to expand. Instead, the Unterwaldner just argued among themselves, resulting in the creation of the cantons of Obwalden and Nidwalden, which are separated by a high moor and a dark forest.

As the centuries progressed, the powerful leaders of Schwyz, the cosmopolitan cattle drivers of Uri and the rather introverted Obwaldner and Nidwaldner – all situated in close proximity to each other in this small area – developed ways of life, economic patterns and political cultures that were distinctively different from one another. Today, the *Urschweiz* cantons are characterised by the political dominance of the Christliche Volkspartei (Christian People's Party), the fond way in which traditions and old customs are upheld and the common religious persuasion (Catholicism). Combined with these qualities is a certain consumer conformism which gives an outsider the happy impression of Inner Switzerland as a rich but smooth stew with the odd hint of archaism. It is considered a charming, but also a rather unimportant, sort of place that tends to be neglected.

Whether this splendid isolation will last is questionable. What with the corridor for goods traffic, the future trans-Alpine rail link coming here and the increasing attraction of the area for holiday and second homes the place may not be able to remain a charming backwater for ever.

The traditional hearty Swiss dish of sausage and chips, washed down with an ice-cold beer.

Going in by the back way

So, to avoid using Luzern as a starting point and to begin a visit to Inner Switzerland at one of its outermost points, it is best to enter **Obwalden** canton from the south via the **Brünigpass** ❶. Today, there is a road as well as the **Brünig Rail-**

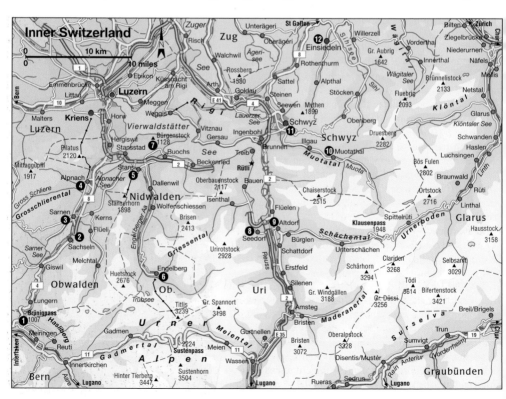

Map
on page
312

way with its carriages offering panoramic views across the pass, making the journey easy, but in the Middle Ages a barrier blocked the way here (denying access to the lords of the Bernese Oberland who were eager to expand their territory) and the steep terrain falling away in the direction of **Lungern** provided the canton with extra protection against conquerors and invaders.

Travelling north along highway 4, after **Giswil** the landscape gets a lot broader and gentler and also provides enough room for the **Sarner See**, a small and typical resort lake, ringed by gentle hills with the higher Alps towering beyond. Even further north, the towns of **Sachseln** ❷, nearby **Flüeli** and the **Ranft** form the centres of an important pilgrimage. Niklaus von Flüe, Switzerland's only saint, was born in Flüeli in 1417; after an active life in local politics he spent 20 years fasting and praying in the remoteness of the Ranft. His remains, visited by about 100,000 pilgrims each year, have been kept in Sachseln's church since 1934. No wonder, then, that the area is full of guesthouses and hotels. Indeed, Switzerland's first motel was built in Sachseln.

It is true that **Sarnen** ❸, the capital of the canton of Obwalden a few kilometres north, has no saints to speak of, but it does have a modern and architecturally remarkable **monastery** and the baroque **Church of St Peter and St Paul**. The town's hill, the **Landenberg**, provided an attractive setting for the *Landsgemeinde* (vote), which from 1646 until 1998 was held outdoors annually on the last Sunday in April. The **Rathaus** (Town Hall) contains the so-called *Weisses Buch* (White Book), which includes the earliest account of the history of the Confederation, written during the 1470s.

Of all the museums in Inner Switzerland, the **Heimatmuseum** (Obwalden local museum; open mid-Apr–Nov Mon–Sat 2–5pm; entrance fee; tel: 041 660 65 22) in Sarnen on Brünigstrasse 127, is the most varied and best endowed, and it provides a comprehensive overview of the culture and history of the region. Exhibits include a number of prehistoric items, Roman material from the settlement of Alpnach, weaponry from the Middle Ages, various examples of religious art and pictures and sculptures by local artists from the 17th century until the present day.

Return to highway 4, leave Sarnen and head for **Alpnach** ❹, 8 km (5 miles) north. At this point you have already reached the lower end of the canton. On one of the oldest rack railways in Switzerland it takes 30 minutes to travel between **Alpnachstad** and **Mount Pilatus** at 2,120 metres (6,955 ft), affording unparalleled views of the Alps and out across the entire lowlands. On the shore of the lake, the remains of a Roman villa were unearthed some time ago – evidence that this part of the country has been inhabited for at least 2,000 years.

The Nidwalden

Anyone wanting to go to **Nidwalden** canton (which covers an area to the north up to the southern shore of the Vierwaldstättersee) from Obwalden can do it via the road that runs along the shores of the **Alpnacher See** in the direction of **Stansstad**, but a more attractive route is northeast via Kerns, through the dark Kernwald and across the practically flat Ice-Age valley to **Stans** ❺.

TIP

If you are a fan of church architecture, have a look inside **Sarnen**'s church, which is beautifully decorated, especially the chapel ceiling.

BELOW: choppy *Föhn* weather on the Urner See.

This is the main village in Nidwalden, and it has a small aircraft industry. The old town has been painstakingly restored and cleaned up over the years and two museums, the "**Höfli**" (open Apr–Oct Wed–Sat 2–5pm, Sun 10am–midday, 2–5pm; Nov–Mar Wed & Sat 2–5pm, Sun 10am–midday, 2–5pm) in its centre and the **Winkelriedhaus** (open Wed & Sat 2–5pm, Sun 10am–midday, 2–5pm) slightly outside the village, reflect the wealth and power of the patricians who once lived here. The early-baroque church, the old Romanesque tower and the Gothic ossuary dominate the broad village square, which also contains the monument to Arnold von Winkelried who, legend has it, helped a Confederate army out of trouble near Sempach in 1386 by throwing himself on to a flurry of enemy lances.

Although it is not strictly within Nidwalden, but is in fact part of Obwalden, **Engelberg ❻**, 25 km (15 miles) south, is simpler to reach on an excursion from Stans. With its excellent walking country, hills and lakes, it is a popular winter and summer resort. Its **Benedictine abbey** was founded in the 12th century and remodelled in the baroque style between 1730 and 1737. The abbey contains an important library and also doubles as a boarding school.

Because of its location Engelberg is an active winter resort area. Skiing and especially snowboarding are popular – there are several schools teaching both skills – but the slopes are not as carved up by trails as they could be and the town has not yet been given over completely to tourism. As a result a visit here makes a pleasant outing, attracting a surprisingly youthful crowd. The **Laub Wall** of the Titlis is a death-defying run, however, for experts only – do not go up there without plenty of experience and insurance.

For a more gentle summertime activity visitors can take the sequence of cable cars and lifts from Engelberg to the summit of the **Titlis**, which at 3,239 metres

TIP

Be sure to take a ride in one of the cable cars at Engelberg which has cabins that rotate, providing riders with a 360-degree view of the surrounding valley.

BELOW: the daily trek through the Alpine pastures.

(10,627 ft) is the tallest peak in this part of Switzerland. Besides astounding views, you will also have the opporunity to walk atop a glacier (along a carefully marked road) and enjoy drinks from a bar built in an ice cave. The ride to the mountain top and glacier can be costly but is worth it for the view across the valley to numerous, jewel-like lakes and other towering peaks including Mount Pilatus (2,121 metres/6,959 ft) near Alpnachstad. Smaller summits such as **Brunni** (1,402 metres/4,600 ft) to the east and **Fürenalp** can also be reached by cable car which operate from the Engelberg area.

High above the lake

Another interesting excursion from Stans, this time heading north via Stansstad, leads to the **Bürgenstock** ❼ mountain (1,128 metres/3,701 ft), which has an imposing group of late 19th-century hotels and an incomparable view of **Lake Luzern**. A small path leads away from the hotels along a rock face to the **Hammet-schwandlift**, a panoramic lift for anyone with a head for heights, which whisks you up to the summit at breathtaking speed. Afterwards, you can go down into the valley by funicular from the hotels.

Alternatively, travel northeast from Stans and you will reach Lake Luzern, which looks almost Mediterranean; there the route disappears into the **Seelisberg Tunnel**, emerging in the canton of Uri a few minutes later. A trip across the lake is also an option. You can board a ship in **Beckenried** on the southern shore and travel east to **Treib**. From there, take the funicular up to **Seelisberg**, and then hike along the "Swiss Path", which was constructed as part of Switerland's 700th-birthday celebrations, high above Lake Luzern and the Rütli meadow. The path goes south 15 km (9 miles) past the little castle of

Map on page 312

Souvenir cowbells, available in all shapes and sizes.

BELOW:
breathtaking views from the lift on Bürgenstock mountain.

Beroldingen, down to **Bauen** and along a passageway cut out of the rock to Seedorf **8**, where you can rejoin the motorway.

The baroque church, the tower of the lords of Seedorf, the small 16th-century castle and the nearby convent form a delightful ensemble, called the Benedictine Kloster, built in 1197 and renovated in 1695. They also make it instantly clear that this place must once have been a very important shipment point for goods coming across Urner See. From here they would have been transported throughout the canton via the St Gotthard Pass towards the south.

East of Seedorf is **Altdorf 9**, the capital of the canton of Uri, which lies on another old route, leading from **Flüelen** via Altdorf east into the **Schächental**, and which also leads in the direction of the St Gotthard Pass. A reminder of the city's former importance and busy traffic is the **Fremdenspital**, a hospital which offered refuge to pilgrims and sick and impoverished travellers. The **Capuchin monastery** high up on the mountainside, where the Counter Reformation in Switzerland had its origins, and the patrician houses give one some idea of the wealth engendered by the brisk trade across the St Gotthard Pass.

Moreover, Altdorf and nearby **Bürglen** are particularly closely connected with the legendary origin of the Confederation. It was in Altdorf that William Tell defied the hated bailiff, Gessler, and as a result was forced to shoot an apple off his son Walter's head *(see page 27)*. Tell's house is believed to have stood in Bürglen and so it is the site of the **Tell Museum**, on Postplatz (open daily July–Aug 9.30am–5.30pm, May–June and Sept–Oct 10–11.30am and 1.30–5pm; entrance fee; tel: 041 870 41 55). However, the archer is commemorated in Altdorf by a much-photographed **monument** by Richard Kissling and by the **Tell Theatre**, built in 1925. Schiller's *Wilhelm Tell* (1805) is regularly performed at the theatre.

Also on the old route to the St Gotthard Pass, a little further south of Altdorf, are the ruins of a **castle** that once belonged to the Lords of Attinghausen.

Traffic past and present

Over a period of roughly 600 years, travellers and goods would leave Flüelen and Altdorf and head south along a route now marked by Autoroute No. 2, in the direction of the St Gotthard Pass and Italy, past the Von Silenen Residence Tower in **Silenen**, past the castle of Zwing Uri near **Erstfeld**, to the 18th-century church in **Wassen**. In the early days the journey was done mostly on foot or, at best, on horseback. Later, after a road had been constructed, people travelled by coach and wagon. From 1882 onwards traffic used the rail tunnel and, since 1980, the St Gotthard road tunnel.

The valley, narrow and dignified, and for centuries dominated only by the thundering sound of the Reuss River, is now filled with the sound of heavy traffic 24 hours a day; even worse, the clear mountain air is being polluted by exhaust fumes. While it is still possible to ascend the wild Schöllenen ravine on foot along the old mountain trail and hike all the way to the St Gotthard Pass, complete silence and really fine hiking can only be found high up in the lateral valleys: in the **Urseren**, and in the **Göschener**, **Maderaner**, **Meien** and **Schächen** valleys.

The castle at Attinghausen was where Freiherr von Attinghausen, who featured in Schiller's William Tell play, died in 1321.

BELOW: well equipped for the active outdoor life.

In the 1940s there was a plan to flood the whole of the Urseren Valley in a massive hydroelectricity scheme. It was only when the locals ejected the gentlemen from the lowland electricity board out of their valley that the entire plan, which seems crazy today, was eventually dropped. Today the valley is one of the few skiing areas in Switzerland that can guarantee snow every winter.

In the Schächen Valley stories are still told about General Suvorov and his Cossack troops, who fought Napoleon and the French on Swiss soil; although he brought war, devastation and hunger to the country, the general's forced marches across the St Gotthard, Kinzig and Pragel passes earned him the respect and admiration of the local inhabitants.

Map on page 312

Elegant edifices

The canton of Schwyz had its own experience of Suvorov: the general, forced to retreat from the French, moved east via **Muotathal ⑩** in the direction of **Glarus** and incurred heavy losses. It is assumed that the **icon** which hangs in the **parish church** (1792) in Muotathal was left behind during this retreat. Nothing is known of the origins of the 8th-century **Merovingian reliquary** that forms part of the church treasure, though the hamlet of Muotathal, as well as nearby **Illgau** and **Morschach**, was populated as early as the 10th century: something quite astonishing for such a remote area, lying deep in a forested gorge of the Muota River.

Northwest of Muotathal, the town of **Schwyz ⑪**, capital of the canton, has seen so much uncontrolled construction over the past 20 years or so that its original housing pattern can scarcely be discerned. The very centre of the town, however, retains traces of its old character, notably the broad square and the richly decorated baroque **Church of St Martin**. At one time a dozen or so town houses, complete with imposing facades and extensive gardens, would have graced the square. Today, only a handful of traditional patrician houses (17th–18th-century) remain and they have been interspersed with modern structures.

BELOW:
the Ital-Reding-Haus in Schwyz.

Particularly noticeable is the baroque-influenced **Ital-Reding-Haus** (open Apr–Nov Tues–Fri 2–5pm, Sat and Sun 10am–noon and 2–5pm; entrance fee; tel: 041 811 45 05). The 700-year-old **Haus Bethlehem**, which is now a museum, stands beside the Ital-Reding-Haus. The Haus Bethlehem is the oldest wooden house in Switzerland, built in 1287 and renovated in 1989. Still quite grand, and kept cool by its air conditioning, is the **Bundesbriefarchiv**, at Bahnhofstrasse 20 in the town centre (open Tues–Fri 9.30–11.30am and 1.30–5pm, Sat and Sun 9am–5pm, opens at 1.30pm Nov–Apr weekends; free; tel: 041 819 20 64). The archives, which contain the **Bundesbrief** of 1291 (the original deed of confederation signed in Rutli), also holds other important documents and written alliances from Swiss and cantonal history, plus a collection of pennants, flags and banners.

Also of interest in Schwyz is the **Rathaus**, opposite the Church of St Martin. It is not open to the public but its splendid facade is decorated with a series of frescoes illustrating different events in Swiss history.

BELOW: ornate panelling inside the Ital-Reding-Haus.

Other places of historical significance to the northwest of Schwyz include the ruins of the **Gesslerburg** in Küssnacht (seat of the Habsburg governor Gessler, killed by William Tell), the ruins on the island of **Schwanau** on the Lauerzer See and the **Hohle Gasse** ("sunken lane", where Tell killed Gessler), near **Immensee**. Visitors may also see the last remaining pieces of *Letzine* (barrages) at Arth, Morgarten, Rothenturm and Brunnen. The ruins and remnants are all testimonies to the series of battles fought against the local nobility and the House of Habsburg at the beginning of the 14th century.

The municipality of **Gersau**, 12 km (7 miles) west of Schwyz, has the warm *Föhn* wind, as well as its sheltered position by the lake, to thank for the fact that it can support both chestnut trees and palm trees; both grow in profusion. A further attraction is the well-constructed road that runs from **Brunnen** to **Küssnacht**, some 28 km (17 miles) to the northwest, along the shore of the Vierwaldstättersee, via Gersau, Vitznau and Weggis. The scenic route is full of bends and, along some stretches, almost like the corniche at Monte Carlo. From Gersau it is about 20 km (12 miles) to the **Astrid Chapel**, between Merlischachen and Küssnacht, overlooking the Vierwaldstättersee. Inside the chapel is the grave of Queen Astrid of Belgium, who died in an accident in the town in the 1930s, and who is venerated almost as much as a saint.

Nearby **Merlischachen**, about 9 km (5 miles) south of Küssnacht, is a small village, containing a few grand farmhouses, which is worth the slight detour to make a pleasant break in your journey. The Swiss Chalet Hotel, brightened by geraniums and small red lanterns, is a thoroughly romantic place to stay, and in the Schloss Hotel – popular with honeymooners – you can sleep in a gondola in a swimming pool (*see Travel Tips, page 334, for contact details*).

Monastic community

The town of **Einsiedeln** ⑫, 20 km (12 miles) north of Schwyz on highway 8, is another focal point in the canton. The surrounding area is an excellent place to enjoy the countryside. The meadows are used for winter skiing, and in the summer the **Sihlsee** is a hotbed of water sports, fishing, lakeside camping and swimming.

Einsiedeln's importance is not a modern occurrence; it dates back to the 10th century, when Eberhard, Dean of Strasbourg, founded a monastic community above the hermitage of a monk from Reichenau, Meinrad, who had been murdered in 861. Duke Hermann of Swabia donated to the monastery a portion of land to farm. For years the Habsburg-controlled abbey was involved in a long and bitter dispute with the people of Schwyz about rights to the cattle-grazing land between the town and the monastery. In 1314 a band of Schwyz men attacked the abbey, took the sleeping monks prisoner, drank the abbey's wine and desecrated the religious relics.

The abbey, whose prince abbots minted their own coins, lost much of its secular power in 1798 as a result of the revolution, but as a place of pilgrimage, and the next stop on the pilgrim route after Santiago de Compostela, Einsiedeln has been a major centre of Catholic Christianity for centuries.

The monastery's heyday, however, was during the 17th and 18th centuries, when pilgrimages to the "Black Madonna" painting in the **Gnadenkapelle** (Chapel of Grace) were at their height. This led to the construction, between 1674 and 1770, of the splendid baroque church and the spacious monastery, both of which have been restored. The buildings are widely considered to be among the finest examples of baroque architecture in Switzerland. ❑

Map on page 312

BELOW: the Benedictine Abbey of Einsiedeln.

INSIGHT GUIDES

TRAVEL TIPS

SWITZERLAND

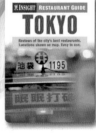

TRAVEL TIPS

T RANSPORT

GETTING THERE AND GETTING AROUND

GETTING THERE

By Air

There are five international airports in Switzerland: Zürich and Geneva are the main points of entry, followed by Basel, Lugano and Bern. Swiss is the national airline. with flights to European and worldwide destinations. Numerous airlines, including budget operators such as Easyjet, have flights from the UK to Geneva and Zürich. Airlines operating flights to Switzerland from the US include American Airlines, British Airways, Air France, Continental, Lufthansa and Delta.

The airports in Zürich and Geneva have their own train stations which are part of the national fast-train network. In both these cities there are several trains each hour running between the airport and the main railway station. Basel-Mulhouse airport is actually situated in France; the journey by bus from there to the railway station in Basel takes about 25 minutes. There are regular connections between the Zürich, Basel and Geneva international airports. Regular and charter airlines as well as local air-taxi services fly in and out of the Bern-Belp, Lugano-Agno, Gstaad-Saanen, Sion and Samedan-St Moritz airfields.

With "Fly-Rail Baggage", train passengers don't have to lug their baggage around the airport any more. Instead, it is unloaded from the plane on to a train and forwarded directly to its destination point (in 117 train stations, mostly in cities and the larger holiday resort areas). The same service applies for the return trip: you can send your baggage – up to 24 hours in advance – directly through to your home town airport from the town where you've been staying. Travellers may also check in at 24 train stations (including Basel, Bern, Geneva, Lausanne, Lugano, Luzern, Neuchâtel, St Gallen and Zürich) and obtain a boarding pass up to 24 hours prior to departure.

Further information regarding Fly-Rail services, plane and railway timetables can be found in the **Fly-Rail Brochure**, available at every train station in Switzerland.

The national carrier is **Swiss** (www.swiss.com). Its offices abroad include:
Canada: tel: 1-877 359 7947
UK: tel: 0845 601 0956
US: tel: 1-877 359 7947

By Train

Comfortable intercity trains connect Switzerland with all larger cities in the surrounding countries. These trains have comfortable first- and second-class compartments and leave every hour. For further information contact the **Swiss Tourist Information Centre** in your country or ring the free number of Switzerland Tourism Call Centre on 00800 100 200 30 (www.myswitzerland.com). From the Swiss Tourist Information Centre you can also obtain the latest train timetables as well as the following travel tickets:

Discount **Gruppenfahrkarten** (group tickets), for groups of 10 or more.

Swiss Pass: a personal network ticket issued for 4, 8, 15 or 22 days or 1 month, or for 3–6 or 8 days out of 15 days or a month (referred to as a **Flexipass**), which enables its bearer unlimited mileage on SBB and many private railways, postbuses and boats (and in 30 cities and towns on buses and trams too).

The **Swiss Card** is good for a round-trip ticket from one of the Swiss borders or airports to a holiday resort area located in Switzerland. The Swiss Card – which is valid for a month – also gives 50 percent reduction on most other journeys you make (check mountain railways, some might not be included).

The **Swiss Transfer Ticket** is a free return ticket from the border or airport to your holiday resort. It is valid for one month. Note that you have to buy it outside Switzerland, ideally at the tourist office in your own country.

Regional Card: Some regions offer a ticket valid for 15 days of which you can travel 5 days for free in a limited region. Ask tourist information in your country.

The **Swiss Half Fare Card** offers 50 percent reduction on normal tariffs for trains, boats and postbuses throughout Switzerland. Direct information from the rail company SBB: tel: 0900 300 300; www.sbb.ch

By Car

Travellers can enter Switzerland by car from all neighbouring countries after passing through border customs, located on main thorough-fares (primarily along motorways). In addition to the major border customs, there are numerous, smaller borders which can be crossed, but keep in mind that these may not be open around the clock.

Motor vehicles weighing up to 3.5 tons (including trailers and caravans) are charged a flat tax of SFr 40 per year for what is commonly referred to as the "motorway vignette" (a sticker you place on your windscreen that permits you to drive on Swiss motorways). This is valid from 1 December to 31 January (14 months). These "*taxes routières*" can be purchased at borders, post offices, petrol stations and garages in Switzerland and in other countries from automobile associations and Swiss Tourist Information centres. The sticker should be fixed to the left edge of the vehicle's front windscreen. Hire cars come with a valid sticker.

Swiss Touring Club (TCS)
Chemin de Blandonnet 4
CH-1214 Genève-Vernier
Tel: 022 417 20 20
www.tcs.ch
Swiss Automobile Club (ACS)
Wasserwerkgasse 39
CH-3000 Bern 13
Tel: 031 328 31 11
Fax: 031 311 03 10
www.acs.ch
Oberzolldirektion
Monbijoustrasse 40
CH-3003 Bern
Tel: 031 322 65 11
Fax: 031 322 78 72
www.zoll.admin.ch

GETTING AROUND

Public Transport

Switzerland maintains an extensive transport network (the second most dense in the world). Nearly every area can be reached comfortably by train, postbus or boat. Many mountains can be reached by rail *(see box)*. **Tickets** for trains, postbus and boats can be obtained at railway stations or at the tourist office; You can also buy tickets directly, though more expensively, on every post bus and Intercity train.

Timetables: You can buy the substantial **Offizielle Schweizer Kursbuch**, in which you can find timetables of all railways, postbuses and boats. In addition to general information on up-to-date offers and railway services, it also contains guidance on the most important connections to foreign countries.

Taxis

Taking a taxi in Switzerland is relatively expensive; rates vary from place to place. There are fixed prices charged for extra services (luggage, etc.) which are posted in the taxi itself. The tip is included in the fare.

ABOVE: wait here for the postbus.

Alternatively, you can get information on train, postbus and boat connections at all railway stations – they will print out the date and time of the connection you need (often complete with departure platform number).

Where there are no rail services, hop on one of the yellow buses owned by the **Swiss Postal Service**. These vehicles don't just serve the most remote areas (for example, Juf, the highest village in Europe that is inhabited year-round, located at 2,126 metres/7,087 ft), but will also make additional journeys.

Regularly scheduled **boats** cruise all the big lakes. There are also **steamships** to put you in a nostalgic mood on Lake Geneva/Lac Léman, Lake Zürich/Zürichsee, Lake Brienz/Brienzer See and Lake Luzern/Vierwaldstätter See. It's also possible to take a trip along the Rhine, Rhône, Aare and Doubs rivers.

In cities, towns and larger villages **trams** and **buses** operate. Some larger destinations such as Zürich have a local train network (S-Bahn) which includes connections to the airport. Every town is organised differently, though usually the ticket you buy is for any form of public transport in that town. Ask for the type of ticket you need at train stations or at the nearest tourist office. There are also ticket machines, but some are a little complicated to use. In case of queries, ask one of the locals.

The Swiss love public transport timetables. You can get them for literally every train, tram or bus. But make sure you arrive in good time, since the country's public transport is extremely punctual.

Swiss Railway (SBB/CFF/FFS): Hochschulstr. 6, 3000 Bern (office

opening hours: Mon–Fri 7.30am–noon, 1–5.30pm); for all rail enquiries, tel: 0900 300 300; www.sbb.ch.

Post Bus: www.postbus.ch Their website is also in English and provides useful information on all kinds of offers by post, including on-line shopping.

By Train

It's easy to get about by train in Switzerland and many Swiss prefer this method of travel themselves. Ask at train stations or at the tourist office for special offers and excursions regularly available for travellers *(see also Tour Operators, page 354)*.

Thanks to regular departures and exceptional punctuality, you won't have to wait very long for a train in Switzerland. Intercity, rapid and regional trains have direct connections to all cities and most holiday-resort regions. **Die Züge** has trains leaving every hour, and sometimes every half-hour between the major cities such as Zürich–Bern, Zürich–Luzern, Bern–Lausanne, Geneva–St Gallen and many others. You can obtain free timetables for either the Intercity or regional trains, or a print-out of times, changes, etc. from all railway ticket desks.

If you don't wish to carry your

Mountain Railways

There are numerous **rack railways** and **funiculars** in Switzerland, complemented by various **cable cars** and **chairlifts** to carry you up some of the highest peaks, as well as **alpine underground railways** (eg, the Metro-Alpin in Saas Fee) where you can travel inside the mountain to an elevation of almost 4,000 metres (13,300 ft). Timetables are available in railway stations and at local tourist information centres.

luggage on an excursion, there's a service where you can send your bags (for 10 francs each/families 8 francs, maximum 25 kg per item) to the destination in advance for later pick-up. International luggage delivery and advance luggage check-in prior to flying are also available. Information is available at railway stations or by visiting: www.sbb.ch, or the **Swiss Rail Service**, tel: 0900 300 300.

There is a **lost property** office at every train station. They are well organised and thanks to computer-linked systems they can trace lost luggage nationwide. If you know the specific train on which you lost an item, staff will phone through

ABOVE: entering the Lötschberg Tunnel.

immediately to see if it can be found, and will send it back to you at the earliest opportunity.

There are trains with dining cars and minibars in operation each day (normally on all intercity and inter-regional trains). If you plan to travel in a large party or during meal times, you'd be wise to reserve a table in advance.

By Car

If you plan to enter Switzerland by car, you are required to be in possession of a passport, a motor vehicle registration and a valid national driving licence.

Wearing a seat belt is mandatory and children under the age of 12 must sit in the back seat. Motorcyclists are required by law to wear helmets. Driving while the alcohol level in your bloodstream exceeds 0.8 mg per millilitre is illegal.

On all country roads the maximum speed is 100 kph (60 mph); on motorways 120 kph (75 mph); within city limits 50 kph (30 mph).

Parking Places

It is becoming more common for motor vehicles to be banned from city centres, and the number of pedestrian zones is increasing. It's wise to leave your car somewhere on the city outskirts or in a car park.

If you want to leave your car in the city centre, there are some short-stay parking areas (from half an hour to a few hours) with parking meters. These only accept small change, so it is useful to carry 20 rappen (cents), 50 rappen, and 1-franc coins with you.

Road traffic queries can be answered by:
Swiss Touring Club (TCS)

Chemin Blandonnet 4
CH-1214 Genève-Vernier, tel: 022 417 20 20; fax: 022 417 20 20; www.tcs.ch
Swiss Automobile Club (ACS)
Wasserwerkgasse 39
CH-3000 Bern 13, tel: 031 328 31 11; fax: 031 311 03 10; www.acs.ch.

Road Information

For information on road conditions in Switzerland (for instance whether or not a road is passable, whether or not ice is present, etc.), contact the TCS – Swiss Touring Club – Information Call Centre, tel: 0844 888 111 (www.tcs.ch).

You can tune into Swiss radio traffic reports issued by the police after the regular news on the hour and at half-past the hour.

During winter, information on road conditions is read out Mon–Sat at 5.30am, 6.30am, 7.30am and 12.15pm, and forecasts for the coming night are broadcast daily after the 6pm and 10pm newscasts. Foreseeable traffic obstructions registered by the police (construction sites, detours, etc.) are announced after the news report at 5.30am, 6.30am, 7.30am and 12.15pm.

Breakdowns

Foreign car drivers can dial 140 (the same telephone number applies throughout Switzerland) for help in the case of a breakdown. One of the five action centres of the Swiss Touring Club (TCS) will answer your call and put you in touch with the closest repair shop or mobile help. If you are in possession of a letter of safe conduct, issued by your own automobile association, breakdown aid will be delivered free of charge by the TCS Road Patrol. There are emergency telephones positioned on the highways at 1.6-km (1-mile) intervals. You'll also find TCS and ACS (Swiss Automobile Club) emergency telephones along remote stretches on pass roads.

In the case of an accident resulting in injury, it is mandatory

Petrol Stations

At many petrol stations along the motorways as well as in cities you'll find machines which accept Swiss notes. These enable you to purchase petrol around the clock with 10, 20 and 50 SFr notes. Prices vary depending on the international fuel market and the location of a particular petrol station. For instance, prices may be higher in the more mountainous regions.

to inform the police. If there are no injuries but damage is done to a vehicle it is still advisable (but not obligatory) to call the police. Throughout Switzerland dialling 117 will connect you with the police.

Special Regulations

Private vehicles with studded tyres are permitted on country roads only between 1 November and 31 March. Such vehicles are forbidden to drive on motorways and major thoroughfares (clearly designated as Autobahn or Autostrasse).

There are special regulations that apply specifically to trailers, caravans and boats. Further information is available from automobile associations or from the Swiss customs officials posted at the borders.

Police

As their different uniforms and patrol cars indicate, Swiss police are organised regionally, by canton. Speed, measured by radar, and blood/alcohol-level controls are common.

Tunnels & Passes

Road Tunnels

The Great St Bernard Tunnel (5.8 km/ 3½ miles) connects Valais to the Aosta Valley (in Italy). The price of the toll is contingent upon the type of vehicle you are driving and starts at SFr 27. If the return trip is made within 30 days cars are awarded a 30 percent discount, and buses 20 percent. It is also possible to purchase a booklet containing several toll tickets.

The Munt la Schera Tunnel (3.5 km/2¼ miles) between Zernez and Livigno (in Italy) is open 8am–8pm. One-way tickets for private cars are SFr 9, plus SFr 2 for each occupant.

It is necessary to obtain a motorway *vignette* for passage through the St Gotthard Tunnel (connecting inner Switzerland to Ticino, 16.8 km/10½ miles) and for the highway leading to the San Bernardino Tunnel (between Graubünden and Ticino, 6.6 km/4 miles). You will not have to pay additional fees inside the tunnel.

Car Hire

Hiring a car in Switzerland is expensive. There are car rental agencies in all cities of any size, so you'll have no trouble renting a vehicle. The minimum driving age is between 20–25 depending on the rental company. In the larger train stations tourists travelling by rail can take advantage of the car rental service operated by the Swiss Federal Railways. If coming from elsewhere in Europe, a cheaper alternative might be to hire a car in advance from your home country.

Car Hire Firms

The main international car hire firms are represented throughout Switzerland. The telephone numbers are listed below:
Avis tel: 0848 811 818
Budget tel: 0844 844 700
Europcar tel: 0848 808 099
Hertz tel: 0848 822 020

Cars on Trains

Cars are transported through Alpine railway tunnels according to a timetable. Additional trains are employed during Christmas and Easter holidays.
Albula tunnel, Thusis-Samedan, up to 10 daily departures; www.rhb.ch
Furka tunnel, Oberwald-Realp, at least 16 daily departures. Tel: 027 927 77 77; www.mgbahn.ch
Lötschberg tunnel, Kandersteg-Goppenstein, at least 33 daily departures. Tel: 0900 55 33 33; www.bls.ch
Vereina tunnel, Klosters Selfranga-Sengalins, daily departures every 30 minutes. Tel: 081 288 37 38; www.rhb.ch
Oberalp tunnel, Andermatt-Sedrun, 4–5 daily departures. Tel: 027 927 77 77; www.fo-bahn.ch
For Albula and Oberalp it is essential to call the embarkation train stations in advance and make a reservation for your car:

Albula: 081 288 37 38
Oberalp: Andermatt 041 888 77 51; Sedrun 081 949 11 37
Furka: Realp 041 887 14 46; Oberwald 027 973 11 41
Lötschberg: Kandersteg 033 675 18 88; Goppenstein 027 939 11 69. At all other embarkation stations it is not possible to reserve in advance.

Further information on schedules and prices (including those applicable to buses, trailers, motorcyclists, etc.) can be obtained at Swiss Tourist Information centres or railway stations.

In order to spare car drivers a time-consuming journey to their holiday destination, European railways offer **Transport Trains for Cars**, with sleepers and/or couchettes.
Vereina: information, tel: 081 288 37 38

Mountain Passes

These are the months when the following mountain passes are accessible:
Albula
(2,312 metres/7,586 ft)
Tiefencastel–La Punt, June–Oct.
Bernina
(2,328 metres/7,638 ft)
Pontresina–Poschiavo, all year (in winter mostly closed at night).
Brünig
(1,008 metres/3,307 ft)
Meiringen–Sachseln, all year.
Croix
(1,778 metres/5,834 ft)
Villars–Les Diablerets, May–Nov.
Flüela
(2,383 metres/7,819 ft)
Davos–Susch, April–Nov (in winter use Vereina Tunnel).
Forclaz
(1,526 metres/5,007 ft)
Martigny–Le Châtelard, all year.

Furka
(2,431 metres/7,976 ft)
Gletsch–Andermatt, June–Oct.
Great St Bernard
(2,469 metres/8,100 ft)
Martigny–Aosta, June–Oct (tunnel passage open all year).
Grimsel
(2,165 metres/7,103 ft)
Meiringen–Gletsch, June–Oct.
Il Fuorn
(2,149 metres/7,051 ft)
Zernez–Santa Maria, all year.
Jaun
(1,509 metres/4,951 ft)
Boltigen–Bulle, all year.
Julier
(2,284 metres/7,494 ft)
Tiefencastel–Silvaplana, all year.
Klausen
(1,948 metres/6,391 ft)
Altdorf–Linthal, June–Oct.
Lukmanier
(1,914 metres/6,280 ft)
Disentis–Biasca, May–Nov.
Maloja
(1,815 metres/5,955 ft)
Chiavenna–Silvaplana, all year.
Mosses
(1,445 metres/4,741 ft)
Aigle–Château d'Oex, all year.
Nufenen
(2,478 metres/8,130 ft)
Ulrichen–Airolo, June–Oct.
Oberalp
(2,044 metres/6,706 ft)
Andermatt–Disentis, June–Oct.
Pillon
(1,546 metres/5,072 ft)
Aigle–Gsteig, all year.
San Bernardino
(2,065 metres/6,775 ft)
Thusis–Bellinzona, June–Oct (tunnel passage open all year).
St Gotthard
(2,108 metres/6,916 ft)
Andermatt–Airolo, June–Oct (tunnel passage open all year).
Simplon
(2,006 metres/6,582 ft)
Brig–Domodossola, all year.
Splügen
(2,113 metres/6,933 ft)
Thusis–Chiavenna, June–Oct.
Susten
(2,224 metres/7,297 ft)
Innertkirchen–Wassen, June–Oct.
Umbrail
(2,501 metres/8,206 ft)
Santa Maria–Stelvio, June–Oct.

BELOW: the narrow-gauge Brünigbahn travels from Luzern to Interlaken.

Bicycle Hire

Bicycles can be rented from Rent-A-Bike (www.rent-a-bike.ch) at many railway stations. Every station that is a starting point in the large network of bike-hiking routes has top-condition, modern bicycles for rent.

Ensure, especially during the summer, that you make bookings in advance. If you are in possession of a Swiss Pass you get a discount. They also provide bikes for children and child seats to attach to adults' bikes.

In some cities, such as Zürich and Bern, you can get free bike rental when you leave your ID card and a small cash deposit with the hire company.

Tours by Train

The Glacier Express

St Moritz–Zermatt and back again (7 hrs 45 mins), or Davos–Zermatt or vice versa (7hrs 15 mins).

This route provides the traveller with 291 km (182 miles) of varied scenery through the enchanting landscape of the Alps. On the slowest express train in the world, complete with a "panorama wagon", you'll make your way through 91 tunnels, over 291 bridges, across the 2,033-metre (6,777-ft) Oberalp Pass and through the longest metre-gauge railway tunnel in existence.

The steepest parts of the stretch are accomplished by virtue of rack railways. You can partake of a midday meal in the tastefully decorated dining car. For more information, pick up a copy of the brochure *Glacier Express* at the tourist office.

The Bernina Express

Chur–Tirano or vice versa (4 hrs 35 mins). The highest crossing of the Alps by train is made on the Bernina Express; with a 7 percent gradient it is the steepest non-rack railway in the world. During the 145-km (90-mile) ride the train first ascends to the Albula Line at 585 metres (2,860 ft) above sea level (Chur), before reaching Pontresina at 1,774 metres (5,913 ft). From here the express heads over the Bernina Pass (2,253 metres/7,510 ft) to descend twisting and turning all the way to Tirano (429 metres/1,430 ft). In just a short while passengers can experience the complete range of vegetation zones from the Piz Bernina Glacier (4,049 metres/13,497 ft) to the palm trees of Tirano in Italy. When the weather is good, some trains offer open "panorama wagons" – an unforgettable experience. Further information is available in the brochure *Bernina Express* at the tourist office. You can travel further on – to Lugano – by a connecting bus in Tirano.

The Palm Express

St Moritz–Palmolino and back again (4 hrs 10 mins), from the end of May until the middle of October, and to Lugano in summer and autumn.

The Palm Express, a recent connection between postbus and railway, travels from the snow and glaciers of the Alps to the palm-fringed regions of southern Switzerland and back again. This express connects the Engadine and Upper Valais with Ticino, St Moritz and Zermatt with Ascona (where passengers remain overnight), before continuing on to Locarno and Lugano.

Additional information can be found in the brochure *Palm Express* at the tourist office, or tel: 033 828 88 38.

The Golden Pass Route

Luzern–Interlaken–Zweisimmen–Montreux or vice versa (5 hrs 6 mins).

This is one of the classic Swiss train journeys. It leads through charming scenery from the banks of Lake Luzern to the Swiss Riviera. You travel on the narrow-gauge SSB Brünigbahn to Interlaken and continue on from there with the BLS to Zweisimmen. At Zweisimmen you'll change back to the narrower gauge MOB tracks all the way to Montreux – an especially pleasurable experience in the panorama wagons with their enormous picture windows.

BELOW: Zürich has free bike hire.

The Lötschberg-Centovalli ExpressTrain

Locarno–Domodossola (1 hr 30 mins).

This narrow-gauge track makes its way through romantic Centovalli and connects the two great European railway lines over the Simplon and Gotthard passes. The journey takes you 52 km (33 miles) over bridges, idyllic gorges and up inclines, some of which have a gradient of 6 percent, as well as through stretches of Italy. The round-trip journey Zürich–Gotthard–Centovalli–Simplon–Lötschberg–Brig–Zürich is an extra-special treat which can be accomplished in a single day.

Swiss Station Experience

Railway stations in Switzerland are often an attraction in their own right, with excellent facilities. You can dine out at a good restaurant on the station concourse, or shop in supermarkets (open in the evenings), or use the 24-hour vending machines which dispense bread, milk, and even salami. There are luggage lockers at all stations except tiny country halts, and they come in three sizes. You can use them for several consecutive days without problem.

Platforms are marked out in sectors and the PA will announce which sector your carriage will be arriving at, to save you running up and down the length of the train. All in all, a civilised experience.

Wilhelm Tell Express

The Wilhelm Tell Express (6 hrs) runs daily from May to mid-October. This route, connecting Inner Switzerland with Ticino, includes passage in a steamboat. You can sit back and enjoy the sights from the huge saloon or panorama wagons.

During the ferry ride a delicious midday meal is served in the "Salon Belle Epoque".

This is a packed and varied day excursion from Luzern to Locarno/Lugano and back again.

Heidi Express

Landquart–Davos–Berninapass–Tirano or vice versa (4 hrs 40 mins). Like the Bernina Express, the 145-km (90-mile) route traverses the Bernina Pass but first leads from Landquart up the lovely Prättigau Valley past Klosters and Davos. After Davos the landscape becomes more rugged, with raging mountain torrents. From the train you can see a wide range of Alpine flowers and in

ABOVE: the rack railway covers the steepest rail inclines.

the Bernina area you will encounter shining glaciers.

After a stopover in Tirano (Italy) the route takes you through the Valtellina Valley back to Lugano (only in summer).

As you will cross the Swiss border during this journey you will need your passport or identity card.

Voralpen Express

Romanshorn–St Gall–Rapperswil-Arth–Goldau–Luzern or vice versa (2 hrs 39 mins). This Prealp Express takes you through the Alpine foothills of Switzerland and along various lake sides. It is worth stopping off en route to make a small excursion to any one of the following: Cloister of St–Gall, Säntis Mountain, Appenzellerland (where the cheese comes from), the Children's Zoo in Rapperswil, Cloister of Einsiedeln, the Wildlife Park in Goldau, Rigi Mountain or the Transport Museum in Luzern.

Allalin Express

Bern or Interlaken–Lötschberg–Brig–Saas Fee or vice versa (2 hrs 50 mins). The journey first takes you from the canton of Bern through one of the highest tunnels in Europe (Lötschberg) into the canton of Valais. From the train you can see the foothills of the Rhone Valley wine region, and also the snowcapped mountains rising all around. In Brig the bus waits to take you on an exciting journey

uphill to Saas Fee, one of the country's famous ski resorts. If you haven't had enough sightseeing yet there is an option to take the Alpine Express from Saas Fee to the world's largest glacier grotto at 3,500 metres (11,480 ft) above sea level.

Note: these scenic routes are also possible on ordinary trains where you pay no extras. Of course, you can just do one part of a route and then return if you wish. Or you can pay for an excursion as part of a package holiday *(see, for example, Railtour Suisse, Tour Operators, page 355)*. In general it is hard to make a long train journey which is not pleasant in Switzerland, since the country is so small and the variety of the countryside so expansive, you'll always have interesting scenery to look at en route.

Road Tours

By Postbus

Swiss postbuses offer a comfortable and safe way of travelling through the Alps. Tours are offered throughout Switzerland. Examples include a triple-pass journey (over the Grimsel, Furka and Susten passes, starting from either Meiringen in the Bernese Oberland or from Andermatt in the canton of Uri), and a quadruple-pass trip (over the Grimsel, Nufenen, Gotthard and Susten passes, commencing in Meiringen) in Inner Switzerland.

During lengthy journeys with the post bus (for example from St Moritz to Lugano), a generous break is allowed to give travellers plenty of time for a bite to eat. You can get more information at the Swiss Tourist Office or at any of the regional offices. Visit www.postbus.ch

By Bicycle

If you are in possession of a valid ticket, you can have your bicycle transported by train or boat. It is also possible to get your bike aboard a postbus, but space is quite limited and you must be sure to make arrangements in advance.

It's no trouble bringing your own bike into Switzerland but you have to buy a *vignette* from a post office.

Cycle routes: There are nine marked long-distance cycle routes throughout Switzerland, as well as many regional paths, mostly well away from traffic. You can obtain a map showing the long-distance routes from tourist offices.
Eurotrek is a tour operator for cycle tours. Contact them at:
Eurotrek
Militärstrasse 52
8021 Zürich,
tel: 01 295 59 59;
fax: 01 295 59 58; www.eurotrek.ch.
Bicycle maps and cycling information are available at:
Bike Explorer, tel: 078 657 22 22; www.bike-explorer.ch and
La Suisse à Velo, tel: 031 307 47 40; www.suisse-a-velo.ch

A CCOMMODATION

HOTELS, YOUTH HOSTELS, BED & BREAKFAST

Choosing a Hotel

There are around 6,000 hotels, motels, pensions, mountain sanatoria and health resorts in Switzerland, amounting to more than 266,000 beds. There are 360,000 beds in chalets and holiday apartments and 7,300 youth hostel beds. Camp sites have a further 238,000 places.

For more information, contact the **National Tourist Office**, Postfach 695, 8027 Zürich, tel: 00800 100 200 30, fax: 00800 100 200 31 (Mon–Sat 8.30am–7pm), online information and bookings: www.myswitzerland.com or one of the **Swiss Tourism Offices abroad** (see page 354).

Hotel Listings

Information and prices can be found in free hotel listings, and the comprehensive *Schweizer Hotelführer* (Swiss Hotel Guide), all available at travel agencies and Swiss tourist offices, including at its branch offices in other countries. Swiss Hotel Association: **Schweizer Hotelier-Verein** (SHV), Monbijoustrasse 130, CH-3000 Bern, tel: 031 370 41 11, fax: 031 370 44 44; www.swisshotels.com

Camping

There are more than 500 camp sites in Switzerland. Of these, 90 are open in winter. You can obtain a listing of regional camp sites along with a map of Swiss camp sites from the tourist office.

Outside the boundaries of official camp sites, caravans and trailers may only be parked with the permission of the property owner, the relevant local authority or from the police. Spending one night at a public car park is tolerated in many cantons. If you decide to do this, it's a good idea to inform the closest police station or the local authorities beforehand.

The **Swiss Touring Club** (TCS) publishes a Camping Guidebook. Ask at TCS, Ch. Blandonnet 4, 1214 Genève-Vernier, tel: 022 417 20 20; fax: 022 417 20 20; www.tcs.ch

A list of Swiss camping and caravan sites is published annually by the following two associations: **Schweizerischer Camping und Caravanning Verband**, Postfach 42, 4027 Basel, tel: 061 302 26 26; fax: 061 302 24 81; www.sccv.ch **Verband Schweizerischer Campings** www.swisscamps.ch

Youth Hostels

The 63 youth hostels in Switzerland run by the **Swiss Youth Hostel Association** are all of very good quality. They are open to anybody, regardless of age. You don't need a membership card, but if you would like to stay for long periods it is worth buying one (22 francs up to 18 years, 33 francs for adults) which is also valid in 4,500 other youth hostels around the world and gets you a price reduction of 5 francs per night. Normally they provide bedding. Double rooms are available in many hostels. The prices vary depending on location and size of rooms. Get the free "Know-How" map with a list of all hostels from the tourist office or from: **Schweizer Jugendherbergen** (SJH), 14 Schaffhauserstrasse, Postfach 8042 Zürich, tel: 01 360 14 14; fax: 01 360 14 60; www.youthhostel.ch

Swiss Backpackers runs about 30 hostels in Switzerland, often centrally located in towns and cities with competing price offers. No membership is required.

They publish their own free newspaper which can be found in tourist offices. For further information contact them at Eisengasse 34, 5600 Lenzburg, tel: 062 892 26 75; fax: 062 892 26 76; www.backpacker.ch

In more peaceful locations, surrounded by nature, you can find **Naturfreunde** hotels (around 100 in Switzerland), which are run by individuals and are often located in picturesque historic buildings. For information, contact: **Naturfreunde Schweiz**, Pavillonweg 3, Postfach, 3012 Bern, tel: 031 306 67 67; fax: 031 306 67 67; www.naturfreunde.ch

The Swiss Alpine Club

There are over 150 club huts in the Swiss region of the Alps. In spite of their magnificent locations, they are not meant to be used as holiday lodgings. They are starting points for mountain-climbing expeditions or high-Alpine ski tours.

You can get an illustrated register of huts complete with a map and other important information from the **Schweizer Alpen-Club** (SAC), Zentralsekretariat, Monbijoustrasse 61, CH-3000 Bern 23, tel: 031 370 18 18; fax: 031 370 18 00; www.sac-cas.ch; e-mail: info@sac-cas.ch.

Holiday Apartments

One of the main agencies for apartments, with approximately 3,500 holiday apartments in Switzerland, is **Interhome AG**, Sägereistrasse 20, 8152 Glattbrugg/Zürich, tel: 043 211 77 77; fax: 043 211 77 79; www.interhome.ch

There are many chalets to hire from other agencies. In popular tourist areas you have to book early.

To find out what chalets and apartments are available, enquire at local tourist offices *(see pages 353–4)* in Switzerland as well as at other Swiss and foreign agencies that serve as clearing houses for the renting of holiday apartments.

Bargains

For travellers on tighter budgets, or for those who prefer simple lodgings, there are plenty of smaller hotels and inns. A listing of these can be found in the following brochures, available at the tourist office: *E+G Hotels*; *Preiswerte Unterkünfte in der Schweiz* (reasonably priced accommodation). In the brochure

Ferien auf dem Lande (Country Holidays) you will find addresses of B&Bs, furnished apartments, collective accommodation, and country inns, farm camping and mountain inns.

You can stay in private rooms (ask at the tourist office) and even sleep on straw at some farms: the brochure *Schlaf im Stroh* is issued by the tourist office.

ACCOMMODATION LISTINGS

BASEL

Hotel Krafft
Rheingasse 12
Tel: 061 690 91 30
www.hotelkrafft.ch
In a building dating from 1872 overlooking the Rhine. Attractive rooms. **$$$**
Merian am Rhein
Rheingasse 2

Tel: 061 685 11 11
Fax : 061 685 11 01
Great view of river and Münster. **$$$–$$$$**
Resslirytti
Theorodsgraben 42
Tel: 061 691 66 41
Fax : 061 691 45 90
Modern establishment near

the Messe Basel. **$$$**
Der Teufelhof Basel
Leonhardsgraben 49
Tel: 061 261 10 10
Fax : 061 261 10 04
www.teufelhof.com
Two small hotels are combined with a small theatre. The Art Hotel has

eight rooms and a suite, each individually designed. The Gallery Hotel consists of 24 rooms in a former convent where artists exhibit their work. Three great restaurants, and a gourmet wine and food cellar. **$$$–$$$$**

BERN AND BERNESE OBERLAND

Adelboden

Adler Sporthotel
Dorfstr. 19
Tel: 033 673 41 41
Fax: 033 673 42 39

BELOW: Bern's Belle Epoque has an impressive art collection.

www.adleradelboden.ch
A nice chalet hotel in the village centre with a swimming pool as well as sauna and solarium facilities. **$$$–$$$$**

Bern

Belle Epoque
Gerechtigkeitsgasse 18
Tel: 031 311 43 36
Fax: 031 311 39 36
www.bellevue-epoque.ch
Seventeen rooms in the picturesque old town, all furnished with beautiful antiques. **$$$–$$$$**
Bellevue Palace
Kochergasse 3–5
Tel: 031 320 45 45
Fax: 031 311 47 43
www.bellevue-palace.ch
The best hotel in town and one of Switzerland's best, with Alpine view and top cuisine. **$$$$**
Goldener Schlüssel
Rathausgasse 72
Tel: 031 311 02 16
Fax: 031 311 56 88
Near the clock tower in the old town, the restaurant serves international and Swiss cuisine. **$$**

Brienz

Brienzerburli
Tel: 033 951 12 41
Fax: 033 951 38 41
Situated in the old part of town with free bus service

from railway station to the hotel. In-house bakery. **$$**

Grindelwald

Hirschen
Tel: 033 854 84 84
Fax: 033 854 84 80
Family-run hotel in the village centre. Excellent cuisine. **$$**

Gstaad

Palace
Tel: 033 748 50 00
Fax: 033 748 50 01
www.palace.ch
Famous luxury hotel reminiscent of a castle on a hill above the village. Swimming pool, sauna, massage and gym facilities. **$$$$**
Posthotel Rössli
Tel: 033 748 42 42

PRICE CATEGORIES

Price for a double room for one night, including breakfast:
$ = less than 120 SFr
$$ =120–200 SFr
$$$ = 200–300 SFr
$$$$ = more than 300 SFr

Fax: 033 748 42 43
Cosy little hotel in an old wooden house in the centre, with modern rooms and Swiss cuisine. **$$$**

Interlaken

Sonne
Hauptstrasse 34
Tel: 033 822 75 41
Fax: 033 823 29 15
Family hotel with a big garden, toys, mountain bikes – and a gourmet restaurant. **$$–$$$**

Victoria-Jungfrau Grand Hotel & Spa
Höheweg 41
Tel: 033 828 28 28
Fax: 033 828 28 80
www.victoria-jungfrau.ch
Very famous, old and luxurious grand hotel. Three restaurants and bars. **$$$$**

Lenk

Alpenruh
Tel: 033 733 10 64
Fax: 033 733 41 64
Central chalet hotel. **$–$$**

Thun

Emmental
Bernstrasse 2
Tel: 033 222 01 20
Fax: 033 222 01 30
www.essenundtrinken.ch
Nice hotel in the centre of the town with international live bands once a week in the bar/restaurant. **$$**

Wengen

Edelweiss
Tel: 033 855 23 88

fax: 033 855 42 88
www.edelweisswengen.ch
Cosy family hotel near the railway station, with sauna, no-smoking rooms, and special prices for children. **$$**

Regina
Tel: 033 856 58 58
Fax: 033 856 58 50
www.wengen.com
Large traditional hotel established in 1894 overlooking the village. Gym and beauty facilities. **$$$–$$$$**

THE NORTHEAST

Appenzell

Appenzell
Hauptgasse 37
Tel: 071 788 15 15
Fax: 071 788 15 51
www.hotel-appenzell.ch
Pretty hotel with its own bakery. **$$**

Braunwald (GL)

Tödiblick
Tel: 055 653 63 63
Fax: 055 653 63 66
www.holidayswitzerland.com
Chalet-style hotel with great view of the Alps. **$$–$$$**

St Gallen

Gallo
St. Jakobstr. 62

Tel: 071 242 71 71
Fax: 071 242 71 61
www.hotel-gallo.ch
Comfortable hotel next to Congress Centre, theatre and concert hall. **$$$**

Stein am Rhein (SH)

Adler
Tel: 052 742 61 61
Fax: 052 741 44 40
Family-run hotel in the centre of the medieval town. The building's facade is painted by the famous Swiss artist Alois Carigiet. **$$**

Trogen

Krone
Dorf 3
Tel: 071 343 60 80

Fax: 071 344 43 76
Magnificent Appenzeller house 10 km (6 miles) from St Gallen, built in 1727 with facade frescoes from 1767, and with fine cooking. **$$**

Zürich

Glockenhof
Sihlstrasse 31
Tel: 01 225 91 91
Fax: 01 225 92 92
www.glockenhof.ch
Traditional, first-class establishment near the station with a garden restaurant. **$$$$**

Zürcherhof
Zähringerstrasse 21
tel. 01 269 44 44
Fax: 01 269 44 45
www.hotelzuercherhof.ch

Centrally located, popular with businessmen, with a famous restaurant. **$$$**

Zürichberg
Orellistrasse 21
Tel: 01 268 35 35
Fax: 01 268 35 45
www.zuerichberg.ch
Situated on Zürich's "house mountain" near the zoo and James Joyce's grave, with terraces, garden and a wonderful view of the lake and mountains.
$$–$$$

Leoneck
Leonhardstrasse 1
tel: 01 254 22 22
www.leoneck.ch
Near the main train station and the shopping area with its own restaurant with Swiss food. **$$**

THE SOUTHEAST

Andeer

Hotel Fravi
Veia Granda 1
Tel: 081 660 01 01
Fax: 081 660 01 02
Grand old castle-like establishment, frequented in the past by notable celebrities **$$$**

Arosa

Alpina
Prätsclistrasse
Tel: 081 377 16 58
Fax: 081 377 37 52
www.alpina-arosa.ch
Cosy hotel near mountain railways, ski facilities; special rates for families and senior citizens.
$$–$$$

Chur

Duc de Rohan
Masanserstrasse 44
Tel: 081 252 10 22
Fax: 081 252 45 37
Facilities in this luxury hotel

include a fitness club and indoor pool. **$$**

Stern
Reichsgasse 11
Tel: 081 258 57 57
Fax: 081 258 57 58
www.stern-chur.ch
Traditional hotel situated on the edge of the old town with a good restaurant.
$$–$$$

Davos

Larix
Obere Albertstr. 9
Davos Platz
Tel: 081 413 11 88
Fax: 081 413 33 49
www.hotel-larix.ch

Chalet hotel run by its owner. Close to the centre. **$$$**

Flims

Curtgin
Flims Dorf
Tel: 081 911 35 66
Fax: 081 911 34 55
Near the mountain railways, quietly situated, with snack bar. **$$–$$$**

Ilanz

Casutt
Glennerstr. 20
Tel: 081 925 11 31
Fax: 081 925 41 47

The building dates from 1903 and the hotel is still in the family. Good starting point for Vals Valley, Obersaxen ski area. $$

Klosters

Chesa Grischuna
Bahnhofstr. 12
Tel: 081 422 22 22
Fax: 081 422 22 25
www.chesagrischuna.ch
Small, romantic hotel in the centre of the village, with excellent restaurant. $$$–$$$$

Lenzerheide

Collina
Voa Val Sporz 9
Tel: 081 384 18 17
Fax: 081 384 62 09
Small, central hotel. Ideal for summer and winter sports. $$$

Maloja

Maloja Kulm
Hauptstr. 1
Tel: 081 824 31 05
Fax: 081 824 34 66
Serves fresh food from their own farm. Exhibitions of paintings by well-known artists. $$–$$$

Müstaïr

Münsterhof
Tel: 081 858 55 41
Fax: 081 858 50 58
Central hotel run by the same family for generations. Antique-furnished rooms and home-cooking. $$

Pontresina

Walther
Hauptstrasse
Tel: 081 839 36 36
Fax: 081 839 36 37
www.hotelwalther.ch
Old hotel with modern

features including swimming pool, fitness centre and tennis court. $$$$

Poschiavo

Suisse
Via da Mez
Tel: 081 844 07 88
Fax: 081 844 19 67
Pleasant hotel in centre of town. $$

St Moritz

Soldanella
Tel: 081 833 36 51
Fax: 081 833 23 37
www.hotel-soldanella.ch
On a mountain slope with spectacular views of the Alps. $$–$$$
Suvretta House
Tel: 081 836 36 36
Fax: 081 836 37 37
www.suvrettahouse.ch
One of St Moritz's grand hotels, the location might be the most ideal. $$$$

Scuol

Filli
Chantröven
Tel: 081 864 99 27
Fax: 081 864 13 36
A comfortable family hotel, with friendly service and excellent cuisine. $$$

Silvaplana

Julier Palace
Tel: 081 828 96 44
Fax: 081 834 30 03
Comfortable, sensibly priced rooms and a recommended restaurant. $$

Zuoz

Klarer
Tel: 081 851 34 34
Fax: 081 851 34 00
www.klarerconda.ch
Small hotel on the *platz* in Zuoz with attractive rooms and apartments. On-site sweet shop. $$–$$$

TICINO

Ascona

Schiff-Batello
Piazza G.Motta 21
Tel: 091 791 25 33
Fax: 091 792 13 15
Situated by the lakeside on the main promenade. Run by the same family for the past 70 years. $$–$$$

Bellinzona

Unione
Via G. Guisan 1
Tel: 091 825 55 77

Fax: 091 825 94 60
www.hotel-unione.ch
At the foot of the Castelgrande, near the railway station. $$$

Locarno

Camelia
Via G. G. Nessi 9
Tel: 091 743 00 21
Fax: 091 743 00 22
www.camelia.ch
Family-friendly hotel, a short walk from town centre and lake. $$

Lugano

Continental-Parkhotel
Via Basilea 28
Tel: 091 966 11 12
Fax: 091 966 12 13
www.continentalparkhotel.com
Near the railway station, with its own swimming pool and special hiking programmes. With a nice view of lake and mountains. $$
Romantik-Hotel Ticino
Piazza Cioccaro 1
Tel: 091 922 77 72

Fax: 091 923 62 78
www.romantikhotels.ch
A small but very good hotel right in the heart of the old town. $$$$
Villa Principe Leopoldo & Residence
Via Montalbano 5
Tel: 091 985 88 55
Fax: 091 985 88 25
www.leopoldohotel.com
Magnificently situated former residence of Prince Leopold of Hohenzollern, situated above the Collina d'Oro. $$$$

VALAIS

Brig

Victoria
Bahnhofstr. 2
Tel: 027 923 15 03
Fax: 027 924 21 69
www.minotel.com
A comfortable hotel in an attractive building in the city centre, with restaurant serving Swiss food and local wines; rooms have all mod cons and mountain views. $$–$$$

Crans-Montana

Eldorado
Rte de Fleurs des Champs
Tel: 027 481 13 33
Fax: 027 481 95 22
www.hoteleldorado.ch
Peaceful hotel five minutes from the city centre with fantastic view of the Alps. $$–$$$
Hostellerie du Pas de l'Ours
Tel: 027 485 93 33
Fax: 027 485 9334

www.pasdelours.ch
This Relais and Châteaux chalet offers nine cosy suites. There are indoor and outdoor pools, and other wellbeing options. $$$$

Leukerbad/Loeche-L.Bains

Weisses Rössli
Tel: 027 470 33 77
Fax: 027 470 33 80

Small hotel near the Alpentherme and the Torrentbahn. $$

Obergesteln

St Hubertus
Tel: 027 973 28 28
Fax: 027 973 28 69
www.hotel-hubertus.ch
Located by the edge of the wood. Ideal for cross-country skiing and other sports. $$–$$$

TRANSPORT
ACCOMMODATION
EATING OUT
ACTIVITIES
A – Z
LANGUAGE

Saas Fee

Feehof
Tel: 027 957 23 08
Fax: 027 957 23 09
www.feehof.ch
Modest and charming hotel
on the village outskirts. **$$**

Sion

Du Rhône

Rue du Scex 10
Tel: 027 322 82 91
Fax: 027 323 11 88
www.bestwestern.ch
Peaceful, if basic Best
Western hotel in the town
centre, with fine cuisine. **$$**

Verbier

Bristol
Route des Creux

Tel: 027 771 65 77
Fax: 027 771 51 50
www.bristol-verbier.ch
Small hotel in the centre of
Verbier. Valaisian
specialities served in the
restaurant. **$$–$$$**

Zermatt

Hotel Dufour
Tel: 27 966 24 00

Fax: 27 966 24 01
This small, central hotel is
a picture-postcard Swiss
chalet. **$$**

Monte Rosa
Bahnhofstrasse 80
Tel: 027 966 03 33
Fax: 027 966 03 30
Mountain inn since 1839,
with a beautiful dining
room. **$$$$**

INNER SWITZERLAND

Einsiedeln

Linde
Schmiedenstrasse 28
Tel: 055 418 48 48
Fax: 055 418 48 49
www.linde-einsiedeln.ch
Very close to the abbey, with
spacious rooms. Excellent
restaurant. **$$–$$$**

Engelberg

Europe
Dorfstr. 40
Tel: 041 639 75 75
Fax: 041 639 75 76
Traditional hotel with
excellent cuisine and
attentive service. **$$–$$$**

Luzern

Château Gütsch
Kanonenstrasse
Tel: 041 249 41 00
Fax: 041 249 41 91
First-class castle-style hotel
on a hill with great views.
$$$$
Goldener Stern
Burgerstrasse 35
Tel: 041 227 50 60
Fax: 041 227 50 61
www.goldener-stern.ch
Small hotel near train
station; good cuisine.
Family room available. **$–$$**
Kurhotel Sonnmatt
Hemschlenstrasse
Tel: 041 375 32 32
Fax: 041 375 39 19
www.sonnmatt.ch
Peaceful spa hotel. **$$$**

Merlischachen

Schloss Hotel
6402 Merlischachen
Tel: 041 854 54 54
Fax: 041 854 54 66;
www.schloss-hotel.ch

Four-star luxurious hotel
with pool, in picturesque
countryside setting. Some
rooms have four-poster
beds. **$$**
Swiss Chalet Hotel
6402 Merlischachen
Tel: 041 854 54 54
Fax: 041 854 54 66
www.schloss-hotel.ch
Under the same
management as the
Schloss Hotel, but less
posh. **$–$$**

Schwyz

**Hirschen Backpackers
Hotel Pub**
Hinterdorfstrasse 14
Tel: 041 811 12 76

Fax: 041 811 12 27
www.hirschen-schwyz.ch
Cosy hostel with unusual
pub. **$**

Vitznau

**Arabellasheraton
Vitznauerhof**
Seestrasse
Tel: 041 399 77 77
Fax: 041 399 76 66
Shorefront Victorian hotel
with wonderful gardens.
$$$$

Weggis

Frohburg
Seestrasse 21
Tel: 041 392 00 60

Fax: 041 392 00 66
www.frohburg.ch
Next to peaceful lake
and gardens; the 12 rooms
all have balconies
overlooking the water.
$$–$$$

Zug

Löwen am See
Landsgemeindeplatz 1
Tel: 041 725 22 22
Fax: 041 725 22 00
www.loewen-zug.ch
Attractive hotel located
on the lakefront in
the heart of Zug's old
town. Rooms have all
mod cons and there is a
restaurant. **$$$**

BELOW: Zermatt's Hotel Dufour.

SWISS MITTELLAND

Baden (AG)

Kappelerhof
Bruggerstr. 142
Tel: 056 222 38 34
Fax: 056 222 55 32
Just outside the town with buses connecting every 10 minutes. Bar and bowling alley. **$$**

Biel/Bienne (BE)

Worbenbad
Hauptstrasse
Tel: 032 384 67 67

Fax: 032 384 79 06
Luxury rooms, indoor pool and sauna. **$$**

Solothurn

Baseltor
Hauptgasse 749

Tel: 032 622 34 22
Fax: 032 622 18 79
www.baseltor.ch
Central and small hotel in 17th-century cannon store in the pretty old town; good prices. Good restaurant and bar. **$$**

WESTERN SWITZERLAND

Chexbres

Préalpina
Rte de Chardonne
Tel: 021 946 09 09
Fax: 021 946 09 50
www.prealpina.ch
Situated in the middle of the Lavaux vineyards (one of the main Swiss wine-making areas) and with a fantastic view of Lake Geneva. **$$$–$$$$**

Fribourg

Duc Berthold
Rue des Bouchers 55
Tel: 026 350 81 00
Fax: 026 350 81 81
Right next to the cathedral in the old town, with a swimming pool and very good food. **$$–$$$**

Geneva

Angleterre
Quai du Mont-Blanc 17
Tel: 022 906 55 55
Fax: 022 906 55 56
www.dangleterrehotel.com
Traditional luxury hotel, with views over the lake. **$$$$**
Balzac
Rue de l'ancien Port 14
Tel: 022 731 01 60
Fax: 022 731 38 47
www.hotel-balzac.ch
Large rooms near lake and railway station. **$$**
Eden Hotel Geneva
Rue de Lausanne 135
Tel: 022 716 37 00

Fax: 022 731 52 60
www.eden.ch
Located between the international district and the old town, overlooking a park and lake. Offers spacious rooms and parking. **$$$**
Luserna
Avenue Luserna 12
Tel: 022 949 56 56
Fax: 022 949 56 36
Quiet little hotel situated in a park with ancient trees, between the railway station and airport. **$–$$**

Gruyères-Moléson

Hostellerie St-Georges
Tel: 026 921 83 00
Fax: 026 921 83 39
www.st-georges-gruyeres.ch
Traditional in the heart of Gruyères with excellent food and a nice view. **$$–$$$**

Lausanne

Lausanne Palace and Spa
Grand-Chêne 7–9
Tel: 021 331 31 31
Fax: 021 323 25 71
www.lausanne-palace.ch
Luxury hotel with a superb view of Lake Geneva, designed by Swiss artist Jean Tinguely. **$$$$**
Du Marché
Pré-du-marché 42
Tel: 021 647 99 00
Fax: 021 646 47 23
www.hoteldumarche-lausanne.ch
Little hotel in the centre of the old town; quiet. **$$**

Montreux

Le Montreux Palace
Grand-Rue 100
Tel: 021 962 12 12
Fax: 021 962 10 25
www.montreux-palace.com
Plenty of *belle-époque* luxury. **$$$$**

Murten/Morat

Adler
Hauptgasse 45
Tel: 026 672 66 69
Fax: 026 672 66 77
www.adler-hotel.ch
Small cosy hotel in the heart of the medieval town. Rooms have been named after the hotel's many famous guests. **$$–$$$**

Neuchâtel

La Maison du Prussien
Au Gor de Vauseyon
Tel: 032 730 54 54
Fax: 032 730 21 43
www.hotel-prussien.ch
Historic hotel in an old brewery with three mills and a menagerie. Nice views. **$$–$$$**

Saignelégier/ Franches-Montagnes.

De La Gare et Du Parc
Rue Gruère 4
Tel: 032 951 11 21
Fax: 032 951 12 32
Family hotel with surrounding park. Renowned cuisine with seasonal specialities. **$$–$$$**

Yverdon-les-Bains

La Maison Blanche
En Calamin
Tel: 024 423 83 11
Fax: 024 423 83 12
www.la-maison-blanche.ch
Near the motorway exit on the A1 (Yverdon-South) in a quiet location with bus stop behind the hotel. **$$**

BELOW: Geneva's Hotel Eden.

E ATING OUT

RECOMMENDED RESTAURANTS, CAFES & BARS

What to Eat

Switzerland's restaurants, inns and bistros have an exciting variety of cuisines. You can order, in addition to the various national specialities, food with a pronounced French, Italian or German influence. Examples of distinctively Swiss dishes include fondue, *raclette* (melted sharp cheese served over potatoes or bread), *Bündnerfleisch* (cured, thinly sliced meat produced in Graubünden), *Bernr Platte* (sauerkraut or green beans with potatoes, bacon, sausage and ribs), *Zürcher Geschnetzeltes* (braised veal with a cream sauce) served with the popular *Rösti* (grated fried potatoes), *Luzerner Chügelipastete* (meat and mushroom pie), *Papet Vaudois* (sausage and leek with potatoes) and risotto (Italian-style savoury rice).

Desserts include *Zuger Kirschtorte* (cake with butter cream and cherry schnapps), a variety of meringues served with whipped cream, and *Zabaglione* (a warm cream made from lots of eggs and wine) in Ticino.

Switzerland has the highest vineyards in Europe. The best-known white wines are Fendant, Dorin, Féchy, Dézaley and Twanner. Well-known red wines include Dôle, Merlot, Gamay and Pinot Noir.

Some of the many different varieties of schnapps (said to be *digestifs*) are *Kirsch* (cherry), *Pflümli* (plum), *Williams* (pear) and *Bätzi* (a kind of mixed-fruit cognac, consisting mostly of apple and pear).

Coffee is served as *kaffee crème* (with cream), *milchkaffee* (German-style), *café renversé* (French-style) with milk, but you can also get the Italian-style *cappuccino* and *espresso*. *Kaffee hag* is coffee without caffeine and *kaffee fertig* is coffee with schnapps (especially nice

in winter to warm you up). As well as the traditional teas, many places serve a variety of herbal teas, including *kräutertee* (German), *infusion* (French) and *tisana* (Italian), which include peppermint, camomile, etc. In summer iced tea is served everywhere.

Hot or cold Swiss chocolate drinks *(schockolade/chocolat)* are ubiquitous, delicious and rich. Also try the healthier *Ovomaltine* milk drink where chocolate is replaced by malt.

A distinctively soft, cold drink is *Rivella*: made from whey and giving you strength for a strenuous day's sightseeing.

There are many beers from different regions, including Feldschlösschen (Basel), Cardinal (Fribourg) and Calanda (Grisons). Shandy is called *panaché* as in France. There is apple juice *apfelsaft/jus de pomme,* and an alcoholic cider called *Suure Most.*

Meal Times

Generally, the midday meal (*dîner* or lunch) is served 11.30am–2pm, and evening meals *(souper)* from 6–9pm in mountain areas, until 10pm in large towns. Inns and restaurants usually stay open until 11.30pm (later at weekends). In larger cities there are always a few places where you can order food until 2am. Many cafés and tearooms offer lighter meals and snacks, which are often cheaper than restaurants.

BELOW: rows and rows of freshly made Swiss cheese at Granjeres.

RESTAURANT LISTINGS

BASEL

Restaurant Löwenzorn
Gemsberg 2/4 (near Marktplatz)
Tel: 061 261 42 13
Fax: 061 261 42 17
Typical Basel restaurant serving a wide range of local dishes. **$$**

St Alban-Eck
St. Alban-Vorstadt 60
Malzgasse
Tel: 061 271 03 20
Cosy, simple wood-panelled restaurant with fresh produce. **$$**

Stucki Bruderholz
Bruderholzallee 42
Tel: 061 361 82 22
The best gourmet restaurant in town, with a fine midday menu and attractive terraces. **$$$**

Zum Goldenen Sternen
St-Alban-Rheinweg 70
Tel: 061 272 16 66
The oldest inn in Basel (1412) with food served in the garden in summer. Good Swiss fare. **$$–$$$**

BERN AND BERNESE OBERLAND

Bern

La Neuveville
Jean-Jacques Rousseau
Prom. J.-J. Rousseau 1
Tel: 032 752 36 52
With a view over St Peter's Island. Local fish specialities.
$–$$$

Zimmermania Le Bistro
Brunngasse 19
Tel: 031 311 15 42
This is a cosy Bernese restaurant with good food and excellent desserts.
$–$$$

Frohsinn
Münstergasse 54

Tel/Fax: 031 311 37 68
Excellent food and relatively inexpensive.
$$

Brasserie Bärengraben
Muristalden 1
Tel: 031 331 42 18
Little restaurant near the bear pit over the river. Bernese specialities, fish, and excellent desserts.
$–$$

Rosengarten
Alter Aargauerstalden 31b
Tel: 031 351 01 43
Glass-fronted restaurant on a hill above the bear pits with glorious views across the city. Food is mostly

Mediterranean. **$$$**

Grindelwald

Fiescherblick
Tel: 033 854 53 53
Rustic atmosphere, excellent food and good wines at fair prices.
$$–$$$

Gstaad

Chesery
Lauenenstrasse
Tel: 033 744 24 51
Old house with rustic atmosphere; best gourmet in town.
$$$

Interlaken

Du Nord
Restaurant im Gade
Höheweg 70
Tel: 033 827 50 50
Very cosy, friendly restaurant in the Hotel Du Nord. International cuisine and good wine at moderate prices. **$–$$**

Thun

Schloss Schadau
Seestrasse 45
Tel: 033 222 25 00
Superb food served in the castle beside the gastronomy museum. **$$**

BELOW: The Swiss are big fans of terrace dining.

EASTERN SWITZERLAND

Appenzell

Säntis
Landsgemeindeplatz
Tel: 071 788 11 11
Excellent regional cuisine
and good wine at
reasonable prices.
$$–$$$

Glarus

Sonnegg
Asylstrasse 30
Tel: 055 640 11 92
Tasty regional cuisine. **$–$$**

Rapperswil

Back & Brau
Hotel Speer
Bahnhofplatz 5
Tel: 055 220 89 00
Excellent regional fare
including home-made
pastries and home-
brewed beer, in the

heart of historic Rapperswil.
$$–$$$

St Gallen

Jägerhof
Hotel Jägerhof,
Brühlbleichestrasse 11
Tel: 071 245 50 22
Classic, creative regional
cuisine and excellent wine.
$–$$$
Peter und Paul
Kirchlistrasse 99
Tel: 071 245 56 25
In the centre of St Gallen
with a panoramic view of
Lake Constance and
excellent food. **$–$$**
Zum Goldenen Schäfli
Metzgergasse 5
Tel: 071 223 37 37
Fax: 071 223 70 45
Situated in a 17th-century
guildhall, "The Golden
Lamb" has lots of local
character. **$$**

Schaffhausen

Gerberstube
Bachstrasse 8
Tel: 052 625 21 55
Serving excellent Italian
food. Stylish decor.
$$–$$$

Winterthur

Walliser Kanne
Steinberggasse 25
Tel: 052 212 81 71
Friendly restaurant with
classic Swiss food. **$**

Zürich

Hiltl
Sihlstrasse 28
Tel: 044 227 70 00
A landmark for more than
100 years. A vegetarian
restaurant offering a
multitude of salads, pastas
and other choices. **$**

Kronenhalle
Rämistrasse 4
Tel: 01 251 66 69
Traditional, French-style
cuisine. Delicious. **$$–$$$**
Kaufleuten
Pelikanplatz
Tel: 01 225 33 33
Fashionable restaurant and
bar with food served until
after midnight. **$–$$**
Rosaly's
Freieckgasse 7
Tel: 01 261 44 30
Restaurant specialising
in Swiss dishes. Many
locals come here to
sample real
Aeplermakkaroni or
Glarner Zigerhörnli. **$–$$**
**Zunfthaus zur
Zimmerleuten**
Limmatquai 40
Tel: 01 252 08 34
Old traditional restaurant in
Guild House with local
specialities. **$–$$**

GRAUBUNDEN

Chur

Obelisco
Vazerolgasse 12
Tel: 081 252 58 58
Lovely, large Italian
restaurant with balcony

seating available. There
is a large menu and a
good selection of wines.
$–$$
Zum Kornplatz
Kornplatz 1
Tel: 081 252 27 59

Popular with both young
and old customers alike.
and offering a delicious
selection of French and
Swiss specialities using
the best local produce.
$–$$

Davos

**Bistro Gentiana et Cafe
des Artistes**
Promenade 53
Tel: 081 413 56 49
Trendy bistro with several
fondue varieties and snail
dishes. **$$**
Bündnerstübli
Dischmastrasse 8
Tel: 081 416 33 93
Cosy restaurant with
Grisons specialities. **$$**

Flims Dorf

Conn
Tel: 081 911 12 31
Excellent regional cuisine
and great view of the Alps.
$–$$

Ftan

Engiadina
Tel: 081 864 04 34
Friendly restaurant in this
lovely Engadine village. **$$**

Le Prese

Le Prese
Tel: 081 844 03 33
Pretty location by the small

BELOW: St Gallen's Zum Goldenen Schäfli is perfect for a relaxed, local meal.

lake of Le Prese in Val
Poschiavo. **$$–$$$**

Pontresina

Saratz
Via Maistra
Tel: 081 839 40 00
Friendly restaurant with an
Art Nouveau hall. Excellent
regional cuisine. **$–$$**

St Moritz

Monopol
Via Maistra 17

Tel: 081 837 04 04
Elegant, excellent
Italian cuisine but
also other specialities.
Great desserts.
$–$$$
Meierei
Via Dim Lej 52
Tel: 081 833 20 60
Dating from the 11th
century, this ancient
inn excels at local cuisine.
$$
Veltlinerkeller
Via del Bagn 11
Tel: 081 833 40 09

This is one of St Moritz's
favourite eating
establishments. The prices
aren't too high and there's
a good selection of dishes.
$$

Scuol/Susch

Traube
Via Stradun
Tel: 081 861 07 00
High-quality regional
dishes served in cosy
surroundings. Try the local
grappa. **$$**

Sils Maria

Waldhaus
Tel: 081 838 51 00
Wonderful restaurant
with a garden terrace
and Alpine view.
Inspired, high-class
cuisine. **$–$$$**

TICINO

Ascona

**Giardino Restaurant
Aphrodite**
Via Segnale
Tel: 091 785 88 88
Luxurious restaurant with
excellent food. **$$–$$$**

Bellinzona

**Castelgrande Grotto San
Michele**
Tel: 091-826 2353
The grotto terrace
restaurant is the cheaper of
the two at Castelgrande. It
offers great food, views
and estate wines. **$$**
Locanda Orico
Via Orico 13

Tel: 091-825 1518
Located at the foot of
Castelgrande. Friendly
atmosphere. **$$–$$$**

Comano

Pedemonte
Via Pedemonte 12
Tel: 091 825 33 33
Pleasant, intimate
restaurant serving fine
local cuisine. **$$**

Gudo

Osteria Brack
Tel: 091 859 12 54
A perfect place for lovers of
pasta. Good wine list.
Located 13 km (7 miles)

from Bellinzona. **$–$$**

Locarno

Il Boccalino
Via della Motta 7
Tel/fax: 091 751 96 81
Near Piazza Grande. Fresh
organic food carefully
prepared. **$–$$**
Carcani-Mövenpick
Piazza Motta
Tel: 091 785 17 17
This atmospheric eatery is
part of the nationwide
Mövenpick chain. It offers a
wide choice of dishes and a
great location right on the
lake. **$$**
Dell Angelo
Piazza Grande

Tel: 091 751 81 75
Busy hotel restaurant
in the heart of the old
town. Ticinese
specialities and regional
wines. **$$**

Lugano

Al Portone
Via Cassarate 3
Tel: 091 923 55 11
Family-run restaurant with
excellent food and wine.
$$–$$$
Osteria Calprino
Via Carona 28
Tel: 091 994 14 80
Excellent regional
specialities offered at
reasonable prices. **$$**

VALAIS

Brig

Schlosskeller
Alte Simplonstrasse 26
Tel: 027 923 33 52
Excellent food with a
French touch in the 16th-
century Stockalper Palace.
Large choice of cheeses
and wines. **$–$$**

Leukerbad

La Malvoisie
Hotel les Sources des Alpes,
Tuftstrasse 17
Tel: 027 472 20 00
La Malvoisie offers a
regional set menu,
including wonderful local
cheeses and wines.
$$–$$$

Saas Fee

Hohenegg
Tel: 027 957 22 68
In summer you can sit on
the terrace with a fantastic
view. But whether you go at
lunch time or for dinner
there is always local fresh
food of a very high quality.
$$–$$$

Sion

Enclos de Valère
Rue des Châteaux 18
Tel: 027 323 32 30
Access via a pedestrian-
only lane in the old town;
very pleasant terrace and a
great selection of dishes.
$$

Relais du Mont d'Orge
La Muraz
Tel: 027 395 33 46
A short distance west of
Sion, this delightful
restaurant offers seasonal
specialities and fish. **$$**

Verbier

La Pinte du Rosalp
Route de Médran
Tel: 027 771 63 23
The bistro of the luxurious
Rosalp restaurant (with
meals cooked by the same
chef). **$$–$$$**

Zermatt

Le Corbeau d'Or
Hotel Mirabeau

Tel: 027 966 26 60
Very cosy, with good food,
including many seafood
specialities. **$$–$$$**
Grill Restaurant Spycher
Hotel Aristella
Tel: 027 967 20 41
This chalet-style restaurant
serves a wide range of
dishes and has an
extensive wine list. Good
for liqueurs. **$$**
Schäferstübli
Romatik Hotel Julen
Tel: 027 966 76 00
Traditional Valais and Swiss
specialities are served,
including fondues and
raclette. The Julen also has
a more upscale restaurant
with an international menu.
$$

INNER SWITZERLAND

Aarau

Chez Jeannette
Vordere Vorstadt 17
Tel: 062 822 77 88
Best restaurant in town
with local fish and
other specialities.
$–$$$

Entlebuch

Drei Könige
Dorf
Tel: 041 480 12 27
Excellent restaurant for
wine lovers, in historical
building. **$–$$$**

Luzern

Old Suisse House
Löwenplatz 4
Tel: 041 410 61 71
Excellent atmosphere and
delicious food and wine. **$$**

Rebstock
St. Leodegarstrasse 3
Tel: 041 410 35 81
Inviting, French-style bistro
with terrace. **$–$$**

Schiff
Unter der Egg 8
Tel: 041 418 52 52
Serves decent traditional
Swiss cuisine mainly
to tourists who come

for the ideal location,
a large terrace right on
the river with a view of
the Kapellbrücke.
$–$$

Wirtshaus Galliker
Schützenstrasse 1
Tel: 041 240 10 02
Traditional specialities
since 1681. Filling
dishes such as *pot-au-feu*
and *leberli* with *rösti*.
$–$$

Vitznau

Park Hotel Vitznau
Seestrasse

Tel: 041-399 60 60
This renowned palatial
hotel is situated at the foot
of Rigi, by the lakeside.
Varied menu. Traditional
Sunday breakfasts.
$$–$$$

Zug

Hecht am See
Fischmarkt 2
Tel: 041 729 81 30
Located right next to the
lake. Founded in 1435
and famous for its
seafood dishes. Excellent
wines. **$$**

WESTERN SWITZERLAND

Delémont

Hotel du Midi
Place de la Gare 10
Tel: 032 422 17 77
There is a bistro and a
restaurant in the same
building with fine food from
various areas. **$$–$$$**

Fribourg

Buffet de la Gare CFF
Place de la Gare 1
Tel: 026 322 28 16

Unbelievably good food,
inside Fribourg's railway
station. **$$**

Café de l'Ange
Rue des Forgerons 1
Tel: 026 322 35 49
Fondue and *raclette* are the
specialities here. In fine
weather sit on the terrace
on the river. **$–$$**

Geneva

L'Auberge d'Hermance
Rue du Midi 12

Hermance
Tel: 022 751 13 68
Nestling on a narrow
street in the quaint village
of Hermance (just before
the French border along
the left bank). Enchanting
French restaurant with
vine-covered terrace in the
summer. Also a small inn
with six rooms. **$$$$**

Café des Négociants
Rue de la Filature 29
Carouge
Tel: 022 300 31 30

Situated just outside
Geneva, but only a short
tram-ride away, in the
popular suburb of Carouge.
One of many excellent
dining options in Carouge.
Extensive wine selection.
Larger groups can eat at a
big table in the wine cellar.
$$$–$$$$

L'Olivier de Provence
Rue Jacques-Dalphin 13
Carouge
Tel: 022 342 04 50
Provençale specialities in
this charming restaurant in
Carouge, to the south of
the old town. **$$$**

Restaurant les Armures
Rue du Puits St-Pierre
Tel: 022 310 34 42
Typical brasserie in the
heart of the old town. Try
regional dishes such as
raclette or *filets de perch*.
$$

Sam-Lor Thai
Rue Monthoux 17
Tel: 022 738 80 55
Authentic Thai cuisine and
great atmosphere. **$$**

Murten/Morat

Le Vieux Manoir au Lac
Rue de Lausanne
Tel: 026 678 61 61
Restaurant in one of the
best hotels in the country,
situated just by the
lakeside. Light French
cuisine and fish from the
lake feature on their menu.
$–$$$

BELOW: a typical Swiss dish of sliced meat with chanterelles, served with rosti.

Neuchâtel

Le Banneret
Rue Fleury 1
Tel: 032 725 28 61
Situated in the old town, this attractive restaurant with a small terrace serves great pasta. **$$**

Maison des Halles
Au Premier
Rue du Trésor 4
Tel: 032 724 31 41
Very good food served in a 400-year-old building. Delicious desserts. **$–$$**

Solothurn

Vini al Grappolo
Prisongasse 4
Tel: 032 623 55 45
Italian restaurant and cellar with a fine selection of mainly Italian wines. Attractive terrace for dining al fresco. **$–$$**

Zum alten Stephan
Friedhofplatz 10
Tel: 032 622 11 09
Famous restaurant with delicious food in its first-floor *Narrenstübli* and street café. **$$–$$$**

Yverdon-Les-Bains

Grand Hôtel du Bains
22, av. des Bains
Tel: 024 424 64 64
Wonderful gastronomic restaurant in the Pavillon restaurant of this spa hotel. **$$–$$$**

PRICE CATEGORIES

Price for a meal for two peope without drinks:
$ = under 50 SFr
$$ = 50–100 SFr
$$$ = over 100 SFr

L'Ecusson Vaudois
Rue de la Plaine 29
Tel: 024 425 40 15
Traditional rustic fare on offer at this characterful restaurant. **$$**

LAUSANNE

Auberge du Raisin
Place de l'Hotel-de-Ville
Tel: 021 799 21 31
A Relais & Chateaux hotel and restaurant, the seasonal menu offers fresh seafood, game and other locally sourced meats. **$$$**

La Rotonde
Place du Port 17–19
Tel: 021 613 33 33
Wonderful old-fashioned restaurant in the Beau-Rivage Palace hotel, with excellent international cuisine and friendly service. **$$–$$$**

L'Age d'Or
Rue Pont-Bessières 3
Tel: 021 323 73 14
Friendly atmosphere, many vegetarian specialities. **$–$$**

Les Chevreuils
Route du Jorat 80,
Vers-chez-les-Blancs
Tel: 021 785 01 01
In a beautiful setting just outside of the town. Gourmet regional cooking and an extensive wine list. **$$–$$$**

Philippe Rochat
Rue d'Yverdon 1, Crissier
Tel: 021 634 0505
Considered one of the best restaurants in Switzerland, Philippe Rochat took over this Swiss insitution from Fredy Girardet (former name) and has maintained its status among the culinary elite. **$$$**

Les Avants

Auberge de la Cergniaulaz
Orgevaux
Tel: 021 964 42 76
Delicious substantial food, with only the best ingredients, 8 km (5 miles) from Montreux. **$–$$**

BELOW: sharing a fondue in one of Fribourg's traditional restaurants.

A CTIVITIES

THE ARTS, FESTIVALS AND EVENTS, NIGHTLIFE, SHOPPING AND OUTDOOR ACTIVITIES

THE ARTS

Music and Theatre

Cultural opportunities in Switzerland run a lively gamut from yodelling clubs and village concerts to drama associations, from jazz and rock groups to literary or musical events and films. All larger cities maintain at least one theatre and a symphony orchestra. There are performances by internationally acclaimed artists and even the smaller outlying communities put on dramatic and musical events. In the concert scene, the leading venue currently is Luzern's new Kultur & Kongress-zentrum (KKL) designed by France's Jean Nouvel *(see details below)*. Zürich's opera has an international reputation with the most new productions per season anywhere in Europe. In general, the theatre and concert season begins in September and ends in June. In summer, highly acclaimed festivals take place in which distinguished musicians and conductors entertain music lovers the world over. The best known of these take place at Lausanne, Zürich, Thun, Braunwald, in the Engadine, Sion, Gstaad, Interlaken, Luzern, Ascona and Vevey.

Jazz and folk music festivals are organised in Bern, Nyon, Montreux, Willisau and Zürich. There are also regular points of rendezvous for the film and television industries: the competition for the Rose d'Or in Luzern (it has moved after 43 years in Montreux), international film festivals in Locarno, Nyon and Les Diablerets, and film and literature days in Solothurn.

In addition to all these offerings, folklore fans from all corners of the world congregate in Fribourg and at the Tell Games in Interlaken. Advance tickets and other information can be obtained by calling **Swiss Ticket Corner**, tel: 0848 800 800; www.ticketcorner.ch (open Mon–Fri 8am–8pm, Sat 8am–6pm, Sun 10am–6pm).

Top Theatres

Basel: **Stadtcasino**, tel: 061 225 93 93 (main concert hall); **Stadttheater**, Theaterstrasse 7, tel: 061 295 11 33 (main theatre). Other live music: **Bird's Eye** (jazz), Kohlenberg 20; www.birdseye.ch; **Kaserne**, Klybeckstr. 1b; www.musikaserne.ch.

Bern: **Casino**, Herrengasse 25 (main concert hall); **Stadttheater**, Kornhausplatz 20 (main theatre). Other live music: **Wasserwerk**, Wasserwerkgasse 5.

ABOVE: the legacy of ancient Rome.

Geneva: **Victoria Hall**, Rue Général-Dufour 14, tel: 022 418 35 00 (main concert hall); **Grand Théâtre**, Place Neuve; **Grand Casino**, Quai du Mont-Blanc 19, tel: 022 908 90 81. Other live music: **Le Chat Noir**, Rue Vautier, Carouge 13; **Sud des Alpes**, Rue des Alpes 10.

Lausanne: **Opéra de Lausanne**, Av. du Théâtre 12, tel: 021 310 16 00; **Salle Métropole**, tel: 021 320 54 28 (main concert hall and ballet performances). Other live music: **Chorus**, Av. Mon-Repos 3; Le Caveau, **Café de l'Hôtel de Ville**, Place de la Palud 10.

Luzern: **Kultur-und Kongresszentrum Luzern** (KKL), Europaplatz 1, tel: 041 226 70 70; www.kkl-luzern.ch (main concert hall and gallery). Other live music: **Boa**, Geissensteinring 41; **Jazz Kantine**, Grabenstr. 8; **Schüür**, Tribschenstrasse 1;

Zürich: **Tonhalle**, Claridenstr. 7,

tel: 01 206 34 34 (main concert hall); **Opernhaus**, Falkenstr. 1, tel: 01 268 64 00; www.operabase.ch (opera house and ballet); **Schauspielhaus** (main theatre), Rämistr. 34; **Schiffbau**, Schiffbaustr. 10, tel: 01 265 58 58; www.schauspielhaus.ch. Other live music: **Rote Fabrik**, Seestr. 395; www.rotefabrik.ch; **Kaufleuten**, Pelikanstr. 18; **Jazzclub Moods**, Schiffbaustr. 6, tel: 01 276 80 00

Art & Architecture

There are abundant patrician and farmhouses, churches, castles and medieval town centres to discover in Switzerland. Traces of the **ancient Romans** have been found in Avenches, Orbe, Augst, Windisch and Martigny. The baptism chapel in Riva San Vitale dates from the **5th century** and the church of Müstair (GR), cultural heritage of UNESCO) was built during the **Carolingian period**. The church of St Martin in Zillis contains the oldest preserved painted-wood ceiling in the Western World.

From the **Romanesque** and **Gothic** period it is interesting to see influences from neighbouring areas: the churches in Ticino are influenced by the **Lombards** from the south, for example, the Romanesque church in Biasca; **Burgundy**-influenced examples are the cathedrals of Lausanne (Romanesque) and Basel (Gothic). The minsters in Bern (Gothic) and Schaffhausen (Romanesque), and the Grossmünster in Zürich are influenced by **German** architecture. Other Romanesque and Gothic cathedrals can be seen in Chur,

Swiss Artists

Many Swiss artists of the 19th and 20th centuries have won glowing international recognition. Names like Arnold Böcklin, Le Corbusier, Ferdinand Hodler, Paul Klee, Alberto Giacometti, Max Bill, Hans Arp, Meret Oppenheim, Bernard Luginbühl, Jean Tinguely and Mario Botta, Herzog and de Meuron, Peter Zumthor – to name just a few – indicate the tremendous creativity alive today in Switzerland. Relevant buildings worth a visit include the **Tinguely Museum** and the **Ste-Marie-des-Anges** on the Monte Tenero near Lugano, by Mario Botta; the **Fondation Beyeler** in Basel, by Renzo Piano; **SPA** in Vals (GR), by Peter Zumthor; as well as private houses in **La Chaux-de-Fonds** by Le Corbusier and others.

Holiday Courses

Courses are offered throughout Switzerland in practically every kind of sport. Those less interested in athletic endeavours can choose from a wide variety of courses focusing on practical, creative or cultural topics including theatre, dance, music, mime, art, crafts or cooking. For more information contact your nearest Swiss Tourism Office.

Geneva and Neuchâtel.The cathedrals in Basel, Chur, Lausanne and Bern have well-preserved sculptures. The abbeys of Romainmôtier and Payerne are well known for their paintings. After the Reformation in 1536 paintings were banned from churches. **Renaissance** buildings include the Hôtel de Ville de Palud in Lausanne, the church in Chêne-Paquer (VS) and the Town Hall in Luzern. In many towns you will see fountains with sculptures dating to the Renaissance period.

The splendour of **baroque** architecture can be seen in the Einsiedeln, Engelberg and Disentis monasteries as well as in the abbey of St Gallen and the churches of Kreuzlingen and Arlesheim. There are other treasures well worth taking a look at in St Maurice (VS), Beromünster and Chur. Swiss architecture in the 18th century has a **French** influence. Painters from the 18th century include Jean-Etienne Liotard (portraits), Anton Graff, Jean-Pierre Saint-Ours, Johann Heinrich Wüst, Heinrich Füssli and Félix Vallotton.

FESTIVALS AND EVENTS

Music and Film Festivals

January–April

Solothurn Film Festival (Jan); **Fribourg Film Festival** (Mar); **Primavera Concertistica**, a classical music festival in Lugano (Apr);

May

Bern International Jazz Festival; **Schaffhausen Jazz Festival**; **Nyon International Documentary Film Festival**; **Rose d'Or International Television Festival**, Luzern.

June

Gurten Open-air Rock and Folk Festival in Bern; **Zürich Caliente**, the biggest Latin festival in Switzerland; **Solothurn Literature Days**; **Zürich**

Festspiele, an arts festival (June–July); **Wilhelm Tell Festspiele** in Interlaken (June–Sept); **Ascona New Orleans Music Festival** (June–July).

July

Saas Fee Alpine International Music Festival; **Festival Jazz** in Lugano; **Montreux Jazz Festival**; **Klassik-Musikwochen** in Braunwald (GL); **Arosa International Jazz Festival**; **Fribourg International Jazz Festival**; **Verbier Music Festival** (end July–beginning Aug); **Yehudi Menuhin Festival** in Gstaad (July–Aug); **Classical concert weeks** in the Engadine (July–Aug); **Luzern International Blues Festival**; **Davos International Music Festival** – young artists in concert (July–Aug); **Open-air theatre performances** in Ballenberg's Freilichtmuseum, near Brienz (July–Aug); **Leukerbad Clown Festival**; Nyon (VA); **Paléo International Open-air Rock Festival**; **Thuner Schlosskonzerte**, classical music festival in Thun; **Tibor Varga**, classical music festival with violin competition in Sion (VS; July–Sept).

August

Neuchâtel Busker's Festival; **Luzern International Music Festival**; **International Festival** for music and lyric poetry in Montreux (Aug–Sept); **Interlaken Music Festival** (Aug–Sept); **Music weeks** in Locarno/Ascona (Aug–Oct); **Locarno International Film Festival**; **Willisau** (Luzern), a jazz festival (end Aug–beginning Sept); **Fribourg International Folklore Festival**.

September–November

Cinemusic in Thun – an international festival on music and film; **International Festival of Alpenfilms** in Les Diablerets; **International Jazz Festival** in Zürich (Nov).

Traditional Festivals and Events

There are numerous festival traditions throughout the year. For more information and tickets contact Switzerland Tourism, tel: 00800-100 200 30 (from Switzerland and abroad) or visit www.myswitzerland.com or Swiss Ticket Corner, tel: 0848-800 800, www.ticketcorner.ch. Another good website is: www.events.ch

January

Vogel Gryff in Basel (*New Year's Eve and 13th*); **Kläusenacht** in Urnäsch near Appenzell (*New Year's Eve*); **Lauberhorn World Cup** downhill ski racing in Wengen (*mid*); **Inferno giant slalom ski race** in Mürren (*late*);

TRANSPORT

ACCOMMODATION

EATING OUT

ACTIVITIES

A – Z

LANGUAGE

international **hot-air ballooning** week in Chateau d'Oex *(late)*.

February

Horse racing on St Moritz's frozen lake *(early)*; **Cresta Run** toboggan competition in St Moritz *(mid)*; **Fasnacht** carnival in Basel and Luzern and many other towns and villages *(mid)*; in the Lötschen Valley there are the terrifying masks of "Dirty Thursday" and the "**Good Lord's Grenadier**" *(mid-February–early March)*.

March/April

Chalanda Marz in Graubünden, with its ringing chimes *(1st)*; **Fridolinsfeuer** in Glarus and the **Good Friday Procession** in Mendrisio *(6th)*; **Sechseläuten** in Zürich (spring festival; *first Monday after 21 March*).

May

May Day celebrations in many places *(1st)*; **Landsgemeinde** in Glarus, public voting on local issues *(early)*; Valaisian champion's meeting of **Cow Fighting** in Aproz *(mid)*.

June

Celebration in many villages of taking cattle up to the Alps *(early)*; **Tour de Suisse** cycle race *(mid)*; Celebration of the **Battle of Murten/Morat** with flower parade *(22nd)*.

July

Swiss Open tennis championship, Gstaad *(early)*; **Aarau Youth Festival** *(first Friday in July)*; **Medieval Festival** in St Ursanne, Jura *(mid)*.

August

Swiss National Day, with fireworks, parades etc. everywhere *(1st)*; **Zürich Street Parade**: giant techno

dance party *(early)*; **Fêtes de Genève** in Geneva *(early)*; **Marché-Concours** horse festival in Saignelégier, Jura *(early)*; **Chur Festival** *(late)*; Lausanne international **Rollerskating Championships** *(late)*; **Fribourg International Folklore Festival**, with yodelling and typical Alpine sports events *(late)*.

September

Bern Festival *(early)*; **Zürich Knabenschiessen**, with funfair *(mid)*; **La Bénichon** in Fribourg, a traditional thanksgiving festival *(mid)*; **Aarau Backfischet**, children's parade with Chinese lanterns *(second Friday in Sept)*; **International Horse Race** in Luzern *(mid)*. There are **grape-growing festivals** in Fribourg, Neuchâtel, Lugano, Lutry, Morges and other villages throughout the month.

October

Celebrations in many villages of bringing cattle down from the Alps *(early)*; **Basel Autumn Fair**, food fair *(late)*.

November

St Martin's Market in Vevey and Porrentruy, a food festival *(early)*; **Zibele-Märit** onion fair in Bern *(4th Monday)*.

December

Claus Hunt in Küssnacht on Rigi and in Arth *(6th)*; **Escalade** in Geneva *(around 11th)*; **Lichterschwimmen** in Zürich, illuminated boats on the Limmat River *(mid/late)*.

Trade Fairs

Switzerland hosts many regional, national and international trade fairs.

A few are listed below but you can find a detailed calendar by visiting www.osec.ch/swisstradefairs. **March**: motorshow in Geneva; **World's Watch and Jewellery Trade Fair** in Basel. **April: The Swiss Sample Trade Fair** in Basel (Muba; late April/early May); **The BEA** in Bern (end of April). **May**: EUROP'ART in Geneva. **June**: the art fair **Art**, held in Basel. **September**: Comptoir **Suisse** in Lausanne. **October**: **Cultura** in Basel; OLMA in St Gallen (agriculture). **November**: EXPOVINA in Zürich (wine).

NIGHTLIFE

Disregard the rumour that nightlife in Switzerland is pretty provincial. In larger cities you'll find a wide variety of bars, clubs, discos and other opportunities to dance. Some of the well-known holiday resort areas also offer attractive places to spend an evening, as well as world-class entertainment programmes. For further, up-to-date information enquire at a local tourist information centre, the hotel concierge, or just ask a likely-looking native.

There are a wide variety of lively cafés (or café-bars) dotted around the Swiss cities which serve alcohol. The best places tend to be crowded. In the larger cities such as Zürich, you will find some exclusively gay bars. There are many venues for rock music and jazz, and the modern club scene has burgeoned recently, many dance venues heaving with newfound energy.

Casinos

There are casinos in Bad Ragaz, Baden, Brunnen, Chur, Courrendlin, Crans, Davos, Engelberg, Geneva, Gstaad, Interlaken, Locarno, Lugano, Luzern, Montreux, Rheinfelden, St Moritz, Thun, Vaduz (Liechtenstein), Weggis, Wettingen, Zug and Zürich.

In Swiss casinos – which are primarily found on the premises of health resorts and hotels – you can stake your money on *Jeu de la boule* (a game similar to roulette).

SHOPPING

What to Buy and Where

There is an enormous choice of mementos to take home. Interesting purchases from different regions could include rock crystals (from Alpine areas), painted ceramics

BELOW: a break for refreshments during a cattle festival.

(different patterns depending on the region), utensils and vessels made out of wood (various areas), glass (Glasi Hergiswil, near Luzern is good), music boxes (the Jura), Ste Croix, dolls in folkloric costumes, carved wood (Brienz area), lace and embroidery, silk shawls and ties (Fabric Frontline in Zürich is good), traditional scarves (Glarner Tüechli in the Glarus region is good), traditional shirts (Toggenburg TG area), bells and leather accessories (Appenzell area), jewellery, chocolate, cheese, wine, schnapps, watches (from the Jura) and Swiss Army knives (choose between Victorinox or Wenger).

If you're searching for something typical and of good quality, take a look in one of the **Schweizerischer Heimatwerke** (Swiss Handicraft) shops, located in many cities and well-populated areas (www.heimatwerk.ch). They are staffed by competent sales assistants who can tell you anything you'd like to know. In smaller towns it's best to purchase articles directly from the source, in other words the company or artist. In Hergiswil (LU) you can visit the glazier's workshop and see how they work in the atelier.

Fabric Frontline in Zürich has designed silk fabric by the metre. For jewellery and watches visit the famous **Bucherer** in Zürich or any other **Bijouterie** shop.

Chocolates

These can be found in any food store. Look out for real Swiss chocolate (brand names include Lindt and Sprüngli, Nestlé and Frey). Home-made chocolates such as pralines are sold in bakeries and confectioners in most villages. In Zürich you will find the best ones at **Sprüngli** and in the lovely old-fashioned **Café Schober**.

The Lindt and Sprüngli Chocolate

ABOVE: fresh produce for sale at a local market.

Factory in Zürich has a museum with a video on chocolate production (Seestrasse 204, 8802 Kilchberg/ZH, tel: 01 716 22 33; open Wed–Fri 10am–noon, 1–4pm; www.lindt.com).

Cheese & Sausages

Swiss cheese is for sale in every grocer's shop, but if you have the opportunity, buy regional cheese directly from village dairies or on mountain farms – they are authentic and taste especially fine. Famous cheeses include: Appenzeller, Emmentaler (Bern region), Gruyère and Vacherin Fribourgeois (Fribourg area), Sbrinz (originally from Brienz), Schabziger (Glarus area), Tilsiter (eastern Switzerland), Raclette (Valais), Tête de Moine (Jura) and Formaggelli (Ticino).

There are various kinds of sausages which originate from different regions. Try to purchase them from a good butcher. Varieties include: Klöpfer (Basel area), St Gallen Schüblige, Bratwürste (pork, beef or a mixture; the Appenzell area), Waadtländer (Vaud), Longeoles (pork; Geneva), Coppa (salami; Ticino), Salsiz (salami; Bündner) Bindefleisch (dried, sliced meat).

Wines

In western Switzerland, Valais, Ticino, Grisons and other wine regions, look out for wine farms. A lot of them sell directly to the customer, or in wine shops and in larger food stores. Wine brands include white Chasselas, Epesses, St Saphorin (from the Lavaux, Geneva/Vaud area), red Dôle (Valais area), red Merlot (Ticino), Maienfelder Blauburgunder and Veltliner (Grisons area).

Confectionery

Try – or take home – the famous *kirschtorte* (cherry schnapps tart) in Zug or the Engadine, *nusstorte* (nut tart) in Graubünden, *Rüeblitorte* (carrot tart) from the Aargau, filled *Meringuen* from Meiringen (BE), *Délices* (a sort of bagel) from Geneva or filled *Amaretti* (Tessin).

Shops normally open daily 8/8.30am–6.30pm, on Saturday until 4pm. A lot of food shops close noon–2pm. Some confectioners in the holiday resorts and larger towns are open on Sundays.

OUTDOOR ACTIVITIES

Winter

Skiing

Rack and funicular railways, ski and chairlifts take fans of winter sports to ski runs which, thanks to the high premium placed on safety, are well-marked and constantly maintained. Some 200 ski schools employ about 4,000 instructors to teach at all levels. Instructors are also available for guided tours. You can rent ski equipment at all winter-sport resort areas.

Mono-ski

In numerous winter-sport centres you can learn how to hotdog ski, do snow ballet and ski jump as well as how to manage on a monoski or snowboard.

Cross-country & Ski-hiking

There are fully developed cross-country ski runs and ski-touring trails in all larger holiday areas of the Alps, Alp foothills and in Jura. You'll find

Markets

In Swiss markets all goods have to be marked with the price by law. Prices are usually by the *Kilo* or by the *Stück*, that is, each item priced individually. Usually the stallholder *(Verkäufer)* will select the goods for you. Sometimes there is a self-service system – observe everyone else. If you are choosing cheese, for example, you may be offered a taste to try first: *Zum Versuchen.*

tasting *die Degustation*
organic *biologisch*
flavour *der Geschmack*
basket *der Korb*
bag *die Tasche*

ABOVE: Switzerland's ski-instructors cater for all ages.

cross-country ski schools everywhere.

Ski Tours
Accomplished skiers can climb up mountain slopes with animal skins attached to their skis and roped to their fellow skiers for safety, then ski back down the slopes at breakneck speed, accompanied by an experienced guide.

Skibobbing
Many areas of the country have now set up special skibob runs.

Ice Skating, Curling and Ice Hockey
Over 300 natural and artificial ice-skating rinks, both indoors and outdoors, await ice-sport aficionados.

Sledding
You'll find everything from the usual sledding slopes to especially prepared and marked runs.

Skijoring
This is an extremely demanding and dangerous sport in which a skier is pulled across a run by a galloping horse. The most famous area for skijoring is St Moritz.

Horse Riding and Sleighs
You can hire horses in many places and most riding schools remain open in winter. If you prefer a more tranquil, contemplative excursion there are more than 70 holiday resort areas where you can sit back and relax in a horse-drawn sleigh.

Winter Hiking
Hiking fans can also get their money's worth even in the snow season; there are about 3,000 km (1,875 miles) of hiking trails open during the winter months.

Summer

Summer Hiking
Hikers are spoilt for choice in Switzerland with approximately 50,000 km (31,000 miles) of marked hiking trails. In addition to these, there are innumerable other paths waiting to be discovered. Yellow signs keep walkers informed on destination points and estimated hiking times.

Look for the useful and detailed guides and hiking maps issued by the Bundesamt für Landestopographie (federal office of regional geography). These are available in book shops, kiosks and some local tourist offices.

Numerous tourist information centres organise guided outings, from wildlife-observation hikes to moonlight and sunrise tours. There are over 300 hiking holiday options, from botanical excursions to senior-citizen hiking weeks, adventure trekking to long-distance tours.

The botanical and geological information-station nature trails, which lead through nature reserves, introduce you to the native flora and fauna of Switzerland.

Mountain Climbing
The Swiss Alps are full of peaks to tempt climbers, and glaciers can be crossed in the company of experienced mountain guides. There are more than 150 huts belonging to the Swiss Alpine Club (SAC). There are also schools which offer mountain-climbing instruction.

Jogging
Around villages, towns and cities there are some 500 woodland paths, each 2–3 km (1–2 miles) long and interspersed with fitness stations where you can rest for a while.

Golf
There are more than 30 beautifully situated golf courses to choose from as well as mini golf.

Tennis & Squash
In practically all cities and in most holiday resort areas there are indoor and outdoor tennis courts; many larger hotels have private courts at their disposal. You'll find squash facilities in about 40 different cities.

Aerosports
It's possible to take a sightseeing tour by plane from many regional airfields. There are numerous air centres which regularly offer courses at beginning, intermediate and advanced levels for gliding, paragliding, delta and hang-gliding.

Swiss Caves

About 10 caves are open for visits with guided tours, among them the third-largest cave system in the world – the Hölloch in the Muota Valley.

Other caves include: Beatushöhlen (near Interlaken), Höllgrotten (near Zug), Grotte aux Fées (near St-Maurice, Valais), Grotte de Milandre in Bancourt (near Porrentruy), Grotte de Réclère (near Porrentruy), Grotte de l'Orbe (near Vallorbe), Grotte de St-Léonard in St-Léonard, Kristallhöhle near Oberriet (SG) and Sandbalmhöhle (near Göschenen). For further information ask at the nearest tourist office.

Winter Sports in Summer
Various high-altitude ski areas have snow all year round and are in operation even during summer. You'll also find some curling, ice-skating and ice-hockey facilities open at this time.

Riding
You can hire horses, either for indoor riding, or hacking through the

Fishing

Approximately 32,000 km (20,000 miles) of running water and about 135,000 hectares (337,500 acres) of lakes are available for fishing througout Switzerland.

Local tourist centres can provide you with information about permits. As the regulations vary in different cantons, anglers should obtain information from the local police, or in advance from the relevant administration in the areas in which they wish to fish.

A brochure is available from Swiss tourist offices which provides details on the restrictions in the most important fishing areas of the country.

countryside at around 90 horse-riding centres. Special trekking weeks are organised and riders can explore the Alps via old mule tracks.

Covered Wagons

If you have a yearning to journey through the Jura in the manner of pioneers and Gypsies, climb aboard a horse-drawn wagon.

Water Sports

Switzerland, with its many lakes and rivers, is suitable for just about every conceivable kind of water sport.

Sailing & Windsurfing

There are sailing and windsurfing schools at most of the lakes in Graubünden and inner Switzerland.

Rowing & Canoeing

Every year international rowing regattas take place on the Rotsee, near Luzern. This lake is reputed to have some of the best rowing conditions in the world. Canoeists make for the Doubs in the Jura and the Muota in the canton of Schwyz.

River Rafting

Rafting trips along some of the turbulent rivers of the Alps (for example the Inn, Rhine, Rhône, Simme and Saane) and more leisurely journeys in canoes (along the Aare, Doubs, Reuss, Rhine, Rhône and Thur rivers) are offered during summer.

Water-skiing

It is possible to water-ski on most lakes in Switzerland. In the larger holiday-resort areas you'll also find water-skiing schools.

Swimming

Swimmers have more than 350

natural bathing areas along lakes and rivers to choose from, in addition to hundreds of indoor and outdoor pools and around 200 hotel pools. There are places to swim even in high-altitude holiday resorts.

Nature Reserves

There are over 500 nature reserves in Switzerland. The most important is the **Swiss National Park**. The Engadine (Graubünden), a region at an altitude of 1,400–3,171 metres (4,593–10,413 ft) with a total area encompassing about 172 sq. km (65 sq. miles), has been turned into a wildlife and plant reserve. The park was established in 1914 and some 150,000 visitors come to walk along the 80-km (50-miles) of hiking trails every year. The single road threading its way through the reserve follows the Spöl, goes over the Ofen Pass (Fuorn) and into the Val Müstair before continuing into Italy. One-third of the park is made up of woods, one third of Alpine meadows and one third of non-productive land. Chamois, marmots, roe and red deer, ibex, and various eagles are found here.

Children under the age of 15 are allowed in the park only if accompanied by an adult; dogs and camping are prohibited. The national park House Zernez and museum are open seven days a week June–October.

BELOW: sailing on Lake Geneva.

Other beautiful nature reserves include the **Aletschwald** (Aletsch Forest). At an altitude of 2,100 metres (6,900 ft) you reach the Valais by hiking across the Aletsch Glacier, the largest ice stream in the Alps. The forest has very old mountain fir trees and many other plants, some of them relatively rare. Guided day excursions in English are available (tel: 027 928 60 50).

In the canton of Ticino there are wonderful flower gardens on the **Isole di Brissago** (Brissago islands) on Lago Maggiore. You can reach them by boat from Brissago or Ascona. As well as fabulous flora, there is Mediterranean vegetation, with the only lemon and orange trees in Switzerland.

From the boat which runs regularly between the cities of Biel and Solothurn on the **River Aare** you can see a wild and very green romantic landscape – home to many birds.

Bird-spotting is also possible in the **Untersee**, the western part of Lake Constance. Here you can observe and listen to many bird species which are rarely found elsewhere.

In all nature reserves it is forbidden to disturb or to take away plants and animals, or to leave waste.

For more Information contact the conservation organisation: **Pro Natura**, Postfach, 4020 Basel, tel: 061 317 91 91; fax: 061 317 91 66; e-mail: mailbox@pronatura.ch; www.pronatura.ch.

A – Z

A HANDY SUMMARY OF PRACTICAL INFORMATION, ARRANGED ALPHABETICALLY

Admission Charges

Charges to get into museums and other places of interest are no higher than anywhere else in Europe, with most museums charging around 8–10 francs. There are discounts for under 16s and children (under 12) often go free. Ask at tourist offices about the **Swiss Museum Pass** (www.museumspass.ch), which covers more than 420 museums around the country. The **Swiss Pass** public transport pass also entitles you to free admission at all museums in the Swiss Museum Passport scheme. An International Student Identity Card (ISIC) entitles the holder to all sorts of discounts on admission prices.

Budgeting for Your Trip

There's no doubt about it, Switzerland can be an expensive place to take a holiday, with costs about 10 percent higher than many other European countries and 20 percent higher than Australia and the US. Even on the most budget of budget trips you'll still need to bank on a bare minimum of 80 francs a day for hostel accommodation, transport, three basic meals and some modest nightlife; 100 francs would be more reasonable and 200 francs would allow you to do more and stay in simple hotels.

Hotel costs are likely to be your biggest expenditure; expect to pay more than the average in big cities and popular ski resorts. You can

BELOW: The Red Cross Museum in Geneva is just one of the many museums that are free with the Swiss Museum Pass.

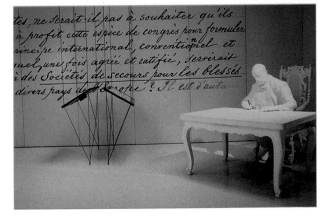

A – Z ◆ 349

TRANSPORT

ACCOMMODATION

EATING OUT

ACTIVITIES

A – Z

LANGUAGE

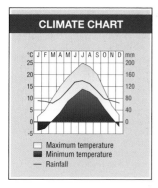

CLIMATE CHART

☐ Maximum temperature
■ Minimum temperature
— Rainfall

save money by staying in hostels (around 35 francs a night) or cheap hotels (around 80 francs a night), which are basic but clean and comfortable.

Eating out can be expensive, but there are plenty of self-service and fast-food restaurants in most towns and cities where you can eat for less. A good tip is to go to the main railway station, which will usually have bars and cafés selling healthy sandwiches, kebabs, roast chicken and hot quiche. Department stores such as Migros and Coop have restaurants where you can get a nourishing meal for around 12 francs.

Business Hours

Business hours cited here apply to the different service industries. Keep in mind that there are local and regional deviations from this general pattern.

Shops open daily 8/9am–6.30pm, until 4pm on Saturday. Zürich will soon have flexible opening hours until 11pm. In some cities you'll find that many stores are closed on Monday mornings. Once a week shops are allowed to open until 9pm (generally on Thursday or Friday).

In smaller towns and outside city centres businesses are usually closed for one to two hours during lunch time. In most holiday areas shops have longer hours and are sometimes even open for a few hours on Sunday.

In large cities, banks and bureaux de change open Mon–Fri 8.30am–4.30pm and are closed at weekends. In the rest of the country, opening hours are Mon–Fri 8.30am–noon and 1.30–4.30pm or 5.30pm.

Bureaux de change situated in airports and railway stations will exchange foreign cash, traveller's cheques and Eurocheques at the going rate. They are open daily 6am–9/11pm. There are also convenient currency-exchange machines at the main airports.

Post offices open 7.30am–6.30pm and are closed in smaller towns from noon–1.30pm. On Saturday they close at 11am. In bigger towns the main post office is often open until 9pm and for some hours on Saturday and Sunday.

Government and other official offices open Mon–Fri 8am–noon and 2–5/6pm.

In general, museums open Tues–Sun 10am–noon and 2–5pm. Some larger museums have also started opening during the evenings, while smaller and regional museums are sometimes only open half days or on weekends. In any case, to avoid disappointment, it's a good idea to find out exact opening hours prior to setting off.

Business Travellers

It's not surprising in a country renowned for its financial expertise and service sector that business travellers are well catered for. Even the trains are geared up for work, with wireless internet access and "quiet carriages" where you won't be disturbed. In major cities there are plenty of adequate mid-range hotels where around 200 francs a night will get you a good room with internet access, and breakfast included in the price.

Because most Swiss speak good English, business travellers find meetings and negotiations easy. Many Swiss dress smartly but informally for the office, although for very important meetings a jacket and tie – a smart suit for women – is a

BELOW: Switzerland is well prepared for children.

Holidays with Kids

Reka-Ferien organises holidays especially for families in more than 140 places in Switzerland (see Farm Holidays, page 354). Ask for the brochure "Familienferien" at tourist offices.

good idea. Business Network Switzerland (www.osec.ch) is a good place for general information about doing business in the country. It also has comprehensive listings including chambers of commerce, trade associations and Swiss products and producers.

C hildren

There are many different possibilities for enjoyable family holidays in Switzerland. Ask at the Swiss Tourist Office for more information (including the brochure Family Holidays).

The list of addresses below contains a variety of family-friendly accommodation. Special playgrounds for kids are often provided, as well as special attractions at reasonable prices. Travelling with children is easy in Switzerland, and the Swiss railway makes special arrangements for families, such as the family card, where children up to 16 years travel free when travelling with their parents. Information is available from all railway stations.

Interhome AG (for apartments and houses): Sägereistrasse 20, 8152 Glattbrugg/Zürich, tel: 043 211 77 77; fax: 043 211 77 79; www.interhome.ch

Utoring AG (hotels and apartments): address as for Interhome; www.utoring.ch

Schweizer Hotelier-Verein (hotels): Monbijoustrasse 130, Postfach, 3001 Bern, tel: 031 370 41 11; fax: 031 370 44 44; www.swisshotels.ch

Swiss Youth Hostels (some specialise in family accommodation): Schaffhauserstrasse 14, 8042 Zürich, tel: 01 360 14 14; fax: 01 360 14 60; www.youthhostel.ch

Schweizerische Reisekasse (Reka; for farm holidays, see also Tour Operators, pages 354–5): Neuengasse 15, 3001 Bern, tel: 031 329 66 33; fax: 031 329 66 01; www.reka.ch

Climate

Located in the centre of Europe, the Swiss climate is influenced by maritime and continental air masses. Summers are mostly warm at lower altitudes, although they can be quite wet with frequent thunderstorms. Winters are generally cold with plenty of cloud, snow and fog.

The high mountains mean great differences can occur within just a short distance – one valley can be sunny and dry while the next is shrouded in mist. The Ticino area bordering the Italian lakes is markedly warmer and sunnier than the rest of the country throughout the year.

Don't forget to bring along a warm fleece, raincoat, waterproof boots and an umbrella, even in the height of summer, and likewise, sunglasses and suntan lotion even in the depths of winter.

Weather Reports

When in Switzerland, for an up-to-date weather report dial 162, or visit: www.meteo.ch. Weather reports are also intermittently broadcast on Swiss radio and television. Since the Alps function as a climatic divide, weather broadcasts distinguish between the north side of the Alps, southern Switzerland and the Engadine.

Crime and Safety

In comparison with other countries, Switzerland is very safe and there is little crime. Nevertheless, it is better not to walk at night-time in some parts of the bigger cities. Ask for advice at your hotel or in a tourist office. Pickpocketing can happen in crowded places, such as on public transport and in supermarkets, so be attentive. The **police emergency number** everywhere is 117.

Customs

Tourists are allowed to take the following goods into Switzerland duty- and tax-free:

● **Personal belongings**, for example clothes, sports equipment, cameras, amateur movie and video cameras (including films), musical instruments, camping and mountaineering equipment, etc.
● **Food for the journey**, not exceeding what can normally be consumed in a single day. This regulation also applies to food stipulated for special diets, babies and pets.
● **Alcoholic beverages**: up to 2 litres of 15 percent proof wine, etc., and up to 1 litre of spirits exceeding 15 percent proof.
● **Tobacco products**: 200 cigarettes or 50 cigars or 250 grams of pipe tobacco. Members of non-European countries can bring double this amount.

Alcoholic beverages and tobacco products may be imported into the country duty-free only by persons at least 17 years old.
● **Articles to be given away as gifts** as long as their total value does not exceed SFr 100 (persons under the age of 17 SFr 50 in total). There are special regulations for fresh meat and meat products).
For further information about customs and special permission contact Swiss Customs head office: **Eidgenössische Oberzolldirektion**, Monbijoustrasse 40 CH-3003 Bern Tel: 031 322 65 11 Fax: 031 322 78 72 www.zoll.admin.ch; also **Zolldirektion Basel** Tel: 061 287 11 11; **Zolldirektion Schaffhausen** Tel: 052 633 11 11; and Geneva, tel: 022 747 72 72.

D isabled Travellers

Contact **Mobility International Schweiz** at Froburgstrasse 4, 4600 Olten, tel: 062 206 88 35; fax: 062 206 88 39; www.mis-ch.ch. They provide a list of easy-access accommodation and a hiking brochure for those with mobility difficulties.

Nautilus Reisen, Froburgstrasse 4, 4601 Olten, tel: 062 206 88 30; fax: 062 206 88 39; www.nautilus.ch organises its own tours and arranges holiday bookings for the disabled. **Cato**, Limmatstrasse 275, 8005 Zürich, tel: 01 440 41 00; fax: 01 440 41 01; www.cato-reisen.ch specialises in activity holidays and guided group tours for the disabled with or without able-bodied companions.

You can get information on special services on public transport for travellers with disabilities at most railway stations. In the UK, **Holiday Care** provide practical advice, support and information for disabled travellers and their families; visit www.holidaycare.org.uk or tel: 0845 124 9971 for information.

A list of ski schools with professional assistance for the disabled is available at **Schweizerischer Zentralverein für das Blindenwesen**, Schützengasse 4, 9000 St Gallen, tel: 071 223 36 36; fax: 071 222 73 18; www.szb.ch

E lectricity

The voltage in Switzerland is 220V, 50Hz so for appliances of 100V or 125V you'll need a transformer. The biggest nuisance is Switzerland's unique plug – a small six-sided affair

that fits snugly into a socket that is often recessed and won't take any kind of adapter, even a universal one. Most hotels will have some older-style non-recessed sockets that will take adapters and they may have adapters you can borrow, but only for standard continental plugs – not for plugs such as the three-pinned UK plug. If you really depend on an appliance and need to make sure it's going to work in Switzerland, the only sure way is to rewire it with an hexagonal Swiss plug, available in supermarkets Coop and Migros.

Embassies and Consulates

Australia: Chemin de Fins 2, 1211 Geneva/Grand-Saconnex, tel: 022 799 91 00.
Canada: Kirchenfeldstrasse 88, 3000 Bern 6, tel: 031 357 32 00. Consulate, Rue de l'Ariane 5, 1202 Geneva, tel. 022 919 92 00.
UK: Thunstrasse 50, 3000 Bern 15, tel: 031 359 77 00. Consulate, Rue de Vermont 37–39, 1211 Geneva, tel: 022 918 24 00.
US: Jubiläumsstrasse 93, 3001 Bern, tel: 031 357 70 11.

Swiss Embassies

Australia: 7 Melbourne Avenue, Forrest/Canberra ACT 2603, tel: 02-6162 8400, fax: 02-6273 3428; www.eda.admin.ch/australia
Canada: 5 Avenue Marlborough, Ottawa, Ontario K1N 8E6, tel: 613-235 1837, fax 613-563 1394; www.eda.admin.ch/canada
New Zealand: 22 Panama St, Wellington, 6001, tel: 04-472 1593, fax: 04-499 6302.
UK: 16–18 Montagu Place, London W1H 2BQ, tel: 020-7616 6000, fax: 020-7724-7001; www.swissembassy.org.uk
US: 2900 Cathedral Avenue N.W., Washington, DC 20008-3499, tel: 202-745 7900, fax: 202-387 2564. Consulate, 633 3rd Avenue, 30th floor, New York NY 10017, tel: 212-599 5700, fax: 212-599 4266; www.swissemb.org

Entry Requirements
Visas & Passports

Travellers from most European countries, the US, Canada, South America, Australia and New Zealand must be in possession of a valid passport but do not need a visa for a stay (for business or pleasure) of up to three months.

Animal Quarantine

Travellers bringing cats and dogs into Switzerland must be prepared to present a certificate issued by a vet stating that the animal has been vaccinated against rabies within the past 12 months. The vaccination has to be given at least 30 days before entry.

Parrots, budgies and rabbits may be taken into Switzerland only after having been granted permission by the federal veterinary office **Bundesamt für Veterinärwesen**, Schwarzenburgstrasse 161, CH-3097 Liebefeld, Bern, tel: 031 323 85 24, www.bvet.admin.ch.

It is possible to take hamsters, guinea pigs, canaries and ornamental fish into Switzerland without a vet's certificate.

Etiquette

The reputation the Swiss have for being ultra-conservative is somewhat misleading. Their apparent reserve is usually superficial and born more out of a deep respect for order and polite behaviour than any sense of superiority. One of the small joys of Switzerland is that people – most of them anyway – turn off their mobile phones when they go to a restaurant; or if they do leave it turned on, they'll step outside to make or take a call. Talking loudly on your mobile in a quiet café or on the bus will not endear you to people, so follow the Swiss example and use your phone with consideration.

The Swiss are usually punctual and will also expect you to be so. A handshake is fine for a first meeting, but if you know people well it's traditional throughout Switzerland to exchange three kisses on alternating cheeks. If you're having dinner, don't start slurping your wine before anyone else; the host will usually propose a toast and you shouldn't drink until he or she has done so. For the toast, hold the wine glass by the base and clink glasses with everyone. Before you eat, wish everyone *bon appetit* or *Guete*.

Dress codes are more relaxed than you might expect. If you're invited for dinner, smart-casual clothes are fine, with neat jeans and open-necked shirts or blouses.

 **G** ay and Lesbian Travellers

Attitudes among the Swiss towards homosexuality are open-minded and progressive. All cities have gay communities and areas where there are gay bars and entertainment venues. The age of consent for gay sex is 16, the same as for heterosexuals. A new law recognising same-sex unions came into effect in

2007. In January 2007, two men from Ticino, aged 89 and 60, became the first couple in Switzerland to join in a same-sex union. Switzerland's de-facto gay capital is Zürich, where around 4,000 gays and lesbians join a massive parade every July. There's a similar annual event in Geneva. Zürich has also been chosen to host the annual EuroPride conference and parade in 2009 (www.europride.com).

H ealth and Medical Care
Medical Treatment

The quality of medical treatment in Switzerland is very high. In case of emergency, go to the **nearest doctor** or to the **Emergency Station** in the nearest hospital.

Dial **144** for an ambulance. Cities and larger villages have an emergency doctor's number. This is printed in the local press and can be gained on the information number 111, which can also give you contact details of 24-hour pharmacies.

I nternet

There are Internet cafés in all of Switzerland's larger towns. Ask at a tourist office for further details. Keep up to date with new internet cafés by visiting: www.netcafeguide.com Here are a couple of typical net cafés, in Bern: **Café Bit**, Neuengasse 36, CH-3011, Bern, tel: 031 318 32 32: cost is 18 francs per hour.

Music Web Café, Musik Hug, Marktgasse 22, Ch-3011, Bern, tel: 031 318 32 32: cost is 10 francs per hour.

L ost Property

Major railway stations and airports have lost-property offices or small police stations where you can

report something missing or try to claim something that you've lost. Police and security guards at stations and airports are zealously efficient and often take bags and suitcases to lost-property offices if the owner isn't nearby, so don't wander off and leave your bag unattended. If it is taken away you'll have to prove that it's yours before you get it back.

M aps

There's no shortage of every kind of map for Switzerland, from road maps that can be bought at petrol stations to maps of cycle routes and high-quality 1:60,000 scale maps of every inch of the country for hikers and climbers. Book shops and adventure-travel retailers in cities and many towns stock a great selection.

Many post offices in Switzerland also stock a range of maps. Maps published by Hallwag, Kummerly and Frey (www.swisstravelcenter.ch, tel: 031 850 3131) are some of the best and are available throughout Switzerland and abroad; they can also be bought online.

Another good online source is eMapStore (www.emapstore.com), which has a wide range including city maps (1 inch = 0.25 miles), cantonal maps and detailed Alpine maps for walkers. Basic city and town maps can be picked up free at a local tourist office.

Media
Newspapers

The Swiss newspaper *Blick* can be found everywhere, from the largest city to the smallest village, as well as in most restaurants and bars. Daily newspapers of a superior quality include the *Neue Zürcher Zeitung*, which is held in high

BELOW: relaxing with a newspaper.

esteem abroad, the *Tagesanzeiger*, and many local and regional newspapers, such as *Luzerner Zeitung*, *Basler Zeitung*, and *Berner Zeitung*. In French-speaking Switzerland the most important daily newspaper is *Le Temps*.

In the cities and bigger holiday resorts you will find the usual selection of foreign newspapers and magazines.

Television and Radio

Television and radio in Switzerland are of a fairly high standard both technically and with regard to content, in particular the news. Swiss television has stations in German, French and Italian. There are also local television stations in some of the larger cities.

In all of the bigger cities and the major hotels and holiday resorts you can receive foreign television stations such as BBC World, CNN and others.

As well as the official Swiss radio stations there are many local stations, from which you may be able to glean information concerning your holiday destination. **Radio Switzer-**

land International has sections in many foreign languages, including English (www.swissinfo.org/eng).

Money Matters

There is no limit regarding the amount of foreign currency, as well as other means of payment, travellers are permitted to take with them upon either entering or leaving Switzerland. The unit of currency in Switzerland is the Swiss franc (Schweizer Franken, SFr), with 100 rappen (Rp) or centimes to a franc. There are 5, 10, 20 and 50 rappen coins, and 1, 2 and 5 franc coins. Notes are issued in 10, 20, 50, 100, 200 and 1,000 francs.

Traveller's cheques, foreign currency and other means of payment can be changed into Swiss money at banks, bureaux de change, train stations, airports, travel agencies and hotels. Most Swiss banks accept Eurocheques. Travellers can often settle their bills in larger hotels, shops, department stores and restaurants with foreign money. Ask for the rate of exchange; in most cases it

will be slightly worse than the current rate.

It is best to carry Swiss Bankers traveller's cheques issued in Swiss francs. You can use these as cash, and in Switzerland they can be exchanged free of charge.

P hotography

You probably don't need reminding that for a country where there are eye-popping photo opportunities everywhere you'll need to take as much film or digital memory as you can. Film is becoming increasingly hard to find, although standard 35mm colour film can be picked up in photo shops everywhere. Finding anything more specialised such as 120mm could be tricky, so take it with you.

Digital memory cards are reasonably priced in Switzerland. At InterDiscount, the country's best-known electronics chain, prices range from 20 francs for 1GB to 120 francs for 4GB. If you want any prints made while you're in Switzerland, they are expensive: about 3 francs each.

Postal Services

The Swiss Post Office (tel: 0848 888 888; www.swisspost.ch) is a paragon of efficiency. Within Switzerland, 98 percent of first-class letters ("A-Post") posted before 6pm arrive the next morning. The charge for a standard letter is 1 franc and for a large letter 2.20 francs. For overseas mail there are three services: the urgent courier service, which is the fastest and most expensive, priority and standard. A priority letter to another European country costs from 1.30 francs to 30 francs, depending on the weight; the higher charges are for letters up to 2kg. To a country outside Europe you'll pay from 1.80 francs to 45 francs. For sending parcels you can buy useful "flatpack" boxes in various sizes which you assemble yourself.

Post offices usually have ATMS

BELOW: you will find plenty of opportunities to use your camera.

ABOVE: stained glass windows at Zürich's Grossmünster cathedral.

where you can get cash advances and many have shops inside where you can buy envelopes, film, computer accessories and maps. Poste restante or postlargende (in German) services are available throughout Switzerland for a charge – usually around 10 francs for two weeks. You'll need to ask senders to address the letter to the branch of the post office where you intend to collect; and you'll need to show your passport.

R eligious Services

Religious services are held in either French or German, although there are a small number of Anglican churches that have a weekly service in English. The website of the Intercontinental Church Society (www.ics-uk.org) lists churches which minister in English, including churches in Wengen, Kandersteg and Thun. In Bern the Anglican church St Ursula's in Jubiläumsplatz has Sunday services at 8.30am and 10am.

S tudent Travellers

An International Student Identity Card (ISIC) entitles the holder to all sorts of discounts on admission prices, air and international train tickets, hostel accommodation, bars, clubs, shopping and ski lifts. You can get your card, along with all sorts of other information about student and youth travel from the International Student Travel Confederation (www.istc.org). If you are not a full-time student, but aged under 26 or you

are a full-time teacher or professor, the International Youth Travel Card (IYTC) or International Teacher Identity Card (ITIC) offer similar benefits and are also available from the ISTC.

T elecommunications

Telecommunications in Switzerland are very good. The dialling code from abroad into Switzerland is ++41. From Switzerland to other countries the dialling code is 0044 (UK), 001 (US and Canada) and 0061 (Australia). Be careful when using hotel telephones: the charge, especially when you are calling abroad, is much higher than from elsewhere. Be aware also that some public telephones no longer accept small change. It is easier to use phone cards. The so-called **taxcard** is available at post offices, train stations and kiosks for 5, 10, 20 or 50 francs. Even better than the taxcard are **pre-paid cards** by Swisscom or Diax (Diax is cheaper). You buy a card between 20–200 francs. After you have dialled the Swiss access number (free call) you dial the number or code of the card and then the actual number. There is a great advantage with this kind of card since you can use it from every phone in the country or abroad (you can even take it home with you to use it up). You can buy all pre-paid cards at kiosks, post offices and some railway stations.

Otherwise many phone boxes accept **credit cards**. The basic fee for using older public telephones is 60 rappen. Generally, charges are much lower at the weekend. Mobile phones are widely used, although the reception is often bad in mountainous regions. While driving, you may use only hands-free mobile phones.

Some important telephone numbers are listed below:
Swiss Directory Enquiries: 111 (minimum charge 2 francs), but most official phone boxes provide an electronic phonebox where you can get inquires for free.
Police Emergency: 117
Tourist Bulletin (summer)/Ski Report (winter): 120 (during the summer, there are reports on events of general interest as well as information on tours and excursions; in German, French and Italian only).
Road Aid: 140
Weather Report: 162 (German, French and Italian only)
Road Conditions: 163
Avalanche Bulletin (winter)/Wind Predictions and Pollen Bulletin (summer): 187 (in German, French

and Italian only; during winter an avalanche bulletin is announced by the Federal Institute for Snow and Avalanche Research, Weissfluhjoch-Davos).

Most hotels have fax machines and at every post office you can send and receive faxes. For a mimimum charge of 1.50 francs you can send e-mails and messages on mobile phones from many public phone boxes.

Tipping

Hotels, restaurants and bars are legally obliged to include a 15 percent service charge in their bills, which means tipping is not necessary. It is, however, appreciated, so if you're satisfied with the service you could round up the bill as locals often do. Bus boys, porters and taxi drivers expect a franc or two.

Toilets

Public toilets are usually very clean and well-maintained, whether they're in railway stations or pubs. The Mr Clean franchise of public toilets operates at many railway stations and airports, where you'll pay either 1 or 2 francs. Supermarkets and department stores also have good toilets. In some restaurants toilets are for customers only and there's a security code to get in – the code for the day is often printed on your receipt, so don't throw it away.

Tourist Information Offices
Tourism Offices Abroad
Australia: 33 Pitt Street, Level 8, NSW 2000 Sydney, tel: 02-9231 3744, fax: 02-9251 6531; e-mail: info@switzerland.com
Canada: 926 The East Mall, Etobicoke (Toronto) Ontario M9B 6K1, tel: 416 695 20 90, fax: 416-695 2774; e-mail: info.can@switzerland.com
UK: Swiss Centre, 10 Wardour St, London W1D 6QF, tel: 020-7851 1700, fax: 020-7851 1720; freephone: 00800-100-200-30, freefax: 00800-100-200-31; e-mail: info.uk@switzerland.com
US: Swiss Center, 608 Fifth Avenue New York 10020, NY, tel: 212-757 5944, fax: 212-262 6116; e-mail: info.usa@switzerland.com Switzerland Tourism, 501 Santa Monica Blvd, Ste 607, Santa Monica, CA 90401, tel: 310-260 2421, fax: 310-260 2923; e-mail: info.usa@switzerland.com

National Tourist Office

The Swiss National Tourist Office provides information, addresses and links on any tourist-related subjects (as well as any other question about the country and its people, which you may wish to ask). They also sell tickets, tours, package tours and make hotel bookings (they hold a data bank of more than 10,000 entries). They will either send you details by fax or e-mail or send brochures.

The tourist office has a vast website with on-line bookings and a department called "Switzerland destination management" specifically for hotel bookings: **Schweiz Tourismus**, Tödistr. 7, 8027 Zürich (open Mon–Sat 8.30am–7pm); free international, tel: 00800-100 200 30; free international fax: 00800 100 200 31; www.mySwitzerland.com; e-mail: info@switzerlandtourism.ch

Local Tourist Offices

Listed below are the local tourist offices responsible for cities, cantons and the larger regions. There are, in addition, local tourist offices in every holiday region and many smaller villages, specialising in their own particular area.

Basel: Basel Tourismus, Schifflände 5, CH-4001 Basel, tel: 061 268 68 68; fax: 061 268 68 70; www.baseltourismus.ch
Bern and Swiss Mittelland: Bern Tourismus, Railway Station, 3011 Bern, tel: 031 328 12 28; fax: 031 328 12 77; www.bernetourism.ch
Bernese Oberland: Berner Oberland Tourismus, Jungfraustrasse 38, 3800 Interlaken, tel: 033 826 53 00; fax: 033 826 53 75; www.berneroberland.com
Bernese Jura: Office du Tourisme du Jura Bernois, Avenue de la Liberté 26, 2740 Moutier, tel: 032 493 64 66; fax: 032 493 61 56; www.jurabernois.ch
Eastern Switzerland: Tourist Information St Gallen, Bahnhofplatz 1a, 9001 St Gallen, tel: 071 227 37 37; fax: 071 227 37 67; www.ostschweiz-i.ch
Fribourg: Pays de Fribourg Information, 1644 Avry-devant-Port, tel: 026 915 92 92; fax: 026 915 92 99; www.pays-de-fribourg.ch
Geneva: Genève Tourisme, Rue du Mont-Blanc 18, 1211 Geneva, tel: 022 909 70 70; fax: 022 909 70 75; www.geneve-tourisme.ch
Graubünden: Graubünden Ferien, Alexanderstrasse 24, 7000 Chur, tel: 081 254 24 24; fax: 081 254 24 00; www.graubuenden.ch
Inner Switzerland: Zentralschweiz Tourismus, Postfach, 6002 Luzern, tel: 041 227 17 17; fax: 041 227 17 18; www.luzern.org
Jura: Jura Tourisme, Place du 23 Juin 6, 2350 Saignelégier, tel: 032 952 19 53; fax: 032 952 19 50.
Lake Geneva Region: Office du Tourisme du Canton de Vaud, Av. d'Ouchy 60, Case Postale 164, 1000 Lausanne, tel: 021 613 26 26; fax: 021 613 26 00; www.lake-geneva-region.ch
Neuchâtel: Tourisme Neuchâtelois, Hôtel des Postes, 2001 Neuchâtel, tel: 032 889 68 90; fax: 032 889 62 96; www.ne.ch/tourism
Northwestern Switzerland: Aargau Tourismus, Untere Brühlstrasse 21, 4800 Zofingen, tel: 062 746 20 40; fax: 062 746 20 41; www.aargautourismus.ch
Ticino: Ticino Tourismo, Casella Postale 1441, 6501 Bellinzona, tel: 091 825 70 56; fax: 091 825 36 14; www.tourism-ticino.ch
Valais: Wallis Tourismus, Rue Pré-Fleuri 6, 1951 Sion, tel: 027 327 35 70; fax: 027 327 35 71; www.valaistourism.ch
Zürich: Zürich Tourismus, Tourist Service im Hauptbahnhof, 8023 Zürich, tel: 01 215 40 00; fax: 01 215 40 44.

Tour Operators

Switzerland has a huge variety of specialised holidays and events. Some of the most popular activities, with their relevant addresses, are listed below. If you have an idea of how you would like to spend your holiday just ask at the **Switzerland Tourism Centre** – they might be able to find the right tour operator in the right region for your needs. Tel: 00800 100 200 30 (Mon–Sat 8.30am–7pm); fax: 00800 100 200 31; www.myswitzerland.com

Adventure Activities

Eurotrek
Militärstrasse 52, 8021 Zürich, tel: 01 295 59 59; fax: 01 295 5958; www.eurotrek.ch
For hiking tours (including painting and photography), mountaineering, snowboarding and skiing tours.
Swiss Adventures
Hotel Bären 3766 Boltigen tel: 033 773 73 73, fax: 033 773 73 74; www.swissadventures.ch
For skiing and snowboarding.
Swiss Ski School Information
Tel: 031 810 41 11; www.snowsports.ch.
Information on tuition for beginners and experts.
Trekking Team AG
Central Switzerland, tel: 041 390 40 40; fax: 041 390 40 39.
Ticino, tel: 091 780 78 00; fax: 091

Matterhorn Guides

If you are planning to climb the Matterhorn, Switzerland's most famous peak (see the feature on page 180), guides can be contracted through Zermatt's **Alpine Centre** (Postfach 403, CH-3920 Zermatt; tel: 027 966 24 60; fax: 027 966 24 69; email: alpincenter@zermatt.ch; www.zermatt.ch/alpincenter). The standard cost is 1070 francs per person, which includes transport and half-board accommodation at the Hörnli mountain hut, but not equipment hire or insurance (there is a cancellation fee in the event of bad weather).

Alternatively, those visitors who would simply like to stay overnight close up against the mountain – and avoid a strenuous hike – can experience a night in the Hörnli hut (tel: 028-67 27 69) or reserve a room at the adjacent Hotel Belvédère (tel: 028-67 22 64), both of which are at an altitude of 3,260 metres (10,696 ft).

780 78 01; www.trekking.ch
For any kind of outdoor adventure; renowned for the famous 007 "GoldenEye" bungee jump in the Verzasca Valley (see page 196) and a bivouac tour into the 180-km/112-mile long Hölloch Cave in the Muota Valley. They also make smaller tours of other caves.
Weit Wandern
Markus Zürcher, Allmigässli, 3703 Aeschiried, tel: 033 654 18 42; www.weitwandern.ch
For climbing, archery, cave tours, tobogganing, etc.

Farm Holidays

Holidays spent on the farm have been increasing in popularity. Schweizerische Reisekasse offers 270 places to stay in Switzerland. Such down-to-earth holidays offer the best opportunity to get to know the country and its inhabitants and are especially suitable for families with children. In some places it is possible for a child (aged 6 to 14) to stay unaccompanied with the farmer's family, allowing them to participate actively in farming life.

The brochure Ferien auf dem Bauernhof (Holiday on the Farm) is obtainable at the tourist office. Or you can book directly at: **Schweizerische Reisekasse** (Reka) Swiss Farm Holidays, Neuengasse 15, CH-3001 Bern, tel: 031 329 66 33; fax: 031 329 66 01; www.reka.ch (Mon–Fri 8am–6pm)

Pro Emmental

Schlossstrasse 3, CH-3550 Langnau, tel: 034 402 42 52; fax: 034 402 56 67; www.emmental.ch (in the farm region of Emmental near Bern).

For one-day educational visits to farms, including meals and other special attractions, contact:

Agroimpuls, Erlebnis Bauernhof

Laurstr. 10, 5201 Brugg, tel: 056 462 51 44; fax: 056 442 22 12; www.erlebnis.ch

If you would like to go on a make-your-own-cheese holiday, contact: **Office de Tourisme**, 1837 Château d'Oex, tel: 026 924 25 25; fax: 026 924 25 26; www.chateau-doex.ch

For young travellers (aged 16–25) there is an opportunity to help with the Swiss wine harvest every autumn. You pay your own travel costs to get there; and meals and accommodation are provided, plus a small daily spending allowance. The only thing you need to know is a little bit of French, enough to get by. There are a range of other active farm holidays throughout the year. For more information, contact:

Landdienst

Zentralstelle Postfach 728, 8025 Zürich, tel: 01 261 44 88, fax: 01 261 44 32; www.landdienst.ch

Cultural Holidays

Martin Randall Travel

10 Barley Mow Passage, London W4 4PH, tel: 020 8742 3355; fax: 020 8742 7766; www.martinrandall.com One-week holidays covering art or music in Switzerland, including 3–6-day trips to the International Jazz Festival in Montreux (July).

Ciao Travel

San Diego, CA, tel: 619 297 8112; www.ciaotravel.com

Art and music holidays.

Plus Travel

Swiss Travel Centre, London W1D 6QF, tel: 020 7734 0383; fax: 020 7292 1599.

Soft adventure and gourmet tours.

Towne & Country Tours

Dendron, VA, tel: 800 487 0479; www.towneandcountrytours.com Wine sampler tour.

Holidays by Train

The Swiss Railway has its own travel agency with special offers on holidays in Switzerland by train. Tours offer packages including train tickets, hotels and special offers for the region you wish to stay in.

Railtour Suisse SA

Chutzenstr. 24, 3000 Bern 14, tel: 031 378 01 01; www.railtour.ch

Health Resorts & Spas

There are many opportunities for relaxed holidays in one of about 80 health hotels spread across Switzerland. For information and brochures contact the **Swiss Tourist Office** at Schweizer Kurhäuser, Oberdorfstr. 53b, 9100 Herisau, tel: 071 350 14 14; fax: 071 350 14 18; www.wohlbefinden.com

The 20 spas in Switzerland all specialise in different medical treatments. Many offer various pools, Roman and Turkish baths, saunas and solariums. The most famous places include La Réserve Genève, Bad Ragaz, Leukerbad, St Moritz, Scuol and Vals. For more details ask at the tourist office or **Schweizer Heilbäder**, Av. des Bains 22, 1400 Yverdon-les-Bains, tel: 024 420 15 21; fax: 024 423 02 52; www.heilbad.org

Generally all Swiss health resorts and spas are open to the public. Just enquire in advance about opening times and prices.

Mineral Springs

There are mineral springs at the following places: Eptingen, Henniez (VD), Weissenburg (BE), Adelboden (BE), Vals (GR), Elm (GL), Rietbad (SG), Passugg (GR). Where it is possible to visit the actual springs, you will have to book in advance. Ask at a local tourist office for details.

Websites

The best place to start surfing is at the **Swiss National Tourist Office** (www.myswitzerland.com), which has a vast site providing all sorts of information about the country as well as hotel bookings, transport details,

BELOW: people bathing in a natural hot water pool in the spa resort at Leukerbad.

snow reports and walking guides. For train travel you can book online at www.sbb.ch, while you can book tickets with the national carrier Swiss at www.swiss.com. For hostels www.youthostel.ch has everything you'll need including online booking, while there's excellent hotel information and reservations at www.swisshotels.ch. Swissinfo (www.swissinfo.com) is an excellent all-round site about all things Swiss, with news, weather, and sections dedicated to music, travel and culture.

Weights and Measures

The metric system is used. Food such as cheese, meat and portions of salad are priced per 100g not per kg.

What to Bring

The golden rule when packing for Switzerland is to pack for all four seasons, whichever season you're travelling in. Summers can be hot so you'll primarily need lightweight clothing, but at altitude it can still be cold, windy and misty, so also make sure you've got some warm gear, especially if you're planning on hiking. In winter you'll need to be well prepared for extreme cold, which means good-quality outdoor clothing, thermals, gloves and hats.

Remember several layers of thin clothing keeps you warmer than one or two layers of cumbersome thick clothing.

Good-quality sunglasses and sunscreen are an absolute must at any time. The sun in the Alps can be sizzling and you'll burn very quickly if you don't take care. Your itinerary will dictate the specifics of what you pack – no need for expensive hiking boots if you're only wandering around the shops in Interlaken and Zürich.

If you're planning a more adventurous trip, you'll need to take or rent gear such as tents and skis. A rain coat or rain jacket is useful at any time of year and for rainy city days it's worth packing an umbrella. There are fountains all over the place where you can fill up a water bottle with potable Alpine water, so pack or buy a decent water bottle and carry it with you in a small day pack.

What to Wear

It's unlikely you'll need to take anything formal, unless you're planning a night at the opera. The Swiss dress well and always look neat, but they are rarely showy. For dinner you'll be fine in smart trousers or jeans with a simple shirt, or a blouse for women. Wear a tie if

you want, but many men don't bother unless it is a very formal occasion. For après-ski people wear comfortable trousers, warm boots and a ski jacket. Visitors to ritzy resorts like Gstaad and St Moritz take things a bit further, but there's no need for an expensive fur coat or ermine boots.

Women Travellers

Switzerland may have taken it's time to give every woman the vote, but it's actually a remarkably egalitarian society, with women holding senior positions in commerce, the arts and politics. The Swiss foreign minister is a woman (Micheline Calmy-Rey) and other high-profile politicians such as Ruth Dreifuss and Christiane Brunner are highly respected.

Women travellers rarely have problems of any sort in Switzerland. Crimes against women, while not unknown, are unusual and tend not to involve tourists. Cities such as Bern, Zurich and Geneva do have a drugs problem and it's worth taking care around railway stations at night when you'll sometimes come across drug addicts asking for money. Boisterous drunks can be a nuisance at weekends, but in most cases their bravado is just that and you can deal with it easily by paying no notice and walking away.

BELOW: A walking tour admires the view at the resort of Zermatt.

LANGUAGE

UNDERSTANDING THE LANGUAGE

What to Speak Where

About 64 percent of Swiss people speak **Schwyzerdütsch**, a variation of German, but don't be afraid to try out the more usual High-German on them (they grow up with High-German at school and it is the official written language). The three other official languages are French, which is used by about 19 percent of the population in the western part of Switzerland; Italian, used by roughly 7 percent of the Swiss in the southern part of Switzerland, especially in the canton Tessin; and Romansch, which is spoken by 0.6 percent of people in some regions of the canton Graubünden. All Romansch-speaking and a lot of Italian-speaking people also understand and speak German. But in the French-speaking part of Switzerland you would be more successful speaking English than German.

Swiss people are in general friendly and patient, and will take the time to listen to foreigners who do not speak their language fluently.

Since a lot of English vocabulary is related to German, travellers will

The Alphabet

Learning the pronunciation of the German alphabet is a good idea. In particular, learn how to spell out your name.

a = ah, **b** = bay, **c** = tsay, **d** = day, **e** = ay, **f** = ef, **g** = gay, **h** = hah, **i** = ee, **j** = yot, **k** = kah, **l** = el, **m** = em, **n** = en, **o** = oh, **p** = pay, **q** = coo, **r** = ehr, **s** = ess, **t** = tay, **u** = oo, **v** = fou, **w** = vay, **x** = eex, **y** = eepseelon, **z** = tset.

often recognise many helpful cognates: words such as *Hotel*, *Kaffee*, *Milch*, *Markt* and *Bett* hardly need to be translated. You should be aware, however, of some misleading "false friends" *(see panel on page 360)*.

There is one rather puzzling characteristic of the Swiss: even if they are speaking real German, they use many words which they borrow from the French, such as *billet*, *lavabo* and *portemonnaie*; this is especially the case if they are speaking about eating.

Basic Rules

Even if you speak no German at all, it is worth trying to master a few simple phrases. The fact that you have made an effort is likely to get you a better response. Increasing numbers of German-speaking people practise their English on visitors, especially waiters in cafés and restaurants and the younger generation. Pronunciation is the key; they really will not understand if you get it very wrong. Remember to **emphasise each syllable**.

Whether to use **"Sie"** or **"Du"** is a vexed question; increasingly the familiar form of "Du" is used by many people. However, it is better to be too formal, and use "Sie" if in doubt. You address people with "Sie" or, if you know their names, you address them **Herr** (Mr) or **Frau** (Mrs), and attach the relevant surname. To say Herr or Frau without surnames sounds in German rather ridiculous. If you say "Du", then you attach (if you know the name) just the first name. When entering a shop always say, **"Guten Tag"**, and **"Danke, auf Wiedersehen"**, when leaving.

Words & Phrases

How much is it?
Wieviel kostet das?
What is your name?
Wie heissen Sie?
My name is... *Ich heisse...*
Do you speak English?
Sprechen Sie englisch?
I am English/American
Ich bin Engländer(in)/
Amerikaner(in)
I don't understand
Ich verstehe nicht
Please speak more slowly
Sprechen Sie bitte langsamer
Can you help me?
Können Sie mir helfen?
I'm looking for... *Ich suche...*
Where is...? *Wo ist...?*
I'm sorry *Entschuldigung*
I don't know
Ich weiss es nicht
No problem *Kein Problem*
Have a good day!
Einen schönen Tag!
That is it *Das ist es*
Here it is *Hier ist es*
There it is *Dort ist es*
Let's go *Lass uns gehen*
See you tomorrow
Bis morgen
See you soon *Bis bald*
Show me the word in the book
Zeigen Sie mir das Wort im Buch
At what time?
Um wieviel Uhr?
When? *Wann?*
What time is it?
Wieviel Uhr ist es?
yes *ja*
no *nein*
please *bitte*
thank you (very much)
danke (vielmal)
you're welcome
bitte or gern geschehen
excuse me *Entschuldigung*

TRANSPORT · ACCOMMODATION · EATING OUT · ACTIVITIES · A–Z · LANGUAGE

hello *Guten Tag* or, more familiar, *Hallo*
OK *In Ordnung*
goodbye *Auf Wiedersehen*
good evening *Guten Abend*
good night *Gute Nacht*
here *hier*
there *dort*
today *heute*
yesterday *gestern*
tomorrow *morgen*
now *jetzt*
later *später*
right away *sofort*
this morning *heute morgen*
this afternoon
heute nachmittag
this evening *heute abend*

On Arrival

I want to get off at...
Ich möchte in ... aussteigen
Does this bus go to...?
Fährt dieser Bus nach...?
What street is this?
In welcher Strasse sind wir?
Which line do I take for...?
Welche Linie muss ich nehmen nach...?
How far is ...? *Wie weit ist ...?*
Validate your ticket
Entwerten Sie Ihr Billet
airport *der Flughafen*
train station *der Bahnhof*
bus station *der Busbahnhof*
bus *der Bus*
bus stop *die Bushaltestelle*
platform *das Perron*
ticket *das Billet*
return ticket *das Retourbillet*
hitchhiking *Autostop*
toilets *die Toiletten*
This is the hotel address
Das ist die Adresse des Hotels
I'd like a room
Ich möchte ein Zimmer
single/double...
Einzelzimmer/Doppelzimmer
...with shower *...mit Dusche*
...with bath *mit Bad*
...with a view *...mit Aussicht*
Does that include breakfast?
Ist das Frühstück inbegriffen?
May I see the room?
Darf ich das Zimmer anschauen?
washbasin *das Lavabo*
bed *das Bett*
key *der Schlüssel*
elevator *der Lift, der Aufzug*
air conditioning
die Klimaanlage

Emergencies

Help! *Hilfe!*
Stop! *Halt!*
Call a doctor
Rufen Sie einen Arzt

Call an ambulance
Rufen Sie eine Ambulanz
Call the police
Rufen Sie die Polizei
Call the fire brigade
Rufen Sie die Feuerwehr
Where is the nearest telephone?
Wo ist das nächste Telefon?
Where is the nearest hospital?
Wo ist das nächste Spital?
I am sick *Ich bin krank*
I have lost my passport/purse
Ich habe meinen Pass / mein Portemonnaie verloren

On the Road

Where is the spare wheel?
Wo ist das Reserverad?
Where is the nearest garage?
Wo ist die nächste Garage?
Our car has broken down
Unser Auto hat eine Panne
I want to have my car repaired
Ich möchte mein Auto reparieren lassen
It's not your right of way
Sie haben kein vorfahrt
I think I must have put diesel in the car by mistake
Ich glaube, ich habe irrtümlicherweise mit Diesel getankt
the road to...
die Strasse nach...
left *links*
right *rechts*
straight on *geradeaus*
far *weit entfernt, weit weg*
near *nahe*
opposite *gegenüber*
beside *neben*
car park *der Parkplatz*
over there *dort drüben*
at the end *am Ende*
on foot *zu Fuss*
by car *mit dem Auto*
town map *der Stadtplan*
road map *die Strassenkarte*
street *die Strasse*
square *der Platz*
give way *den Vortritt lassen*
dead end *die Sackgasse*
no parking *Parkieren verboten*
motorway *die Autobahn*
toll *die Gebühr*
speed limit *die Tempolimite*
petrol *das Benzin*
unleaded *bleifrei*
diesel *der Diesel*
water/oil *das Wasser/das Oel*
puncture *die Reifenpanne*
bulb *die Batterie*
wipers *die Scheibenwischer*

On the Telephone

How do I make an outside call?
Wie telefoniere ich nach auswärts?
I want to make an international (local) call

Sightseeing

town *die Stadt*
old town *die Altstadt*
abbey *die Abtei, das Kloster*
cathedral
die Kathedrale, das Münster
church *die Kirche*
mansion *das Herrschaftshaus*
hospital *das Spital*
town hall *das Rathaus*
nave *das Kirchenschiff*
stained glass *das Glasfenster*
staircase *das Treppenhaus*
tower *der Turm*
walk *der Rundgang*
country house/castle *das Schloss*
Gothic *gothisch*
Roman *römisch*
Romanesque *romanisch*
museum *das Museum*
art gallery *die Kunstgalerie*
exhibition *die Ausstellung*
tourist information office
das Verkehrsbüro
free *gratis*
open *offen*
closed *geschlossen*
every day *täglich*
all year *das ganze Jahr über*
all day *den ganzen Tag*
swimming pool *das Schwimmbad*
to book *reservieren*

Ich möchte eine internationale (lokale) Verbindung
What is the dialling code?
Wie lautet die Vorkennzahl?
I'd like an alarm call for 8 tomorrow morning
Ich möchte morgen früh um acht Uhr geweckt werden
Who's calling?
Wer ist am Apparat?
Hold on, please
Warten Sie bitte
The line is busy
Die Leitung ist besetzt
I must have dialled the wrong number
Ich bin falsch verbunden

Shopping

Where is the nearest bank (post office)?
Wo ist die nächste Bank (Post)?
I'd like to buy something
Ich möchte(etwas) kaufen
How much is it?
Wieviel kostet das?
Do you take credit cards?
Nehmen Sie Kreditkarten?
I'm just looking
Ich schaue nur ein bisschen
Have you got...?
Haben Sie...?

I'll take it
Ich nehme es
I'll take this one/that one
Ich nehme das hier/das dort
Anything else? Noch etwas?
size die Grösse
cheap billig
expensive teuer
enough genug
too much zu viel
a piece... ein Stück...
each das Stück
(eg, bananas, 4 Fr. das Stück)
emergency exit Notausgang
bill die Rechnung
chemist die Apotheke
bakery die Bäckerei
butcher die Metzgerei
book shop die Buchhandlung
library die Bibliothek
department store
das Warenhaus
grocer's
das Lebensmittelgeschäft
tobacconist
der Tabakladen, der Kiosk
market der Markt
supermarket der Supermarkt
junk shop das Brockenhaus

Dining Out

breakfast das Frühstück
lunch das Mittagessen
dinner das Abendessen
meal die Mahlzeit
first course die Vorspeise
main course die Hauptspeise
made to order auf Bestellung
drink included Getränk
inbegriffen
wine list die Weinkarte
the bill die Rechnung
fork die Gabel
knife das Messer
spoon der Löffel
plate der Teller
glass das Glas
napkin die Serviette
ashtray der Aschenbecher

Frühstück und Snacks/
Breakfast and Snacks

Brötchen rolls
Brot bread
Butter butter
Ei egg
... weiche Eier boiled eggs
... Eier mit Speck bacon and eggs
... Eier mit Schinken
ham and eggs
... Spiegeleier fried eggs
... Rührei scrambled eggs
Honig honey
Joghurt yogurt
Konfiture jam
Crêpe pancake
Pfeffer pepper
Salz salt
Zucker sugar

Hauptgerichte/Main courses

Fleisch Meat
Blutwurst black pudding
Braten roast
Bündnerfleisch dried meat
Ente duck
Entrecôte beef rib steak
Fasan pheasant
Froschschenkel frog's legs
Gans goose
Gnagi, Schweinsfuss
pig's trotters
Huhn/Poulet chicken
Kalb veal
Kalbsleber calf's liver
Kaninchen/Hase rabbit
Lamm lamb
Leber liver
Leberwurst liver sausage
Nieren kidneys
Schinken ham
Schwein pork
Salami salami
Schnecken snails
Spiessli kebab
Steak steak
Voressen stew of veal, lamb or
chicken with creamy egg sauce
Wildschwein wild boar
Wurst sausage
Zunge tongue
wenig gebraten, bleu rare
mittel gebraten, à point medium
gut gebraten, bien cuit well done
grilliert grilled
gefüllt stuffed

Fisch/Fish

Aal eel
Auster oyster
Egli small regional fish
Felchen regional white fish
Forelle trout
Hecht pike
Hummer lobster
Kabeljau, Dorsch cod
Krevetten shrimp
Lachs salmon
Langustine large prawn
Muscheln, Moule mussel
Meerfrüchte seafood
Sardellen anchovies
Schalentiere shellfish
Thunfisch/Thon tuna
Tintenfisch squid

Gemüse/Vegetables

Artischocke artichoke
Aubergine eggplant/aubergine
Blumenkohl cauliflower
Bohne bean (green or dried)
Chips potato crisps
Cornichon gherkin
Erbsen peas
Grüner Salat green salad
Haselnuss hazelnut
Kartoffel potato
Kefen snow peas
Knoblauch garlic
Kohl cabbage

Lauch leek
Linsen lentils
Mais corn
Nuss nut, walnut
Pastinake parsnip
Petersilie parsley
Pilze mushrooms
Pommes frites French fries
Radieschen radish
Reis rice
Salatgurke cucumber
Sellerie celery
Spargel asparagus
Spinat spinach
Steinpilz boletus mushroom
Trüffel truffle
weisse Rübe turnip
Zucchini zucchini/courgette
Zwiebel onion
roh raw
gedämpft steamed
gekocht boiled

Obst/Fruit

Ananas pineapple
Apfel apple
Birne pear
Erdbeere strawberry
Feige fig
Grapefruit grapefruit
Himbeere raspberry
Kirsche cherry
Limone lime
Mango mango
Mirabelle yellow plum
Pfirsich peach
Pflaume plum
Rotebeere redcurrant
Traube grape
Zitrone lemon
Zwetschge prune

Desserts/Dessert

Glacé ice cream
Käse cheese
Kuchen cake
Schlagrahm whipped cream
Torte tart
Vermicelles
Chestnut purée with whipped cream

Table Talk

I am a vegetarian
Ich bin Vegetarier
I am on a diet Ich bin auf Diät
What do you recommend?
Was empfehlen Sie?
Do you have local specialities?
Haben Sie lokale Spezialitäten?
I'd like to order
Ich möchte bestellen
That is not what I ordered
Das ist nicht, was ich bestellt habe
Is service included?
Ist der Service inbegriffen?
May I have more wine?
Ich möchte noch Wein, bitte.
Enjoy your meal
Guten Appetit!

In the Café

drinks *Getränke*
alcoholic drinks *Alkoholische Getränke/Drinks*
coffee *Kaffee*
... with milk or cream
... mit Milch oder Kaffeerahm
... decaffeinated *koffeinfrei*
... black espresso *Espresso*
... American filtered coffee *filtre*
tea *Tee*
... black tea *Schwarztee*
... herbal infusion *Kräutertee*
... peppermint *Pfefferminze*
... rosehip *Hagebutte*
... camomile *Kamille*
... vervain *Eisenkraut*
hot chocolate
heisse Schokolade
milk *Milch*
mineral water
Mineralwasser
fizzy *mit Kohlensäure*
non-fizzy
ohne Kohlensäure
fruit-flavoured carbonated water
Mineralwasser mit Aroma
freshly squeezed orange juice
frisch gepresster Orangensaft
full (eg, full-cream milk) *voll*
fresh or cold *kalt*
beer *Bier*
... bottled *in der Flasche*
... on tap *offen*
wheat beer *weissbier (white, cloudy beer)*
pre-dinner drink *Aperitif*
with ice *mit Eis*
neat *trocken*
red *rot*
white *weiss*
rosé *rosé*
dry *herb*
sweet *süss*
sparkling wine *Schaumwein*
house wine *Hauswein*
local wine *Landwein*
Where is this wine from?
Woher kommt dieser Wein?
carafe/jug
Karaffe/Krug
... of water/wine
... Wasser/Wein
half litre
einen halben Liter
mixed *panaché (beer with lemon mineral water) or gespritzt (white wine with water)*

False Friends

False friends are words that look like English words but mean something different, for example:
Der Car **coach**
Es geht can sometimes mean walk, but is usually used to mean working (the TV, the car etc.) or going well.

Feedback

We do our best to ensure the information in our books is as accurate and up-to-date as possible. The books are updated on a regular basis, using local contacts, who painstakingly add, amend and correct as required. However, some mistakes and omissions are inevitable and we are ultimately reliant on our readers to put us in the picture. We would welcome your feedback on any details related to your experiences using the book "on the road". Maybe we recommended a hotel that you liked (or another that you didn't), as well as interesting new attractions, or facts and figures you have found out about the country itself. The more details you can give us (particularly with regard to addresses, e-mails and telephone numbers), the better. We will acknowledge all contributions, and we'll offer an Insight Guide to the best letters received.

Please write to us at:
Insight Guides
PO Box 7910
London SE1 1WE
United Kingdom
Or send e-mail to:
insight@apaguide.co.uk

after-dinner drink *Digestif*
cherry brandy *Kirsch*
pear brandy *Williams*
plum brandy *Pflümli*
cheers!
Gesundheit! or Zum Wohl!
I have a hangover
Ich habe einen Kater

In Switzerland table wine, and sometimes also mineral water, is served in measures of 100cl (one decilitre). Usually you order 2 *Dezi*, 3 *Dezi*, einen halben Liter or einen Liter. If it is a very good wine, you have to order a whole bottle, which can vary in size.

Numbers

0 *null*
1 *eins*
2 *zwei*
3 *drei*
4 *vier*
5 *fünf*
6 *sechs*
7 *sieben*
8 *acht*
9 *neun*
10 *zehn*
11 *elf*
12 *zwölf*
13 *dreizehn*
14 *vierzehn*
15 *fünfzehn*
16 *sechzehn*
17 *siebzehn*
18 *achtzehn*
19 *neunzehn*
20 *zwanzig*
21 *einundzwanzig*
30 *dreissig*
40 *vierzig*
50 *fünfzig*
60 *sechzig*
70 *siebzig*
80 *achtzig*
90 *neunzig*
100 *hundert*
1,000 *tausend*
1,000,000 *eine million*

Days & Months

Days of the Week

Monday *Montag*
Tuesday *Dienstag*
Wednesday *Mittwoch*
Thursday *Donnerstag*
Friday *Freitag*
Saturday *Samstag*
Sunday *Sonntag*

Months

January *Januar*
February *Februar*
March *März*
April *April*
May *Mai*
June *Juni*
July *Juli*
August *August*
September *September*
October *Oktober*
November *November*
December *Dezember*

Saying the Date

20 October 2004 *der zwanzigste-Oktoberzweitausendundvier.*

Seasons

spring *der Frühling*
summer *der Sommer*
autumn *der Herbst*
winter *der Winter*

FURTHER READING

Book Shops and Websites

A large selection of books in English can be found in the **Orell Füssli** book shop in Zürich, Bahnhofstr. 70, Postfach, 8022 Zürich, tel: 01 211 04 44; fax: 01 215 72 05; www.books.ch; e-mail: english-orders@books.ch. Also have a look on www.bergli.ch

Background

The Music Guide to Belgium, Luxembourg, Holland and Switzerland: Brody, Elaine; Prentice Hall (USA), 1999
La Place de la Concorde Suisse: McPhee, John; Farrar, Straus & Giroux (USA), 1984
Why Switzerland?: Steinberg, Jonathan; Cambridge UK, 1998
Ticking along with the Swiss 1988, **Ticking along too**, **Ticking along free** 2000: Dicks, Dianne; Bergli Books LTP. Collections of personal stories from English-speaking writers, teachers, translators, etc., living in Switzerland.
Cupid's Wild Arrows: inter-cultural romance and its consequences, Dicks, Dianne; Bergli Books LTP, Basel 1993. Personal experiences of 55 authors of many nationalities.
Perpetual Tourist: Bilton, Paul; Bergli Books Ltd, 1994. The Englishman who lives in Switzerland started to write his diary in short notes to remind him what to write to his family in England.
Culture Shock!: En-Wong, Shirley; Graphic Arts Center Publishing Company, 1996. A guide to customs and etiquette.
Inside Outlandish: Tuttle, Susan; Bergli Books Ltd, 1997. Snapshots in prose about the never-ending questions: What am I doing here? Can I call this place home?
Laughing Along with the Swiss: Bilton, Paul; Bergli Books. Describes the funny side about Switzerland and the Swiss.
Who put the Wit in Switzerland: Epstein, Eugene; Benteli Publishers, Bern 1988. A collection of wits.
A Taste of Switzerland: Style, Sue and Miller, John; Bergli Books Ltd. Descriptions of Swiss food, folklore, history and 50 recipes and tips on restaurants and hotels.
The Surprising Wines of Switzerland: Sloan, John C.; Bergli Books. The best book on Swiss wine, describing the wine tradition, products and places, with lots of practical tips.

Fiction

Hôtel Du Lac: Brookner, Anita; Penguin Books, 1993.
Prisoner of Chillon: Byron, Lord; Woodstock Books (UK), 1993.
A Pocketful of Rye: Cronin, A.J.; New English Library Ltd, 1986.
The Manticore: Davies, Robertson; Penguin Books, 1977.
Man in the Holocene: Frisch, Max, Harcourt (USA), 1994.
Peter Camenzind: Hesse, Hermann; Penguin Paperbacks, 2000.
Not To Disturb: Spark, Muriel; Penguin Books, 1974.
Heidi: Spyri, Johanna; Morrow & Co. Inc., 1996 and Puffin, 1994.
The Magic Mountain: Mann, Thomas. Mann's greatest work on a group of patients and their discussions about love, death and war, in a sanatorium in Davos during World War I.
The Pollen Room: Zoë, Jenny, Bloomsbury. The 1974-born young star writer describes in her first novel a marriage break-up through the eyes of a child.
Steppenwolf: Hesse, Hermann; Penguin Books. Hesse's best-known novel is about profound social deconstruction.
Masquerade and other stories. Poems and short stories about the writer's life in Zürich, Berlin, Biel and Bern.
Daisy Miller: James, Henry. The witty novel tells about an American tourist who falls in love near Lake Geneva and finally ends up by the Château de Chillon.

Other Insight Guides

The 190-title Insight Guides series is the main series in the Insight stable, known for its superb pictures, in-depth background reading, detailed maps, excellent coverage of sights and comprehensive listings section.
Insight Guide: Great Railway Journeys of Europe features the best of European rail travel from the Orient Express to little-known branch lines. There are full details on all of Switzerland's superb Alpine routes.

Insight Pocket Guide: Switzerland is a personal guide to the country, with 15 itineraries of varying length from city tours to Alpine treks. Fold-out map included.

Insight Compact Guide: Switzerland is a mini-encyclopædia packed with concise information on the country's many attractions.

Insight Fleximap: Switzerland combines clear cartography with useful travel information in an easy-to-fold, rain-resistant laminated finish.

TRANSPORT ACCOMMODATION EATING OUT ACTIVITIES A - Z LANGUAGE

ART & PHOTO CREDITS

PICTURE SPREADS

INDEX

Numbers in italics refer to photographs

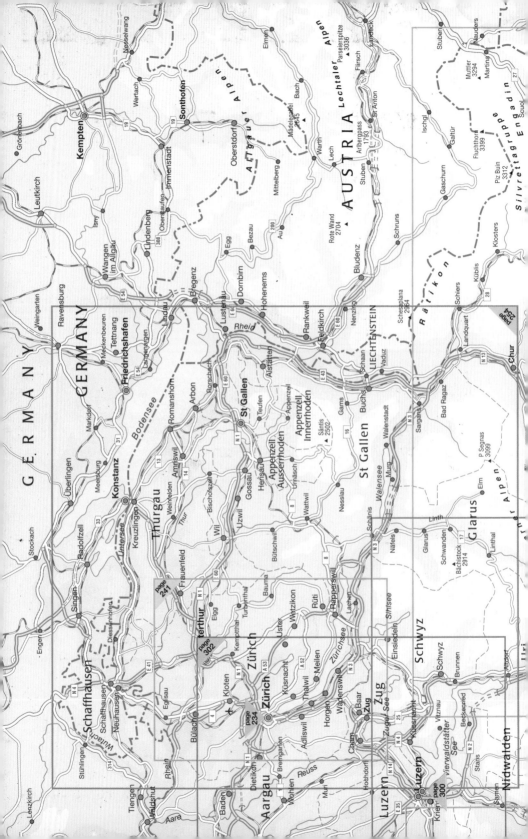